# PROSPECT:
# THE REAL ESTATE LEAD GENERATION MANUAL

BRIAN ICENHOWER

PROSPECT: The Real Estate Lead Generation Manual
Authored by Brian Icenhower
© 2018 Copyright Icenhower Coaching & Consulting, LLC
ISBN: 9781723906886

# TABLE OF CONTENTS

Foreword .................................................................................................................iii

Chapter 1:
Welcome To The Only Prospecting Plan You'll Ever Need .................................. 1

Chapter 2:
Making Presentations With Scripts ................................................................... 40

Chapter 3:
Your Sphere of Influence (SOI) ......................................................................... 81

Chapter 4:
Prospecting for Expired Listings ..................................................................... 123

Chapter 5:
Prospecting Through Open Houses ............................................................... 159

Chapter 6:
Property Previews ........................................................................................... 208

Chapter 7:
Time Management .......................................................................................... 233

Chapter 8:
FSBO Prospecting .......................................................................................... 275

Chapter 9:
Circle Prospecting .......................................................................................... 296

Chapter 10:
Your Prospecting Arena .................................................................................. 317

Chapter 11:
Mindset - Maintaining a Proper Perspective .................................................. 337

Chapter 12:
The Art of Closing .......................................................................................... 357

Chapter 13:
Tracking_Truth In Numbers ............................................................................ 400

Chapter 14:
Holding Yourself Accountable ........................................................................ 425

Chapter 15:
Next Level Commitment ................................................................................. 441

# Icenhower Coaching & Consulting (ICC)

Icenhower Coaching & Consulting (ICC) provides customized & structured coaching & training programs for real estate agents & team leaders, representing many of the top-producing agents in North America. ICC also offers broker/owner consulting on agent recruiting, training & retention. ICC has over 120 clients coached by a team of talented and experienced coaches. This progressive company provides one-on-one and group coaching, online courses, educational podcasts, training materials, speaking events, training workshops, video modules and real estate books.

ICC coaching programs offer much more than just weekly calls with our real estate coaches. ICC coaches are experienced real estate business consultants that offer strategic planning and a full library of training resources to elevate agents' businesses and their careers. Coaching clients are continuously engaged with their coaches through ICC's Online Coaching Platform where agents can communicate with their coach, watch video training modules, track their activities, attend training courses, monitor their businesses, and access the ICC training library.

Brian Icenhower, CEO & Founder of ICC, understands that people learn and retain information in a number of different ways. Whether it be visually, audibly, verbally, kinetically, or through engaging interaction, ICC's programs are designed to accelerate the learning process while engaging clients more effectively. Brian set out to supplement one-on-one and group coaching by creating training materials you can print and touch, videos you can watch, calls you can listen to, and workbooks that really break down procedures and truly involve agents in the process. ICC's vast resource library is made up of training modules, videos, scripts, tools, job descriptions, budgets, business plans, workflows, systems and other interactive tools to help clients grow their business systematically.

## ICC TRAINING MATERIALS

Brian Icenhower's real estate productivity coaching, training and recruiting programs have propelled a number of real estate companies to be repeatedly recognized as some of the highest producing and fastest growing offices in North America by a number of major industry media sources. ICC's production department now produces video training modules on a wide variety of productivity-focused topics. These modules come complete with agent workbooks, instructor's manuals and audio files that can be white-label branded for any real estate company. Additionally, ICC's broker/manager coaches are available to consult with company leadership to ensure proper understanding and implementation of brokerage retention, training & recruiting systems.

## ICC SPEAKING & TRAINING

Brian Icenhower, along with a number of ICC's trainers and coaches, are available to speak and train on a variety of real estate and business topics by request. Event programs can feature any combination of real estate, educational, motivational, business or leadership focused training as well. Brian's interactive training style provides a high level of energy that keeps attendants engaged and receptive to learning throughout the entire event.

Brian Icenhower has presented for many organizations across a wide number of industries. He has presented at real estate companies, trade conferences, Realtor associations, financial institutions, non-profit & service groups, and a variety of national corporations. Mr. Icenhower has also been a keynote speaker for numerous organizations. Event sessions can be conducted by the hour, half-day, full day or over multiple days depending on the topic and audience. Audience sizes have ranged from a group of ten to a room of thousands.

# Welcome To The Only Prospecting Plan You'll Ever Need

Welcome to a goldmine of strategies, insights, tools and techniques for developing your prospecting skills and building your own business from the ground up. This course has been designed to help you serve more people and experience greater success in the real estate industry. We're really glad you're here.

We're assuming you picked up this book because you're at a turning point in your life and your career. Perhaps you're fresh out of school and are drawn to selling real estate; you know that prospecting success won't just fall into your lap, but you don't quite know where to begin. Or perhaps you've been prospecting for some time with little success; you're dissatisfied with the results you've been getting and are afraid of wasting more time, but you believe there must be a better alternative.

Congratulations—you've come to the right book and the only prospecting plan you'll ever need.

This book will teach you:

- Discovered truths about prospecting—what it really is, and why it works.
- How to implement the techniques *proven* to boost sales.
- How to recreate the framework to do it again, and again, and again.

Specifically, we will teach you everything you need to know about the following prospecting methods:

- Prospecting for Expired and Cancelled Listings
- Prospecting through Open Houses
- Property Previews
- Prospecting For Sale By Owners (FSBOs)
- Circle Prospecting
- Generating business through your SOI Referral Database

Additionally, this book is peppered and punctuated with the tools and strategies necessary to secure your success:

- Learning Scripts
- Time Management
- Tracking Numbers
- Holding Yourself Accountable
- Maintaining a Proper Mindset

Maintaining a proper mindset and perspective is the most important lesson you'll learn. As you'll soon see, we cannot repeat or emphasize this enough!

## How To Use This Book

It should come as no surprise that success will require some active participation on your part. Throughout this book, we invite you to experiment with new techniques, adopt new practices and perspectives, and adapt them to your own style. Each chapter will include Exercises and Challenges for you to consider and complete.

As well as this book, you'll need the following few materials, including:

 A notebook and/or journal for note taking and reflecting

 A database of personal contacts

 Something to write with

 A calculator

 A computer with Internet access

 A schedule: either paper or digital, preferably both

## Getting Started: Balance & Perspective

We know you're eager to dive right in and get working on the practical aspects of prospecting. By the end of this chapter, you will have learned the nuts and bolts of learning the business, the three pillars of prospecting success, how to create a daily work schedule, and how to implement a systematic organized sales process.

Before we dive into the details, however, it's important that we establish the fundamental importance of **mindset, attitude, and perspective** when it comes to prospecting.

In this chapter, we will examine various prospecting stereotypes, negative connotations, conventional thinking, and false beliefs. We will ask you to explore the ties that bind you and address the things that are holding you back. We will stress the importance of taking the long view and approaching each day with a positive attitude and your future success in mind. Positive energy changes everything, and we will ask you to commit to making positivity a habitual practice in your daily life.

If you're thinking: "I just want to prospect—this sounds like a lot of head shrinking," then pay extra close attention: this chapter has been written especially for you.

Until you understand that your attitude and perspective is the fundamental bedrock of your business, it's unlikely that anything we teach you throughout this book will stick or generate meaningful results in the long term. You might learn a few nifty tricks or techniques to get you started, but that can only take you so far. To truly succeed and go the distance in your prospecting career, you will need to adopt and maintain a positive mindset to fuel and reenergize you through the failures, setbacks, and rejections that lay before you.

*To truly succeed and go the distance in your prospecting career, you will need to adopt and maintain a positive mindset to fuel and reenergize you through the failures, setbacks, and rejections that lay before you.*

Perhaps that sounds negative and contradicts our insistence that you remain positive! But being positive isn't about denying reality or pretending that everything will always be great or that every technique you apply will generate instant and wild success. Maintaining a positive mindset is about keeping those inevitable failures and rejections in perspective, learning from them, and not allowing them to break you or take away from your achievements.

Another thing we want to establish from the outset is the **importance of maintaining balance in your work as well as a work-life balance.**

By prospecting, we're specifically talking about *business generation* and doing a regular activity each and every business day in order to generate leads and identify potential clients. Servicing existing clients is important but, oftentimes, agents tip the balance towards customer-service and neglect to actually prospect for new leads. When working, it's important to prioritize business-generation and your long-term career goals.

To achieve this, you must be efficient with your time and balance servicing existing clients with generating new business. It's not unreasonable to carve out 25% of each day and 25% of each week to generating new business.

*"More business cannot equal less personal time. Your goal is to increase your business and income to increase your personal freedom." – Brian Icenhower*

Efficiency at work increases income, which, in turn increases work-life balance and helps you to achieve the life you want. Sooner or later our business life will suffer if our personal life goes away. We will perform poorly and burn out. At some point, there won't be anything left to work for. You need to have personal goals and interests in order to drive and fuel your business over the long term.

In everything we teach you here, it's important to understand that **more business cannot equal less personal time.** Your goal is to increase your business and income to increase your personal freedom. Any business model that doesn't achieve both of those things is flawed and outdated.

Of course there will be times when you'll burn the midnight oil and have to work a little bit longer than you want to, but understand that we always want you working towards a place where that will no longer happen, and you'll be able to tip the balance back in the other direction. As you progress through each stage of this book, your goal is an efficient, systematized, rich and balanced life.

With all of that in mind, let's review our targets for what you'll learn in this chapter.

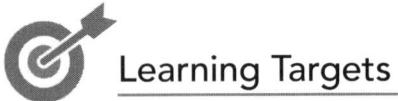 Learning Targets

- Understand the Three Pillars of Prospecting Success
- Develop a *Success Library* as your Motivational Fuel to Succeed
- Differentiate between the skillsets of prospecting and selling
- Learn the techniques in creating a schedule for prospecting

Now that you know what to expect, we really can get started!

# THE BIG 3

Prospecting success depends upon three things:

1. Skill Level
2. Frequency
3. Number of Contacts

Each of these elements is necessary. When all three are in balance, they provide the structure and support that is essential for success.

Think of it like a three-legged stool. A stool with one or two legs will collapse, and although four or more legs would strengthen the platform, they require extra time and expense. That fourth leg will cause the stool to wobble if you try to use it on uneven ground. Having more legs is not efficient. Three is the perfect number: Skill Level, Frequency, and Number of Contacts.

This winning trifecta is the ultimate goal. However, most people don't begin their prospecting journey with three legs of the same length, so it's essential that you understand from the outset that these three elements are an end goal rather than an immediate given. Like any quality, long-lasting piece of furniture, prospecting success is something you have to measure, plan, build, and perfect piece by piece and day by day.

## SKILL LEVEL

When it comes to prospecting, too many people evaluate how good they are far too early. They judge their skill level right off the bat or, often, before they even begin. They quit too soon, and some of them don't start at all because they assume they don't have the skills it takes. They prematurely assess themselves as a poor prospector and say, "I guess this isn't for me after all."

These people fail to understand—because nobody ever told them—that Skill Level is developed. What's more, your ability to succeed is based on the skills you develop through the other two pillars: Frequency and Number of Contacts.

*"Your success is more about your availability than your natural ability."* - Brian Icenhower

We repeat: prospecting is a developed skill.

Yes, some people possess certain personality or behavioral traits that make them more 'natural' salespersons. They have an aptitude or inborn potential for the business.

However, time and time again, we have seen people with amazing natural ability flounder and fail. They try to get by with their innate skills and dismiss the importance of the other two pillars. Meanwhile, we have seen people with the lowest skill levels become some of the most successful prospectors out there, because they worked on their skill development as they were actively prospecting for business.

*Skill levels increase in direct proportion to time on task and making the right connections.*

These people understood that their skill levels increased in direct proportion to time on task and making the right connections. Their commitment and availability conquered their natural ability. Their persistence and their attitude overcame their aptitude.

## Frequency

How often do you prospect? What is your consistency level?

If you work another full-time job (which is often the case for new prospectors), perhaps you're trying to squeeze in some prospecting time during your lunch break or after you get home and are already exhausted from a long and busy day.

We hate to say it, but if you're prospecting with low and irregular frequency, this career will probably not pan out for you.

*You cannot increase your skill level if you don't spend a substantial amount of time practicing and performing prospecting activities.*

Successful prospecting requires repeated and frequent time on task. Time on task makes you much more efficient and gets you much better results. You cannot increase your skill level if you don't spend a substantial amount of time practicing and performing prospecting activities. Real estate is a numbers game. You must develop consistent habits and you must begin prospecting with high frequency to develop your skills and see steady and recurring results.

## Number of Contacts

As we said, real estate is a numbers game, and this is especially true when it comes to prospecting. Prospecting success hinges on making connections. You must have contact information and connect with a certain number of people so that you can prospect with high frequency and develop your skill level.

However, your skill level will not increase through frequency alone—you must have the right people to contact. In time, you will develop different databases of people to contact. There are many different prospecting methods and ways of generating leads, sourcing contacts, and exponentially building your sphere of influence. We'll explore that in more detail throughout the book.

*Your skill level will not increase through frequency alone—you must have people to contact.*

For now, your contacts are primarily the people in your Sphere of Influence. Simply put, these are people that know you by name and are in a position to refer you business. They include your close friends and family, as well as acquaintances like your child's teacher or the person who cuts your hair.

 ## EXERCISE: Contact Count

Try this quick exercise: check your Facebook and LinkedIn pages. How many connections do you have? How many followers do you have on Twitter and Instagram? Write the numbers below and add them up:

| | |
|---|---|
| Facebook | _____ |
| LinkedIn | _____ |
| Twitter | _____ |
| Instagram | _____ |
| TOTAL | _____ |

You probably already have hundreds of contacts, and these are people you know. That's an excellent beginning. We'll work on growing your number of contacts at each stage of this book.

In summary, your prospecting skill level increases in direct proportion to frequency, time on task, and making the right connections. Take care of these three pillars, and your prospecting business will take care of you. Each of these things is in your reach, and your control, right where you sit. Whether you're brand new to prospecting, or you were around when they invented the word, these three factors can level the playing field.

## BREAK THE TIES THAT BIND YOU

The Christian bible tells us that a cord of three strands is not quickly broken, and this metaphor is true no matter your religious or spiritual beliefs—your prospecting skills are overwhelmingly strengthened and reinforced when you prioritize and attend to all three elements.

However, so often we see people that are chained down, limited, and constrained by cords of a different kind.

Perhaps you're familiar with the story of the man who encountered some elephants in a trainer's enclosure and was confused by the fact that these enormous, powerful animals were being held by a very thin rope, tied to their front leg. No heavy chains. No padlocked cages. It was clear that the elephants could, at any time, break the ties that held them, and escape from the enclosure, but for some reason they did not..

Confused, the man asked the trainer why the elephants just stood there and made no attempt to run away.

"Because," the trainer said, "the cord you see tied to their leg is the same cord we used to tie them in place when they were babies. At that young age, it's enough to hold them. And as they grow up, they are conditioned to believe that they cannot break away. They believe the same thin cord is still strong enough to keep them where they are, so they don't even attempt to break out of bondage."

The man was astounded. These strong and powerful animals could break free from their weak cords at any time, but because they believed that they couldn't, they remained right where they were.

## What's Holding You Back?

Too often we see people that are constrained and held back by a false belief that they cannot do something. Too often, we allow ourselves to be tied to old goals and outdated practices. We are restricted and restrained by our former failures. We believe that what happened in the past is what will happen in the future. As time goes on, we don't even attempt to break free.

Is the same thing true for you? Are you tethered to practices that don't achieve results? Are you held back by false beliefs? Have you been conditioned to believe that you don't have the skills it takes to even attempt prospecting?

Let's revisit **The Big 3**. Is there a cord or false belief that is holding you back from achieving one, or more, of the three pillars? If you had to pick your weakest area, which would it be? What would a consultant choose if they were to shadow you and observe your activities for a week? What would you tell them is tying you down or constraining you?

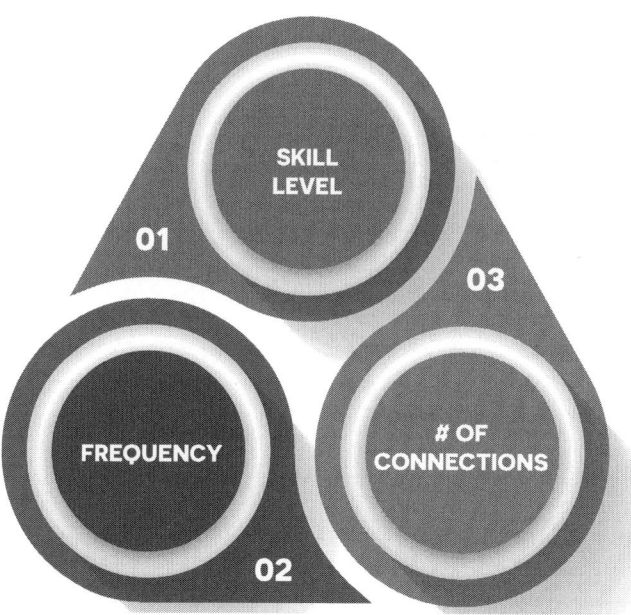

Whatever that cord or belief is for you, it doesn't have to hold you back or prevent you from exploring greener pastures. You, too, are stronger and more powerful than you think you are. You can break free of the ties that bind you and experience greater freedom and greater abundance. All you have to do is be open to letting go of the behaviors that no longer serve you and replace them with practices—and perspectives—that guarantee greater success.

*"The most important thing is this: to be able, at any moment, to sacrifice what you are, for what you will become!"  - Eric Thomas, Secrets to Success*

## Prospecting Is Sales, Not Selling

In Martin Scorsese's *The Wolf of Wall Street*, Leonardo DiCaprio, playing famed stockbroker Jordan Belfort, takes an ordinary pen out of his pocket and challenges an audience of novice salespeople to sell him the pen.

There's nothing particularly remarkable about the pen but, one by one, each of them begins describing how amazing and wonderful and life changing the pen is.

They think that in order to sell the pen, they need to pitch its features and qualities and make it as attractive and enticing and extraordinary as possible.

*"Sell me this pen"  - Jordan Belfort*

In a previous scene, however, Belfort's drug dealer friend Brad approaches the challenge in a completely different way. He sees that selling the pen is not about the pen—it's about the needs and problems of the buyer. He takes the pen from Belfort and turns it around on his fingers but, instead of describing how incredible the pen is, Brad turns to Belfort and says, "*Write this down for me*," to which the now pen-less Belfort replies, "*I don't have a pen…*"

This is the difference between selling and sales. It doesn't matter whether the pen is amazing or ordinary. Brad has something that Belfort needs. This is how he sells the pen. As you'll see, this difference in attitude and perspective is everything.

### Your Perspective, Their Perspective

Prospecting is the very same. Prospecting is Sales, and Sales is about the needs of the buyer. Attitude and perspective is everything. What we think, and how we feel, about prospecting influences our ability to be successful at it and approach it with insight and an open mind.

Oftentimes, prospecting has a negative connotation in the real estate industry. Sometimes, people have a wary or skeptical attitude towards it. They picture someone aggressive and pushy, like the stereotypical slick and seedy used car salesman. They picture somebody pitching and selling. Even those who are interested in and attracted to the industry think: "I don't want to be a salesman, I don't want to be a salesman." Perhaps there's a part of you that's thinking that too.

HUNGRY

*What we think and how we feel about prospecting influences our ability to be successful at it and approach it with insight and an open mind.*

Well, guess what? You are a sales person. Making sales is precisely what you're supposed to be doing. However, often our attitude and perspective about selling, prospecting, and what it means to be aggressive holds us back from making sales and meeting the needs of the buyer.

Before we drill down on true prospecting, let's explore your attitude and perspective about prospecting.

 ### EXERCISE 1:  Meeting of the Minds

Just below this paragraph, you'll see a diagram, consisting of two overlapping circles.

- In the circle labeled *My Perspective*, list all the words you can think of that go with the term 'Prospecting'. Take about 30 seconds to brainstorm this, but don't overthink it—the idea is to capture the immediate and honest impressions that come to mind.

- Repeat this process for the circle labeled *Their Perspective* from the viewpoint of a potential client.

- In the area where the circles overlap, write any words shared by you and potential clients.

- Next, take a look at the words that you wrote down. Put a plus symbol next to any words that you feel are positive. Put a minus symbol next to any that are negative. Tally your results:

# +s _____     # -s _____

Having more pluses or minuses reveals your attitude—and what you believe your prospective clients' attitudes are—about prospecting. An abundance of minuses may mean that you'll need to explore your feelings about prospecting so that you can embrace it completely.

 **CHALLENGE:** If Your Perspective Is Negative, Does It Change With Different Information?

What if we told you that, time and again, surveys by the National Association of Realtors (NAR) confirm that buyers and sellers want an aggressive agent?

It's true, but what exactly does that mean? For starters, please rid yourself of the image of a slick and seedy, pushy bully. To be an aggressive prospector means something else entirely.

Buyers and sellers want someone that will advocate hard on their behalf. Sellers want an agent that will market their home aggressively, energetically, and dynamically. They want an agent that is determined to get it sold for the highest price in the quickest amount of time. Buyers want an agent that is tenacious, purposeful, and persistent in helping them find their dream home. And, when you've found their dream home, they need an agent that will negotiate forcefully on their behalf in an increasingly competitive market.

If your perspective was somewhat negative in the exercise above, swap out some of those words with positive connotations like:

- Assertive
- Confident
- Dynamic
- Determined
- Energetic
- Forceful
- Purposeful
- Persistent

We all want to be proud of and good at our jobs. Being good at prospecting means being good at customer-service, being good at helping people, and being good at meeting people's needs. Buyers and sellers care mainly about their pain points and what you can do to help them solve their problems. Selling, searching, and negotiating are your clients' biggest needs. This is what they want from you, and you serve them best by representing them confidently, assertively, and with pride in what you do.

 **EXTRA CREDIT:** Explore Shared Attitudes And Common Perspectives.

You might also find it interesting to analyze the responses that you wrote in the center of the diagram. The feelings and attitudes that you and your prospective clients share about prospecting may provide common ground for establishing rapport and relationships.

It can also uncover how *vital* it is to investigate perceptions and expectations early on in the sales process with clients. If you're working under different impressions than someone else, it can make for an awkward reveal, or worse, an expensive mistake that costs all parties.

Getting clarity on intentions is also the sign of a professional during negotiations, so this skill will echo through a number of different services you provide.

Your goal is to serve as many clients as possible at as high a level as possible. There are few things that save more time than clarifying intentions.

## PROSPECTING UNEARTHED

We have established that **Prospecting is Sales, not Selling**—now let's unpack that further.

Oftentimes, prospecting has a negative connotation among some real estate agents because they don't really understand what it is and the logic behind it. They think that there's a good way and a bad way to do business, a correct way and an incorrect way. In short, they see things very differently.

Agents that operate an SOI referral database business are horrified at the idea of cold calling or reaching out to people that they don't know. Whereas, for prospectors, the last thing they want to do is call up their friends and acquaintances to ask them for business or a referral. They don't want to bother them or create an impression that they're only staying in touch for personal gain. Instead, they would rather contact people that they know want to sell their house (such as an expired listing), and that need their help. To a prospector, that's not a cold call at all—it's a warm lead.

> *Prospecting is a sales method. It is a technique and a systematic process with its own structure and logic.*

**Prospecting is a sales method.** It is a technique and a systemic process with its own structure and logic. Like any sales method, it has its advantages and drawbacks, but your successful application of the method comes largely down to your mindset. Neither sales method is correct or incorrect, or better or worse than the other. They both work. The difference between them working and not working is your perspective.

## A BRIEF HISTORY OF PROSPECTING

The word 'prospecting' emerged in the mid-1800s when thousands of hopeful people travelled across the United States, lured by the promise—or prospect—of silver, gold, and other precious metals.

Prospecting is the *first stage* of examining land with a view to mining a claim. As such, prospecting was a very physical and repetitive activity. Prospectors traversed and combed the countryside on foot and horseback. They explored for gold along rivers and creek beds, sifting through mounds of sand and mined ore, hoping to catch that thrilling glimmer of a gold nugget in the bottom of their pans.

They did this *over and over again*, multiple times, endlessly, all day long. Even back then, prospecting was a numbers game, where people experienced a tremendous amount of failure but nevertheless persisted because the rewards—when they came—were more than worth it.

Though the famous 49ers of the Gold Rush are now a distant memory, the same principles apply to real estate prospecting methods:

- Prospecting is the *first stage of examining the lead landscape* with a view to securing prospects and future clients.

- Prospecting is a *physical and exploratory activity*: Circle-Prospecting, for example, involves knocking on doors and physically approaching people within a specific geographic area. Prospectors are as familiar with nearby neighborhoods and the local landscape as the 49ers were with the mountains and rivers of California!

- Prospecting is *repetitive*: there is no quick trick—you will have to sift through an enormous amount of dead leads to unearth your glimmers of gold.

More than anything, though, as with prospecting for silver and gold, the real estate prospecting method is a game of numbers and, as you'll see, when playing the game of numbers, it helps to take the long view.

## Prospecting Is A Game of Numbers: Take The Long View

Traveling further back in time, the word 'prospecting' comes from the word 'prospect', which, in turn, comes from the Latin word prospectus. In the 15th century, the word prospect meant to literally look into the distance. In the 17th century, it came to mean "expectations" or "things looked forward to." And in the early 20th century, the word took on a sense of a person or thing considered promising. It's funny, then, that prospecting can sometimes have a negative connotation when, in fact, it has such positive and optimistic origins.

As a prospector, you will sift through large numbers of people and wade through a lot of incorrect and bad information to find that one person who needs your help. You will do this over and over again, endlessly, all day long. Depending on your mindset, this may sound very dispiriting or downright crazy, but understand that this is a normal part of the technique. Yes, there will be a lot of false leads, failure, and rejection. But the rewards, when they come—and they will come—will be more than worth it.

Apart from the obvious financial rewards, a major benefit of the prospecting method is that your success rate—that is, your conversion rate—is largely within your control. While you will encounter a lot of people that don't need your help, you can be extremely successful by playing the numbers, embracing frequency and repetition, and adopting a long-view perspective.

> *Apart from the obvious financial rewards, a major benefit of the prospecting method is that your success rate—that is, your conversion rate—is largely within your control.*

For example, veteran Expired Listing prospectors with good conversion rates typically contact between 20 and 25 seller-leads (prospective clients or 'prospects' for short) in order to get a listing appointment. While some people may see that as 19 to 24 resounding No's, prospectors that possess a broad, long-term perspective immediately understand that, if they can commit to talking to 25 people every single day, that could be 5 listing appointments in a week. For every *No* you experience on a daily basis, that's a great deal of *Yes's* when you add it up over the course of a year.

At ICC, we coach several agents that prospect for expired listings who list anywhere from 70 to 100 homes a year. (Expired Listings are when a property hasn't been sold by the end of the period stipulated in the listing contract. When a listing expires, sellers can choose to stay on with their current agent, or they can decide to work with a new agent without incurring any penalties. We cover this in-depth in Chapter 4). They're in control of their business and their income because they're committed to systematized practices that assure specific conversion rates.

Now, 70 to 100 listings a year isn't too shabby at all, let us tell you! Prospecting is a game of numbers and it is also a mental game of perspective and attitude. What these agents have in common is that when they're panning through that metaphorical sand at the bottom of the creek bed, they don't see the 24 No's—they see the promise of that 1 thrilling nugget of glittering gold. In the same way that investors take the long view when considering where to put their money, prospectors take the long view and see those 25 calls as a daily investment in their overall future.

## Organized Sales Process

As we said a moment ago, prospecting is a sales method. It is a technique and a system with its own structure and logic. To be more exact, it is an Organized Sales Process: a systematic, repeatable series of steps and actions that map out and track interaction with leads and prospects, from their first point of engagement with your business through to a close.

Broadly speaking, it is a three-step sales process where we take an individual from **Lead** to **Prospect** to **Client** or, in other words, from **Contact** to **Appointment** to **Contract**.

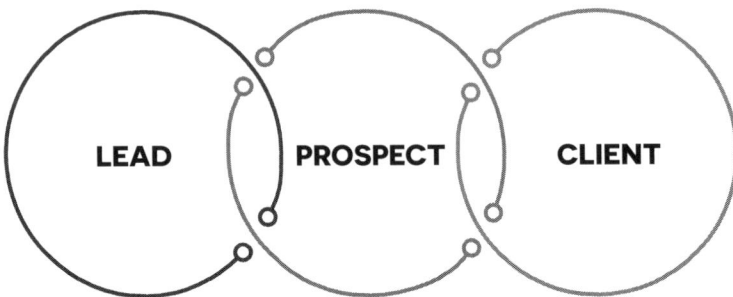

However, within these three broad steps, **additional actions and activities** must be performed in order to move people forward to the next step.

As we will explore in Chapter 12, the art of closing is the art of transitioning an individual from one stage to the next in the organized sales process. Closing is not a one-time event. Closing happens at every stage in the process, whether you're trying to close an appointment, a contract or agreement, a price-reduction, a counter-offer, and every other event where you present a scenario, vision or option to an individual and ask them if they're ready to make a decision and move forward.

Some see the Organized Sales Process as a timeline; others see it as a checklist. Though the actual actions and activities may vary, here's an example process that we'll reference throughout the material:

- Prospecting (Generate Leads & Contacts)
- Source and Qualify Leads
- Nurture & Cultivate
- Set & Confirm Appointment
- Prepare for Appointment/Sales Call
- Deliver Successful Sales Presentation
- Close for the Sale
- Calendar and Schedule Transaction
- Review, Request Feedback & Referrals
- Close Again
- Execute & Follow Up

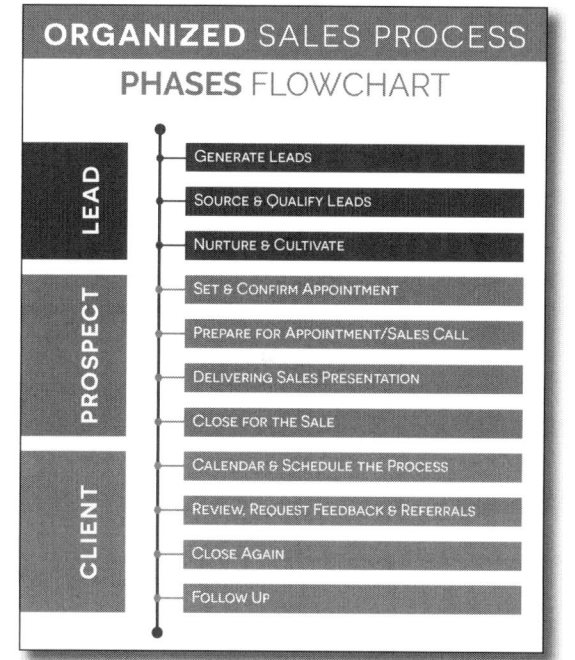

As you can see, some of the actions and activities overlap and occur at each stage of the process. Often, the actual details of the process will depend on the lead source. Depending on the lead source, you will employ a very different qualification process.

At all stages, leads and prospects must be nurtured and cultivated, and prospectors must determine whether a lead is a qualified prospect that is ready, willing, and able to buy or sell real estate. BANT

At this point, it might be helpful to pause for a moment and clarify some of these terms and phrases.

## DEFINITIONS

### Lead

A lead is nothing more than a name and contact information for someone who is a possible future client. Often, a lead is referred to as a contact. Depending on the lead source, you might not even have a name, but if you have a way to contact and connect with someone, that is a lead.

Many leads are dead ends that come to nothing. Prospectors must sift through a lot of bad information—old phone numbers, misspelled email addresses etc. Be prepared to come across a lot of fake phone numbers: 1-800-SHOVEOFF is one of our favorites!

### Lead Source

Simply put, a lead source is where your leads originate or come from. Leads are sourced in a variety of ways, from online leads such as home-search sites, social media and email marketing to offline leads such as open houses and referrals. We will explore this in more detail throughout the book.

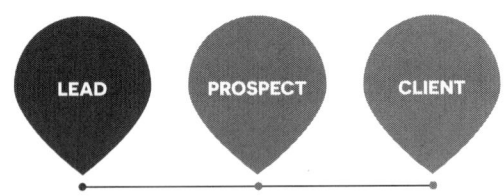

### Prospect

You could say that everyone you meet is a prospect but, for now, a prospect is a prospective client that is further along in the sales process than a lead.

While many leads come to nothing, a prospect is a qualified and interested lead that has demonstrated (through interacting or communicating with the agent) that they are interested in making a buying or selling decision.

Additionally, a qualified prospect is someone that is *ready, willing, and able* to buy or sell real estate. Oftentimes, prospects want to buy or sell—they are more than willing—but, for one reason or another, they are currently unable to do so.

Prospectors engage in a variety of long and short term nurturing and cultivating activities to determine whether a prospect is qualified to move forward to the final stages in the process.

### Ready, Willing, Able

"Ready, willing and able" is a phrase used in real estate to refer to a prospective client who is legally capable and financially able to consummate the deal.

It is crucial to determine that a client is ready, willing, and able to actually make a sale. Too often, agents are so focused on their commission check at the end that they neglect to complete the additional steps and actions in between. It's essential to communicate clearly and determine answers to the following questions:

**READY?**
- Is the prospect truly ready to buy or sell?
- Are they expressing doubts or raising objections?
- Is something preventing them from moving forward?

**WILLING?**
- Is the prospect eager, engaged, and excited?
- Is the prospect willing but under pressure or held back by an unwilling partner or spouse?
- Is there a clear expectation agreed to that they will take action?

**ABLE?**
- Does the prospect have funds to purchase?
- Are they prequalified or prepproved to obtain financing from a lender?
- Are they unable to buy or sell for any other financial or legal reason?

BANT

As we said, oftentimes, prospects are willing to buy or sell but, for one reason or another, they are not quite ready or able to do so. Think of the tumblers inside a lock: all three tumblers must unlock to qualify an individual as a truly qualified prospect.

In a dream world, every lead and prospect would check all three boxes upfront at the same time, but don't be at all surprised or discouraged if that's not the case. You will develop systems and skillsets to guide your prospects to meet all three criteria.

The connections you make where the individual's readiness, willingness, and ability are farther off the radar become a long-term investment of nurturing and cultivation. You should never dismiss a prospect based on their current situation. Be a skilled investor with a balanced portfolio of both prospects and future prospects. For insight on converting rejections to potentials, look for *6 Things No Means* in the Appendix.

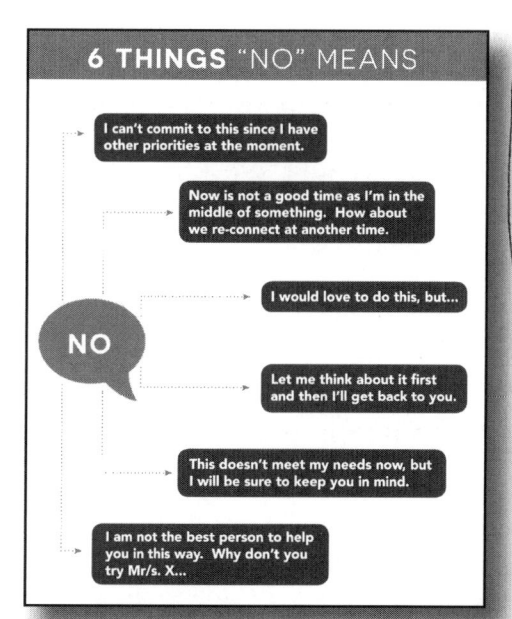

*Nurturing & Cultivating*

Most prospects are in the "just looking" or "just thinking about it" stage, so it's important to follow-up and build rapport with potential clients before meeting with them in person or moving them through the next stage in the process. Essentially, nurturing is about developing and deepening relationships with leads and prospects, and listening to their needs so that you can maintain their interest and help serve them best.

Nurturing or cultivating a lead or prospect can be done in a variety of ways, from content email marketing and social media to direct communication by phone or in person. Often, the tactic or frequency of nurturing will depend on the type of lead.

For example, nurturing a 'Cool Lead' who plans to move in the next 9-18 months might involve a phone call or text every couple of months, while nurturing a 'Hot Lead' who plans to move in 30 days or less could involve contacting them 3 times a week with a combination of calling, texting, meeting in person, and/or showing them properties.

*Voice note*

Depending on the lead source, prospectors might have to do much more nurturing or cultivating of a lead.

Online leads, for example, require much nurturing, as you have to build a relationship with a stranger that you basically met on the Internet!

For Sale By Owner leads obviously want to sell their home without the help of an agent. So, nurturing a FSBO might involve staying in touch over a period of time, building rapport, and providing some assistance so that when they eventually give up and decide to list with a realtor, you'll be first of mind and they'll appreciate that you built a relationship over time.

### Appointment

*Prospectors are constantly focused on moving leads and prospects forward to the next stage in the process. Ultimately, you want to move them to the client/contract stage, but in order to advance that far, you must successfully complete the appointment part of the process.*

*An appointment could be a Listing Presentation or a Buyer Consultation. Think of them as a job interview where you have one chance to show them why you're the best agent to represent their needs and interests.*

### Client/Contract

A successful Listing Presentation results with a signed Listing Agreement—a contract between the agent and the owner/seller of a property granting the agent the authority to act as the seller's representative in the sale of the property.

Prospective buyers, on the other hand, might sign a Buyer Exclusive Agency Agreement. This contract outlines the obligations of the agent and the responsibilities of the buyer. Crucially, this contract stipulates that the buyer may not retain the services of more than one agent to assist him or her.

In either case, a signed contract means that you have successfully taken that individual from a virtually anonymous lead to a qualified prospect all the way to a bona fide client!

Congratulations! Now, all you have to do is rinse and repeat and follow the same organized sales process again and again…..aaaaaaand again and again!

Are you starting to see how a positive mindset is crucial to a successful career in prospecting?

## Positive Energy Changes Everything

Would you agree that, in just about every profession, the businesses that seem to thrive, excel, and grow at a rapid pace are the ones that exhibit a positive, wide-eyed passion for what they do?

Customers are clamoring to get in the door and interact with this experience because it makes them feel better and validates their value.

How you show up to everything you do makes a difference, of course, but increasingly it can make *the* difference. With the round-the-clock access businesses have to our attention spans, competition is fierce. People are attracted to high energy and positivity. If you want to build rapport and nurture clients, you must capture their attention with positivity and remain smiling, even in the face of rejection and negativity.

## Positivity Is A Skill

Oftentimes, real estate agents are 'nuts and bolts' types of people:

> *"Just tell me what to do, and I'll do it. Tell me what to say, and I'll say it."*

While we certainly admire that, we're afraid that a practical attitude in itself will not work. Believe it or not, positivity is not just an incidental mood or feeling, separate from your business practices—it's actually a skillset and should be practiced and developed as diligently and seriously as any prospecting skill you're trying to learn.

There is a tremendous amount of rejection, failure, and negativity in prospecting. It's crucial that you always work to remain positive in everything you do. Apart from your personal wellbeing, which is obviously very important, positive energy will also increase your conversion rates.

In the following pages, we will suggest some strategies that will help you perform an overhaul and maintenance plan on one of the most valuable tools you'll be using day in and day out—your mindset.

---

*"Your attitude determines your altitude."* - Zig Ziglar

---

But, before we dive into that, let's establish a benchmark of where you are now, so that as you progress, you'll be able to chart how far you've come. Small successes are vital to celebrate and keep you going.

# EXERCISE: Map It!

Take a few minutes to complete the **Attitudinal Energy Level** Chart below. This exercise maps your work-life balance and takes a personal inventory of your life through 6 different lenses: Relationships, Health, Education/Training, Finances, Work-Life Balance, and Career.

Mark your satisfaction level in each of these areas. On this scale, '10' indicates the highest level of satisfaction and '1' indicates a low level of satisfaction.

- How would you rate your relationships? Relationships can include your friends and family as well as personal relationships with your spouse or partner.

- How is your health and wellness? Health includes your fitness and diet as well as your mental and spiritual health.

- What about your education and training? How are you doing with increasing your knowledge and developing the skills you need to succeed in your career?

- How are your personal finances? What is your level of debt? Are you saving money? How is retirement looking?

- How would you rate your work-life balance? Are you spending enough time at home with your family? Do you have time for hobbies and pursuits outside of work?

- Where do you think you are in your career? Are you satisfied with your career? How would you rate your attitudinal energy level when looking at your life through this lens?

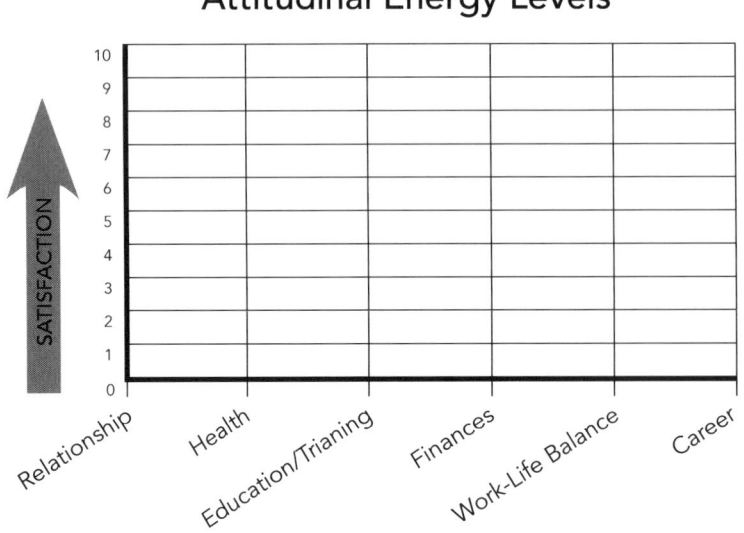

*How Did You Do?*

- Which area is your lowest?

- Which area is your highest?

- Which area would you most like to work on?

- If a friend or family member were asked about your levels, would the numbers change?

The energy levels of most people resonate just under the halfway mark, at 4 or less. If you marked 6 or above in an area, it's likely that you are either at the top of your game or on your way there.

In other words, you can categorize your energy levels like this:

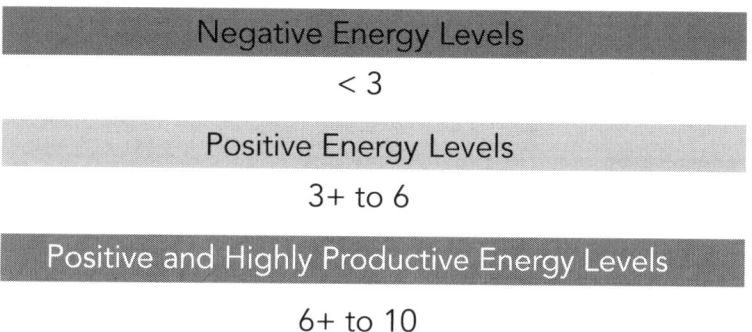

Energy levels can be visualized this way:

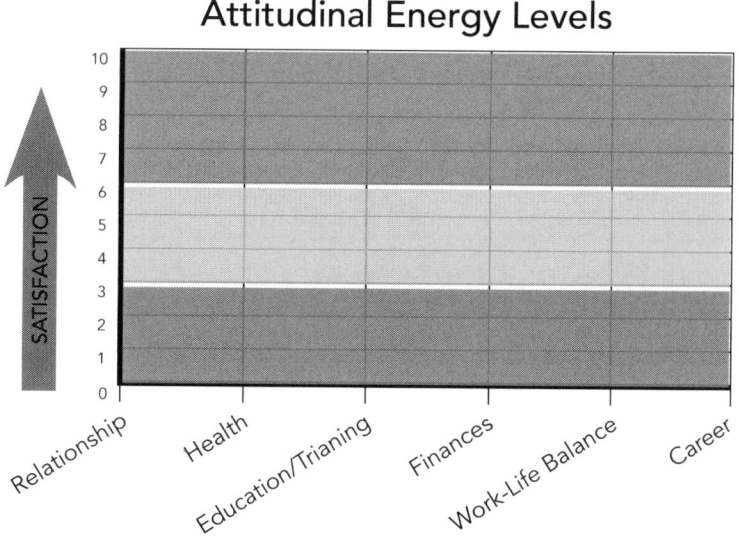

Areas in the lower red zone are emergency-level areas that need a lot of your attention right now. It's wonderful if your energy levels are in the medium to high zones, but understand that if you're lagging in one area, you will soon start to feel the knock-on effects in other areas in your life.

Though you may currently be highly satisfied with your Career and Finances, those lower level areas will eventually catch up with you and begin to chip away at your positive attitude. A great career won't seem so great when your family and health is suffering. If you want to be successful in prospecting for real estate, you need to have balance in your entire life.

Identifying and implementing strategies for improving a particular life area can enhance your energy level. The increased energy will result in better overall satisfaction, whether you seek to improve your satisfaction with your health, finances or career. Often, these areas overlap. Working in one area helps to improve all others.

> *"From time to time, it's important to step back from who we are and where we are and what we're doing and take another look at who we are and where we are and what we're doing. If we don't do that, we get caught up in our own little worlds, and that's a dangerous place." - Matthew Kelly, author of 'The Dream Manager'*

A proven way to ensure you are on track is to work with a mentor and a coach who can help you break through blocks and remain accountable for improvement. It's also essential that you begin to make positivity a habitual practice!

## Make Positivity A Practice

It's extremely important that you work to develop the crucial skillset of positivity. Frequent interactions with your contacts will increase your skills and ability, and help to generate more business for you.

Of course, we're only human. Nobody actually feels positive and energetic all day every day. Sometimes, we have to fake it till we make it, but don't think that this is being deceptive or false.

Oftentimes, we think that our actions are simply an outward reflection of our inward feelings but, in fact, the opposite is true. Sometimes, we have to act our way into a feeling. We do this by habitually practicing the actions and traits associated with the feeling we want to reflect and exude.

At first, it may feel corny or cheesy to smile or speak with exuberance or excitement. In time, however, this habitual practice will become completely natural and help you to become genuinely positive and optimistic.

> *Sometimes, we have to act our way into a feeling. We do this by habitually practicing the actions and traits associated with the feeling we want to reflect and exude.*

Whether speaking on the phone or speaking in person, a positive attitude and high energy level always generates the best results.

People can 'hear' your mood. Your attitude comes through in your tone and even in your facial expressions. In fact, when speaking with leads and prospects on the phone, a lot of top prospectors keep a mirror in front of them that reminds them to smile and keep their chin up. We've all heard the expression, but did you know that keeping your chin up actually opens up our lungs and throats and helps us to speak more positively and confidently? Conversely, dropping your chin results in a drop in your demeanor and causes you to speak in a monotonous, mundane, and low energy voice.

When you break down positive energy to its basic elements, there remains a series of conscious choices of how to act and behave in any given moment. B.F. Skinner remarked that "our behavior isn't controlled by thoughts, thoughts are actually behavior."

If positive energy has eluded you, it may simply have been an absence of conscious choices. As you move forward in your career, practice the following habits so that they become the character traits that come to mind when people think of you.

**10 — Know When To Say "No"**
to something without the feeling of loss.

**09 — Accept Your Faults And Mistakes,**
and own them candidly.

**08 — Build People Up In A Genuine Way.**
Reframe faults into opportunity.

**07 — Empathize And Forgive,**
even when no one's watching.

**06 — Avoid Complaining.**
It's bad marketing for your voice.

**05 — Recognize What's In—And Out Of—Your Control.**
Literally write it down.

**04 — Smile. Wave. High Five. Nod. Make Eye Contact**

**03 — Take Care Of Yourself, Physically And Mentally.**
Get enough sleep. Work out and watch your diet. Be kind to yourself. Avoid self-deprecating, even in jest.

**02 — Be Genuinely Excited About What You're Doing.**
If it's repetitive, be resourceful and creative in your work.

**01 — Find The Best In Everyone.**
Some people hide it well—so keep searching. Asking great questions is the key

## CHALLENGE: Work It Out

Think of the above traits as skills that can be worked on and developed. When working out and staying in shape, some days we focus on our abs, and some days we focus on our cardio. Book a 'workout plan' each week to focus on two of the above practices.

Track the activity you chose. Give it your all, and use real evidence as to how you'd like to continue. Remember that improving your attitude is not about checking in for approval on your transformation: it's about authentic internal growth.

Find the positive in everything you do, and your optimistic outlook will create enough energy to catapult you forward. You'll also have unlimited combinations of decisions to help you get started. These are opportunities.

As with the glass that's half full or half empty depending on your perspective, where you place hope and look for opportunity depends on where you draw the line. Mark the waterline at less than halfway, and you'll perceive that it will take more effort to move forward. Draw the line at the halfway mark, and you'll feel like you are halfway to an accomplishment.

### Make Up Your Mind

Getting ready to prospect is a Catch-22. This expression, from the 1961 Joseph Heller novel *Catch-22*, is still used to mean a tricky or no-win situation. It seems like prospecting often falls into that category: either we're afraid to prospect because of the rejection that goes with it, or the rejection steals our motivation to prospect in the first place. Though we know the Catch-22 is based entirely in our mind, it can be hard to maintain perspective and motivate ourselves to get started let alone keep going.

> *"There are only two ways to influence human behavior: you can manipulate it or you can inspire it."* – Simon Sinek

Think back to a project you've undertaken where, early on in the process, it got hard. Early wins were hard to come by. Maybe the tasks involved got a little repetitive. Sometimes you even got a little lost, or felt overwhelmed? Then progress stopped, and just like that, expectations met reality. The adventure that first fired you up fizzled out.

Perhaps someone encouraged you to hang in there with a thoughtful card or uplifting insight. Perhaps they kindly suggested a different approach altogether. Maybe an experienced colleague reframed the outcome, shared some strategies that work for them, and your energy was renewed.

*"Be a collector of good ideas. Keep a journal. If you hear a good idea, capture it. Write it down. Don't trust your memory." - Jim Rohn*

Do you remember what they said that reenergized and inspired you? If so, write it down right now and don't ever forget it. Collect success whenever you see it and store it up to motivate you in those tricky and seemingly no-win situations.

 ## EXERCISE: Your Success Library

Build and nurture a library filled with evidence of success—yours, as well as other peoples. Curate the kind of successes that will motivate you, renew you, and empower you in as many different areas you can think of, from health & wellness, to relationships, and your career.

You may be wondering, why not draw from just my own business success? There are two powerful reasons to refrain from doing so:

1. When we see someone take on something daunting and win, it's inspiring. We think: If they can do *that*, I can do *this*.

2. When we've had a win it builds confidence, and creates a benchmark. We think: If I can do *this*, I can definitely do *that*!

Start it as an exercise, and it will evolve into a ritual. Like any great salesperson, once you "know the inventory" of your success library, you'll be able to draw on it continually.

*"The best time to plant a tree is twenty years ago. The second best time is today."*
*– Chinese proverb*

Start today. Here's why:

- Success stories become "case studies" you might cite or leverage with clients.

- Most successes lend perspective that might be different than yours; there's a business maturity you'll develop like no other from this.

- Motivation can be like pushing a car; it's a lot easier to keep it moving, than to start from a standstill.

- Successful people implement immediately; it's just what you do.

 ## EXERCISE: My Success Library Blueprint

Each script, strategy, and technique that has made millions has also been taped to someone's wall. Let's begin our framework with a few questions from the *Success Library Blueprint*. Take A Moment To Sketch What Your Library's Success Stories Will Look Like.

- What will some of the topics be?
- Where can you locate these resources?
- Will they be local, national, or global? What would happen if you have a blend?
- What time of day will be most effective for reviewing these?
- What will be the most efficient?
- Who do you know that has this ritual already?
- Who could you partner with on this to help you stay on track?
- What is your definition of success?

Time and again, two outcomes show up as benchmarks of success in real estate: increased productivity and a better work-life balance, year after year.

Having one without the other is dangerous. Focusing exclusively on work-life balance takes away time from work: productivity drops and, when you're less productive, you have less to enjoy. If you devote all your time to productivity, however, you'll burn out sooner than later. Or worse, you'll live until you're 110, all the while never really having lived.

### Powerful Prospectors

No one knows more about maintaining work-life balance and high productivity levels in prospecting than Brian Icenhower. He's been where you are now, and he'll tell you that you don't have to accept the results you've been getting.

For decades he has coached and trained many of the top producing real estate agents, teams and industry leaders on methods and systems to increase their performance while preserving balance in their personal lives. After all, can you truly call yourself a success if you don't have time to enjoy it?

Productivity and Work-Life Balance form the core of success in real estate. You'll find them in your own success story as you develop the prospecting skills to amplify your sales and create abundance.

As you build your library, think about what factors make up your productivity, and what factors pour into your work-life balance. Then seek out successes that will keep them both in the foreground for you.

To get your Success Library started, let's read about H. Ross Perot, the founder of EDS (Electronic Data Systems), and how a unique promotion paired with a high skill level tells the story of a legend:

> H. Ross Perot founded EDS as a way to provide data services to his customers, ultimately selling his company for $2.4 billion. He was a true prospector.
>
> Perot says that he learned about customer service when working for IBM, where he peddled computers. He had already proven himself an excellent salesman, and through commissions, he earned significantly more than many of the executives at IBM.
>
> And though he was a proven talent who deserved to move up, the IBM leadership couldn't promote Perot to a higher position because doing so would cut the man's pay. Instead, they decided to cut the figurative rope holding Perot back.
>
> In exchange for the opportunity to increase his sales volume without IBM's direct supervision, Perot agreed to an 80% cut in commission fees. IBM set the new goals for Perot and turned him loose at the beginning of January 1961.
>
> Perot returned to the IBM offices on January 19th to check in and verify the quota that IBM had set for him in February.
>
> Stunned, upper management explained that the quota they had assigned Perot in January was his quota *for the year*.

Let's do some reflection:

- What were some business lessons in this story?
- How did you feel when you read, "*80% cut* in commission fees"?
- What would make this worth it to you?

Your own sales success will depend on your willingness to implement the prospecting strategies you learn in the course and how consistently you use them.

### EXERCISE: What Motivates Me

Take a moment to reflect; what's the most motivating sales story you've heard or witnessed? Write it down in a paragraph or two. Be sure to include how you felt when you heard it. Then write a paragraph about a similar experience you've personally experienced, or hope to experience.

Your reflection sets the stage for us to dive deeply into our next stage.

## CREATING A DAILY WORK SCHEDULE

One of the first things to do when elevating your prospecting skills is to develop a routine that you can follow, day in and day out. Calendaring and scheduling is one of the most essential tools that you can use as a prospector. By establishing a routine, you'll find that you have plenty of time to get everything done in a day.

There's a warehouse somewhere filled with facts, figures, and statistics about why schedules are important, what gets in the way, the tweaks you must make, as well as a myriad of hacks and workarounds. We'll delve into that a little more when we discuss time-management and your monthly plan in Chapter 7. For now, we have our own schedule to keep if we're to stay on track with this book, so we'll allow you to explore these undeniably important factors in your own time—just don't forget to put it on your calendar!

*"A schedule defends from chaos and whim. It is a net for catching days. It is a scaffolding on which a worker can stand and labor with both hands at sections of time."  - Annie Dillard, author*

## Learning the Business

To help you create your daily schedule, you might benefit from a general overview of what your next steps will likely be as you start out on your prospecting journey.

In the beginning, you'll devote most of your time to learning the business. It often takes six months to develop prospects and processes that result in closed sales. After all, you must first develop and nurture leads before converting them into appointments. Then you'll need to spend time helping your clients locate a property to purchase or waiting for a listing to sell. Once your clients are under contract to purchase or sell a home, you'll then take the transaction through a standard 30-60 day closing process before ultimately earning a commission.

The length of time it takes to get paid has more to do with the real estate *servicing process* than with the particular business-generation techniques themselves. The quicker you learn these processes and train on what you've learned, the quicker you'll be able to cultivate prospects and make money.

Training is different than learning. Training is practice, feedback, and testing with repetition. Learning about a triathlon is vastly different then training for one, and only training guarantees you reaching the finish line. Needless to say, the best way to learn these processes is by practicing on actual people! You will learn the business as you generate business and train kinetically through your clients.

As we move through the book and examine the different prospecting methods in detail, you will need to carve out time in your schedule to practice and hone your skills for each specific type of method. There is a lot to learn and train on.

In the beginning, however, you will need to master the following three things:

- What to Say
- What to See
- Who to Talk To

To get you started in creating your schedule and honing your skills, let's begin with the basics:

- Learning Scripts for various scenarios
- Previewing Listings
- Growing your Sphere of Influence

Remember that we will cover these topics in much more detail in future chapters.

## Learning Scripts

Real estate scripts help you say the right things to prospects. Real agents with real prospects have tested our scripts, and the scripts have been refined to help you communicate effectively with your prospects.

A practiced dialogue also keeps you on track, saves you time, and shows that you are prepared. If you'd ever like to experience the polar opposite of being in the zone, start a dialogue where you're not sure what to say next, and then bask in the awkward silence when you and your client come to the same conclusion that you're not the best choice.

Your primary directive is to memorize the scripts until you can recite them in your sleep. It's recommended that you devote the morning hours to working with your scripts, but you can choose other hours if that's your best time of day. Like exercising, the best time is as soon as you get up, followed closely by the next time you're willing to do it

**CANNED HEAT:** There's an undercurrent of pushback around scripts. The argument is that prepared questions or presentations sound "canned." Don't buy it; they can't sell it anyway. Musicians learn scales and follow sheet music, world-renowned chefs learn and follow recipes, and athletes learn plays and practice them. Debt collectors and fast food workers learn them, too. Please heed the recommendations here, and you'll sound like the confident professional you are.

We'll devote time throughout this book to the various scripts you'll need.

## Previewing Listings

A real estate agent who doesn't know what's available in the market won't generate many sales. Neither will the agent who doesn't understand how certain neighborhoods and their amenities attract a specific clientele.

**Note:** The afternoon is preferred for perusing pre-listings.

You'll learn more about previewing listings in Chapter 4, along with information on how to identify what's available in the real market you are working in.

## Making Connections (Sphere of Influence)

We've talked about working with your connections – the people you know. We call that your 'Sphere of Influence' (SOI). As you probably discovered during the exercise where you tallied the number of connections and followers you have, your SOI is larger than you thought.

Chapter 3 of this textbook will help you explore ways to strengthen and even increase your SOI.

## Don't Forget Work-Life Balance!

When creating your daily work schedule, it's important to remember work-life balance and all six areas of your life. These areas won't improve or develop themselves. You must dedicate focused and conscientious time towards them. If you don't prioritize those areas and block out time for them in your calendar, the likelihood is that they won't be addressed and they will deteriorate even more.

If you rated your Health at 2, for example, we would like to see you factor that area into your daily work schedule. If you need more education and training, then you need to schedule time in your calendar to make sure that happens.

### *Your Daily Schedule*

So, what will your daily schedule look like? There's no better time than now to decide. Remember: you'll need time for working with scripts, previewing listings, expanding your Sphere of Influence, as well as making time for your personal relationships, health, and hobbies.

Be specific when creating your schedule. If you wake up and simply walk into 'work' without a specific plan, the nothingness of 'busy work' will soon take over, you'll get distracted by one type of activity when you're in the middle of another type of activity, and you'll find you didn't actually do or achieve very much of any one thing.

What *must* get done in your day? If you are like most people, life's got you booked in a couple places, with family, errands, and previous recurring commitments. Enter the 'non-negotiable' items on your schedule first.

Enter your start and end times. These are the times you can commit to being physically in the office and on the job.

Next, identify when you'll take lunch. Your schedule may seem a little empty at first, but as you go through this book, you'll be blocking out time to do the following:

- Increase your Sphere of Influence (SOI)
- Reach out to owners of Expired Listings
- Hold Open Houses
- Preview Property
- Contact *For Sale By Owner* (FSBO) properties
- Conduct Circle Prospecting
- Monitor Accountability Numbers, and more

For now, begin by blocking out the time you will devote to learning these three business aspects: Scripts, Listings, and Connections.

With that completed, you are more than ready to get started on taking the next steps!

## Proposed Work Schedule

| Time | Monday | Tuesday | Wednesday | Thursday | Friday | Friday |
|---|---|---|---|---|---|---|
| 8:00 AM | | | | | | |
| 9:00 AM | | | | | | |
| 10:00 AM | | | | | | |
| 11:00 AM | | | | | | |
| 12:00 PM | | | | | | |
| 1:00 PM | | | | | | |
| 2:00 PM | | | | | | |
| 3:00 PM | | | | | | |
| 4:00 PM | | | | | | |
| 5:00 PM | | | | | | |

# Summary

The three pillars of prospecting success are Skill Level, Frequency and Number of Contacts. When all three are in balance, they provide the structure and support that is essential to success. Skill levels increase in direct proportion to time on task and making the right connections.

Prospecting is sales, not selling. Take pride in your ability to advocate hard for your clients and meet their needs.

Prospecting is an Organized Sales Process: a systematic, repeatable series of steps and actions that take an individual from Lead to Prospect to Client or, in other words, from Contact to Appointment to Contract.

Your persistence in adhering to your schedule will reward you, and the motivational stories you collect will inspire you even when some days are tougher than others.

More business cannot equal less personal time. Your goal is to increase your business and income to increase your personal freedom.

Mindset, attitude, and perspective are the bedrock of your business. Positive energy changes everything. Smile.

With that in mind, you're now ready to get to the real work of prospecting. See you in Module 2!

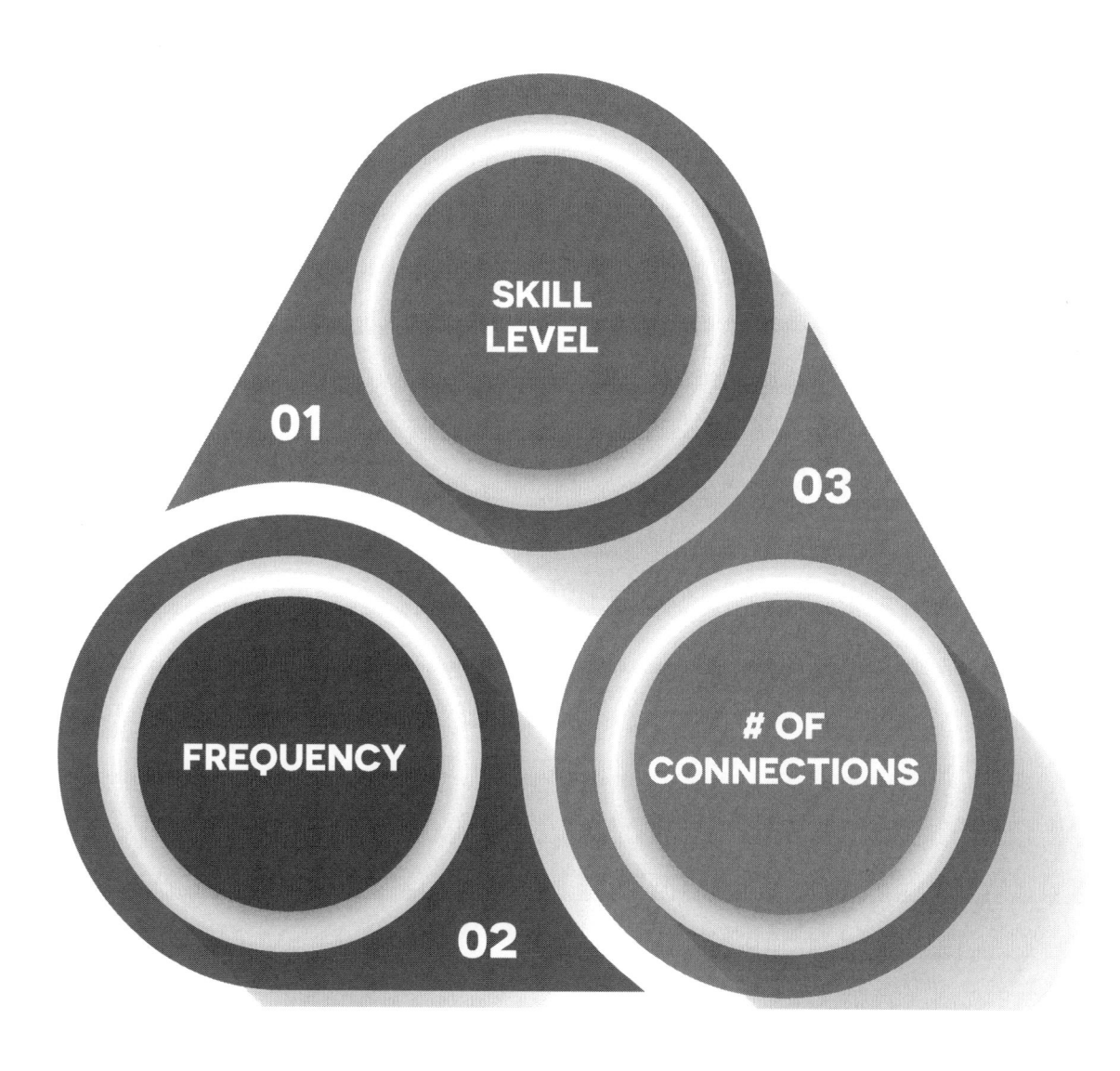

# THE BIG 3 OF PROSPECTING SUCCESS

01 — SKILL LEVEL

02 — FREQUENCY

03 — # OF CONNECTIONS

MODULE 1 　　　　　　　　　　　　　　　　　　　　　　　APPENDIX 1.2

# PROSPECTING: MEETING OF THE MINDS

　　　　　　My Perspective　　　　Their Perspective

- Next, take a look at the words that you wrote down. Put a plus symbol next to any words that you feel are positive. Put a minus symbol next to any that are negative. Tally your results:

　　　　# +s _____　　　　　　# -s _____

© Copyright Icenhower Coaching & Consulting, LLC. All rights reserved.

MODULE 1 — APPENDIX 1.3

# ORGANIZED SALES PROCESS
## PHASES FLOWCHART

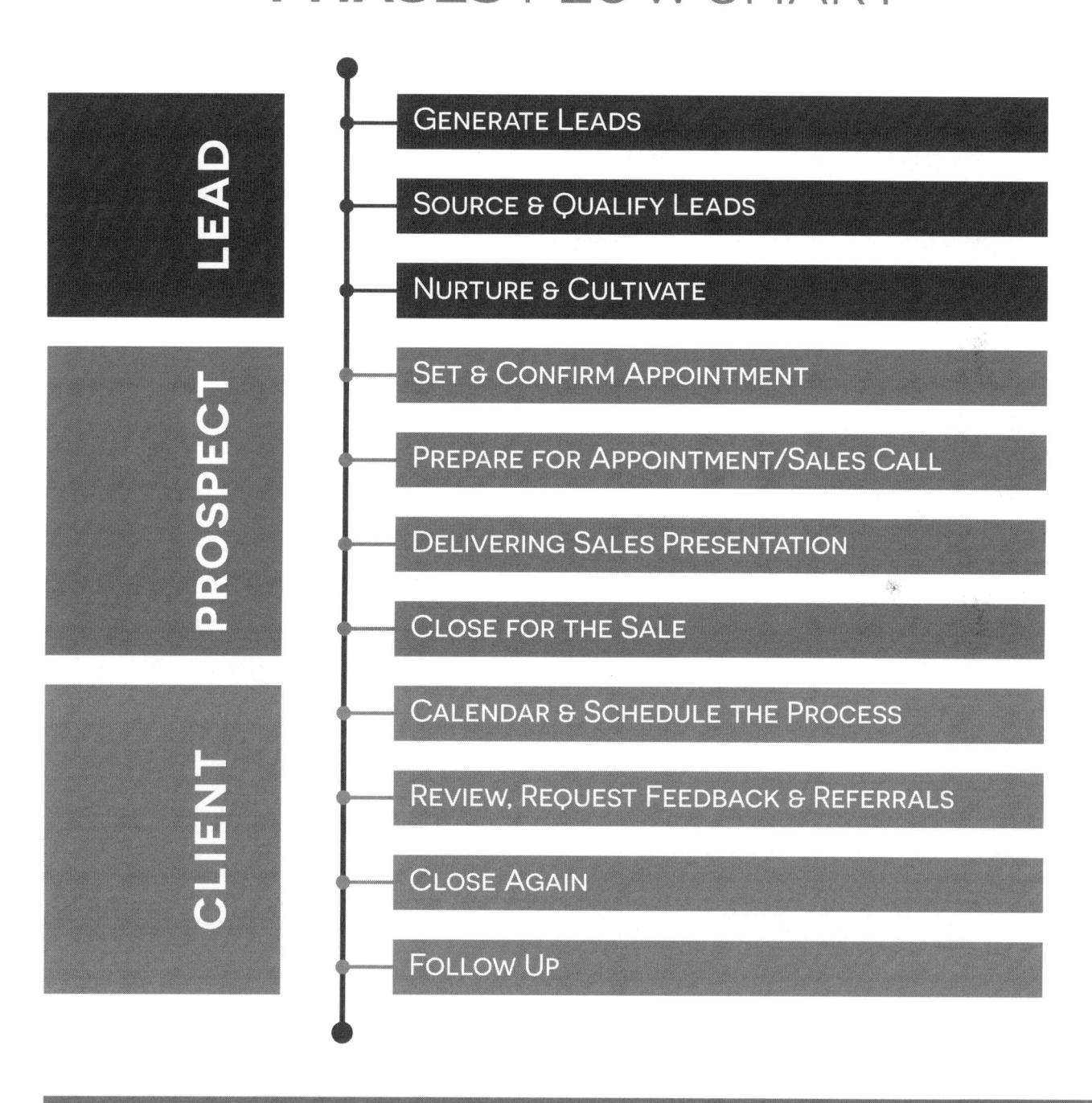

**LEAD**
- Generate Leads
- Source & Qualify Leads
- Nurture & Cultivate

**PROSPECT**
- Set & Confirm Appointment
- Prepare for Appointment/Sales Call
- Delivering Sales Presentation
- Close for the Sale

**CLIENT**
- Calendar & Schedule the Process
- Review, Request Feedback & Referrals
- Close Again
- Follow Up

© Copyright Icenhower Coaching & Consulting, LLC. All rights reserved.

# READY? WILLING? ABLE?

## READY?

- Is the prospect truly ready to buy or sell?
- Are they expressing doubts or raising objections?
- Is something preventing them from moving forward?

## WILLING?

- Is the prospect eager, engaged, and excited?
- Is the prospect willing but under pressure or held back by an unwilling partner or spouse?
- Is there a clear expectation agreed to that they will take action?

## ABLE?

- Does the prospect have funds to purchase?
- Are they prequalified or prepproved to obtain financing from a lender?
- Are they unable to buy or sell for any other financial or legal reason?

# 6 THINGS "NO" MEANS

**NO**

- I can't commit to this since I have other priorities at the moment.
- Now is not a good time as I'm in the middle of something. How about we re-connect at another time.
- I would love to do this, but...
- Let me think about it first and then I'll get back to you.
- This doesn't meet my needs now, but I will be sure to keep you in mind.
- I am not the best person to help you in this way. Why don't you try Mr/s. X...

© Copyright Icenhower Coaching & Consulting, LLC. All rights reserved.

# 10 HABITS TO IMPROVE POSITIVE ENERGY

**10 — Know When To Say "No"**
to something without the feeling of loss.

**09 — Accept Your Faults And Mistakes,**
and own them candidly.

**08 — Build People Up In A Genuine Way.**
Reframe faults into opportunity.

**07 — Empathize And Forgive,**
even when no one's watching.

**06 — Avoid Complaining.**
It's bad marketing for your voice.

**05 — Recognize What's In—And Out Of—Your Control.**
Literally write it down.

**04 — Smile. Wave. High Five. Nod. Make Eye Contact**

**03 — Take Care Of Yourself, Physically And Mentally.**
Get enough sleep. Work out and watch your diet. Be kind to yourself. Avoid self-deprecating, even in jest.

**02 — Be Genuinely Excited About What You're Doing.**
If it's repetitive, be resourceful and creative in your work.

**01 — Find The Best In Everyone.**
Some people hide it well—so keep searching. Asking great questions is the key

© Copyright Icenhower Coaching & Consulting, LLC. All rights reserved.

# MODULE 1
## APPENDIX 1.7

## PROPOSED WORK SCHEDULE

| Time | Monday | Tuesday | Wednesday | Thursday | Friday | Friday |
|------|--------|---------|-----------|----------|--------|--------|
| 8:00 AM | | | | | | |
| 9:00 AM | | | | | | |
| 10:00 AM | | | | | | |
| 11:00 AM | | | | | | |
| 12:00 PM | | | | | | |
| 1:00 PM | | | | | | |
| 2:00 PM | | | | | | |
| 3:00 PM | | | | | | |
| 4:00 PM | | | | | | |
| 5:00 PM | | | | | | |

© Copyright Icenhower Coaching & Consulting, LLC. All rights reserved.

## MAKING PRESENTATIONS WITH SCRIPTS

In the early days of pro football, quarterbacks made spontaneous and instinctual game-time decisions—play calls were made on the field, in the huddle, throughout the course of the game.

Starting in the 1970s and 1980s, however, coaches turned to a better tactic. The late Bill Walsh, famed coach of the San Francisco 49ers (named for the settlers who ventured to the city during the gold rush of 1849), is widely credited with developing the practice of scripting the first 15-25 offensive plays of the game.

In a 1996 *New York Times* interview, Walsh described scripting as "contingency planning." Practicing scripted plays reduced the need to make kneejerk, real-time decisions. Scripts enabled the team to focus on their strengths. Scripts gave the team a plan to follow, no matter what happened, and no matter whom they were up against.

"It takes real nerve," Walsh told the *Times*. "If things aren't working, you can lose your nerve. The script makes you stay in the game plan and make it work."

It's true. Scripts work, and top business professionals use them because the level of return outperforms cases when they are not used. As in the NFL, execution is paramount when making real estate sales presentations. And, as you'll see throughout this chapter, honing, practicing, and internalizing a carefully considered script increases your ability to execute and close the sale.

## Learning Targets

In this chapter, we'll provide you with seven core scripts to kick-start your prospecting career. You will also learn:

- The importance of having a positive perspective around the use of scripts.
- Strategies for memorizing and internalizing scripts.
- Tips for effective script delivery.
- The necessity of time on task and building a practice schedule around the use of scripts.

## FLIP THE SCRIPT

In the last chapter, we discussed the importance of attitude and perspective. We also explored some of the negative connotations associated with prospecting. As you learned, what we think, and how we feel, about prospecting influences our ability to be successful at it and approach it with insight and an open mind.

A lot of agents have a negative mindset about prospecting with scripts. Some people will tell you that:

- Scripted presentations are a thing of the past.
- Scripts don't help salespeople connect with their clients, and can actually irritate and alienate them.
- Scripts feel too canned, almost as if they are sterile, lifeless, or even manipulative, monologues.

Those same people that have an extreme aversion to using scripts can usually repeat this list of arguments over and over again, word-for-word, no matter their audience. It's almost as though their well-organized, repeatable insights create a more compelling and convincing argument! Interesting, eh?

When real estate agents claim that they never use scripts, we say: "Tell that to the last twenty prospects that signed a Listing Agreement after that same agent delivered a stellar listing presentation!"

Those agents may not *think* they use scripts, but they *do*.

*When people respond positively to something you say, and your words translate into successful results, it's both natural and shrewd that you'd say the same thing to the next person.*

Once you've conducted a handful of listing presentations, you'll find yourself saying the same things over and over again. To some extent, all presentations must follow some sort of formula. Essentially, you're explaining your services and what you will do to market and sell the property. You're also overcoming objections in approximately the same way from prospect to prospect.

So, when people respond positively to something you say, and your words translate into successful results, it's both natural as well as efficient and shrewd that you'd say the same thing to the next person.

Does a good comedian tell the same joke, night after night, if it isn't getting a laugh? No. Believe it or not, the world's best and funniest comedians work from constantly evolving scripts. In fact, many top stand-ups will watch videos of their performance and rework their script to increase their laugh-per-minute targets. They either hone their script to make the build-up and the punch line better, or they cut it from their performance altogether.

When real estate agents say they don't use scripts, what they mean is that they don't use somebody else's script, or that they're not reciting from a pre-written text. But, whether they write their words down or not, all agents create, rehearse, and perform from scripts that they have developed, tweaked, and internalized over time.

Like we said, those agents may not *think* they use scripts, but they *do*. There is no reason at all to worry or object to the use of scripts.

> *If you're feeling in any way averse or uncomfortable, "flip the script" and embrace the opposite of what your natural instinct is.*

As with anything in prospecting for real estate, when you first start using scripts, you're going to feel very uncomfortable and unnatural. With time and practice, this initial discomfort will all but disappear and using scripts will feel much more natural and intuitive.

Before we go any further, therefore, we would ask you to examine your perspective and rid yourself of any negative preconceptions you may have about making presentations with scripts. If you're feeling in any way averse or uncomfortable, try to "flip the script" and embrace the opposite of what your natural instinct is. In order to use scripts successfully, you must learn do so with a positive attitude and an open mind.

## A Scaffold, Not A Crutch

Isaac Newton once wrote: "If I have seen further than others, it was only by standing on the shoulders of giants."

As he rightly and humbly pointed out, our present and future success is built on the previous successes and discoveries of those who have gone before us. These great people have already succeeded through much trial and error, so why would you waste time and energy building yourself up to their giant level when you can stand on their shoulders—and use their hard-won knowledge—to reach incredible heights right away?

> *"If I have seen further than others, it was only by standing on the shoulders of giants."-Isaac Newton.*

At ICC, we want you to reach new heights and succeed as quickly as possible. We want to save you the stress of recreating dialog off the top of your head with each new encounter.

We don't want you have to go through the trial and error of developing your own scripts over time. We don't want you to wait weeks or months to get to the highest and best conversion rates from your prospecting activities.

Our scripts have been tested and proven by some of the most successful real estate agents in North America. By providing you with ready-made scripts, you can get a handle on the business of prospecting far sooner than if you had to figure out what works and doesn't work by yourself.

However, these scripts are not intended to be crutches that enable you to perform the steps unthinkingly or without being fully engaged in the delivery.

Rather, think of a well-written and well-rehearsed presentation script as a scaffold.

Scaffolding, as you know, is a temporary structure used to support a work crew in the construction of a building. Scaffolds provide access to heights that would otherwise be difficult or time-consuming to get to. And, scaffolds, of course, are eventually removed while the finished building remains standing on its own.

Our scripts are not crutches: they are a support system that enable you to immediately connect with your prospects and see results that would otherwise be time-consuming or incredibly difficult to achieve. Through time on task and frequent practice, you will eventually memorize and internalize these scripts to the point where you won't need a physical piece of paper anymore.

Soon, you will have constructed a solid room within yourself that you can endlessly draw from, as well as modify and tweak to suit your evolving needs and style. At that point, the physical scripts can be removed but what you have honed and internalized will stand strong.

# EXERCISE: The Benefits Of Scripted Presentations

Put a checkmark next to anything you think is a positive benefit of scripted presentations. If you checked at least one, let's move forward in agreement that scripts will make you a better prospector.

- ☐ Commitment to practice
- ☐ Understanding of the material
- ☐ Preparation
- ☐ Consideration for the client
- ☐ Organization of ideas
- ☐ Discipline
- ☐ Planning
- ☐ A mapped sequence of what works
- ☐ Humility

## SEVEN CORE SCRIPTS

ICC has prepared **seven core scripts** to launch you into successful real estate prospecting:

1. SOI Scripts
2. Expired Listing Scripts
3. FSBO Scripts
4. Circle Prospecting Scripts
5. Buyer Pre-Qualification & Conversion
6. Seller Pre-Qualification & Conversion
7. Objection Handling

Each of the script scenarios have been specially crafted from thousands of hours spent working with both agents and prospects. In each script, the *sequence*, *keywords*, and *questions* are arranged to produce powerful and persuasive prospecting potential.

Keep in mind that within each of these seven script categories are endless variations that have been developed for specific situations. For example, our SOI scripts have a dozen or so variations targeted to delivering updates, reconnecting with past clients, getting referrals, and more. There's a script for every scenario you can imagine.

This chapter offers a basic prospecting script for each core area, but there are hundreds of scripts available for you to include in your repertoire.

Also, be careful not to assess whether or not you like a script too early on. In fact, we would go so far as to say that, if you have just started prospecting, it's not possible for you to know whether you like a script or not at this point.

It will take time for you to develop your skills and to become good enough, and efficient enough, at prospecting to see how the scripts work. Though they may feel uncomfortable to you right now, your skill level is too low at this point to determine and foresee what you will need to say in order to be a successful prospector.

At this stage in your career, you must adopt an open-minded, positive attitude and trust that we are providing you with tested and proven scripts that successful prospectors are using today. With that in mind, let's examine the seven core scripts in turn. Once we have introduced you to each type of script, we will look at strategies for memorizing and internalizing scripts as well as tips for effective script delivery.

## SOI Scripts

Typically, when we think about real estate business-generation techniques, prospectors and referral-based agents appear to be poles apart and completely separate, but in fact it's more like a spectrum.

On one end of the spectrum are prospectors: people, like you, that actively reach out to people they don't know, whether they do it with a door knock, or they do it with a phone call. On the other end of the business-generating spectrum, referral agents are working the people they do know through a 'Sphere of Influence', or what we call an SOI. Many agents do both. At ICC, we coach a lot of clients that employ a blend of business-generation activities.

Although you're a prospector, working your SOI will be the foundation of your business. With this business-generating strategy, you will be cultivating and growing a group, or sphere, of people *you know* who might use you for their real estate needs and who, in turn, might refer you to the people that *they* know (hence the name referral business).

> *With the SOI method, if you're marketing to 100 people in your sphere of influence, and they all know 100 people too, then you're effectively marketing to 10,000 people when you're using a script like the one below that explicitly asks for a referral.*

With the SOI method, you're staying in touch with the people you know and exponentially expanding your network of possible referral contacts. With the SOI method, if you're marketing to 100 people in your sphere of influence, and they all know 100 people too, then you're effectively marketing to 10,000 people when you're using a script like the one below that explicitly asks for a referral.

As you can see, this script is quite straightforward, but very effective. It can be used systematically when you're committed to a disciplined daily SOI contact plan. Or it can be tweaked for those unanticipated moments when you happen to bump into someone you know at the grocery store or the dentist's office. Oftentimes, this script is used to top off or wrap up a conversation with someone. It's important to make sure that your friends and acquaintances know that you appreciate their referral business.

You will notice that this script is very direct and gets straight to the point. Believe it or not, people in your SOI prefer this, even if they know you socially outside of work. While you may feel that you need to warm up to the request and spend some time catching up and being social, members of your SOI don't like overly long SOI calls. They might not tell you that, but it's true! Sticking to the script helps you to stay on point and deliver your message professionally and efficiently.

> ## SOI Script: Asking for Referrals
>
> ① "Hi _____, this is John Smith at ABC Realty, how have you been? This is a quick call about business. I'm reaching out to remind you that I'm in real estate! You see, statistics show that our clients are going to run into 6 to 10 people over the next 12 months that are looking buy or sell a home. So can I ask you for a favor?"
>
> (If yes . . .)
>
> ② "I prefer to grow my business by word of mouth. So when you bump into these people, would you be willing to refer my services and call me with their contact information?"
>
> *(Pause and wait patiently for a response. Let silence do the heavy lifting here)*
>
> ③ "Thanks! Oh and since I've got you on the phone, do you happen to know anyone that is thinking about buying or selling a home right now?"
>
> ④ "Thanks for all your help. I'll be in touch!"
>
> *(Note: A follow up "Thank You" card can have a very positive impact.)*

## Expired Listing Scripts

Expired listings are when a property hasn't been sold by the end of the period stipulated in the listing contract. When a listing expires, sellers can choose to stay on with their current agent, or they can decide to work with a new agent without incurring any penalties.

There are many ways to search for and find expired listings; we'll explore that in detail in Chapter 4. However, for now, we will say that there is a difference between expired listings and withdrawn listings. Withdrawal doesn't break the contract between a seller and an agent. Until the contract has expired, a new agent cannot represent a seller who has withdrawn their listing, so it's important to understand the difference when you're searching for and reaching out to people with expired listings.

Sellers let their listings expire for a variety of reasons. Either they weren't committed to selling the home in the first place, or they were hoping to find another real estate agent with whom to work. Sometimes they are at a loss as to what to do next.

Maybe you'll get a hold of the seller on the phone. More often, however, you'll have to leave a message. Below are some scripts for both situations. Again, these are very brief and simple scripts. With expired listings, you're typically just trying to get an appointment rather than an agreement to list the property over the phone.

Ideally, you should choose one script that you like and feel comfortable with, and then use that one script over and over again so that it becomes automatic and very natural to you.

## Expired Listing Scripts: For When They Answer

**SCRIPT 1:** "Hi, I'm looking for _____. This is John Smith with ABC Realty, and I'm calling because, as I'm sure you've figured out, your home has come up as an expired listing. So I'm calling to see when you plan on hiring the right agent to sell your home?"

**SCRIPT 2:** "Hi, I'm John Smith with ABC Realty, and I'm calling about the house that was listed in the multiple listing service that expired, and I wanted to interview for the job of getting your home back on the market and sold. I'd like to show you the techniques I use to get my listings sold."

**SCRIPT 3:** "Hi this is John Smith with ABC Realty, and I noticed that your listing on 123 Pepperwood Court is no longer active. I wanted to see if you are going to take this opportunity to interview a different agent. If so, I'd love to share my marketing methods for getting homes sold quickly."

## Expired Listing Scripts: For Leaving Voice Messages

**SCRIPT 1:** "I'm calling about your home for sale. My number is 555-123-4567."

**SCRIPT 2:** "Hi this is John Smith and I'm calling about the house you had listed in the multiple listing service, and I'd like to talk to you about the house. Would you please call me back as soon as possible? Call me at 555-123-4567."

**SCRIPT 3:** " Hello this John Smith with ABC Realty and I'm calling about your listing that is no longer on the market. If you are interested in taking this opportunity to interview a different agent, call me at 555-123-4567."

Agents who are contacting expired listings need to understand that these sellers are getting lots of phone calls from other hopeful prospectors. Sellers with expired listings might receive upwards of twenty phone calls in a single morning, especially the day after the listing has expired. While sellers need your help on the one hand, this can be very overwhelming and aggravating from another perspective.

## OVERCOMING OBJECTIONS

Prospects with expired listings are often quick to object so, to assist you, we have included a script for handling one of the more common objections. We will provide you with dozens of different objection handlers throughout this book. When overcoming objections, it's crucial that you maintain continuous conversation, build rapport, and keep the dialog going. As you can see from the scripts, curiosity is the key to continuing the conversation: it's important to *ask a lot of questions*.

---

**COMMON OBJECTION:**
**"WE'RE NOT PUTTING IT BACK ON THE MARKET"**

LINE of QUESTIONING:

1. "Really? Well if it had sold, where were you moving to?"

2. "How soon do you want to be there?"

3. "What do you think stopped it from selling?"

4. "If I were to present you with a strong offer to purchase your home, would you be still be willing to at least take a look at it?"

5. "Well that's exactly what I would like to talk to you about. What would be the best time for me to quickly drop by, 4:00 today or tomorrow?

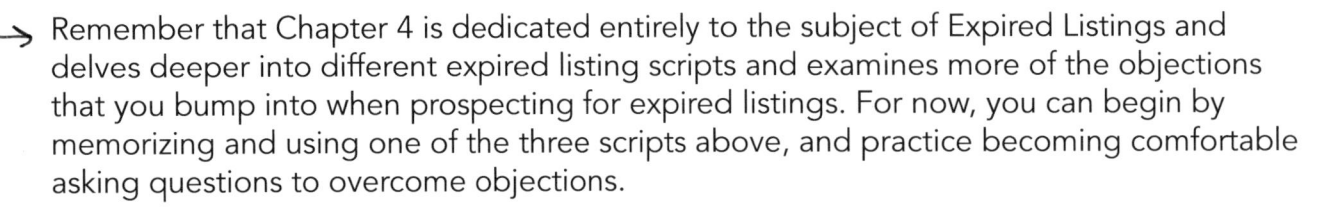

---

Remember that Chapter 4 is dedicated entirely to the subject of Expired Listings and delves deeper into different expired listing scripts and examines more of the objections that you bump into when prospecting for expired listings. For now, you can begin by memorizing and using one of the three scripts above, and practice becoming comfortable asking questions to overcome objections.

## FOR SALE BY OWNER (FSBO) SCRIPTS

Homes designated as For Sale By Owner (FSBO) can be a real estate gold mine.

Sellers sometimes go the FSBO route to save money on the real estate agent's commission. However, when the sellers discover that they do not have the time, skills, or perseverance to sell the home, they may find themselves in limbo, wondering what steps to take next.

Savvy real estate agents know how to step in and validate the FSBO experience and convince the homeowner to list the property with a professional.

Often, you will find FSBO listings on online sources like Zillow, Craigslist or any other place in your local area where FSBO sellers are listing their homes publicly for sale. When you make first contact, you will typically ask the following three questions in order to filter through these sellers and establish if you have a chance of listing the property for sale with them.

They may seem like simple questions, but they are powerful tools to help move the prospect forward. Remember the Organized Sales Process from the previous chapter. Oftentimes, FSBO sellers will initially be unwilling to list with an agent, but careful nurturing and cultivating can convince them to list with you when their solo efforts have failed. The following scripts are a way to initiate the sales process with a long-term view to taking them from lead to prospect to client.

> **FSBO 3 Key Questions Script**
>
> ① *"If I brought you a qualified buyer, would you be willing to pay me a 3% commission?"* If yes, continue on to the next question.
>
> ② *"How long are you going to try to sell your home on your own before you explore other options?"* Shorten their timeline by half. If they say "3 months", they will likely list in 45 days. If their answer is "6 months or less", continue on to the next question.
>
> ③ *"If you don't sell your home by that time, what other options will you consider?"* Again, this is to ensure that another agent is not their relative or best friend and you don't waste too much time and effort. If they are open to the possibility of interviewing agents in the future, place them in your lead follow-up campaign and move on to contacting the next FSBO seller!

## CIRCLE PROSPECTING SCRIPTS

Circle prospecting involves knocking on doors and physically approaching people within a specific geographic area (a radius, or a circle) to ask them for their business. This technique allows you to concentrate on a unique area of homes, perhaps a particular neighborhood or price range in which you've been hoping to gain entry.

Oftentimes, when you're circle prospecting, you will be talking to people who don't currently want to sell their house. In these situations, you can initiate dialog and maintain conversation by talking to them about **Just Listed** or **Just Sold** properties in their neighborhood. The idea is to plant a seed in their mind about buying or selling.

Or, if they're 100% not interested in selling, you can ask them if they know of anyone who is. This can be as blunt as saying, "Hey there, we have your neighbor's house under contract, and we're looking for more listings because we have a shortage of inventory in your neighborhood. Do you know anyone looking to buy or sell real estate?"

Again, you will see that the scripts you will be working with are a series of questions.

Most good scripts involve a *systematic line of questioning*. Good scripts are not about telling. As you'll recall from the previous chapter, prospecting is sales, not selling. It's about identifying the needs of the buyer so that you can serve them best and secure their business.

Here are the two scripts you'll need to begin circle prospecting.

## JUST LISTED SCRIPT

1. Hi, I'm (John Smith) with (ABC Realty). We just listed a home for sale in your neighborhood on (123 Main Street) for ($250,000), and we often find that the ultimate buyer of a home is a friend, family member or acquaintance of someone that lives in the same neighborhood. Since we are doing everything we can to sell your neighbor's home, I'd like to ask you if you know anyone looking to move into your community? *Answer: "No"*.

2. Great! I truly appreciate your taking the time to try and help. So tell me, when do you plan on moving? *Answer: "No plans"*.

3. Fantastic! How long have you lived in your home? *Answer: "Five years"*.

4. Terrific! Where did you live before that? *Answer: "Denver, Colorado"*.

5. Excellent! How did you pick this community? *Answer: "To be near family"*.

6. Wonderful! So if you were to move, where would you move next? *Answer: "To Florida"*.

7. Exciting! And when would that most likely be?

**If their answer is "6 months or less", continue:**

8. Did you know that it can take up to 6 months to get a home prepared, marketed and sold in today's market? *Answer: "No"*.

9. Great! So do you want your home sold in 6 months, or do you want to start the process of selling then? *Answer: "Sold"*.

10. Perfect! All that we need to do to start you on your way to (Florida) is pick a time to get together. How does that sound? *Answer: "Great"*.

11. Excellent! Would Wednesday or Thursday at 4:00 pm work better for you?

## JUST SOLD SCRIPT

1. Hi, I'm (John Smith) with (ABC Realty). We just sold a home for sale in your neighborhood on (123 Main Street) for ($250,000), and when one neighbor sells a home, typically 2 or 3 more homes in the same neighborhood sell right away. So I was curious as to when you plan on moving? *Answer: "No plans"*.

2. Great! How long have you lived in your home? *Answer: "5 years"*.

3. Terrific! Where did you live before that? *Answer: "Denver, Colorado"*.

4. Excellent! How did you pick this community? *Answer: "To be near family"*.

5. Wonderful! So if you were to move, where would you move next? *Answer: "To Florida"*.

6. Exciting! And when would that most likely be?

**If their answer is "6 months or less", continue:**

7. Did you know that it can take up to 6 months to get a home prepared, marketed and sold in today's market? *Answer: "No"*.

8. Great! So do you want your home sold in 6 months, or do you want to start the process of selling then? *Answer: "Sold"*.

9. Perfect! All that we need to do to start you on your way to (Florida) is pick a time to get together. How does that sound? *Answer: "Great"*.

10. Excellent! Would Wednesday or Thursday at 4:00pm work better for you?

## Prequalification and Conversion: Seller and Buyer Questionnaires & Lead Sheets

One of the most important things you'll do in the real estate business is prequalify your prospects. If you don't take the time to prequalify them, you'll waste endless hours that could have been spent more productively, both for you and for them.

Prequalification helps you:

- **Assess** how motivated your prospects are to purchase a home or sell their own home or investment property. It's easy for people to want a new home, but committing to the process of selling their current home, making an investment, or ending a lease and moving can be a huge undertaking.

- **Determine** if the buyers have realistic expectations of property values, both for what they are selling, and for what they are hoping to buy. The equity in their current home will also be a factor in the prequalification process. Buyers may need to turn to other funding sources to complete the transaction.

- **Validate** that they're working with a detail-oriented consultant that creates a clear path of what needs to happen, which establishes crucial trust in the early stages of the agent-prospect relationship.

Again, the process involves a series of questions. When you have identified an individual who wants to sell or buy a home in the next 6 months, you start working through the 'Seller Questionnaire & Lead Sheet' or the 'Buyer Questionnaire & Lead Sheet' like the ones you see below.

These forms will help you to engage the prospect, identify their needs, maintain an open dialog and systematic line of questioning, and ultimately convert them to sign a listing contract, exclusive buyer agency agreement, or possibly an offer to purchase a home.

We recommend using this **Seller Lead Sheet** to help you assess, determine, and validate the prospect's readiness and motivation to sell.

### Seller Questionnaire & Lead Form

Date:
Name: _____ Spouse Name: _____
Property Address: _____ City: _____ State: _____ Zip: _____
Phone #s – Mobile: _____ Spouse Mobile: _____ Home: _____ Work: _____
Email: _____ Spouse Email: _____
Family / Children (include ages): _____

1. Have you spoken with any other agents? ☐ Yes ☐ No
2. Have you considered selling the home yourself? ☐ Yes ☐ No
3. Why do you want to move?
4. Do you know where you want to move to?
5. What date do you want to be moved by?
6. Are there any negatives to not moving by then? (suggest lifestyle sacrifices, job, costs, schools, family, etc.)
7. Tell me all the negatives of not moving at all? (same suggestions above)
8. Tell me all the benefits of buying a new home: (dig deep & find out WHY?)
9. On a scale of 1 to 10, how would you rank your motivation to move? With 10 being highly motivated: _____
10. When did you buy your home? _____ What price did you pay? _____
11. Do you know how much you still owe on it?
12. Have you made any major improvements to the home since? ☐ Yes ☐ No
13. Do you happen to have an idea as to what you think it's worth, or should sell for?
14. Do you have a price you won't sell your home below?
15. Tell me about the positive & negative features of your home:
16. How many BR: ___ Baths: ___ SqFt: ___ Stories: ___ Other: _____
17. How did you hear about me/us?
18. Are you interviewing any other agents? ☐ Yes ☐ No Who? _____ When? _____
19. "Thank you! The next step is for me to take a quick look at your home and I can answer any other questions you may have. Then you can decide what we do next. How does that sound?" (pause)
   "Great! Does 4:30 tomorrow or 5:00 Wednesday work for you?"

Appointment Date/Time: _____
DISC Behavioral Profile: _____ Why? _____

**1**

This is the Buyer's Lead Sheet we recommend to our agents:

## Buyer Questionnaire & Lead Sheet

Date: _____ Lead Source: _____
Name: _____ Spouse Name: _____
Property Address: _____ City: _____ State: _____ Zip: _____
Phone #s – Mobile: _____ Spouse Mobile: _____ Home: _____ Work: _____
Email: _____ Spouse Email: _____
Family / Children (include ages): _____

1. Have any other agents shown you homes? ☐ Yes ☐ No
   If Yes, do you have a signed agency agreement? ☐ Yes ☐ No
2. Is anyone buying the home with you?
3. Are you renting, or do you own a home? ☐ Homeowner ☐ Renter
   a) HOMEOWNER:
      - Do you need to sell your home before you buy? ☐ Yes ☐ No
      - Have you signed a listing agreement to sell your home? ☐ Yes ☐ No  *If "No" use Seller Lead Sheet.*
   b) RENTER:
      - When does your lease end?
4. What date do you want to be moved by?
5. Are there any negatives to not moving by then? (suggest lifestyle sacrifices, job, costs, schools, family, etc.)
6. Tell me all the benefits of buying a new home: (dig deep & find out WHY?)
7. On a scale of 1 to 10, how would you rank your motivation to move? With 10 meaning you must buy as quickly as possible, and 1 meaning you're not sure you'll really buy anything: _____
   - What's missing? What would it take to make you a 10?
8. Do you know where you want to move to?
9. Will you be paying cash or getting a mortgage? ☐ Cash ☐ Mortgage
10. Have you been pre-approved by a lender? ☐ Yes ☐ No
11. How much will your down payment be?
12. What price range are you looking in?
13. How many BR: _____ Baths: _____ SqFt: _____ Stories: _____ Other: _____
14. What else are you looking for in a home?
15. Will anyone else be involved in your home buying decision?
16. "Thank you! I'd love to help you find your perfect home. All that we need to do is to set an appointment so that I can help you find the home you're looking for. Does 4:30 tomorrow or 5:00 Wednesday work for you?"

Appointment Date/Time: _____
DISC Behavioral Profile: _____ Why? _____

## OBJECTION HANDLING

Prospectors face a lot of objections and resistance from leads and prospects. Depending on the lead source, you will face different types of objections. The most common objection is that the lead is "just looking" or "just thinking" right now, and they are not yet ready to work with an agent.

But even when your prospects want to sell their home or have found a property they love, the sale isn't in the bag. You may find yourself facing objections that can range from the color of the walls to the asking price of the property. Even the most enthusiastic sellers may still have questions and want you to prove your worth.

No home is going to be perfect, and few conversations about selling or purchasing a home are without conflict or concern. By learning how to handle objections, you may help prospects see the actual value in the property they are considering purchasing, or the service they're inviting you to perform.

There are a variety of scripts for handling objections because buyers come up with so many reasons to avoid selling or purchasing a home! Objection handling scripts will help you remove risk and confirm that you're the compassionate, confident, and effective representative they're looking for.

We've included three of them here.

### We are just looking right now...

- That's good to hear. You should look thoroughly before you buy anything. Out of curiosity, what type of home are you looking for?
- That's great. Are you looking to purchase a home?
- Absolutely. How many homes have you looked at so far?
- I understand. How did you find out about this home?
- Good idea. What are you looking for?

### We aren't ready to work with an agent yet . . .

- Do you have a home you need to sell first?
- I understand. How are you planning on finding your next home? Would it help if you could see all of the homes for sale that fit your criteria at home on your computer first? That way you could just contact me when you want to see the inside of one?
- I see. Have you spoken to a lender to determine a price range and monthly payments yet?
- May I ask what expectations you have for the agent that ultimately represents you?
- Many of my clients have felt the same way at first. Until they discovered that searching for homes by driving around and looking at scattered listings on line was not very efficient. What if I set you up on your own customized online search so that you could see all of the homes for sale by all REALTORS® that fit your criteria? You would also receive email notifications for homes the instant they come up for sale so that you would be one of the first to see them before they sell?

### We are going to wait. We aren't ready now . . .

- I see. What specifically are you waiting for?
- Do you have a home to sell before you can buy?
- When do you want to move into a new home?
- On a scale of 1 to 10, with a 10 meaning you want to buy as soon as possible, where do you think you fall? And why?
- Understood. There is a lot to get in order before buying a new home: preparing your current home for sale, meeting with a lender, insurance, inspectors, repairs, finding a home, etcetera…. Would you like some help with all of that?

Making a deal is about drilling down to client needs. The idea is to give and achieve something important to everybody involved in the deal. Sellers and buyers may not get everything on their wish lists, but through careful negotiations, agents should ensure that their most important needs are met. It is the real estate agent that mediates and advises. Being able to handle objections effectively can mean the difference between:

1. Coming to agreement with another party.
2. Keeping your contracts together.
3. Walking away from a deal.

Identify what each party needs regarding price, closing date, or other concerns so that you'll be able to address each need to both parties' satisfaction.

# EXERCISE: A Balanced Portfolio

A savvy investor knows that diversifying a real estate portfolio helps you weather even the toughest markets. You'll be investing a lot of time and energy to learn these scripts, and each investment will help you work with a different portfolio of needs or desires, like buyers, sellers, or even FSBOs.

What scripts could you put in each portfolio below to increase your success? Match the investments with the portfolio. Yes, you can use each multiple times (we hope that you do!).

| INVESTMENT | PORTFOLIO |
|---|---|
| SOI | Buyer |
| Objection Handling | Seller |
| Prequalification/Seller | Sphere of Influence Contact |
| Prequalification/Buyer | Expired Seller |
| Showing a Listing | FBSOs |
| Expired/FSBOs | Investor |

## May I Leave A Message?

At one point or another, we've all had the experience of walking away from a conversation with no idea of what the person was actually talking about.

Clarity of message helps you stay on message. When a prospect hangs up the phone after a conversation or presentation, they should be able to describe the purpose of your call in ten words or less.

Every presentation script has a fundamental message. This message is the primary objective, whether it's generating leads, prequalifying a prospective client or handling objections. The message you deliver builds rapport and establishes confidence and trust.

If someone calls you and says, "Hi, I was curious if you'd like tickets to the opera this weekend?" you could say their message means: *If you need opera tickets, we're the service you're looking for!*

However, if a moment later they're asking you to invest in the local Rio Rancho development to qualify for winning the tickets, you might feel like you're being taken for a ride. It's important, therefore, to lead with the actual message and purpose of your call.

Inserting the phrase "the reason for my call" instead of "how are you doing today" at the beginning is a short fix, yet you're in this for the long haul. Let's explore a little deeper.

## EXERCISE: What's the Big Idea?

Select a single script previously presented in this book, and identify the main idea. Write the script type and main idea here: (or write it in your notebook or on the companion worksheet).

```
[                                                                    ]
```

If what you just wrote is longer than ten words, rewrite it so that your summary consists of ten words or less. The reason for writing the message in such few words is so that you can articulate it easily. If you can't describe your message in ten words, it's unlikely your prospects will be able to either.

*"There's great power in words, if you don't hitch too many of them together."* - Josh Billings

## BREAKING IT DOWN

Once you have identified the main idea of the presentation script, it's time to break it down into meaningful sections.

By segmenting, or breaking down the message, you'll be able to learn the script more efficiently.

These sections are the sub-topics, and each one of these has supporting details.

## EXERCISE: Script Breakdown

Using the same script from the activity above, identify the purpose and supporting details here (or write in your notebook or on the companion worksheet):

Purpose: _____

Detail: _____

Detail: _____

Detail: _____

Repeat this activity for every topic you find in the script.

When you are ready to memorize the script, begin with only one script at a time. We recommend that you begin with the SOI script, asking for referrals, since it is quite short and will be one of the first scripts you use.

Once you know and understand the message, read your script aloud 3-4 times.

Now you're ready to begin memorizing it!

## SCRIPT MEMORIZATION

Now that we have introduced you to the seven core scripts for prospecting, we will explore some strategies for memorizing and internalizing scripts, followed by some tips for effective script delivery.

You have to memorize your presentation scripts. There's no other way around it.

When you see a great movie or even a stand-up routine, countless hours of practice and preparation have gone into creating a performance that appears to be natural, spontaneous, and improvised.

Memorizing seven or more scripts might seem overwhelming, but doing so serves two important purposes:

1. First, you will learn the topics well.
2. Secondly, the memorization will help you know exactly what to say in a variety of situations with prospective clients.

In the previous chapter, we told you that the 3 pillars of prospecting success are: Skill Level, Frequency, and Number of Contacts. The best way to memorize scripts and increase this skillset is through frequent practice, repetition, and time on task.

However, depending on your number of contacts and the rate at which you contact them, it will take you a long time to increase this skillset if you only practice in real-life, real-time situations and scenarios. Rather than being the quarterback who makes decisions on the field or in the huddle, you need to *increase this learning curve by practicing scripts* and how you're going to play things ahead of the game.

Practice will help you to set the habit, improve your comfort level, and increase your conversion rates more quickly. Below are some best practices for role-playing and memorizing scripts.

## SCRIPTS ROLE-PLAY BEST PRACTICES

**①** Positivity: Voice Inflection & Tonality

Our tone of voice expresses our attitude, feelings and emotions about something, and it's important that you exude positive attitudes and emotions around leads and prospects, whether in person or on the phone.

In order to deliver your scripts and sales presentations with positive energy, you must show a lot of tonality and inflection in your voice.

Though you will often have scripts in front of you while contacting leads and prospects, this phase of practice allows you to use the scripts as guides rather than crutches. Emphasis and voice inflection, when practiced, can project confidence, empathy, curiosity, and concern.

Rather than saying that something is great in a flat and lifeless monotone, your voice should be effusive, emphatic, and engaging. Emphasize your words and include variations in your tone. Speak in a bright, warm, and affirming voice with a positive upswing: "That's wonderful!" or "I'm so happy to hear you say that."

This may feel uncomfortable at first, but don't be afraid to show excitement, enthusiasm and positive emotion.

On the other hand, we want you to be enthusiastic but not dramatic or over the top. The overuse of upswings will come off as obvious, sarcastic, or insincere and will actually have the opposite effect.

Downswings are as important as upswings. Variety is key.

Often, upswings are used when we're asking a question or expressing something that we're not 100% sure of. It's important, then, to use downswings as well as upswings or you risk sounding uncertain or that you lack authority. Downswings help you to sound confident and convincing.

Balance is key. You want your voice to sound curious, not clueless. You want your voice to project confidence, not cockiness.

In order to assess whether you're exuding the perfect degree of positivity and authority, agents will often record their script practice and listen back to it. It's also an extremely good idea to partner up and work in pairs.

### ❷ Partner Up: Work in Pairs

No man is an island. Feedback is important. Whether it's over the phone or in person, partnering up and working in pairs is a great way to get feedback and increase your skill level.

A partner will catch when you've missed a crucial part of the script. They can also help you with inflection and tonality and help you hone the perfect positive pitch. By switching partners and working with multiple people, you will experience hearing a variety of tones and voice inflections. Peer activity incites peer activity. When people implement a "back and forth" practice pattern, they cut their repetition and rendition practice in half.

Working in pairs also provides a level of accountability. If someone is depending on you for feedback, you don't want to disappoint him or her by failing to show up. Simply checking in with a partner can hold you accountable to maintaining a regular and frequent practice.

What's more, working with a partner can help you to warm up in advance of making actual prospecting calls. New agents often schedule practice with a partner first thing at 8AM before they start making real calls at 8:30AM.

If you have ever prospected, you'll know that your first few calls are fairly awkward and uncomfortable. It takes a while to feel the rhythm and get in the zone. Role-playing with a partner helps take the morning edge off. That way, when you pick up the phone and start doing the real thing, you're already in the zone, you've hit your stride, and you won't miss out on some potentially great contacts because you're still warming up.

### ❸ Posture: Stand Up!

Along with tone of voice, posture is a critical component for projecting positive energy. Whether you're role playing or making actual prospecting calls, be sure to stand up straight!

Standing up increases oxygen flow and circulation. Your voice will be clearer and you will have far more energy than if you slouch in your swivel chair all day long.

Stand up and keep your shoulders back. Keep your chin up! Be sure to hold the script high, as your voice inflection will tend to follow where your head is facing. People who are considered sad, bored, or depressed usually have their head down, and speak in low tones.

The positive energy that comes from voice and posture will build rapport and attract people to you. It will help to keep the conversation going, and the longer you can keep them on the phone, the more receptive they'll be to meeting you in person or making an appointment.

### ❹ Practice Scripts in Parts

When overloaded, the human brain will usually recall only the beginning and end points of any piece of information. As we demonstrated in the previous exercise, when learning a new script, we can enhance and speed up memorization by breaking it down into smaller parts. To do this, we literally break the scripts into pieces, segmenting longer conversations into shorter talking points, or longer paragraphs into brief sentences that are easier to recite and internalize.

- Start with the first line. Read it aloud. Repeat it. Now close your eyes and try to say it word for word.
- If the sentences are too long to remember, try memorizing the first half of the sentence. Add the rest of the sentence when you have the first part memorized.
- Once you have the first sentences committed to memory, begin on the second sentence. Use the last word or words of the previous sentence to set up a "trigger" that will cue you as to what's coming next.
- Practice reciting these two sentences before adding the third one to your memory.
- Continue reciting the memorized sentences and adding one new sentence until the entire script is embedded in your memory.
- Continue to recite the script in its entirety.

Another great way to memorize a script is by reciting it into a phone. Record the script standing up, and with very strong voice inflection, and listen to it throughout the day. Whether you're in the shower, eating lunch, or driving in your car, you can always find the time to listen and passively practice your script by osmosis.

Make sure to practice and/or record the script the way that you would like to say it to actual clients: with big, positive energy, emphasizing your points with a lot of voice inflection and tonality. Continue to do this until you are able to recite any given script in its entirety, without having to refer to the page in front of you, without stopping, and without having to break it down any further.

## CHALLENGE

Even when you've learned all of your scripts, you'll still need to practice them so they are constantly fresh in your mind. Here are a couple of ideas to keep your practice interesting! Remember, when you feel yourself improve, that will be motivation enough: be wary of too much game, and not enough improvement.

- ROLL THE DICE CHALLENGE: Assign each script a number, 1-7. Roll a die and recite the script assigned to the number that appears. Add more dice as you learn more scripts.
- BEAT THE BUZZER CHALLENGE: Role play with a partner, and give them the menu of 7 to choose from. Set the timer for 5 minutes and see how many of the scripts you can complete before the buzzer goes off!

## Raise The Bar...Before Raising The Curtain.

Memorization is not enough to deliver an effective script. Sales calls and presentations are only effective in so far as they build rapport, identify the particular needs of the prospect, and maintain a two-way dialog and continuous conversation.

If you're so focused on delivering your next lines and simply making it through the script from beginning to end, you will break rapport and deliver a rushed or rambling run-on monologue instead of an effective dialog.

*"It is the stuff between the lines that makes it a great performance."* – Alan Alda

Long-running monologues and run-ons can alert your client that you're nervous. Coupled with a fast rate of speech, your audience could miss something, and misunderstanding or mistrust could take root very quickly.

Before raising the curtain on your first prospecting performance, you can raise the bar on your script delivery by taking a breath, slowing down, and creating space in your script for a purposeful pause.

## PURPOSEFUL PAUSES & EMBEDDED COMMANDS

For example, if you say, "So, what would it take for you to list with me...?" and then pause before hurrying into the next sentence or question in the script, it places emphasis on the *'list with me'* portion of the sentence. What's more, the *'what would it take'* portion of the sentence creates a mental space for the potential client to imagine and think about what you're asking them.

Effectively, the entire sentence above functions as a subliminal embedded command that tells the prospect, *"List with me, list with me, list with me,"* without giving the impression that you are over-eager or begging for their business.

> **NOTE!** Effective embedded commands are typically used with a *downswing* in tonality. You can see how the meaning of the above sentence, "So, what would it take to list with **ME**?" changes significantly with the use of an upswing. Upswings keep things positive but, in certain circumstances, they can have an air of desperation.

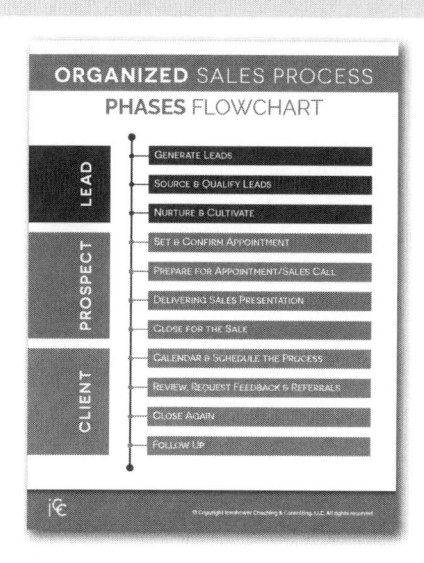

As you'll recall from the organized sales process in the first chapter, the idea is that you are always moving the lead or prospect forward to the next stage in the sales process, taking them in the right direction from contact to appointment to contract. An embedded command is a *linguistic tool that moves the prospect's mind in the direction you want it to go.* It does so in a non-intrusive or domineering way because it's subtly embedded in the structure of the sentence.

Importantly, including a purposeful pause at the end of the sentence adds weight and emphasis to the subliminal command.

Purposeful pauses can be used for three reasons:

1. Purposeful pauses allow time for the other person to ask a question or to answer a question that you have asked.

2. Purposeful pauses create a natural break in the script and prepare the listener for what you're about to say next. Purposeful pauses create anticipation.

3. Purposeful pauses allow for a moment of reflection after you've made a very important point that you want to hit home.

## PUNCTUATE YOUR PAUSES

When people talk, they naturally use pauses. Some of these pauses are longer or shorter than others. The deliberate interludes establish rhythm and patterns in speaking, and they help to convey meaning.

In written language, punctuation is used to tell readers when to pause and for how long. Without punctuation, pausing becomes much harder. Prosody is non-existent, and when there is no prosody, your speaking is mechanical and canned. You may as well have a robot read the words to your prospect!

This is especially true if the pauses accentuate your phrases and clauses (related groups of words). For example commas indicate a brief pause whereas a period indicates a longer pause or breath before the next sentence. Colons and semi-colons fall between the comma and the period in length of pause.

When speaking, it's important to use a variety of short, medium, and longer pauses. If you pause for too long, in the wrong place, it may sound like you're uncertain or confused or have forgotten what you were talking about!

An ellipsis (the little dot-dot-dot at the end of a sentence) indicates an intentional omission of a word or sentence without altering the meaning of the overall sentence. An ellipsis shows that something has been left out and, when used effectively, it invites the reader or listener to fill in the blanks.

When you say, "So, what would it take for you to list with me…?" you are effectively leading the prospect to finish the sentence for you, with the best possible ending.

When practicing and memorizing your scripts, diagram the sentences to include intentional pauses and breaks, or to emphasize and linger on certain words. These small but powerful punctuations will help raise the bar on your performance before the curtain goes up on that first crucial call!

## 8 More Tips for Effective Script Delivery

1. **Read the script.** This should go without saying, but you'd be surprised how many people don't read their scripts as closely and carefully as they should. Really read it so you understand each section and its purpose.

2. **Identify key points.** Every main idea is a section by itself. Learn the section that corresponds with each main idea so that the presentation will make more sense.

3. **Memorize the script.** Commit the entire piece to memory. Recite it daily.

4. **Practice saying 150-160 words per minute.** That's the average talking speed for English. Speak any slower, and your client will lose interest. Speak too fast, and the client won't be able to keep up with what you're saying.

5. **Avoid verbal ticks and crutches.** Speakers tend to fill in silent pauses with fillers, like "um", "ah", and "so", but doing so will make you seem more like an amateur than a professional. If you continue to rely on these words, join a speaking club, like Toastmasters, where the members will help you improve your delivery.

6. **Focus on the clients and the words you are saying.** If you sound like you are reciting from memory, you'll lose not only the sale but also the prospect.

7. **Make a recording of your delivery and critique it.** Most people don't like to hear recordings of their voice, but listening to the way that you speak and deliver presentations is a good way to evaluate which areas still need work.

8. **Practice, practice, practice.** Then practice some more. It's the only way your presentations will become fluent. As you increase the number of scripts committed to memory, be sure to practice them daily. Start with the scripts you already know, and add new content to your repertoire.

## Your Practice Schedule

Remember this moment, right here, when we promised you that there will be a time when your presentation is smooth, well-delivered, and internalized so completely that you're more *excited* than *nervous* to deliver it!

By scheduling your practice now, you're scheduling that point in time in the future.

*" I run on the road long before I dance under the lights."*   Muhammad Ali

Proficiency at scripts is not a lighting strike, and there are hours ahead for you, but those hours need to be calendared and scheduled. We tend to find that people won't just naturally practice and role-play before they prospect, but if it's in their calendar they do. And, when it's in their calendar, we have seen those people get much higher conversion rates, much higher success levels, and get better at generating business much more quickly.

Let's take a look at a practice schedule. As we mentioned before, we highly recommend practicing the scripts before making your actual prospecting calls, as it's a great way to warm up and take the edge off.

## YOUR SCRIPT WORKOUT PLAN

| MON | TUES | WED | THUR | FRI |
|---|---|---|---|---|
| 8-8:30 | 8-8:30 | 4:30-5 | 8-8:30 | 8-8:30 |
| SOI | EXPIRED | FSBO | CIRCLE PROS | PREQ/BUY |
| PREQ/SELL | OBJ HAND | SOI | EXPIRED | FSBO |
| CIRCLE PROS | PREQ/BUY | PREQ/SELL | OBJ HAND | SOI |

Varying your practice will round out your scripts, while making sure you're not specializing to a point where you're ignoring other business-generating strategies. You'll notice that we've included the option of practicing scripts in the evening one day a week.

Entertain this idea for your schedule, because as life happens sometimes in the morning, your schedule will be dynamic enough where you can account for it, without halting your progression. Would you be surprised to know that there are some people who get so upset they missed going to the gym, that they skip going the rest of the week?

Self-sabotaging behaviors can show up anywhere. Don't let those behaviors take over your script practice.

Last pointer: don't be chained to just practicing at these times if you're eager to become great.

High school football teams use double sessions—a morning practice and an afternoon practice—to get their freshmen teams in shape in a short amount of time. Those workouts are grueling, yet by the end of three weeks, the conditioning that's taken place is amazing.

You can reap similar benefits from intensified script practice.

## SUMMARY

Every real estate agent uses scripts. They may not think they do, but they do.

Scripts work. They give you a plan to follow, no matter what happens, and no matter whom you're up against. Prospecting can be uncomfortable and nerve wracking at first. Like Bill Walsh said, "If things aren't working, you can lose your nerve. The script makes you stay in the game plan and make it work."

As with anything in prospecting, when you first start using scripts, you're going to feel very uncomfortable and unnatural. If you're feeling in any way averse or uncomfortable, try to "flip the script" and embrace the opposite of what your natural instinct is. In order to use scripts successfully, you must learn do so with a positive attitude and an open mind.

Our scripts are not crutches: they are a scaffolding support system that enable you to immediately connect with your prospects and see results that would otherwise be time-consuming or incredibly difficult to achieve. Through time on task and frequent practice, you will eventually memorize and internalize these scripts to the point where you won't need a physical piece of paper anymore.

Like everything in prospecting, memorizing and perfecting effective script delivery takes practice, and plenty of it! Agents that schedule and calendar practice and role-play time have higher conversion rates than those that don't.

By practicing and internalizing the scripts for every prospecting scenario, you'll be prepared to handle each client concern, including any number of objections. The ease with which you deliver the scripts will put you in the expert seat as you meet with prospects and take care of their real estate needs.

# SOI SCRIPT
## Asking for Referrals

"Hi _____, this is [Agent Name] at [Real Estate Company], how have you been? (pause) This is a quick call about business. I'm reaching out to remind you that I'm in real estate! You see, statistics show that our clients are going to run into 6 to 10 people over the next 12 months that are looking buy or sell a home. So, can I ask you a favor?"

(if YES, continue with the script . . .)

"I prefer to grow my business by word of mouth. So, when you bump into these people, would you be willing to refer my services and call me with their contact information?"

(Pause and wait patiently for a response. Let silence do the heavy lifting here)

"Thanks! Oh, and since I've got you on the phone, do you happen to know anyone that is thinking about buying or selling a home right now?"

(if YES, get name/contact info, or at least get permission to follow up later)

(If NO, continue with the script . . .)

"Thanks for all your help. I'll be in touch!"

(NOTE: A follow up "Thank You" card can have a very positive impact)

© Copyright Icenhower Coaching & Consulting, LLC. All rights reserved.

# EXPIRED LISTING
## When They Answer & Voice Message Scripts

## WHEN THEY ANSWER SCRIPTS

### SCRIPT 1:

"Hi, I'm looking for _____. This is John Smith with ABC Realty, and I'm calling because your home has come up as an expired listing. So I'm calling to see when you plan on hiring the right agent to sell your home?"

### SCRIPT 2:

"Hi, I'm John Smith with ABC Realty, and I'm calling about the house that was listed in the multiple listing service that expired. I wanted to interview for the job of getting your home back on the market and sold. Are you still interested in moving?"

### SCRIPT 3:

"Hi this is John Smith with ABC Realty, and I noticed that your listing on 123 Pepperwood Court is no longer active. I wanted to see if you are going to take this opportunity to interview a different agent. If so, I'd love to share my methods for getting homes sold quickly."

## VOICE MESSAGE SCRIPTS

### SCRIPT 1:

"I'm calling about the home for sale. My number is 555-123-4567."

### SCRIPT 2:

"Hi this is John Smith and I'm calling about the house you had listed in the multiple listing service, and I'd like to talk to you about the home. Would you please call me back as soon as possible at 555-123-4567?"

### SCRIPT 3:

"Hello this John Smith with ABC Realty, and I'm calling about your house listing that is no longer on the market. If you are interested in taking this opportunity to interview a different agent, please call me at 555-123-4567."

© Copyright Icenhower Coaching & Consulting, LLC. All rights reserved.

# EXPIRED LISTING
## Objection Handlers

These expired listing objection handlers can be used to address the five most common objections that agents face when contacting expired listings by phone. Please review them all first since many of them can be used interchangeably as well.

### 1. OBJECTION: "We're Not Putting it Back on the Market"

1. "Really? Well if it sold, where were you moving to?"

2. "How soon did you want to be there?"

3. "What do you think stopped it from selling?"

4. "If I were to present you with a strong offer to purchase your home, would you be still be willing to at least take a look at it?"

5. "Well that's exactly what I would like to talk to you about. What would be the best time for me to quickly drop by, 4:00pm today or tomorrow?"

### 2. OBJECTION: "Waiting for the market to get better"

1. "Well I understand, this market has been challenging for some. Just out of curiosity, if you did sell, where were you moving to?"

2. "What's important to you about moving there?"

3. "You see, I specialize in selling houses that didn't sell the first time around. Many homes don't sell the first time they're on the market, and it just takes a different approach to get them sold. If I could show you a way to make that happen would you be interested?"

4. "Great! Would 4:00pm today or tomorrow work for you?"

### 3. OBJECTION: "I'm going to re-list with the same agent"

1. "I understand. It makes sense that you might feel obliged to allow your last agent another chance to sell your home. But what do you think they will do differently this time that they didn't do the last time?"

2. "Do you think that you're at least owed the opportunity to interview other agents to see what they can do differently to get homes sold at this time?"

3. "Well that's all I would like to do . . . apply for the job to get your home sold quickly and for the highest price possible. Would 4:00pm today or tomorrow work for you?"

© Copyright Icenhower Coaching & Consulting, LLC. All rights reserved.

# Module 2 — Appendix 2.3 continued

## 4. OBJECTION: "I'm going to sell it myself" (FSBO)

1. "After what you have been through I can certainly understand. What do you think went wrong the first time you had it up for sale?"

2. "Well I can certainly understand the need to make a change. But are you sure that you want to keep your home out of the multiple listing service when about 90% of all buyers use an agent to purchase homes?"

3. "You see, marketing homes to both the general public AND to other agents are crucial to getting homes sold quickly for the highest price possible. And many great houses don't sell the first time around. So don't you think it's at least worth 15 minutes to learn what I do differently to get homes sold before you make your decision?"

## 5. OBJECTION: "I've already found a different agent"

1. "I see, have you already filled out paperwork with them?" (If so, thank them and wish them good luck. If not, then continue with the script . . )

2. "Great. You know even the best houses don't sell the first time around. In fact, I specialize in selling homes that didn't sell the first time. Would you mind telling me what your next agent is planning on doing differently this time?"

3. "I see. Do you think you owe it to yourself to interview multiple agents for the job to ensure that the home sells for the highest price possible . . . at the very least for another opinion on your home's listing price?"

4. "It shouldn't take up too much of your time and I'd be happy to swing by at your convenience. Would 3:00 or 4:00pm today be good for you?"

© Copyright Icenhower Coaching & Consulting, LLC. All rights reserved.

# FSBO "3 Questions" Phone Script

1. **"If I brought you a qualified buyer, would you be willing to pay me a 3% commission?"**

   If YES, continue on to the next question...

2. **"How long are you going to try to sell your home on your own before you explore other options?"**

   Cut their answer in half for practical purposes. So, if they say 2 months, they will likely list in a month. If their answer is 6 months or less, continue on to the next question . . .

3. **"If you don't sell your home by that time, what other options will you consider?"**

   This question is to ensure that an agent is not their relative or best friend and you don't waste too much time and effort. If they are open to the possibility of interviewing agents in the future, place them in your lead follow-up campaign and move on to contacting the next FSBO seller!

**Points to Consider:**

FSBO sellers are very receptive to calls concerning the sale of their home. They are also often eager to get calls from agents that might have a buyer for their home and they might be willing to pay half the commission to an agent that brings them a buyer.

Prospecting for FSBO listings is a numbers game, and even the most effective agents will list no more than 20% of the FSBO sellers they contact. Therefore, it is essential to filter through FSBO sellers quickly over the phone by asking the qualifying questions above. Don't always attempt to aggressively close an appointment on the first call or you might find yourself wasting a lot of evenings on fruitless appointments. They may never intend to us an agent or they might be obligated to use an agent that is a family member of friend if they ever do list their home.

# CIRCLE PROSPECTING
## Just Listed Script

Hi, I'm (John Smith) with (ABC Realty), and we just listed a home for sale in your neighborhood on (123 Main Street) for ($250,000), and we often find that the ultimate buyer of a home is a friend, family member or acquaintance of someone that lives in the same neighborhood. Since we are doing everything we can to sell your neighbor's home, I'd like to ask you if you know anyone looking to move into your community?

Answer: "No".

Great! I truly appreciate your taking the time to try and help. So tell me, when do you plan on moving?

Answer: "No plans".

How long have you lived in your home?

Answer: "5 years".

Where did you live before that?

Answer: "Denver, Colorado".

Excellent! How did you pick this community?

Answer: "To be near family".

Great! So if you were to move, where would you move next?

Answer: "To Florida".

And when would that most likely be?

**If their answer is 6 months or less, continue:**

Did you know that it can take up to 6 months to get a home prepared, marketed and sold in today's market?

Answer: "No".

Great! So do you want your home sold in 6 months, or do you want to start the process of selling then?

Answer: "Sold".

Perfect! All that we need to do to start you on your way to (Florida) is pick a time to get together. How does that sound?

Answer: "Great".

Excellent! Would Wednesday or Thursday at 4:00pm work better for you?

© Copyright Icenhower Coaching & Consulting, LLC. All rights reserved.

# CIRCLE PROSPECTING
## Just Sold Script

Hi, I'm (John Smith) with (ABC Realty), and we just sold a home for sale in your neighborhood on (123 Main Street) for ($250,000), and when one neighbor sells a home, typically 2 or 3 more homes in the same neighborhood sell right away. So I was curious as to when you plan on moving?

Answer: "No plans".

Great! How long have you lived in your home?

Answer: "5 years".

Terrific! Where did you live before that?

Answer: "Denver, Colorado".

Excellent! How did you pick this community?

Answer: "To be near family".

Wonderful! So if you were to move, where would you move next?

Answer: "To Florida".

Exciting! And when would that most likely be?

**If their answer is 6 months or less, continue:**

Did you know that it can take up to 6 months to get a home prepared, marketed and sold in today's market?

Answer: "No".

Great! So do you want your home sold in 6 months, or do you want to start the process of selling then?

Answer: "Sold".

Perfect! All that we need to do to start you on your way to (Florida) is pick a time to get together. How does that sound?

Answer: "Great".

Excellent! Would Wednesday or Thursday at 4:00pm work better for you?

© Copyright Icenhower Coaching & Consulting, LLC. All rights reserved.

MODULE 2                                                                                          APPENDIX 2.7

**ICENHOWER**
COACHING & CONSULTING

## Seller Questionnaire & Lead Form

Date: _____

Name: _____ Spouse Name: _____

Property Address: _____ City: _____ State: _____ Zip: _____

Phone #s – Mobile: _____ Spouse Mobile: _____ Home: _____ Work: _____

Email: _____ Spouse Email: _____

Family / Children (include ages): _____

1. Have you spoken with any other agents?  ☐ Yes  ☐ No  _____
2. Have you considered selling the home yourself?  ☐ Yes  ☐ No  _____
3. Why do you want to move? _____
4. Do you know where you want to move to? _____
5. What date do you want to be moved by? _____
6. Are there any negatives to not moving by then? (suggest lifestyle sacrifices, job, costs, schools, family, etc.)
   _____
7. Tell me all the negatives of not moving at all? (same suggestions above)
   _____
8. Tell me all the benefits of buying a new home: (dig deep & find out WHY?)
   _____
9. On a scale of 1 to 10, how would you rank your motivation to move? With 10 being highly motivated: _____
10. When did you buy your home? _____ What price did you pay? _____
11. Do you know how much you still owe on it? _____
12. Have you made any major improvements to the home since?  ☐ Yes  ☐ No
    _____
13. Do you happen to have an idea as to what you think it's worth, or should sell for? _____
14. Do you have a price you won't sell your home below? _____
15. Tell me about the positive & negative features of your home: _____
    _____
16. How many BR: ____ Baths: ____ SqFt: ____ Stories: ____ Other: _____
17. How did you hear about me/us? _____
18. Are you interviewing any other agents?  ☐ Yes  ☐ No   Who? _____ When? _____
19. "Thank you! The next step is for me to take a quick look at your home and I can answer any other questions you may have. Then you can decide what we do next. How does that sound?" (pause)
    "Great!  Does 4:30 tomorrow or 5:00 Wednesday work for you?"

Appointment Date/Time: _____

DISC Behavioral Profile: _____ Why? _____

© Copyright Icenhower Coaching & Consulting, LLC. All rights reserved.

# MODULE 2

# APPENDIX 2.8

**ICENHOWER**
COACHING & CONSULTING

## Buyer Questionnaire & Lead Sheet

Date: _____ Lead Source: _____

Name: _____ Spouse Name: _____

Property Address: _____ City: _____ State: _____ Zip: _____

Phone #s – Mobile: _____ Spouse Mobile: _____ Home: _____ Work: _____

Email: _____ Spouse Email: _____

Family / Children (include ages): _____

1. Have any other agents shown you homes?  ☐ Yes ☐ No
    - If Yes, do you have a signed agency agreement?  ☐ Yes ☐ No
2. Is anyone buying the home with you? _____
3. Are you renting, or do you own a home?  ☐ Homeowner ☐ Renter
    a) HOMEOWNER:
       - Do you need to sell your home before you buy?  ☐ Yes ☐ No
       - Have you signed a listing agreement to sell your home?  ☐ Yes ☐ No  **If "No" use Seller Lead Sheet.**
    b) RENTER:
       - When does your lease end? _____
4. What date do you want to be moved by? _____
5. Are there any negatives to not moving by then? (suggest lifestyle sacrifices, job, costs, schools, family, etc.)
   _____
6. Tell me all the benefits of buying a new home: (dig deep & find out WHY?)
   _____
7. On a scale of 1 to 10, how would you rank your motivation to move? With 10 meaning you must buy as quickly as possible, and 1 meaning you're not sure you'll really buy anything: _____
   - What's missing? What would it take to make you a 10? _____
8. Do you know where you want to move to? _____
9. Will you be paying cash or getting a mortgage?  ☐ Cash ☐ Mortgage
10. Have you been pre-approved by a lender?  ☐ Yes ☐ No
11. How much will your down payment be? _____
12. What price range are you looking in? _____
13. How many BR: ____ Baths: ____ SqFt: ____ Stories: ____ Other: _____
14. What else are you looking for in a home? _____
15. Will anyone else be involved in your home buying decision? _____
16. "Thank you! I'd love to help you find your perfect home. All that we need to do is to set an appointment so that I can help you find the home you're looking for. Does 4:30 tomorrow or 5:00 Wednesday work for you?"

Appointment Date/Time: _____

DISC Behavioral Profile: _____ Why? _____

© Copyright Icenhower Coaching & Consulting, LLC. All rights reserved.

# OBJECTION HANDLERS

Objection: "I'm just looking…"

Handler:

- I understand MR/MRS Prospect, A lot of people, just like you, are coming to our website just looking at homes, but also have some interest in the homes they are looking at.
- In fact, we took a look and found most people are between 9 and 18 months away from purchasing their home. So, I'm just curious, if we could wave a magic wand here, when would you like to be in your next home?

Objection: "I'm just looking…"

Handler:

- "Of course, MR/MRS Prospect. I understand. I want to assist you in any way I can. May I ask you a few quick questions so that I can help as much as possible in your search"?

Objection: "I'm just looking…"

Handler:

- "Got it, and thank you so much for looking here MR/MRS Prospect. I want to make this as painless for you as possible. If I can ask you just a couple of quick questions, I can make this very easy on you."

Objection: "I'm just looking…"

Handler:

- MR/MRS Prospect, as you can see, there are a lot of choices on the market. Is there a particular area or neighborhood I can direct you to, so you can look?
- There are a few different ways to search for property, you've probably seen a few already! This way you can at least look at the things you want to look at. So tell me, what are a few of the areas you're curious about looking at?

Objection: "We're all set"

Handler:

- "I can appreciate that MR/MRS Prospect! Most of the people I speak with are 'all set' and that's why I'm reaching out to you now – I want to give you an option for the next time you're in need of any help. Let me ask you…"

Objection: "We're all set"

Handler:

- "MR/MRS Prospect, no problem; in fact it's great to hear that you're on your way already! Let me ask you, the next time you're in need of help or information, what's number one on your wish list?"

## MODULE 2 — APPENDIX 2.9 CONTINUED

Objection: "We're all set"

Handler:

- "I understand – I didn't expect to catch you in the market right now. MR/MRS Prospect, instead, let me get an idea of your perfect home, and then I'll send you some choices you can keep on file for the next time you're searching. In fact, if you'd like, I can tailor an automatic search to give you a head start! So, tell me…"

Objection: "We're all set"

Handler:

- "I can appreciate that MR/MRS Prospect, our best prepped clients are usually 9-12 months away for a firmer relationship. Let me ask you, when is your next buying season for this?"

Objection: "We're all set"

Handler:

- "That's fine, MR/MRS Prospect I totally understand. And let me ask you – the next time you're in the market for this, how many agents are you going to reach out to, or is this the first step you've taken?"

Objection: "Let me think about it…"

Handler:

- MR/MRS Prospect, whenever I tell someone I need to think about it, I usually mean one of three things: 1 - I'm not going to be a deal for whatever reason and I just want to get them off the phone, 2 - I kind of like the idea but I'm going to have to find the money or talk to my partner, or something else is holding me back, or 3 - I really like the idea and I just have to move something around before I say yes. Be honest with me; which one of those things is it for you right now?"

Objection: "Let me think about it…"

Handler:

- MR/MRS Prospect, I've heard the only thing costlier than making a bad decision is not making one at all. If you don't change things, then things won't get better for you. You've mentioned that you're in the beginning stages of a very important process…
- Then do what my other clients do, and put me and my company to work for you. Once you see the positive results that we both know are possible here, you'll be saving time, money, AND energy… and that's going to be a win/win for us both, isn't it? Then here's what we need to do…"

Objection: "Let me think about it…"

Handler:

- MR/MRS Prospect, since we both agree this has a great chance to work for you, let me do this:
- While we're on the phone right now, I'm going to email you three customer testimonials from clients just like you, who were hesitant as well.

- And, when you read about how successful they were with us, you'll have peace of mind to take a step further. Once you see for yourself how this works, then we can talk about further involvement, is that fair?"

Objection: "We're not ready yet... or Not a good time"

Handler:

- I completely understand, can we find a 30-minute window next week to talk more?
  - Prospect: Send me an email. I'll take a look at my calendar to see if it's possible.
- Not a problem. What's the best email to send that to within the next 5 minutes?
  - Prospect: 123abc@client.com
- Great, I'll send you an email and include some possible times. Just so I propose some reasonable times, is there a day that works better for you?
  - Prospect: Tuesdays or Wednesdays.
- Mornings or afternoons?
  - Prospect: Afternoon Tuesday.
- Great, 3pm Tuesday works for me. I'll send you a calendar invite as a placeholder. Look for that in the next 5 mins. Is there a hurdle you're having that I can solve to make our time together worth it for you?

Objection: "We're not ready yet... or Not a good time"

Handler:

- I can appreciate that, MR/MRS Prospect, let's very quickly schedule 5 mins when it's better for you, or do you have 5 mins now? GREAT! One last thing, what can I research for you in the meantime, to make it worth it for you to pick up the phone when I call back?

Objection: "We're not ready yet... or Not a good time"

Handler:

- Understood, MR/MRS Prospect. There is a lot to get in order before buying a new home: preparing your current home for sale, meeting with a lender, insurance, inspectors, repairs, finding a home, etc. Would you like some help with all of that?

Objection: "You have the wrong number..."

Handler:

- I'm sorry! Well, now I have a problem, and maybe you can help me solve it.... My name is X and I work for Y, and we've got at least Z buyers looking for their next home; the market doesn't have enough to offer them. Have you ever considered taking a look at homes like yours online to see what they're being offered for?

Objection: "We don't want a pushy salesperson"
Handler:
- Good MR/MRS Prospect, because I consider myself a customer service professional, not a salesperson. My job today is to address your needs and provide you with professional guidance and assistance during the research process.

Objection: "We don't want a pushy salesperson"
Handler:
- Perfect. I would never want to be pushy. MR/MRS Prospect, I believe in listening to a client's needs and helping them to find the perfect property for them. So, what are you looking for in a home?

Objection: "We don't want a pushy salesperson"
Handler:
- I wouldn't want one either MR/MRS Prospect, but can I share something quickly with you? I might want help during the early research phase, someone who's proactive in finding me a few homes I wanted to buy... as two minds on this could be better than one... does that make sense?

Objection: "Our credit isn't good enough yet"
Handler:
- MR/MRS Prospect, I understand. Have you spoken to a lender to find out? That's very common. I've also had many clients find that their credit is better than they thought after speaking to a mortgage lender. Plus, a lender can help you start working to fix any credit issues right away. Could I have a lender that I trust at least give you a call?

Objection: "Our credit isn't good enough yet"
Handler:
- OK. Did you know that there are many loan programs available that have very different credit requirements? Wouldn't it make sense to at least meet with a lender to find out exactly where you stand?

Objection: When you hear a complaint... apologies/frustrations
Handler:
- Feel, Felt, Found-
  - FEEL: "I can appreciate that you feel..."
  - FELT: "and we know that some of our clients who've felt... didn't take the time to bring it to our attention; so first, thank you for that."
  - FOUND: "What we've found helpful at this point is to..." and then move to reconciling their need.
- "I'm sorry that we did not meet your expectations. Please let me apologize and ask.... What's troubling you most with this?" Taking responsibility is not taking blame; you're recognizing there

## Module 2

## Appendix 2.9 continued

was a fault, or a gap, and you're saying that you're willing to take steps to help them get over or through their hurdle.

- *"What can we do to make it up to you?"* Be aware you're opening yourself to any request; let them share their ideas, share a few of yours, and base what happens next to what's within your scope of ability.
- *"Here's what I'm going to do to make it right."* Follow with two suggestions, and invite them to choose one; repeat it back to them, then set an action to follow back up with them, and confirm the issue has been handled.

Objection: "We are already working with someone"
Handler:

- *MR/MRS Prospect, I'm sure a motivated person like you is already working with another firm to handle your home search needs. The reason I contacted you is because you'd registered on our site and we move quickly the way you do. Based on my experience working with clients who are searching online, online searches usually create immediate questions or the need for help right at that moment. So, how can I help you?*

Objection: "We are already working with someone"
Handler:

- *MR/MRS Prospect, almost every person interested in the housing market is searching in a few different places… how many sites have you searched on already? Doesn't it make sense to have a backup to make you feel more secure?*

Objection: "We are already working with someone"
Handler:

- *That's great, MR/MRS Prospect. Since you've already begun the process of searching, would you mind if I asked what they're doing great? We're always looking for great tips. Thank you for that… now, if there was one place they could improve, where would that be? Could we put our name in as a back-up? What can we do to earn that place in the next few days/weeks?*

Objection: "We want to find another home before we put ours on the market"
Handler:

- *"I agree, MR/MRS Prospect, finding your new home is important… can I share a thought with you? It may take as long as 2 to 4 months for your home to sell.*
- *Then it will take another 30-45 days to get the closing done; and in that time, another buyer may have seen the quality you saw, someone who could act quickly without a home to sell first; that can be heartbreaking, and I am definitely not in the heart-breaking business.*
- *Let's start the process to get your home on the market right now and get to work on getting your home sold, so you don't have to wait any longer than necessary to get moved into your new home… does this plan work for you?*

MODULE 2　　　　　　　　　　　　　　　　　　　　　　APPENDIX 2.10

# ORGANIZED SALES PROCESS
## PHASES FLOWCHART

**LEAD**
- Generate Leads
- Source & Qualify Leads
- Nurture & Cultivate

**PROSPECT**
- Set & Confirm Appointment
- Prepare for Appointment/Sales Call
- Delivering Sales Presentation
- Close for the Sale

**CLIENT**
- Calendar & Schedule the Process
- Review, Request Feedback & Referrals
- Close Again
- Follow Up

© Copyright Icenhower Coaching & Consulting, LLC. All rights reserved.

## Your Sphere of Influence (SOI)

As we discussed in the previous chapter, although you are a prospector—generating business from people you have never met and do not know—your SOI database should be the foundation of your business. With this business-generating strategy, you will be cultivating and growing a group, or sphere, of people *you know* who might use you for their real estate needs and who, in turn, might refer you to the people that *they* know.

These two different strategies are quite distinct, but it is very common for real estate agents to employ a blend of business-generation activities. Of the top-producing agents in North America, at least 50% of their business comes from contacts in their Sphere of Influence, and often that number is closer to 80-100%.

Almost all strong teams know that it's important to have a solid SOI foundation to anchor and augment their prospecting activities. Agents that only prospect for leads tend to plough through a lot of business. They're good at taking an individual lead from prospect to client, but they never have that repeat business coming back to them over time, because they don't operate a database system underneath.

> "The richest people in the world look for and build networks. Everyone else looks for work." - Robert Kiyosaki.

Even as a prospector, it's crucial that you grow and cultivate an SOI referral database along with other lead-generation activities and sources at the same time. As you prospect for leads, you are going to meet a great deal of new people—people that you should be adding to your SOI database. In this chapter, we will show you exactly how to do that so that you build a productive and profitable SOI rather than the dreaded watered down database that is, unfortunately, so common.

Over time, you may even find that it's difficult or unnecessary to prospect for new business because you have so much business coming from your SOI database network. A lot of agents eventually stop prospecting for business. Rightly or wrongly, they're getting so much business from their SOI that they don't really need to prospect anymore.

However, prospecting is an absolutely legitimate business-generation method, so you can certainly continue to prospect for new business as long as you have enough people on your growing team to handle it.

But perhaps we're getting ahead of ourselves. While we certainly hope that your business multiplies to the point that you're expanding and leading your own team, for now let's begin with the basics and everything you need to know to identify, grow, and nurture your own Sphere of Influence.

## Learning Targets

In this chapter, you will learn how to:

- Appraise the value of an SOI database.
- Organize your SOI database.
- Memorize a new set of SOI scripts for meeting new people
- Apply the Rule of 7 Touches to introduce new people to your SOI database.
- Calculate return of investment on your SOI.
- Formulate goals for growing your SOI database.
- Review strategies for implementing your Annual Database Contact Plan.

Throughout this chapter, we encourage you to adopt and maintain a growth mindset and commit to the effort it will take to reap the rewards of a successful, systematic SOI database and annual contact plan.

> *All growth depends upon activity. There is no development physically or intellectually without effort, and effort means work." – Calvin Coolidge, American President*

## WHAT'S IN A NAME?

A professor distributed the final exam in a class on successful business practices.

Most of the students felt that they were prepared to share what they had learned during the semester of study with this teacher in her night class.

The professor's students worked their way through the test, answering questions until they came to the last one. This question seemed to stump most of the students. Some of the class did a double take when they saw it. Others laid down their pencils and looked around the room as if they'd find the answer on the walls.

> "What is the name of the custodian who cleans our classroom?"

Only a few were confident enough to answer the question with the one-word response it required.

The students had seen the custodian, an older woman, night after night as she went about emptying the trash, sweeping and mopping. Their classroom was the last class to finish, and the custodian often waited on a bench until the class was over so she could complete her work in this hallway before moving on to the next floor.

The custodian's name was Doris. Few students ever forgot that lesson—or the name of the woman who inspired the question in the first place.

> *For someone to qualify to be in your SOI, you must know that person by name, and they must know you by name.*

By now, you should realize that the people in your Sphere of Influence are people that you already know. Specifically, they are people that you know by name, who also know you by name in turn.

**This is very important:**

*For someone to qualify to be in your SOI, you must know that person by name, and they must know you by name.*

It's crucial that you do not water down your database with people who don't know you by name. Think quality, not quantity, when it comes to the people in your circles.

## THE DANGER OF A DILUTED DATABASE

Maintaining contact with members of your SOI takes precious time and money. The last thing you want is a watered-down database of 2,000 people who don't know who you are.

It's extremely difficult to personally call 2,000 people in a database each and every year, and it's prohibitively expensive to send mailers to 2,000 people. A watered-down database is overwhelming and can cause agents to resort to ineffectual email drip campaigns instead of powerful, systematic contact plans.

An effective SOI database should be efficient and manageable and provide you with a solid return of investment. Don't allow your truly valuable SOI members to become buried and lost within a sea of faceless anonymity. Don't waste your efforts and resources on people who don't know who you are. Eventually, you won't even remember who they are, and you will sorely regret the painstaking and time-consuming process of scrubbing a watered-down SOI database.

The people in your database don't have to be your best friend. And they don't necessarily have to be a past client, or a vendor or affiliate you work with. All of those people will be in your SOI, of course, but at a basic level, if someone were to say, "Hey, you know who Ann Johnson is?" and that person says, "Yeah, I think I know who she is—she's in real estate right?" that person is in your sphere of influence.

On a simple, human level, the story about Doris the custodian, reminds us to treat everyone with respect, regardless of who they are or what they do. It also reminds us that the potential for connection is all around us.

Like we said, your SOI database should never include people that you haven't met or who don't recognize you by name. However, there's a simple way to remedy that. All it takes is the ability to notice those around you, and the willingness to say hello, introduce yourself, and get to know the people that you meet.

## Your Sphere Of Influence

As its name suggests, your Sphere of Influence is a circle with several layers, much like our planet.

You, of course, are the center of the sphere.

Around you is your inner circle, the network of family and close friends that enfold you. These are the people who love you and support you no matter what.

Beyond them are those acquaintances that make up your outer circles. Although your acquaintances may not be as familiar as your close friends, you enjoy meeting with them and they know who you are.

In the outermost layer are your professional and industry contacts—the people you do business with, and who are in a position to refer business to you too.

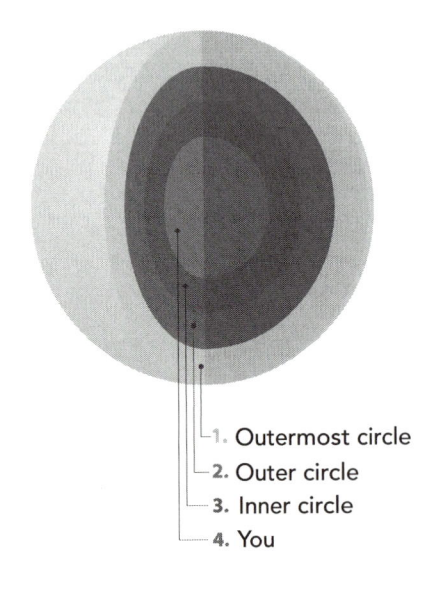

1. Outermost circle
2. Outer circle
3. Inner circle
4. You

**OUTERMOST CIRCLE**
- Industry Contacts

**OUTER CIRCLE**
- Organizations, Clubs & Groups
- Professional Service Providers

**INNER CIRCLE**
- Family & Friends
- Neighbors
- Former Co-Workers

1. Outermost circle
2. Outer circle
3. Inner circle
4. You

## Inner Circle

Your inner circle consists of your loved ones, your closest allies and your advocates. These are the people who want you to be successful in your real estate business, and they'll do whatever they can to help you out.

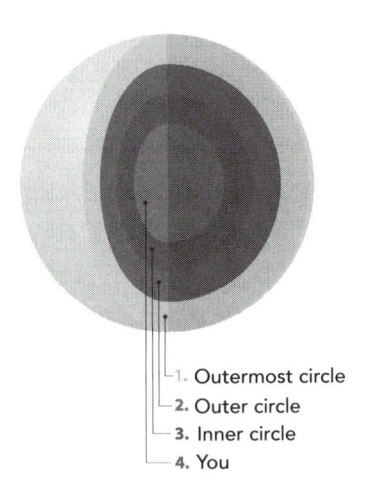

Typically, your strongest advocates can be found in the following categories (and, by extension, the network of each of these people):

- Your spouse or partner
- Parents, siblings, and immediate family members
- Close friends
- Relatives who live nearby
- Close neighbors
- Former co-workers

### EXERCISE: Who's In Your Inner Circle?

Write down as many names as you can think of in the above categories. One of the quickest ways to identify all of your contacts is to begin with your social networks. Take a quick look at your family, friends, and followers in your social media platforms. This is the beginning of your SOI database.

### CHALLENGE: Kick-Start Your SOI Database

Reaching out to your inner-circle will kick-start your SOI database.

Obtain or update the contact information for the key people in your life. At a minimum, you should obtain the following information:

- Full Name
- Physical Address
- Email Address
- Phone Number

Challenge yourself to include additional information, such as:

- **Their relationship to you** (to avoid confusion with a large database that may contain similar names).
- **Their profession, industry, or line of work** (to kick-start conversations and provide value through mutual connections and referrals).
- **Their date of birth** (so that you can send them a card or call them on their birthday)
- **Important life updates** (for example, if they're expecting a baby, make a note of it and remember to congratulate them as well as ask how the family is doing whenever you call).

### CHALLENGE: Ask For Help

As a collective group, the connections in your inner circle will help spread the word that you are in the real estate business. They can hand out your contact information and provide important testimonials about who you are as a person. These people are easy to contact because you know them the best, and they genuinely want you to do well.

You have to ask your inner-circle for help, however. While they care about you and want you to do well, don't assume that they will automatically champion your cause. Your friends and family won't provide the assistance you need unless you're vulnerable enough to ask for it. What's more is that you will need to tell them precisely what you're looking for.

It's not enough to say, "Hey, I'm in real estate now, so spread the word."

A better approach is to ask a direct question, one with a yes or no answer, like this:

> *"Do you know anyone thinking about moving this year?"*

If they say yes, ask your friend or family member to forward your contact information to those who are thinking about moving. Better yet, ask for their contact information so that you can follow up with them.

If your family and friends can't think of anyone moving in the next twelve months, ask for their support:

> *"If you do run into someone thinking about moving, can I count on you to recommend me and get their phone number for me?"*

You are more likely to get the help you need if you ask for it directly. Challenge yourself to ask for an inner-circle referral from the next fifteen friends and family you run into.

## OUTER CIRCLES

When you have tapped into the assistance of your inner circle, you are ready to engage the acquaintances in your outer circles and expand your SOI sources.

Contacts in this group include people you know from:

- Clubs
- Civic Groups
- Church Groups
- Other Organizations

It is quite easy to obtain membership rosters and directories from clubs, your church, or your HOA.

Include people you know from the gym or sports groups. If you have children, think about your kid's teachers or coaches on their sports teams as well.

Make sure to include professional service providers that you're personally acquainted with—everyone has a dentist or a family doctor, and perhaps you have a personal accountant or an attorney, too.

Your outer circles are potentially limitless. When growing your SOI database, the question you should constantly and continually be asking yourself is: *"Who Do I Know?"*

You may not be close personal friends or see each other all the time, but you know these people, and they each have their own spheres of influence. Even if they are not going to be in the market for a new home in the next year, you can still ask them to forward your contact information to someone they may know who will be house-hunting.

> **CHALLENGE:** Deepen & Develop Your Database

As your list of names begins to grow exponentially, it's time to develop a more systematic database.

In the long term, as your SOI database grows and grows, you will likely need to implement a Customer Relationship Management (CRM) system to stay efficient and highly organized.

Most real estate CRMs come with pre-made mailing templates for agents. Some CRMs even contract directly with a mailing service to send scheduled mailers to your entire database throughout the year. CRMs take very little of your time once they are set up and managed efficiently.

For now, you can use simple software tools like Microsoft Excel or iOS Numbers to develop your database.

Include column headers for the following:

- Name
- Contact information (phone, email, physical address)
- Date of Birth
- Business/Industry
- Relationship (family, friend, acquaintance, business, other)
- Comments

Later you'll add a few more columns to the database, including how many times you contacted these resources, and in what format: phone call, direct mail, in person, email, etc.

For now, take the time to get the names recorded. You can add the rest of the information later.

## OUTERMOST CIRCLES

Once this part of your outer circle is complete, it's time to think of the outermost layer. These are people you know too, but not as well as those in the first layer of your outer-circle. The list might include:

- The manager at your favorite restaurant
- An artist whose work you admire
- A store director
- The person who sold you your last vehicle

As you can see, the common denominator amongst these SOI contacts is that each of them works in a particular profession or industry.

Each and every day, we take advice from all sorts of professionals, and often on matters outside their field of expertise! Accountant recommendations come from doctors and dentists. Taxi drivers give advice on where to eat and drink. And hairstylists share information about everything from day care providers to personal trainers and chimney cleaners!

We take their advice because we know and trust them. The people we give business to are likely to give us business back in return.

Like you, people in various industries and professions encounter a lot of different people on a daily basis. Most people meet a lot of realtors but will forget about them over time. By including these contacts in your SOI database, you're keeping your name on the tip of their tongue so that you'll stay first of mind when people think, *"Who do I know who is a real estate agent?"*

### EXERCISE: Who Do I Know Who Is A _____?

Take a look at the list of industries on the following page and use it as a memory trigger. For each profession, ask yourself, "Who do I know who is a _____?"

As always, add as many names and contact information to your developing database as you can think of. Don't just stop at one: you might know three or four people in a particular profession.

The more people, the bigger your SOI spider web, so be purposeful about increasing this number to be as large as possible. For these contacts, don't worry if you don't have an email address or physical mailing address. As long as you know their name, you can fill in the gaps at a later point.

There's a caution to keep in mind, however. Each contact you include must be someone you're personally acquainted with. Culling the name of every hairdresser or carpet cleaner in town and inserting them into your database won't help you build a successful Sphere of Influence. They may fatten your list, but there's no real muscle backing it up.

Treat the list honestly, and you'll see it become a powerful networking tool.

## GROW YOUR SOI

If you're starting off with an SOI of 300 contacts, that's great, but you don't have to stop there. Once you've exhausted all the people you already know, you should continuously put yourself in positions where you're connecting with other people and growing your SOI.

This will happen naturally as you generate business and close deals. By maintaining contact and continually nurturing your existing relationships, your current clients are more likely to become repeated clients in the future, as well as refer you to other potential clients.

# WHO DO YOU KNOW FROM THESE INDUSTRIES?

Accountants
Alarm/Home Security Companies
Appraisers
Appliance Stores
Architects
Asbestos Mitigation
Attorneys (General Practice, Real Estate, Family/Divorce, Wills, Trusts, Estates & Probate)
Auto Body Shops & Repair
Auto/Car Dealerships
Auto Mechanics
Baby-Sitters
Banks (Personal & Business)
Builders (New Home & Improvements/Add-ons)
Cabinet Supply & Installation
Caterers & Party Planners
Carpenters
Carpet Cleaners
Carpet Supply Stores
Chimney Cleaning
Chiropractors
Cleaning Services
Computer & Networking Servicers
Concrete, Cement & Pavers
Construction Contractors
Countertop Supply & Installation
Credit Unions
Day Care
Deck Construction/Repair
Dentists
Dermatologists
Doctors
Dry Cleaners
Dry Wall Companies
Electricians
Engineers (Civil & Structural)
Estate Sale Companies
Event & Community Centers
Excavating Services
Fencing Companies
Financial Planners
Fireplace Supply & Repair
Flooring Companies
Florists
Furniture Stores
Garage Door & Repair
Garden & Nurseries
Geological & Soil Testing
Gyms & Fitness Centers
Hair Stylists
Handyman Services
Home Inspectors
Home Stagers
Home Warranties
HVAC Companies (Heating & Cooling)
Insurance (Auto, Health, Homeowners, etc.)
Interior Designers
Jewelry Stores
Landscapers
Lawn Care
Locksmiths
Masonry
Mold Inspection & Mitigation
Mortgage Lenders
Movers (local & national)
Mud-Jacking Companies
Music (DJ & party services)
Nannies
Notaries
Office Machines (copiers & printers)
Office Supply & Furniture Stores
Optometrists
Orthodontists
Painter
Pediatricians
Pedicure Shops
Personal Trainers
Pest Control Companies
Pet Kennels
Pet Sitters
Photographers
Plumbers
Pool Contractors
Pool Care & Supply
Pressure Cleaning
Printing Companies
Property Management
Radon Inspection & Mitigation
Rain Gutter Installation & Repair
Restaurants
Roofing Companies
Senior Living Communities (Convalescent Homes & Assisted Living)
Septic & Sewer Companies
Siding & Stucco Contractors
Sign & Banner Companies
Snow Removal
Spa & Tub Supply/Service
Sprinkler/Irrigation Supply/Repair
Stock Brokers
Storage Companies
Surveyors
Tax Exchange (1031 Tax Exchange Consultants/Accommodators)
Tailors
Tile & Grout Contractors

But you can grow further than that. Continue your SOI expansion with strategies like these:

**① Create Community**

- Join a local civic group or club.
- Volunteer with a charity you're passionate about.
- Become a member of a Board of Directors.
- Get involved with different trade associations.
- Go to community events like cook-offs and neighborhood sales.
- Participate in events like golf tournaments, etc.

While at these events, get the most out of your investment by:

- Showing up ahead of time for anything you attend so you can strike up conversations.
- Practicing your active listening skills.
- Talking clearly and persuasively about your passion when asked.
- Following up with the people you meet.

**② Follow Up To Build Influence**

Surprisingly, this strategy is one that many people fail to do, and yet it's one of the simplest and easiest things you can do to build rapport and create a meaningful connection. All it takes is a quick phone call or email!

> *Hi Susan,*
>
> *I was going through my notes and found your card, so I thought I'd call to send you the information I told you about.*
>
> *If you don't mind, I'd like to occasionally send you some real estate information you might be interested in. I do this for people with interests similar to yours, and I'd love to include you.*
>
> *Can I count you in?*

The above follow-up script sample follows a pattern that can be endlessly replicated depending on the situation:

| | | |
|---|---|---|
| 1. Greeting | Hi _____, | *(person's name)* |
| 2. Introduction | I was going through my notes and found your card, so I thought I'd call to _____. *(mention something you discussed, offer something of value, and make the person feel that you remember them personally)* | |
| 3. Permission | If you don't mind, I'd like to occasionally send you some real estate information you might be interested in. I do this for people with interests similar to yours, and I'd love to include you. | |
| 4. Verification | Can I count you in? | |

# EXERCISE: Create Your Own Follow-Up Email Template

Staying in touch with your SOI database should not be more time-consuming than it needs to be. Don't waste time typing out the same message every time you follow up with someone you've just met. Create your own follow-up email using the pattern above, and save it as a message template in Outlook or Gmail, etc. This way, you can quickly customize and personalize your follow-up connections.

Remember to always include a:

- Greeting
- Introduction and reminder of how you met
- Permission to contact
- Verification

## ❸ TAP INTO SOCIAL MEDIA

Social media is a big source of business and a great way to grow your SOI and connect with large groups of people. However, most agents make the mistake of adding and following a ton of new people and then promptly forgetting all about them!

Remember: Your goal is to stay first of mind and for people to know and recognize your name. Social media is an easy, inexpensive and effective way to achieve that goal.

A lot of agents spend too much time posting on social media and creating all kinds of new and original content. A lot of people confuse social media with traditional print marketing, which is all about output.

While it's important to put yourself out there and stay in front of people, believe it or not, your posts are less important than interacting and engaging with what the people in your SOI are posting.

> "You can make more friends in a month by being interested in them than in ten years by trying to get them interested in you." -Charles Mengel Allen

People love to be validated and affirmed. No matter who you are, when someone likes or comments on your posts, it feels good, so it's natural that you would have positive associations with the people who interact positively with the things you post and share.

Taking the time to engage and validate people in your social media networks will ensure that members of your SOI have positive feelings towards you and appreciate your friendship.

People pay attention to people who interact with them. The more your name appears in their newsfeed and notifications, the more you're deepening rapport and staying top of mind with them. What's more, you'll see that they will interact more frequently and positively with your posts too.

- Carve out 15-30 minutes a day to interact on social media and spread joy and happiness. Growing your SOI should always come from a place of contribution and positivity.
- Remind the person of how you met and that you have a service to offer. When you add a new connection on Facebook or follow someone on Instagram, add a short personal message, such as, "Enjoyed listening to your band at the street fair today, looking forward to sending you those market updates we talked about afterwards!"
- Post daily on Facebook and other social media platforms to stay present in people's minds. Your posts can be automated and scheduled in advance to increase efficiency. Don't get caught up in spending hours per week posting your own content. Engagement with other people's post is a better investment of your time.

> **CHALLENGE:** Social Media Follow-Up Targets

Business professionals who want to see traction know that even social media follow-up is going to take time. But time won't magically materialize by itself: you have to set an appointment in order to hit your targets. Here's a sample you can model to make sure you're doing whatever it takes. Schedule the time on your calendar, and identify the number of contacts you'll follow up with in this manner.

| Day 1 | Day 2 | Day 3 | Day 4 | Day 5 |
|---|---|---|---|---|
| 8-8:30AM | 8-8:30AM | 8-8:30AM | 8-8:30AM | 8-8:30AM |
| 10 Contacts | 10 Contacts | 10 Contacts | 10 Contacts | 10 Contacts |

For added impact, transfer your Facebook friends to your CRM or other SOI database, along with their known email addresses, telephone numbers, and physical addresses. They then become part of your broader SOI Database Contact Plan.

By now, you should be realizing that you know a lot more people than you first imagined. Your Sphere of Influence is starting to expand, and you have made solid progress by kick-starting your SOI database with contact information and additional notes.

Your next step is to start making those growing numbers count!

## THE NUMBERS GAME

Real estate is a numbers game, and in our decades of coaching and training real estate agents, and tracking their results, we have discovered how important the number seven is for real estate sales.

In the following pages, we will teach you to:

- Apply the Rule of 7 Touches to imprint yourself on people you've just met, and introduce them to your SOI contact plan.
- Achieve a 7:1 conversion rate with a 40-touch annual database contact plan.
- Use the number 7 to calculate potential commission figures and return of investment from each member of your SOI.

## The Rule of 7 Touches

There is no such thing as a dead lead in real estate. Everyone you meet is a potential prospect. According to data from the most recent U.S. Census Bureau, the average person in the United States moves residences more than 11 times in his or her lifetime. While they might not need your services right now, it's highly likely they will at some point in the future!

However, it could be months or even years between now and then, so how do you make sure that you're the agent they think of when the time eventually arrives? If you're thinking, "I'll just give them my business card and wait for their call," here's another statistic for you:

88% of business cards handed out are thrown away within a week, and 63% of those are thrown away because the person who received it doesn't currently need the service.

To fully imprint yourself on people that you've just met, you'll have to do a little more than a one-time introduction.

**The rule of 7 Touches is an 'Introduction Program' to your SOI, for people you've just met.**

Anytime you meet somebody, and you're not 100% sure that they are going to remember you by name, you should apply the rule of 7 Touches.

Say you host an open house over the weekend and strike up a lively, interesting conversation with a nice couple that wandered in on their weekly Sunday stroll around the neighborhood. They're 100% not interested in buying or selling anytime soon, but you enjoyed talking to them and would like to stay in touch with them over time.

While it's tempting to add them to your SOI database the minute you meet, this is a terrible long-term strategy, as we discussed before. As you should know by now, quality not quantity is the key to a successful SOI: don't dilute your database with people you don't really know. Having a good conversation with somebody doesn't guarantee that they'll remember you.

---

*Anytime you meet somebody, and you're not 100% sure that they are going to remember you by name, you should apply the rule of 7 Touches.*

---

Instead, you will apply the rule of 7 Touches, which involves contacting new acquaintances 7 times, over 7 consecutive weeks, as an introduction to you and your service. Once you have imprinted your name in the mind of the prospect, you can then add them to your normal SOI database contact plan.

It's important to diversify your touches through different communication channels. Don't call them 7 times for 7 weeks, whatever you do! Instead, you could try the following approach, depending on the situation and how you originally met them.

- **Week ①** Send them a note card saying, "It was nice to meet you." Remember to remind them of how you met.

- **Week ②** Send them a follow-up email, using the 4-part template provided above. Remember to come from a place of contribution. Mentioning something the two of you previously discussed will make them feel that you remembered them personally, and the email will feel less 'salesy' and more genuine.

- **Week ③** Connect with them on social media. Friend them on Facebook or follow them on Instagram. Begin slowly by liking or commenting on a couple of their posts, but not too many! Be positive, but subtle!

- **Week ④** Send them a direct message on Facebook. Again, remember to come from a place of contribution, such as sharing something you think would be of interest to them.

- **Week ⑤** Invite them to an event via social media. For example, if you met them at an open house, you could let them know you're hosting another open house in the neighborhood.

- **Week ⑥** Send them an event reminder via email saying, "I hope to see you there, so we can continue our great conversation!"

- **Week ⑦** Ideally, they would attend the event and you could solidify the connection in person! If not, email or call to verify any missing contact information, such as their physical mailing address.

At this point, you will have made a meaningful and lasting impression, and you can add them as a bona fide member to your growing SOI database.

## LUCKY NUMBER 7

Real estate is a numbers game, and real estate is a game of touches. So is your annual Database Contact Plan.

As you'll soon see, a Database Contact Plan is a *systematic* process of staying in contact with the members of your SOI, and an effective plan with a solid conversion rate involves making *40 contacts—or touches—per year with each individual SOI member.*

Based upon decades of coaching, training, and tracking the results of real estate agents, we know that a Database Contact Plan with 40 annual touches (using a variety of contact methods) will result in 1 closed transaction for every 7 people in your SOI database.

For example, if you have 300 SOI members in your database, a 7:1 conversion rate results in 43 closed transactions a year.

- 300 SOI Referral Database members receive 40 annual contacts, resulting in 12,000 total touches per year for your business, most of which are automated.

- Applying our 7:1 annual conversion ratio, 300 ÷ 7 = 42.86 (rounded up to 43).

- That's 43 closed transactions in one year from your SOI database alone!

**CAUTION:** To be clear, these results are a culmination of your systematic efforts to this high level. Some agents will look at 40 annual contacts, and start to calculate shortcuts: *If I only make 20 touches, then maybe I'll get a 14:1 ratio, and that's not that bad!* This is dangerous for your business, so for importance sake, consider the 40 touches for a 7:1 conversion ratio a prescription, not a suggestion. Half the cure won't make you better. Stick to the formula.

At this point, it should be clear why building your SOI database is critical to your success. The more people are in your SOI, the more opportunities you will have for contacting people and nurturing them into promising prospective clients.

The more contacts you have, the more conversions you produce. All you have to do is develop a plan of action for contacting each member of your SOI 40 times per year using a variety of contact strategies.

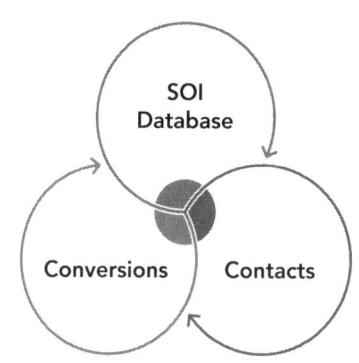

## 40 ANNUAL CONTACTS

An effective Database Contact Plan involves making a minimum of 40 contacts, or touches, per year with each SOI member. Communication with your SOI referral database must be systematic and consistent in order to generate predictable results.

SOI communication is not a hard sell, however. Remember: your SOI members are people that you know, so it's quite a different process to making prospecting calls.

An SOI contact plan should always come from a place of contribution. It's important that you don't harass or alienate members of your SOI. Further below, we provide additional scripts for you to learn that will assist you in making those contacts and conversations.

Additionally, certain contact methods have more or less value or effectiveness than others, and each contact strategy should make up a specific amount or percentage of your 40 annual touches.

There are predominantly four ways to make contact with people in your Sphere of Influence:

1. Email
2. Mailers
3. Telephone Calls
4. Social Media

We have already covered the impact of social media, so we'll now turn our attention to emails, mailers, and telephone calls.

Understand, however, that this chapter provides only a basic overview of these strategies. At ICC, we teach an entire SOI course that goes into a lot more detail about growing and developing a real estate agent's sphere of influence.

Employing a variety of contact strategies ensures that you are not contacting or targeting your SOI members too frequently through one method of communication. Remember that these are people that you have relationships with and that you want to refer business to you, so it's important that you don't offend or constantly bombard them with a single type of contact.

### EMAILS

One of the first ways to reach out and connect with people in your SOI is through email. Email is cost-efficient and takes minimal time and effort to manage. They can also be automated to increase efficiency. After being written and scheduled, emails can be sent to your SOI automatically throughout the year. What's not to like?

Plenty, as it turns out.

Emails, especially when used in isolation of any other strategy, have some of the lowest conversion rates of any marketing strategy. Although an SOI Contact Plan composed of 40 emails a year may seem both inexpensive and efficient, it is also relatively ineffective.

No more than 65% of the 40 contacts made in your SOI Contact Plan should be through email. We'll cover that more in just a moment. For now, understand that email campaigns only work well when used with other marketing strategies. You will have to engage in additional ways to contact your SOI members.

You may wonder, then, why you should bother at all with an email campaign?

Emails are used to generate awareness, not to collect business. Their purpose is to get your brand in front of your audience on a frequent and consistent basis. Email gives you an immediate and regular presence in people's minds, or what marketers call 'mind share'.

Effective mind share marketing establishes you as the first person people think of when they think of a real estate agent. Even if people in your SOI don't open and read every single one of your emails, simply seeing your name in their Inbox will create mind share. When someone asks them if they know a good real estate agent, your name will be first on the tip of their tongue.

### MAILERS

Mailers are any printed material that arrives in your mailbox. Mailers reach your SOI members and potential clients directly. The beautiful thing about a mailer is that it has a longer life than an email.

Most people who receive a mailer will pick it up and look at both sides. They may even hang on to it for a while, *especially if it's useful*, such as a conversion chart for kitchen measurements, a holiday recipe, or essential community phone numbers. Even a photo of a recently sold property in the neighborhood can be cause for taking a good look at a mailer. If a homeowner likes the way you presented the property, he or she may contact you when they are ready to list their home.

Most real estate CRMs (Customer Relationship Management systems) come with pre-made email-templates and mailing-templates for agents. Some CRMs even contract directly with a mailing service to send scheduled mailers to your entire database throughout the year.

So, as with email, physical mailers take very little of your time once they are set up and managed efficiently.

Obviously, however, mailers are not free. Printing and postage will cost as much as $1.25 per mailer. As a rule, any agent's marketing costs should not exceed 10% of their Gross Commission Income (GCI), and mailers should never be more than 5% of the GCI.

In an agent's first year of business, mailers may have to be used on a limited basis if there is not much commission income coming in yet.

## Telephone Calls

The best marketing strategy is to talk to someone. You won't be able to make it door to door to talk to your contacts on a daily basis, but you can pick up the phone and check in with them.

Remember, these are people you already know, so this is not a cold call—it's a warm reconnection. A few minutes spent on the phone can help you foster the connections you have with your SOI, and they may help you generate some leads, especially if you ask if they know of anyone planning to sell their home in the next twelve months.

As easy as the phone call is to make in theory, finding the time or the nerve to do it can be difficult. Agents come up with all kinds of excuses for avoiding making SOI calls. Your days are full and busy, but the ten minutes it takes to make the calls can help you expand your sphere and grow your business.

At the end of this chapter, you will find several new and different SOI scripts that cover a range of situations and scenarios:

- Asking current clients for referrals
- Asking SOI members for updated contact information and referrals
- Following up with former clients
- Contacting neglected past clients
- An SOI request for listings in a hot market
- A neighborhood auto email drip script that keeps your SOI up-to-date on home values and new listings in their existing neighborhoods.

Make sure to start practicing and internalizing these scripts using the methods we discussed in the previous chapter.

Over the course of a single year, you can use a variety of these sample scripts when making scheduled SOI calls as part of your systematic contact plan.

Let's take a closer look at some real-life examples of an annual database contact plan.

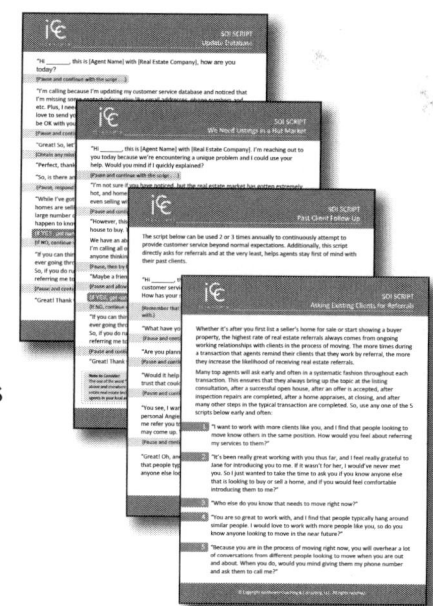

# Sample SOI Database Contact Plans

Below are three SOI contact plans that will give you a sense of what we mean by a systematic communication plan. Depending on your specific needs and circumstances, you can of course adapt these plans to suit your SOI database.

However:

- You must make 40 contacts a year for a 7:1 conversion rate.
- No more than 26 of the 40 contacts in your SOI contact plan can be emails.
- The cost of mailers must not exceed 5% of your gross commission income (GCI)
- Your contact plan must include at least 2 phone calls to each member of your SOI every year.

Let's take a look at the Basic Plan, the Value-Based Contact Plan, and the Efficient Plan.

## The Basic Plan

When you're just starting out, it's highly advisable to begin with the basic plan.

With the Basic plan, your SOI contact goals look something like this:

### 40 Annual Contacts

- 26 emails (once every 2 weeks)
- 12 mailers (sent once a month)
- 2 phone calls (made once every 6 months)
- Post regularly on social media

Over the course of a year, you will build your mind share, gather a following, and see a 7:1 conversion rate if you put in the effort and do your work.

## Value-Based Contact Plan (or Giving to Get)

It's been said that people don't care how much you know until they know how much you care. The same is true in real estate, or in any service-based industry for that matter. To show that you care, you'll need to give away a little something and provide value to your SOI members, whether it's giving away a small gift or some of the knowledge you have.

Giving gifts can quickly become expensive. We recommend this plan only be used on smaller SOI databases or just those SOI members that you can count on the most.

New prospectors, beware! *This is a next-level plan.*

We include it here as inspiration for when your SOI database is more established and you're starting to see a solid 7:1 return of investment.

With the Value-Based Contact Plan, your SOI contact goals look something like this and can be adapted and modified according to the size and complexity of your business and your SOI:

- 18 Emails (automated in CRM to send every 3 weeks)
- 3 Phone Calls

- 1 Drop-By (for example, pumpkins delivered to doorsteps in October)
- 1 Client Appreciation Event
- 4 Invitations to Client Appreciation Event: 2 emails, 1 mailer, and 1 phone call
- 1 Post-Event Email showing photos of event highlights and announcing event contest winners
- 12 Value-Based Mailers (sent once a month)

For Value-Based Mailers, try the following or come up with your own ideas!

- **January**: Happy New Year "*Thank You for Making it a Great Year*" postcard w/ photo of team
- **February**: Flyers/Coupons for local area Home, Garden & Patio Show
- **March**: Local College & Pro Sports Schedules
- **April**: Local & National Market Update
- **May**: Flower & Garden Seed Packets
- **June**: Summer Local Events Update (Graduations, Water Park Coupons, Summer Camps, etc.)
- **July**: Local & National Mid-Year Market Update
- **August**: Back to School Shopping Coupons & Sales
- **September**: Flyers/Coupons for local area Home, Garden & Patio Show
- **October**: Local & National Market Update
- **November**: Canned Food Drive (leave bags on doorstep to pickup) & include Holiday Recipe
- **December**: Happy Holidays Cards

## THE EFFICIENT PLAN

The Efficient Plan combines the strategies of the Basic and the Value-Based Contact plans but is much more efficient and less costly. This plan puts less emphasis on gifts and mailers and more emphasis on agent activities like phone calls.

The Efficient Plan looks something like this:

- 4 Quarterly Newsletters (mailed out every 3 months)
- 26 Emails (automated in CRM and sent every 2 weeks)
- 1 Client Appreciation Event
- 4 Invitations to Client Appreciation Event: 2 emails, 1 mailer, and 1 phone call
- 3 Phone Calls to SOI
- 1 Facebook direct message (to update database contact information)
- 1 Drop-By Visit (with treats)

## CALCULATE YOUR COMMISSION

No doubt some of you who are reading this are somewhat daunted by the sample SOI Contact Plans. Remember to begin with the basic plan. Don't bite off more than you can initially chew! Your SOI database should be manageable, not chaotic, exorbitantly expensive, or overwhelming.

But make no mistake. Managing an SOI database and committing to a systematic 40-touch Annual Contact Plan is not easy. It requires hard work, focus, and discipline to achieve that

7:1 return of investment.

The rewards, however, speak for themselves.

Let's say that your average sales price is $250,000, and let's assume that you charge a 3% commission. This means you will earn $7,500 in gross commission income (GCI) per closed transaction. If you're closing 43 transactions from a 300 member SOI database, your return is pretty impressive:

- 43 Transactions x $7,500 GCI = $322,500 in annual gross commission income
- $322,500 simply by staying in contact with 300 people, 40 times a year

This is a phenomenal number. It may sound crazy, in fact, and you may be asking yourself, "Why doesn't everyone do this?"

Like we said: maintaining an effective SOI takes time, discipline, and devotion. Quite simply, the reason that most agents don't see 7:1 results is:

- They're unwilling to invest the time and effort it takes to grow a solid SOI database with a high number of quality members.
- They're unwilling to invest the time, money and effort it takes to implement and maintain a Customer Relationship Management (CRM) system.
- They're unwilling to invest the time, money, and effort it takes to implement and maintain a 40-touch annual database contact plan.

Granted, all of this is a lot easier said than done, but those few that are willing to do what it takes will reap the riches and rewards.

## WHAT 40 CONTACTS ARE WORTH

It's worth your time to make those 40 annual contacts with each SOI member, because each concluded transaction brings in thousands of dollars.

- 7:1 Ratio with 40 Contacts for each SOI member, with one transaction= $7,500.

While we've cautioned you several times to not shortcut your number of annual touches, we know that many of you are looking at the 7:1 ratio and thinking, "That's a lot of work, and I'm not getting a commission for 6 out of 7 people here."

That's a risky mindset.

Consider it from this perspective:

When you complete 40 touches for 7 members in your SOI, you could earn $7,500 per closed transaction. But rather than viewing this dollar amount as being connected to a single person, you should see it as a collective effort.

- $7,500 ÷ 7 people = $1,071.43

Instead of seeing those six people as being worthless or a waste of your time, the reality is that every single member of your SOI is potentially worth more than a thousand dollars every year.

Of course, they're worth so much more than that because they're people that you know and care about. Our point is that, with a positive mindset, you can start to see how every person and every action you take is a valuable investment.

## SAMPLE CHART BASED OFF COMMISSIONS

| AVG. COM | PER 7:1 | AVG. COM | PER 7:1 | AVG. COM | PER 7:1 |
|---|---|---|---|---|---|
| $2000 | $286 | $5000 | $714 | $12,000 | $1714 |
| $2500 | $357 | $6000 | $857 | $15,000 | $2142 |
| $3000 | $429 | $7000 | $1000 | $20,000 | $2857 |

While some of the numbers might not be staggering at first, consider what it's costing you if you miss out on contacting 15 members of your SOI.

If you are willing to commit to developing your SOI and working the numbers, you will achieve greater sales than you ever thought possible. Your business will bloom, and it's all in the numbers!

> **CHALLENGE: SOI Contact Calculation**

Using your own database numbers, calculate how much your SOI investments are worth to you, annually.

What are you thoughts when you look at this number? Is it still daunting? Or can you now see that it's worth it?

- Are you willing to invest the time and effort it takes to grow a solid SOI database with a high number of quality members?
- Are you willing to invest the time, money and effort it takes to implement and maintain a Customer Relationship Management (CRM) system?
- Are you willing to invest the time, money, and effort it takes to implement and maintain a 40-touch annual database contact plan?

If the answer is yes, your next step is to schedule the time to make sure that these things happen.

*"Decide what you want, decide what you are willing to exchange for it. Establish your priorities and go to work."* -HL Hunt

## MAKE THE TIME

Business-generation must always come first. You'll be tempted to let it go and focus your attention on customer-service activities. Numerous distractions lurk throughout your day, preventing you from focusing on the most important part of your business: generating leads.

We give you permission to focus first on prospecting and lead-generation rather than clients. You must do the same for yourself. Schedule customer-service activities after you have hit your lead-generation time targets. This can be tricky for solo agents who don't have administrative assistance. ICC teaches an entire course that can help you systematize your real estate process, so that the majority of your time is spent on business-generating activities.

## Your Sample Schedule

If a significant portion of your day should be spent contacting the prospects in your database, what should your schedule look like?

First of all, you need to devote at least one hour a day to contacting the prospects in your SOI database. That means contacting your new contacts and previous clients as well.

Some of your scheduled "SOI Contact" time will involve creating emails, mailers, and social media posts. Remember that much of this can be created in advance and automated. SOI Contact activities should be as structured and efficient as possible.

> *"Habits are first cobwebs, then cables."* - Napoleon Hill

However, you will need to maintain a systematic phone call schedule in order to contact everyone in your SOI twice a year. The larger your SOI database, the more phone calls you will need to make each day and week.

For example, if you have 300 SOI members that you need to call twice a year, that's 600 annual phone calls, which works out at 12 phone calls a week or 2-3 phone calls per day. While 600 sounds like a daunting number, it is easy to hold yourself accountable for making a couple of SOI Contact phone calls a day.

Set aside another section of your day to follow up with people you previously attempted to contact but weren't able to reach.

| Day | DAY 1 | DAY 2 | DAY 3 | DAY 4 | DAY 5 |
|---|---|---|---|---|---|
| Time Activity | 9-10AM SOI Contact | 9-10AM SOI Contact | 5-6PM SOI Contact | 9-10AM SOI Contact | 9-10AM SOI Contact |
| Time Activity | 10-10:30AM Follow-Up | 10-10:30AM Follow-Up | 6-6:30PM Follow-Up | 10-10:30AM Follow-Up | 10-10:30AM Follow-Up |

**DAY 1:** Use days of the week or, as we've shown here, the day numbers you decide to work during the week. As real estate agents will sometimes choose to work weekend days, this method of scheduling allows you to still plan your week.

**FOLLOW UP:** Include follow-up as a separate event from your prospecting to make sure this vital piece of your communication gets taken care of. You can add names to your follow-up call list during prospecting and simply keep cultivating this throughout the week and into the next one.

EVENING WHERE: Entertain the idea of choosing one day a week to prospect or connect with your SOI, during the evening; what works with your prospecting time may not work with theirs, and a dynamic plan will increase your odds of connection, and your success!

If you haven't been in contact with previous clients, now is the time to reconnect. You can call them on the phone and apologize. When the prospect asks why you're apologizing, explain that you didn't send out the market updates to them as you had intended, but you want to do so now.

According to the National Association of REALTORS® statistics, the average homeowner moves every six years. By contacting previous clients, you're planting a seed that the time may be right to consider purchasing a new home.

Follow your schedule with integrity, use the SOI scripts coming up in the next section, and you will be able to predict your sales results with accuracy.

Stay front-of-mind by staying in systematic contact.

# 7 Sample SOI Scripts

As promised, here are some new and different SOI scripts that cover a range of situations and scenarios. Make sure to memorize and internalize these scripts and incorporate them into your SOI business generation strategy.

## SOI Script: Asking Current Clients for Referrals

Whether it's after you first list a seller's home for sale or start showing a buyer property, the highest rate of real estate referrals always comes from ongoing working relationships with clients in the process of moving. The more times agents remind their clients that they work by referral during a transaction, they increase the likelihood of receiving real estate referrals.

Many top agents will ask early and often in a systematic fashion throughout each transaction. This ensures that they always bring up the topic at the listing consultation, after a successful open house, after an offer is accepted, after inspection repairs are completed, after a home appraises, at closing, and after many other steps in the typical transaction are completed. So use any one of the 5 scripts below early and often:

### Asking Current Clients for Referrals

1. "I want to work with more clients like you, and I find that people looking to move know others in the same position. How would you feel about referring my services to them?"

2. "It's been really great working with you thus far, and I feel really grateful to Jane for introducing you to me. If it wasn't for her, I would've never met you. So I just wanted to take the time to ask you if you know anyone else that is looking to buy or sell a home, and if you would feel comfortable introducing them to me?"

3. "Who else do you know that needs to move right now?"

4. "You are so great to work with, and I find that people typically hang around similar people. I would love to work with more people like you, so do you know anyone looking to move in the near future?"

5. "Because you are in the process of moving right now, you will overhear a lot of conversations from different people looking to move when you are out and about. When you do, would you mind giving them my phone number and ask them to call me?"

© Copyright Icenhower Coaching & Consulting, LLC. All rights reserved.

## SOI Script: We Need Listings in a Hot Market

The following script can be used to contact your SOI to ask for help with listings in a hot market.

**Note to Consider:** The use of the word "we" as used in the sentence "We have an abnormally large number of buyers . . ." in paragraph 4 and elsewhere throughout the script is intended to allow you to refer to any buyers that other agents in your entire real estate brokerage have looking for homes as well. This use of "we" could also be implied to represent all of the agents in your local area as well.

---

### We Need Listings in a Hot Market

1. Hi _____, this is (AGENT NAME) with (REAL ESTATE COMPANY). I'm reaching out to you today because we're encountering a unique problem and I could use your help. Would you mind if I quickly explained?

2. I'm not sure if you have noticed, but the real estate market has gotten extremely hot, and homes are selling faster than we can put them up for sale. Houses are even selling with multiple offers above asking price!

3. However, this has also created a problem for our buyer clients trying to find a house to buy. This virtual housing shortage is the reason I'm calling you today.

4. We have an abnormally large number of buyers that we need to find homes for, so I'm calling all of the people I know . . . like you . . . to see if you happen to know of anyone thinking about selling their home within the next year?

   – *PAUSE – then try to help them...*

5. Maybe a friend, family member or even a co-worker?

   – *PAUSE – allow silence to do the heavy lifting here.*

6. If you can think of anyone, we may even be able to get their home sold without ever going through the expense and hassle of putting the home up on the market. So if you do run into anyone that's considering selling, would you have any problem referring me to them and letting me know? *(PAUSE)*

7. Great! Thank you so much for helping us!

© Copyright Icenhower Coaching & Consulting, LLC. All rights reserved.

# SOI Script – Update Database

This script is self-explanatory.

## Update Database

1. Hi _____, this is (AGENT NAME) with (REAL ESTATE COMPANY), how are you today?

2. I'm calling because I'm updating my customer service database and noticed that I'm missing some contact information like email addresses, phone numbers and etc. Plus, I need to do a better job of staying in touch with people I know, and I'd love to send you something over the holidays and from time to time. Would that be OK with you?

3. Great! So let's see, it looks like we need your (EMAIL ADDRESS) . . . (*Obtain any missing information needed*) . . . . Perfect, thank you for your help!

4. So is there anything that we can do for you right now? (*Respond if applicable*).

5. While I've got you on the line, we are in a hot real estate market right now where homes are selling faster than we can put them up for sale. So we suddenly have a large number of buyers that we need to find homes for. With that said, do you happen to know of anyone thinking about selling their home within the next year?

6. If you can think of anyone, we may even be able to get their home sold without ever going through the expense and hassle of putting the home up on the market. So if you do run into anyone that's considering selling, would you have any problem referring me to them and letting me know?

7. Great! Thank you so much for helping us!

© Copyright Icenhower Coaching & Consulting, LLC. All rights reserved.

# SOI Script – Update Database & Ask for Referral

In this script, you call with the excuse of updating your database and transition to asking for a referral.

## Update Database & Ask for Referral

1. Hi _____, this is (AGENT NAME) with (REAL ESTATE COMPANY), how are you today?

2. I'm calling because I'm updating my customer service database and noticed that I'm missing some contact information like email addresses, phone numbers and etc. Plus, I need to do a better job of staying in touch with people I know, and I'd love to send you something over the holidays and from time to time. Would that be OK with you?

3. Great! So let's see, it looks like I need your (EMAIL ADDRESS) . . . (Obtain any missing information needed) . . . . Perfect, thank you for your help!

4. So is there anything that I can do for you right now? (Respond if applicable).

5. While I've got you on the line, I wanted to ask you who you might know that might be looking to move in the near future. Maybe a friend, family member or co-worker? Can you think of anyone right now?

6. If you do bump into anyone looking to move, would you have an problem referring them to me?

7. Great! Thank you so much for helping me!

© Copyright Icenhower Coaching & Consulting, LLC. All rights reserved.

## SOI Script: Contacting Neglected Past Clients

Life happens and sometimes you'll fall out of a systematic contact schedule. Try not to let this happen but, if it does, reenergize your contact plan by reconnecting with neglected past clients.

### Contacting Neglected Past Clients

1. "Hi _____, this is (AGENT NAME) at (REAL ESTATE COMPANY), and in case you don't remember, I'm the agent that sold your home and forgive me for not calling for so long how have you been?"

2. "I'm ashamed to say that I haven't checked in sooner because I had a bad client database system and we are now upgrading that, and I just wanted to touch back and see how your new home is treating you. Is everything going OK with it?"

3. "Well from now on please feel free to look to me as your total home resource . . . like your own personal Angie's List. If you ever need any repairs or improvements done to the home, you can contact me to refer you to a tested and trusted professional that I can personally hold accountable. How does that sound?"

4. "Great! Since we're in the process of trying to update our databases and do better at staying in communication, is it okay if I send you something over the holidays and from time to time?"

5. "Excellent! Is this still your correct home address? How about your email address?"

6. "Thank you! And thanks for letting me apologize for not following up and staying in better touch with you, and if there is anything I can do to be of service in the future please let me know?

© Copyright Icenhower Coaching & Consulting, LLC. All rights reserved.

## SOI Script: Past Client Follow Up Script

The script below can be used 2 or 3 times annually to continuously attempt to provide customer service beyond normal expectations. Additionally, this script also directly asks for referrals and at the very least helps agents stay first of mind with their past clients.

### Past Client Follow Up Script

1. Hi _____ , it's (AGENT NAME) at (REAL ESTATE COMPANY). I'm just calling as a customer service to check in with you to see how you're doing in your new home. How has your new home been treating you? (Remember that the key is to continue to ask questions to uncover a need that you can help with.)

2. What have you done to it?

3. Are you planning on doing any work or improvements to it in the future?

4. Would it help if I gave you the contact information of some professionals that I trust that could help you get that done at a reasonable cost?

5. You see, I want you to think of me as your total home resource. Like your own personal Angie's List. So you can save yourself some time & frustration by letting me refer you to a tested & trusted company for any homeownership needs that may come up. Would that benefit you?

6. Great? Oh and by the way, I want to work with more clients like you, and I find that people typically hang around similar people. So with that said, do you know anyone else looking to move in the near future?

© Copyright Icenhower Coaching & Consulting, LLC. All rights reserved.

# Neighborhood Auto Email Drip Script for Sphere of Influence (SOI) or Geographic Farms

Use this script to let people know you've set them up on an MLS Listing E-Alert/ Neighborhood Update tool. We'll discuss this feature in-depth in Chapter 5.

---

### Neighborhood Auto Email Drip Script

Hi it's [AGENT NAME] with [REAL ESTATE COMPANY],

I wanted to give you a heads up that I've set you up on our new Neighborhood Update Tool and would love to hear your feedback on it. My clients really love it. When one of your neighbors puts their home up for sale, you'll immediately get an email with all the listing information and photos of the home. This way, you'll be able to:

1. Look through all the **photos of your neighbor's homes**;

2. Compare the **amenities, features & size** of the listings to your own home;

3. Know the **price of each new listing** to get a rough idea of the current value of your own home.

4. See **how quickly each home sells**, and the **prices that they sell for**;

5. This will give you a good idea of **how the value of your home is increasing** from month-to-month,

6. It will also **keep you up to date** on your local neighborhood market conditions.

I really think you'll find this customer service tool useful since most of my clients already do. But if for some reason you decide that you'd rather not receive these updates, you can unsubscribe yourself or just simply reply to an email and we'll discontinue it for you. However, I'd love to hear what you think about it first.

All that I need from you is to verify that I have the correct home address and email address for you. Sound good?

© Copyright Icenhower Coaching & Consulting, LLC. All rights reserved.

## Summary

Although you are a prospector—generating business from people you have never met and do not know—your SOI database should be the foundation of your business. It is very common for real estate agents to employ a blend of business-generating activities.

For someone to qualify to be in your SOI, you must know that person by name, and they must know you by name.

Don't water down and dilute your SOI database. Don't waste your time, energy, and resources on people that you do not know.

Develop the ability to notice those around you. Cultivate a willingness to say hello, introduce yourself, and get to know the people that you meet. Anytime you meet somebody, and you're not 100% sure that they are going to remember you by name, apply the Rule of 7 Touches as an introduction to your SOI database and annual contact plan.

Your Sphere of Influence is greater and has more impact on your success than you may realize.

A Database Contact Plan with 40 annual touches (using a variety of contact methods) will result in 1 closed transaction for every 7 people in your SOI database. If you have 300 SOI members in your database, a 7:1 conversion rate results in 43 closed transactions a year.

Every single member of your SOI is potentially worth more than a thousand dollars every year. With a positive mindset, you can see how every person and every action you take is a valuable investment.

If you're serious about a career in real estate, you can't afford *not* to devote the time to growing and tending to your Sphere of Influence.

# MODULE 3

# APPENDIX 3.1

## WHO DO I KNOW WHO IS A _____?

- Accountants
- Alarm/Home Security Companies
- Appraisers
- Appliance Stores
- Architects
- Asbestos Mitigation
- Attorneys (General Practice, Real Estate, Family/Divorce, Wills, Trusts, Estates & Probate)
- Auto Body Shops & Repair
- Auto/Car Dealerships
- Auto Mechanics
- Baby-Sitters
- Banks (Personal & Business)
- Builders (New Home & Improvements/Add-ons)
- Cabinet Supply & Installation
- Caterers & Party Planners
- Carpenters
- Carpet Cleaners
- Carpet Supply Stores
- Chimney Cleaning
- Chiropractors
- Cleaning Services
- Computer & Networking Servicers
- Concrete, Cement & Pavers
- Construction Contractors
- Countertop Supply & Installation
- Credit Unions
- Day Care
- Deck Construction/Repair
- Dentists
- Dermatologists
- Doctors
- Dry Cleaners
- Dry Wall Companies
- Electricians
- Engineers (Civil & Structural)
- Estate Sale Companies
- Event & Community Centers
- Excavating Services
- Fencing Companies
- Financial Planners
- Fireplace Supply & Repair
- Flooring Companies
- Florists
- Furniture Stores
- Garage Door & Repair
- Garden & Nurseries
- Geological & Soil Testing
- Gyms & Fitness Centers
- Hair Stylists
- Handyman Services
- Home Inspectors
- Home Stagers
- Home Warranties
- HVAC Companies (Heating & Cooling)
- Insurance (Auto, Health, Homeowners, etc.)
- Interior Designers
- Jewelry Stores
- Landscapers
- Lawn Care
- Locksmiths
- Masonry
- Mold Inspection & Mitigation
- Mortgage Lenders
- Movers (local & national)
- Mud-Jacking Companies
- Music (DJ & party services)
- Nannies
- Notaries
- Office Machines (copiers & printers)
- Office Supply & Furniture Stores
- Optometrists
- Orthodontists
- Painter
- Pediatricians
- Pedicure Shops
- Personal Trainers
- Pest Control Companies
- Pet Kennels
- Pet Sitters
- Photographers
- Plumbers
- Pool Contractors
- Pool Care & Supply
- Pressure Cleaning
- Printing Companies
- Property Management
- Radon Inspection & Mitigation
- Rain Gutter Installation & Repair
- Restaurants
- Roofing Companies
- Senior Living Communities (Convalescent Homes & Assisted Living)
- Septic & Sewer Companies
- Siding & Stucco Contractors
- Sign & Banner Companies
- Snow Removal
- Spa & Tub Supply/Service
- Sprinkler/Irrigation Supply/Repair
- Stock Brokers
- Storage Companies
- Surveyors
- Tax Exchange (1031 Tax Exchange Consultants/Accommodators)
- Tailors
- Tile & Grout Contractors

MODULE 3 — APPENDIX 3.2

# FOLLOW-UP SCRIPT PATTERN

Hi Susan,

I was going through my notes and found your card, so I thought I'd call to send you the crockpot recipe I told you about.

If you don't mind, I'd like to occasionally send you some real estate information you might be interested in. I do this for people with interests similar to yours, and I'd love to include you.

Can I count you in?

---

**1. Greeting**  Hi _____,  (person's name)

**2. Introduction**  I was going through my notes and found your card, so I thought I'd call to _____. (mention something you discussed, offer something of value, and make the person feel that you remember them personally)

**3. Permission**  If you don't mind, I'd like to occasionally send you some real estate information you might be interested in. I do this for people with interests similar to yours, and I'd love to include you.

**4. Verification**  Can I count you in?

© Copyright Icenhower Coaching & Consulting, LLC. All rights reserved.

# RULE OF 7 TOUCHES

**WEEK 1**: Send them a note card saying, "It was nice to meet you." Remember to remind them of how you met.

**WEEK 2**: Send them a follow-up email, using the 4-part template provided above. Remember to come from a place of contribution. Mentioning something the two of you previously discussed will make them feel that you remembered them personally, and the email will feel less 'salesy' and more genuine.

**WEEK 3**: Connect with them on social media. Friend them on Facebook or follow them on Instagram. Begin slowly by liking or commenting on a couple of their posts, but not too many! Be positive, but subtle!

**WEEK 4**: Send them a direct message on Facebook. Again, remember to come from a place of contribution, such as sharing something you think would be of interest to them.

**WEEK 5**: Invite them to an event via social media. For example, if you met them at an open house, you could let them know you're hosting another open house in the neighborhood.

**WEEK 6**: Send them an event reminder via email saying, "I hope to see you there, so we can continue our great conversation!"

**WEEK 7**: Ideally, they would attend the event and you could solidify the connection in person! If not, email or call to verify any missing contact information, such as their physical mailing address.

© Copyright Icenhower Coaching & Consulting, LLC. All rights reserved.

# Module 3

## Appendix 3.4

## SOI Contact Schedule

| Time | Monday | Tuesday | Wednesday | Thursday | Friday | Friday |
|---|---|---|---|---|---|---|
| 8:00 AM | | | | | | |
| 9:00 AM | | | | | | |
| 10:00 AM | | | | | | |
| 11:00 AM | | | | | | |
| 12:00 PM | | | | | | |
| 1:00 PM | | | | | | |
| 2:00 PM | | | | | | |
| 3:00 PM | | | | | | |
| 4:00 PM | | | | | | |
| 5:00 PM | | | | | | |

© Copyright Icenhower Coaching & Consulting, LLC. All rights reserved.

# Module 3 — Appendix 3.5

## SOI SCRIPT
### Asking Existing Clients for Referrals

Whether it's after you first list a seller's home for sale or start showing a buyer property, the highest rate of real estate referrals always comes from ongoing working relationships with clients in the process of moving. The more times during a transaction that agents remind their clients that they work by referral, the more they increase the likelihood of receiving real estate referrals.

Many top agents will ask early and often in a systematic fashion throughout each transaction. This ensures that they always bring up the topic at the listing consultation, after a successful open house, after an offer is accepted, after inspection repairs are completed, after a home appraises, at closing, and after many other steps in the typical transaction are completed. So, use any one of the 5 scripts below early and often:

1. "I want to work with more clients like you, and I find that people looking to move know others in the same position. How would you feel about referring my services to them?"

2. "It's been really great working with you thus far, and I feel really grateful to Jane for introducing you to me. If it wasn't for her, I would've never met you. So I just wanted to take the time to ask you if you know anyone else that is looking to buy or sell a home, and if you would feel comfortable introducing them to me?"

3. "Who else do you know that needs to move right now?"

4. "You are so great to work with, and I find that people typically hang around similar people. I would love to work with more people like you, so do you know anyone looking to move in the near future?"

5. "Because you are in the process of moving right now, you will overhear a lot of conversations from different people looking to move when you are out and about. When you do, would you mind giving them my phone number and ask them to call me?"

© Copyright Icenhower Coaching & Consulting, LLC. All rights reserved.

# MODULE 3

## APPENDIX 3.6

### SOI SCRIPT
### We Need Listings in a Hot Market

"Hi _____, this is [Agent Name] with [Real Estate Company]. I'm reaching out to you today because we're encountering a unique problem and I could use your help. Would you mind if I quickly explained?

(Pause and continue with the script . . .)

"I'm not sure if you have noticed, but the real estate market has gotten extremely hot, and homes are selling faster than we can put them up for sale. Houses are even selling with multiple offers above asking price!"

(Pause and continue with the script . . .)

"However, this has also created a problem for our buyer clients trying to find a house to buy. This virtual housing shortage is the reason I'm calling you today.

We have an abnormally large number of buyers that we need to find homes for, so I'm calling all of the people I know . . . like you . . . to see if you happen to know of anyone thinking about selling their home within the next year?"

(Pause, then try to help them if necessary . . .)

"Maybe a friend, family member or even a co-worker?"

(Pause and allow silence to do the heavy lifting here.)

(if YES, get name/contact info, or at least get permission to follow up later)

(If NO, continue with the script . . .)

"If you can think of anyone, we may even be able to get their home sold without ever going through the expense and hassle of putting the home up on the market. So, if you do run into anyone that's considering selling, would you be open to referring me to them and letting me know?"

(Pause and continue with the script . . .)

"Great! Thank you so much for helping us!"

**Note to Consider:**
The use of the word "we," as used in the sentence "We have an abnormally large number of buyers . . ." in paragraph 4 above and elsewhere throughout the script, is intended to allow you to refer to any buyers that other agents in your entire real estate brokerage have looking for homes as well. This use of "we" could also be implied to represent all of the agents in your local area as well.

© Copyright Icenhower Coaching & Consulting, LLC. All rights reserved.

## SOI SCRIPT
### Update Database

"Hi _____, this is [Agent Name] with [Real Estate Company], how are you today?

(Pause and continue with the script . . .)

"I'm calling because I'm updating my customer service database and noticed that I'm missing some contact information like email addresses, phone numbers and etc. Plus, I need to do a better job of staying in touch with people I know, and I'd love to send you something over the holidays and from time to time. Would that be OK with you?"

(Pause and continue with the script . . .)

"Great! So, let's see, it looks like we need your [EMAIL ADDRESS] . . ."

(Obtain any missing information needed) . . .

"Perfect, thank you for your help!"

"So, is there anything that we can do for you right now?"

(Pause, respond if applicable and continue with the script . . .)

"While I've got you on the line, we are in a hot real estate market right now where homes are selling faster than we can put them up for sale. So, we suddenly have a large number of buyers that we need to find homes for. With that said, do you happen to know of anyone thinking about selling their home within the next year?

(if YES, get name/contact info, or at least get permission to follow up later)

(If NO, continue with the script . . .)

"If you can think of anyone, we may even be able to get their home sold without ever going through the expense and hassle of putting the home up on the market. So, if you do run into anyone that's considering selling, would you be open to referring me to them and letting me know?"

(Pause and continue with the script . . .)

"Great! Thank you so much for helping us!"

© Copyright Icenhower Coaching & Consulting, LLC. All rights reserved.

# MODULE 3    APPENDIX 3.8

## SOI SCRIPT
### Update Database & Ask for Referral

The script below can be used 2 or 3 times annually to continuously attempt to provide customer service beyond normal expectations. Additionally, this script directly asks for referrals and at the very least, helps agents stay first of mind with their past clients.

"Hi _____, this is [Agent Name] with [Real Estate Company], how are you today?

(Pause and continue with the script . . .)

"I'm calling because I'm updating my customer service database and noticed that I'm missing some contact information like email addresses, phone numbers and etc. Plus, I need to do a better job of staying in touch with people I know, and I'd love to send you something over the holidays and from time to time. Would that be OK with you?"

(Pause and continue with the script . . .)

"Great! So, let's see, it looks like I need your [EMAIL ADDRESS] . . ."

(Obtain any missing information needed) . . .

"Perfect, thank you for your help!"

"So, is there anything that I can do for you right now?"

(Pause, respond if applicable and continue with the script . . .)

"While I've got you on the line, I wanted to ask you who you might know that may be looking to move in the near future. Maybe a friend, family member or co-worker? Can you think of anyone right now?"

(if YES, get name/contact info, or at least get permission to follow up later)

(If NO, continue with the script . . .)

"If you do bump into anyone looking to move, would you be open to referring them to me?"

(Pause and continue with the script . . .)

"Great! Thank you so much for helping me!"

© Copyright Icenhower Coaching & Consulting, LLC. All rights reserved.

## SOI SCRIPT
### Contacting Neglected Past Clients

"Hi _____, this is [Agent Name] at [Real Estate Company], and in case you don't remember, I'm the agent that sold your home and forgive me for not calling for so long how have you been?"

*(Pause and continue with the script . . .)*

"I'm ashamed to say that I haven't checked in sooner because I had a bad client database system and we are now upgrading that, and I just wanted to touch back and see how your new home is treating you. Is everything going OK with it?"

*(Pause and continue with the script . . .)*

"Well from now on please feel free to look to me as your total home resource . . . like your own personal Angie's List. If you ever need any repairs or improvements done to the home, you can contact me to refer you to a tested and trusted professional that I can personally hold accountable. How does that sound?"

*(Pause and continue with the script . . .)*

"Great! Since we're in the process of trying to update our databases and do better at staying in communication, is it okay if I send you something over the holidays and from time to time?"

*(Pause and continue with the script . . .)*

"Excellent! Is this still your correct home address? How about your email address?"

*(Pause and continue with the script . . .)*

"Thank you! And thanks for letting me apologize for not following up and staying in better touch with you, and if there is anything I can do to be of service in the future please let me know?"

© Copyright Icenhower Coaching & Consulting, LLC. All rights reserved.

# MODULE 3 　　　　　　　　　　　　　　　　　　　　APPENDIX 3.10

## SOI SCRIPT
### Past Client Follow Up

The script below can be used 2 or 3 times annually to continuously attempt to provide customer service beyond normal expectations. Additionally, this script directly asks for referrals and at the very least, helps agents stay first of mind with their past clients.

"Hi _____, this is [Agent Name] at [Real Estate Company]. I'm just calling as a customer service to check in with you to see how you're doing in your new home. How has your new home been treating you?"

(Remember that the key is to continue to ask questions to uncover a need that you can help with.)

"What have you done to it?"

(Pause and continue with the script . . .)

"Are you planning on doing any work or improvements to it in the future?"

(Pause and continue with the script . . .)

"Would it help if I gave you the contact information of some professionals that I trust that could help you get that done at a reasonable cost?"

(Pause and continue with the script . . .)

"You see, I want you to think of me as your total home resource. Like your own personal Angie's List. So, you can save yourself some time & frustration by letting me refer you to a tested & trusted company for any homeownership needs that may come up. Would that benefit you?"

(Pause and continue with the script . . .)

"Great! Oh, and by the way, I want to work with more clients like you, and I find that people typically hang around similar people. So, with that said, do you know anyone else looking to move in the near future?"

© Copyright Icenhower Coaching & Consulting, LLC. All rights reserved.

## Neighborhood Auto Email Drip Script
### for Sphere of Influence (SOI) or Geographic Farms

Hi it's [AGENT NAME] with [REAL ESTATE COMPANY],

I wanted to give you a heads up that I've set you up on our new Neighborhood Update Tool and would love to hear your feedback on it. My clients really love it. When one of your neighbors puts their home up for sale, you'll immediately get an email with all the listing information and photos of the home. This way, you'll be able to:

1. Look through all the **photos of your neighbors' homes;**

2. Compare the **amenities, features & size** of the listings to your own home;

3. Know the **price of each new listing** to get a rough idea of the current value of your own home;

4. See **how quickly each home sells,** and the **prices that they sell for;**

5. Have a good idea of **how the value of your home is increasing** from month-to-month;

6. **Keep up to date** on your local neighborhood's market conditions.

I really think you'll find this customer service tool useful since most of my clients already do. But if for some reason you decide that you'd rather not receive these updates, you can unsubscribe yourself or just simply reply to an email and we'll discontinue it for you. However, I'd love to hear what you think about it first.

All that I need from you is to verify that I have the correct home address and email address for you. Sound good?

© Copyright Icenhower Coaching & Consulting, LLC. All rights reserved.

## Prospecting For Expired Listings

At ICC, our passion is coaching, training, and mentoring the real estate agents of today and tomorrow. ICC founder, Brian Icenhower, has been coaching and training agents for many years, but he will tell you that if he were to get back into selling real estate today, he would do it two primary ways:

1. Focus on, and prioritize, his 'Sphere of Influence' referral database.

2. Layer 'Expired Prospecting' as his second biggest source of business.

Everyone is different, of course. There are many great ways to generate business, and different people are naturally inclined to gravitate towards different methods and activities. We teach an entire course on how our personality (or behavior profile) influences everything we do, including which lead-generation methods typically work best for different types of people.

There are some misconceptions about prospecting for expired listings. There are people who are not attracted to this method whatsoever. However, at ICC we teach agents that you don't have to like or enjoy a particular business-generating activity in order to practice it and see amazing results.

The reason Brian Icenhower would layer expired listings as his second biggest source of business is that he knows the phenomenal results that you can get from them. As we'll explain throughout the chapter, prospecting for expired listings has some of the best conversion ratios in the business.

Another benefit of prospecting for expireds is that it is a low-cost, low-overhead business method. The old adage that it takes money to make money doesn't apply as much here. Rather, this is a high activity-driven method that costs very little money.

All it takes is focus, a strong skill set, time on task, and a good deal of time-management and self-discipline. You've got this.

## Learning Targets

In this chapter, we will teach you:

- The difference between expired, cancelled, and withdrawn listings.
- The reasons listings fail to sell and ultimately expire.
- Why it's better to be 2nd than 1st when prospecting for expireds.
- Where to find phone numbers and the benefits of using an auto-dialer.
- The importance of a lead follow-up campaign.
- The best way to handle objections.
- The importance of prequalifying your sellers.
- How to close the appointment.

## CONVERSION IMMERSION

Before we delve into the exact details of how to prospect for expired listings, let's cast our minds back to fundamental lessons learned in the first chapter—the first being that *prospecting is a repetitive game of numbers.*

There is no quick trick—you will have to sift through an enormous amount of sand to unearth your glimmers of gold. And, depending on the business-generation method, you will have to sift through different levels of sand to land that single nugget.

Different business-generation methods have different average conversion rates.

When working your Sphere of Influence, for example, you now know that a database contact plan with 40 annual touches will result in 1 closed transaction for every 7 people in your SOI database.

And, when it comes to Expired Listings, skilled and experienced prospectors with good conversion rates typically contact between 20 and 25 expired-seller leads in order to get a single listing appointment.

> *Skilled expired prospectors have a 25:1 conversion rate. For every No you experience on a daily basis, that's a great deal of Yes's when you add it up over the course of a year.*

This is a very good conversion rate. If an expired prospector has 25 conversations or "contacts" with expired sellers per day, an agent with a 25:1 conversion ratio that works Monday through Friday should set 5 listing appointments per week. If the agent works 48 weeks out of a 52-week year, the agent will set 240 listing appointments (48 weeks x 5 appointments = 240 appointments).

If the same agent is only able to convert 60% of these listing appointments into signed listing agreements, the agent will list 144 properties in a single year (240 appointments x 60% = 144 signed agreements). Now assume that only 75% of those 144 listings actually sell and close. In that case, the agent will close 108 transactions in that year (144 listings x 75% = 108 listings sold). As you can see, prospecting for expired listings can be very profitable and predictable.

Plus, it takes four times as much time to work with one buyer lead from an online source like Zillow or Trulia than to work with one expired seller. Now, these are very good sources of business too, and ICC has courses that teach you exactly how to generate leads that way.

Buyers are wonderful, but they take more time. You spend a lot of time setting buyer consultations, showing property, organizing inspections, and getting the client qualified with the lender.

Representing sellers is no walk in the park, but it's far less time-consuming, and you can do 3-4 times more business by focusing on expired listings.

Despite the fact that much of the general population has gone online to look for property, the same technological trends have not impacted the seller market. Expired prospectors are doing just as well now as they were before the rise of the Internet. In fact, if you choose to prospect for expired listings, you will be working with decreased competition. So many agents are gravitating towards online leads that there are now fewer expired prospectors than ever before.

> *If you choose to prospect for expired listings, you will be working with decreased competition. So many agents are gravitating towards online leads that there are now fewer expired prospectors than ever before.*

What's more, if you are able to convert 80-100 listings per year, that's 80-100 more people that you're adding to your SOI referral base, so these are wonderful business methods to work together.

When you first start out, your conversion rates will not be as high as 25:1. Your skill level will not yet be as good. You won't be as fluid and efficient as you need to be to achieve a 25:1 ratio.

However, another fundamental lesson we want you to keep in mind is that *your skill level can be developed through time on task and connecting with as many people as possible.*

You can significantly improve your conversion rates through time on task and a commitment to contact as many people as humanly possible each and every day. Over time, a 40:1 conversion rate will become a 30:1 conversion rate, which will then become a steady 25:1 conversion rate.

> *You can significantly improve your conversion rates through time on task and a commitment to contact as many people as humanly possible each and every day.*

At ICC, we coach quite a few clients with 20:1 conversion rates and even some that have 18:1 and 15:1 ratios. These A-grade agents are prospecting at a very high level thanks to frequency and number of contacts, as well as a great deal of discipline and time-management.

You can achieve amazing results too, but be aware from the outset that you will experience a lot of rejection along the way. It's not abnormal or unusual to go three, four, five days without getting a listing, but you will see that the numbers always catch up. So if you go a week without getting a listing, please don't despair—the week after that you could get upwards of four or five listings that more than make up for the lean days.

The key is to have faith that this prospecting method has been tested and is continually proven year after year after year. The numbers will always average out to a 25:1 conversion rate. For every *No* you experience on a daily basis, that's a great deal of *Yes's* when you add it up over the course of a year.

Please maintain this mindset and remember to take the long view as we guide you through everything you need to know about prospecting for expired and cancelled listings.

## Expired, Cancelled & Withdrawn Listings

To begin, let's take a moment to clarify some terminology. So far, we have been using the term Expired Listings, but there are some important differences to be aware of between expired, cancelled, and withdrawn listings.

A **withdrawn listing** means that the property is no longer listed on the Multiple Listing Service (MLS), but it is technically still listed for sale with another real estate agent.

- Withdrawal doesn't break the contract between a seller and an agent.
- Until the contract has expired, a new agent cannot represent a seller who has withdrawn their listing.
- Other agents should not approach the seller, as there is technically a valid listing in place.

An **expired listing** means that the property hasn't been sold by the end of the period stipulated in the listing agreement. The sellers may or may not have received offers. They may have even accepted an offer, but something happened that caused the transaction to fail, and the listing to expire. Either way:

- The contract between the seller and the original agent has effectively come to an end.
- Sellers can choose to stay on with their current agent, or they can decide to work with a new agent without incurring any penalties.
- Other agents are free to approach the seller, as there is no valid listing in place.

A **cancelled listing** means that the seller and the original real estate agent have terminated the listing and the listing agreement, typically prior to the expiration date on the contract. Perhaps the previous agent was fired, or the relationship broke down in some irreparable way. The end result is the same as before:

- The contract between the seller and the original agent has come to an end.
- Others agents are free to approach the seller, as there is no valid listing in place.

For simplicity's sake, we will refer to both of these as expired listings from now on, as they are effectively the same thing from a prospecting perspective.

Be aware of the difference as you search through the MLS, however. An 'Expired' versus a 'Cancelled' listing can provide initial clues about why the property didn't sell. Understanding the common reasons behind an expired or cancelled listing can be used to your advantage when you make first contact with the prospect.

## WHAT FAILS IN THE MARKET: THE REASONS LISTINGS EXPIRE

The table below illustrates recurring failures that occur in every supply-and-demand market.

The first column is from a study, performed by Forbes, about *why new businesses fail.* The second column is a list compiled by consultants who researched the last five years of *failed products that were ultimately removed from the market.* The third column is our own research, based on decades of experience in real estate and talking with our clients about *why listings fail to sell, and ultimately expire.*

There are some slight variations, but note the commonalities between all three.

| Why New Businesses Fail | Why New Products Fail | Why Listings Fail to Sell & Ultimately Expire |
|---|---|---|
| Failing to Communicate with customers frequently enough or deeply enough | Failure to Understand Needs and Wants of the Consumer | Priced Too High (compared to like properties, or based on neighborhood) |
| Lack of Unique Value Proposition: no real differentiation from competition | Fixes a Non-Existent problem | Weak or Poor Marketing |
| Failure to Communicate Value in a clear, concise, and compelling fashion | Targeting the Wrong Market | Showing Property was too difficult |
| Inability to nail a Profitable Business Model with proven revenue streams | Incorrect Pricing | Pricing wasn't adjusted often enough, if at all, to recapture interest of buyers |
| Leadership Breakdown at the top | Weak Internal Capability & Infrastructure | Poor or weak communication between client and listing agent |
|  | Delayed Market Entry | Condition of home, terms of contract were too restrictive |
|  | Poor Execution or Delivery | Previous Agent's Reputation: poor/weak/unprofessional representation deterred other agents from showing/writing offers |

Though there are several reasons why listings fail to sell and ultimately expire, again and again, the primary reasons for failure in any business are: pricing, communication, and a failure to understand the wants and needs of the client or consumer.

## Pricing

Oftentimes, listings expire because the home was priced to high to begin with. Either the previous agent didn't do a good job of explaining comparisons, or they failed to overcome the seller's objections to price.

Often, pricing can be adjusted to cover any problems with the condition of the home. However, sellers can be stubborn and they often over-estimate the actual value or condition of their home.

As real estate agents, we must own this problem. If the seller is unyielding on price and refuses to price the home correctly, the agent must take ownership of that problem and find a way to effectively communicate the actual market value of the home, and how an appraisal report works, etc.

When listings fail to sell "because of price," something deeper is often going on. Most pricing problems are actually communication problems at heart.

## Communication

Poor communication is one of the most frequently mentioned reasons that a listing expires or is terminated.

When we talk to sellers of expired listings, they often complain about a complete lack of communication and having to reach out to the agent for feedback, updates and even basic information. Agents alienate and frustrate their clients when they fail to proactively communicate on a regular and systematic weekly basis.

However, good communication is not only measured by *how often* you speak with the client but by *how well* you can explain the information to them and get your point across. Failure to communicate in a clear and compelling fashion that everyday people can understand is as damaging as no communication at all.

Generally, we tend to communicate in the way that we would like to be communicated with. As we mentioned a moment ago, our behavior profile influences everything we do, including our communication style.

However, your prospects and clients may have a different behavior profile and communication style, and it is up to you to meet the client where they are at, rather than the other way around. This may mean speeding up so as not to frustrate their impatience, or it may mean slowing down and taking the time to go over things methodically and patiently. Oftentimes, the most effective communication is simply listening to what the seller is saying.

At ICC, we teach an entire course about the preferred forms of communication for each behavior and how to match different people's communication style when generating new business and guiding existing clients through the process (*Behavior: Improve Communication & Sales Performance In Real Estate*). We encourage you to make communication a top priority for your growing business.

When prospecting for expired listings, it is essential that you don't repeat the same communication mistakes as the agent that came before you. Pay attention to sellers when they tell you what the other agent *did* and *didn't* do when it came to communication.

## WANTS & NEEDS OF THE SELLER

One of the reasons prospecting for expired listings has such a good conversion-rate is that sellers *want* to sell their homes.

Forgive us for stating the obvious, but we're often surprised that people negatively perceive this prospecting method as cold-calling when, in fact, it's a very warm lead.

Too often, agents define 'cold-calling' as any interaction with a lead that they don't personally know. However, the 'warmth' of a call is determined not by your familiarity with the individual, but with the *motivation, wants, and needs* of the lead or prospect.

> *The 'warmth' of a call is determined not by your familiarity with the individual, but with the motivation, wants, and needs of the lead or prospect.*

With most other prospecting methods, you will typically have no idea whether the person has any interest in buying or selling a home. You will rarely know what most lead's current wants and needs are. Not so when prospecting for expired listings.

Good prospectors understand that the ultimate motivation for these people is to sell their home and move on with their life. Good prospectors understand that the seller's life is on hold due to one or more of the reasons listed above. Good prospectors know that they must communicate to the seller that they are reaching out in an effort to help them achieve what they most want and need.

As an expired prospector, each of these reasons presents an opportunity and way for you to help a frustrated, regretful, and disappointed seller.

When prospecting for expired listings, you can learn from and capitalize on the failures of the *first agent* in order to differentiate yourself from the competition, communicate your value in a clear, concise, and compelling fashion, and assure the seller that the *second person is the best person* for the job.

## WHO'S UP NEXT?

The answer to that question is very likely, "*You.*"

We are conditioned from birth to believe that winning is everything and being second amounts to being nowhere: "Nobody remembers who came in second," said American golfer, Walter Hagen.

However, when it comes to prospecting for expireds, it's better to be the second listing agent, not the first. As American racecar champion, Bobby Unser said, "Nobody remembers who came in second—except the guy who came in second." When it comes to expired listings, the runner-up takes the prize.

> *"Nobody remembers who came in second except the guy who came in second." – Bobby Unser, American racecar champion*

Now, understand, the first agent was probably perfectly fine. They may have marketed the home quite capably. They likely told the sellers the exact same things you will tell them, and cautioned them against the very same dangers and drawbacks that you will.

While it can be the case that the previous agent was bad at their job and has a truly terrible reputation, oftentimes their only failure was to have the misfortune of being first in line.

For the first agent, it can be difficult for them to communicate and convey information in a way that does not become adversarial to the point of total failure and termination. This is why we urge you to learn how to communicate in the best way for each particular client, so that *you* don't become the first agent that loses out to the second guy.

> *Good expired prospectors realize that they represent a clean slate for the sellers and an opportunity to move on with their lives.*

Sometimes, it takes a second or third time in the ring before sellers will actually hear what an agent is saying. This is another reason why prospecting for expired listings has great conversion rates and is a wonderful business-generation method.

Second-round sellers are not impressed by glossy marketing flyers or wowed by your website. They still want to sell their home for the most amount of money in the least amount of time.

By the time you come along, however, the seller is typically over any of the denials and delusions they had about the condition and value of their home.

For the second agent, it's far easier to handle any pricing objections that arise, and it's a lot easier to make pricing adjustments should the market not bear the price. For the second agent, it's also easier to take a hard look at the home and have candid conversations about making corrections and improvements.

Second-round sellers are generally much more realistic, much more focused, and much more urgent about the bottom line of selling the home.

> *By the time you come along, the seller is typically over any of the denials and delusions they had about the condition and value of their home. Second-round sellers are generally much more realistic, much more focused, and much more urgent about the bottom line of selling the home.*

Good expired prospectors tap into this focus and urgency. Good prospectors realize that they represent a clean slate for the sellers and an opportunity to move on with their lives—without ever having to admit their own mistakes and contribution to the home not selling the first time round.

You present an opportunity for them to make different decisions and do it right this time round. You can be their white knight that saves the day—if you can convince them to make an appointment with you and hear you out.

This is key. As you'll soon see, when you make first contact with the seller, your goal is not to secure the listing right away over the phone. Your mission is to get a meeting with the owners of the home in order to present a full list of alternatives to what was done before, and set expectations for a new process.

You're repositioning their 'product'—that is, their home—for a new, more effective launch onto the market. And you are also setting this appointment with urgency because the competition for these appointments will be fierce. Remember, you are not the only prospector hoping to be remembered for coming in second!

## FINDING PHONE NUMBERS

Before we move on to scripts and making initial contact with prospects, one of the first things you might be thinking is, "Where do I get their telephone number?"

Methods and sources for obtaining telephone numbers have evolved over the years.

Since the advent of the Internet, when listings first went online, prospectors can search 'Hot Sheets' for expired and terminated listings in the Multiple Listing Service (MLS). You can do this manually, or you can set up a notification system that alerts you to every expired listing that comes up each morning.

As listings come up, you can see the property address, listing and pricing history, and other valuable information about the property, but it's unlikely you will find a contact phone number in the MLS.

To find their phone number, you can do a few things:

### SKIP TRACING

The term 'skip tracing' typically refers to the process of searching for a person that has skipped town, leaving minimal clues behind for how to trace them.

In the case of prospecting for expired listings, skip tracing is a process of manually searching for phone numbers using free search-sites like whitepages.com or 411.com, etc.

This is an extremely time-consuming method and, with the proliferation of cell phones, many people no longer have landlines, and will not show up in any of your searches.

Though it's inexpensive, there are not too many prospectors that will use this method. Manually searching for phone numbers cuts into the time when you could be making phone calls. It's very difficult to make 25 calls a day when you're sifting through dead ends and bad information on the Internet.

## SEND A MAILER

Some agents will send a postcard or listing packet and introduction letter to expired listing properties. Their idea is that the seller is probably being bombarded with phone calls, and would prefer the softer method of receiving something in the mail.

In their mind, this allows the seller to review the mailer at their leisure and reach out to the agent with their phone number.

While it's true that prospective sellers are inundated with phone calls in the days after their listing expires, people are equally irritated by what they perceive to be mountains of unsolicited junk mail.

Besides, by the time your postcard or packet makes it to their mailbox, it's highly likely that another real estate agent will have secured an appointment or even the listing.

Instead, most top-producing prospectors will save their money on mailers and spend it on something that saves them precious time and energy.

## PAY FOR PHONE NUMBERS

Generally, prospecting for expired listings is a no-cost/low-cost business-generation method. Paying for phone numbers will be your primary expense, if you choose to do so. In many areas, just one closed commission will more than pay for this expenditure, so it's a good return of investment and very much worth your valuable time.

You can pay anywhere from $50 a month to $300 a month for quality expired phone numbers. Oftentimes, you'll get cell phone numbers, and at the upper end of that price-range, you may even get email addresses and multiple cell phone numbers if there is more than one person living in the home.

The quality of contact information depends on the service you use and the amount of money you want to spend each month. There are so many services and companies, and more are popping up each minute—the best sources change all the time. We therefore suggest that you research different companies and services by yourself, or ask an ICC coach for up-to-date recommendations, insights, and discounts that we offer through our coaching service.

## PROSPECTING THE EXPIRED LISTING: FIRST CONTACT

No matter how you find your phone numbers, when you make first contact with the seller, you will have the support of a tested, proven, and *practiced* script in front of you.

Below are three short opening scripts provided by some of our top expired prospectors and ICC coaches. Take a moment to read through them in turn.

| | |
|---|---|
| Expired Script 1 | "Hi, I'm looking for _____. This is John Smith with ABC Realty, and I'm calling because, as I'm sure you've figured out, your home has come up as an expired listing. So, I'm calling to see when you plan on hiring the **right** agent to sell your home." |
| Expired Script 2 | "Hi, I'm John Smith with ABC Realty, and I'm calling about the house that was listed in the multiple listing service that expired, and I wanted to interview for the job of getting your home back on the market **and sold**. I'd like to show you the techniques I use to get my listings sold." |
| Expired Script 3 | "Hi this is John Smith with ABC Realty, and I noticed that your listing on 123 Pepperwood Court is no longer active. I wanted to see if you are going to take this opportunity to interview a different agent. If so, I'd love to share my marketing methods for getting homes sold **quickly**." |

As you'll recall from the second chapter on working with scripts, every script has a core message that can be summed up in ten words or less. And, as you can see, each of these scripts is simple, clear, concise, and gets straight to the point.

In essence, the core message of each of these scripts is, "Your listing has expired, and I would love the job."

No more, no less. That's it.

## STICK TO THE SCRIPT

Remember that your skill level develops and improves through time on task and number of contacts. In order to achieve high conversion rates, you will be calling a minimum of 25 people a day. You must learn to "deliver your lines" effectively but efficiently.

You don't need to get into a high level of detail when you make first contact with the seller of an expired listing. Squash any desire you have to impress them with your research and knowledge. Keep it quick and simple, and stick to the script.

Of those 25 calls, you're going to encounter a lot of rejection and hear a great many *No's*. Some of these people will be angry or frustrated with you. Remember that you're not the only agent prospecting for expired listings—these sellers receive an enormous number of calls on the day their listing expires.

Don't get into battles with people. Don't argue or try to convince or persuade. When you encounter hostility or rejection, all you need to do is quickly say, "I'm sorry ma'am," then hang up and move on.

Don't take it personally. Shake it off and move on to the next call.

Your goal is not to talk those 24 *No's* into saying *Yes*. Your goal is to sift through the sand, deliver your core message, and make it through those 25 calls to find your one *Yes*.

When you first start out, this number may be higher. Even so, the process is the same. All you have to do is get through 30-40 *short and simple* interactions. By sticking to the script and getting straight to the point, you will begin to quickly filter through these calls and find the people that really need your help.

Expired prospecting is a numbers game. You have to play the numbers.

---

### THE EARLY BIRD CATCHES THE WORM

Competition is fierce on the morning that a listing expires. Plan to time-block your expired listing calls *first thing* in the morning.

Left until later in the morning can put you at caller #20 on their incoming call list.

In that time, sellers will have formulated all sorts of responses for getting agents off the phone.

- "We're going to leave it off the market for a while, and take a break."
- "We're going to relist with the same agent/a friend."
- "We're going to go FSBO and sell it ourselves."
- "We are interviewing other agents, but if lowering the price is the only thing you do… save your breath."

By the time they get to their twentieth inquiry, angry and frustrated sellers waste no time in disconnecting with callers. They may even disconnect their phone completely!

Your goal is to be first in line to be their second listing agent.

---

## WIN THE CLIENT, WIN THE DAY: YOUR LEAD FOLLOW-UP CAMPAIGN

If you are connected to the prospect's voicemail, keep it short and to the point:

| Voicemail Script 1 | "I'm calling about your home for sale. My number is 555-123-4567." |

| | |
|---|---|
| Voicemail Script 2 | "Hi, this is (AGENT NAME) with (REAL ESTATE COMPANY), and I'm calling about the house you had listed in the multiple listing service, and I'd like to talk to you about the house. Would you please call me back as soon as possible? Call me at 555-123-4567." |
| Voicemail Script 3 | "Hello, this is (AGENT NAME) with (REAL ESTATE COMPANY), and I'm calling about your listing that is no longer on the market. If you are interested in taking this opportunity to interview a different agent, call me at 555-123-4567." |

Waiting for a return call could be the longest wait of your life, however. Experienced agents are persistent about calling back multiple times, and continuing the connection with a systematized follow-up campaign.

Good prospectors understand that it can be a very emotional experience for a seller on the day their listing expires. They're tired, they're upset, they're disappointed, and they're frustrated. Oftentimes, their initial reaction on that first day is to give up on the entire process.

When the dust settles, however, they soon begin to realize that they do still want to move. They remember the reasons that they wanted or even needed to move in the first place, and a good prospector will make sure to nurture the lead and continue to build rapport and relationship.

You can win over the seller of an expired or cancelled listing if you are willing to be empathetic, patient, and persistent. There's a fine line between being persistent and becoming a pest, however. Your task is to do the first, without becoming the second. The way to do that is to first establish curiosity with prospects, then trust, and eventually, a relationship.

Trust is earned. Relationships are earned. If you can create a compelling curiosity long enough for the prospect to test you for trust, they'll be open to building the sales relationship. Now, building relationships can take time, so you must commit to a follow-up plan with the seller of an expired or canceled listing.

For people that you couldn't make contact with, remember to set up a lead follow-up reminder in your CRM system and try them again later in the day or possibly even the next day. Persist until you've made that all-important first contact.

For people that you did make contact with, you can extend that brief initial call by maintaining contact with them in a variety of ways, from follow-up phone calls to mailers or physically dropping off a listing package at their home.

Often, prospectors will email e-alerts for other active listings in the area that may inspire them to list again. You can also use services like Sly Dial and Sly Broadcast that connect you directly to their voicemail and schedule voice messages for a day or two later. The key is to keep in touch.

Oftentimes, prospectors will employ a blend of communication strategies over the following week. Effectively, this is an accelerated variation of the Rule of 7 Touches where you introduce people to your services, establish name-recognition, and slowly tap back into the prospect's motivation to sell their home.

| | |
|---|---|
| Prospect | 1234 Main Street: Dave & Mary Allen EXP |
| Day 1 | Call, Thank You Note, Email with 7 Questions |
| Day 2 | Call, Visit/Preview |
| Day 3 | Call, Testimonial Email |
| Day 4 | Call, Email Report of Comparative Homes that Sold |
| Day 5 | Call, Drop Off List of Buyers |
| Day 6 | Call |
| Day 7 | Call, Move to 40 Touch SOI Database |

Notice that, if you establish that the seller has truly decided to hold off on re-listing their property for the time being, you can move them to your 40-touch SOI database (with a note about how you met) and nurture the relationship over time.

You can also create an Expired Listing Call log to accompany your Daily Contact Sheet.

Most real estate agents give up after the initial contact or two. Stay the course, and check back regularly to see how things are going. Offer a solution to the seller's problem, and you will have a better chance of getting the listing. If trust, communication, and keeping promises were problems with their previous agent, following up with them and building relationship could build compelling curiosity and set you apart from agents who fall at the first hurdle.

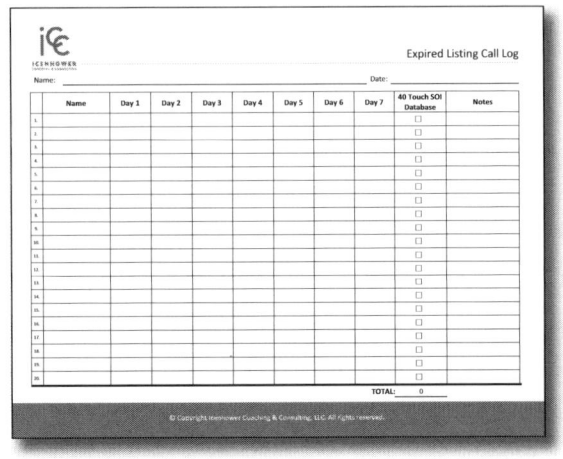

# CLOSING THE APPOINTMENT

As we discussed at length in the very first chapter, prospecting is an Organized Sales Process: a systematic, repeatable series of steps and actions that map out and track interaction with leads and prospects, from their first point of engagement with your business through to a close. Broadly speaking, it is a three-step sales process where we take an individual from *Contact* to *Appointment* to *Contract*.

Prospectors are constantly focused on moving leads and prospects forward to the next stage in the process. Ultimately, you want to move them to the client/contract stage, but in order to advance that far, you must successfully complete the appointment part of the process.

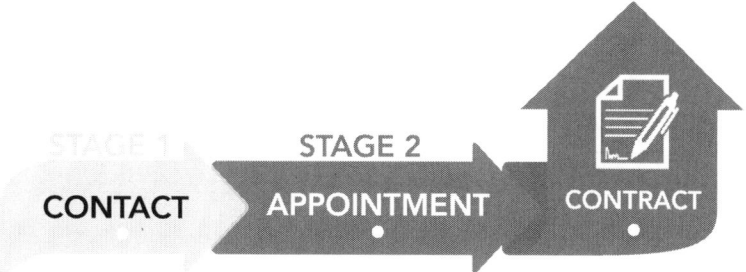

When you dial the phone and connect with the seller or decision-maker on an expired listing, that's considered a contact—that's stage one. At this point, your sole focus should be on moving the prospect forward to stage two: agreeing to meet in person and scheduling an appointment.

Unfortunately, many inexperienced prospectors are so focused on the commission in the distance that they neglect to complete the additional steps and actions in between. It's very important that you do not make the mistake of trying to list the property over the phone. At the first stage of initial contact, the only thing you're trying to close is the appointment and persuading them to meet you in person.

The reason we stress this is that we want you to be as successful as possible. While experienced prospectors with good conversion rates typically contact between 20 and 25 expired-seller leads in order to get a single listing appointment, the listing appointment conversion ratio is a little lower than other forms of business-generation.

If you're setting a listing appointment with a member of your SOI, there's a social peer relationship between you and that person that makes them more inclined to list with you rather than interviewing other agents. With your SOI, you might convert 85-90% of your listing appointments.

When prospecting for expired listings, you don't have a previous relationship, so your conversion rates will be slightly lower. If you're doing well, you might convert 70% of your listing appointments, but when you're starting out that number might be closer to 50%.

Now, 50% isn't bad if you're making enough contacts to set a listing appointment a day. That means every other business day, you're getting a listing and, in a typical 5-day week that's 2.5 listings per week. That's 10 listings over the course of a month, or 120 listings a year. Not too bad at all!

Still, the likelihood of a prospect listing with you is much, much higher if you meet with them in person. Understand that people don't want to interview and invite a whole ton of real estate agents into their home. If you are the first or one of the first people in their home, and you're standing in front of them with a contract ready to sign, you have a far higher likelihood of converting that appointment into a listing.

## I Object!

As you know, however, you will encounter a great many objections and excuses when you speak with expired listing sellers on that first phone call. For example, during the initial telephone call, sellers will often raise objections to listing such as:

- "If we price our home lower we can't afford pay a commission."
- "We need to find a home to buy before we're going to sell."
- "We don't really need to sell now anyway."
- "I think we are going to try and sell our home ourselves."
- "We need to wait to be able to get a little bit more equity out of our home."
- "We can't afford to pay a full commission. How much will you charge us?"

As you can see, the objections above are not objections to meeting with you in person. In fact, all of these objections are actually objections to listing the property for sale.

In other words, they are objections to signing a listing contract.

Agents that get stuck in telephone conversations by these types of objections are getting ahead of themselves by trying to close the contract instead of the appointment—which should be your sole focus at this stage.

Therefore, the key to handling these objections is to not attempt to overcome their objections to listing while on the phone: the time and the place for that is at the listing appointment. Rather, every time you're faced with an objection, you will handle it by using it as a *reason to meet in person*.

The best way to *handle* objections and *close* the appointment is to *validate* the seller by repeating their objection back to them and showing them that you've heard them.

Here are some ways that top producers handle common objections.

# OBJECTION VALIDATION HANDLE AND CLOSE

| Objection/ Rejection | Validation | Handle & Close |
|---|---|---|
| We're leaving it off the market/taking a break. | That's an option; it's also taking a break from the plans you had when you did want to move. Where were you going? | What I'm excited to meet with you about is when you DO move to _____ , the net from your home sale is enough to buy down your next interest rate, pay for moving costs, *if our program is a fit for you.* Let's book time right now. |
| We're going to re-list with a friend/same agent | What benefit do you expect to get by re-listing with the same agent? | What I'd like to do is walk you through how my system finds more options like the one I'm suggesting to you now; you can turn down all of them, if you like; I'm asking for 10 minutes to show them to you, and make it your choice. This evening is good for me. |
| We're going to sell ourselves, go FSBO | Well, welcome to the industry! You're going to be represented in the market, maybe you'd be interested in a partnership and see what we bring to the table? | There are about 7 places you can concentrate on to avoid what happened last time; would you be open to working with me, to see if we can tackle 4 or 5 together in 15 minutes? Would you like to start tonight? |
| We're interviewing, but not dropping price. | Price is crucial; and we'll both talk about price. Let's be up front about it. | What we'll talk about first are a few key points that I'd like to show you in person… 10 minutes, and then you decide if I stay or if I go. And I can be there at 3. |

As you can see, every objection is repeated and validated but ultimately handled as a reason to meet in person. Good expired prospectors convert 70% of their listing appointments, so the game is to secure as many appointments as possible. It's far easier to overcome objections to list in person and convert the appointment into a contract.

## REPEAT AFTER ME

Everyone wants to feel heard. The seller whose hot listing has expired may feel as though no one has listened to him or her, but listening in itself is not always enough.

Behavioral studies show that repeating people's words helps to build empathy and trust, and establish rapport. When we're actively listening, we use the words the other person uses, repeat their words back at them, and summarize our conversations to show that we've really heard them.

In effect, we reflect their identity and feelings back at them in the words we use when talking to them. We go into this in great length in our course *Behavior: Improve Communication & Sales Performance In Real Estate*.

Essentially, your goal is not to change the seller's feelings. Those feelings have developed from past events that you had no control over. Instead, your goal is to validate their experience and empathize with their feelings with a view to reframing the situation and offering up new information that might bring new perspective. Validation consists of a statement affirming that the seller's feelings are understood, a recitation of the causes they've mentioned, and insight as to what they're NOT saying.

- *I completely understand how you feel;*
    - One moment, it feels like there's no one who wants to sell your home, and today, there are 20; you might wonder, "Where were they last month?"
    - To be honest, I wish I knew.
    - Can I share with you what will make sure last month never happens again?

- *Of course you're frustrated that the previous agent didn't stay in contact with you throughout the listing contract.*
    - You're left to wonder if you've had any interest, and meanwhile you're still keeping your end of the agreement,
    - There's a broken promise there.
    - Anyone in your situation would feel that way.
    - How would you like me to stay in contact with you when I represent your property?

- *No wonder you're upset.*
    - It's only natural to expect that there would be more than one or two showings of your home.
    - Did you know that if showings aren't occurring, there's a way to invite more showings?
    - Here's what I would like to do for you…

Validation helps the seller see that moving forward is not only possible, but it is desirable. While it may be just another transaction for the average real estate agent, a good prospector knows that selling a home is a physical and emotional upheaval for the client. If they've committed to move, and then the sale doesn't happen, that can be a truly devastating and disheartening experience. When you dial their phone number, remember that there is an emotional human being on the other end of the line.

### EXERCISE: Do You Validate?

Let's test your validation savvy here:

Create a list of reasons that might make a seller frustrated regarding their expired or canceled listing. Then write a validation for each of the reasons. Be sure to include an action statement at the end to show how you will help the seller move forward. A sample has been provided for you.

| Validating the Seller's Emotions |||
|---|---|---|
| Validation | Affirmation | Resolution |
| Having to cancel a listing is an awful feeling. | No one wants to be in a position of giving up. | I don't like to give up, either, so here's what I do for my listings… |
|  |  |  |
|  |  |  |
|  |  |  |

## PRE-QUALIFY YOUR LISTING CONSULTATION APPOINTMENTS

Closing appointments feels amazing, but there's no sense preparing for, driving to, and conducting listing appointments that you never had a realistic chance of converting in the first place.

Once you've validated their concerns, overcome their objections, and closed the appointment, don't forget to ask for permission to pre-qualify the seller before you spend too much time preparing for the listing appointment.

Pre-qualifying your prospects ensures that you're not wasting your time and it also helps you to prepare for any other objections you might encounter when you finally meet with them in person.

To assist you with this crucial part of the sales process, we have provided the following **Listing Consultation Pre-Qualification Script**.

This script is designed to help uncover the most common issues that might prevent you from listing and selling expired listings. Each question is designed to reveal issues like lack of seller urgency, list price expectations, a deal-breaking lack of equity in the home, and whether they are interviewing other agents or even considering selling the home themselves as a For Sale By Owner (FSBO).

Remember to use the following script **AFTER** the listing consultation appointment has been scheduled with the client. A larger copy of the script has also been provided at the end of this chapter.

## LISTING CONSULTATION
## PRE-QUALIFICATION SCRIPT

1. I'd like to ask you a few quick questions to help me better prepare before our appointment. Would that be alright?

2. After you sell your home, where are you planning on moving?

3. How soon would you like to move there?

4. Do you know your current outstanding loan balance on the home?

5. At what price do you think your home should be listed for sale?

6. Could you tell me some of your home's best features and selling points?

7. Have you ever considered selling your home yourself?

8. If you are comfortable with me, are you planning on listing your home for sale when we meet?

9. Are you interviewing any other agents to sell your home?   *See First or Second below*

   (if "yes") Are you meeting them before or after our scheduled appointment?

10. I'll also be sending you an informational packet prior to our appointment. It will tell you a bit more about me and the services I provide, so could you look that over before we meet?   *See Head Start Hand Delivery on page 223*

11. Do you have any questions for me at this time?

12. Great! I look forward to meeting with you on _____ at _____.

## FIRST OR SECOND?

It's hugely helpful if you know in advance whether you're up against any competition. And it's even more helpful if you know whether you're interviewing before or after them.

If they have a choice, some agents prefer to go second. They will first make sure to ask the client for their assurance that they will not sign any paperwork or list with the first agent until after they've sat through the second appointment and listened to everyone. A lot of agents that interview second wind up getting the listing because the sellers don't want to go back and meet with the first listing agent all over again. You're right there in front of them, so they'll often just sign with you.

Other agents feel more comfortable going first. They're very confident they can close. What's more, they will often offer to cancel the other appointments on the home seller's behalf. Obviously, this is a fantastic result for that agent, but it can be very frustrating if you're on the receiving end of that phone call, so it's important to know if you're up against other competition ahead of time.

### Head Start Hand Delivery

Hand delivering a Listing Packet prior to your presentation can help give you an all-important head start on setting yourself apart from the competition.

Pre-Listing Presentations or Listing Packets will include your Bio, important checklists, and answer the most common questions that typical sellers have.

A well-thought-out package inspires confidence in the client and establishes you as a professional in the real estate industry. When a potential client reviews the information you've collected, they realize that you are an expert in your field. A thoughtful, detailed package can alleviate their worries by helping them to understand the process.

Another benefit of buyer and seller packages is that they can save everyone valuable time. Oftentimes, you can walk into the appointment and get right down to bottom-line conversations like price. Once you agree on a price, you can pull out a listing agreement and move confidently forward from there.

You can also email a copy of the Listing Packet as a PDF or send them a Pre-Listing video. The key is to help sellers feel comfortable and confident around you before they've even met you!

## Time's A Wastin'

Prospecting expired listings is all about working the numbers. Your objective is to contact as many expired listings as quickly as humanly possible each and every day, not to mention nurturing and cultivating those contacts with a systematic follow-up campaign, as well as holding listing appointments and servicing your existing clients.

Most expired prospectors try to contact 20 to 30 sellers of expired listings a week day. If you don't have that many expired listings to contact each day in your particular area, most information services will also let you purchase the contact information for older listings that expired over the course of the past 1 or 2 years to call as well.

When you have a to-do list as long as your arm, what techniques and strategies can you use to perform your role in the best and most efficient way possible?

ICC offers an in-depth course on systematizing your real estate business, which provides a host of organizational and time-management strategies and solutions (*ADMIN: Systematize Your Real Estate Administrative Process*).

Everyone has the same amount of time each day, but the reason some people get more done is because they are much better at using their time for maximum benefit to themselves and to others.

## TRACK & MONITOR

At many real estate companies, administration managers have their agents submit weekly contact forms to track and monitor how many contacts an agent makes each day, week, or month. For those of you who are solo agents, ICC has courses that teach you how to hold yourself accountable and track and monitor your prospecting progress.

## TIME BLOCK

Another important strategy is to time-block lead-generation, lead follow-up, and listing appointments in your calendar.

Any meeting or appointment that involves multiple people should be scheduled well in advance as you will need to factor in response times from several parties as well as coordinating any rescheduling in the event that someone cannot make the appointment.

If your goal is to make a minimum of 25 contacts a day, you will need to time-block 2-3 hours per day to focus exclusively on that activity with no other distractions. If you can carve out 2-3 hours of your day, and have 25 conversations, you'll typically set one listing appointment a day.

Prioritize and perform your lead-generating calls and activities first thing each morning. For starters you'll be fresh and have more energy, but there are also generally fewer distractions in the morning. Sellers usually want to conduct listing appointments in the afternoon or early evening.

## SAMPLE WEEKLY CALENDAR

|  | Mon 3/13 | Tues 3/14 | Wed 3/15 | Thu 3/16 | Fri 3/17 |
|---|---|---|---|---|---|
| 6a |  |  |  |  |  |
| 7a |  |  |  |  |  |
| 8a | 8:30 - Prepare for Business | 8:30 - Prepare for Business | 8:30 - Prepare for Business | 8:30 - Prepare for Business | 8:30 - Prepare for Business |
| 9a–10a | 9 — 11 Marketing/Business Generation | 9 — 11 Marketing/Business Generation | 9 — 11 Marketing/Business Generation | 9 — 11 Marketing/Business Generation | 9 — 11 Marketing/Business Generation |
| 11a | 11 — 12p Business Servicing | 11 — 12p Business Servicing | 11 — 12p Business Servicing | 11 — 12p Business Servicing | 11 — 12p Business Servicing |
| 12p | 12p-1p Lunch | 12p-1p Lunch | 12p-1p Lunch | 12p-1p Lunch w/ Wife | 12p-1p Lunch |
| 1p | 1p — 2p Lead Conversion & Follow-Up | 1p — 2p Lead Conversion & Follow-Up | 1p — 2p Lead Conversion & Follow-Up |  | 1p — 2p Lead Conversion & Follow-Up |
| 2p | 2p — 3p Business Servicing | 2p — 3p Business Servicing | 2p — 3p Business Servicing | 2p — 3p Lead Conversion & Follow-Up | 2p — 3p Business Servicing |
| 3p |  |  | 3:30p — 6p Watch David's T-Ball Game | 3p — 4p Business Servicing |  |
| 4p–5p | 4p — 5:30p Listings Presentation - 123 Cottonwood Ct | 4p — 6p Show Homes to Johnsons |  | 4:30p — 5:30p Buyer Consultation w/ Taylors | 4p — 6p Listings Presentation - 456 Spring Creek Way |
| 6p |  |  |  |  |  |
| 7p |  | 6:30p — 8p Family Dinner |  |  | 6:30p — 8:30p Family Birthday Party |
| 8p |  |  |  |  |  |
| 9p |  |  |  |  |  |

Start adopting a new mindset that you are no longer available in the mornings. Block out that time on your calendar or it will get gobbled up by less important obligations.

### Power Dial

As well as blocking out dedicated prospecting time, your aim will also to become faster and faster to make the best use of that time. We have many clients who can contact 25 expired sellers in an hour and a half, certainly in under two hours.

Earlier, we discussed the benefits of paying for phone numbers rather than the time-consuming method of skip tracing and manually searching for numbers on free search sites like whitepages.com.

Manually searching for phone numbers cuts into the time when you could be making phone calls. It's very difficult to make 25 calls a day when you're sifting through dead ends and bad information on the Internet.

Likewise, many top agents also choose to invest in an auto-dialer or power-dialer. This is typically a nominal expense, often much less than the cost of the phone numbers. We recommend consulting with your ICC coach for tips about the best product to meet your needs.

As it's name suggests, an auto-dialer is an electronic device or software that automatically dials phone numbers (oftentimes, you will receive your phone numbers as a database CVS file that can be uploaded into your dialing system).

An auto-dialer dials through this database of phone numbers until someone picks up. Once the call has been answered, the auto-dialer either plays a recorded message or connects the call to a live person. An auto-dialer/power-dialer dials a pre-set number of lines when the agent completes the previous call. Some power-dialers will call multiple phone lines at once and automatically hang up on the other calls when a first person picks up.

Many agents don't use an auto-dialer, but a lot of pros that have been prospecting for a long time prefer it. They know that they need to power through as many calls a day, as quickly as humanly possible, in order to achieve a solid conversion rate.

As we discussed in the second chapter, it can take a while to establish a rhythm when using scripts and reaching out to people. It can also be quite nerve-wracking, especially to begin with. Auto-dialers can help you stay in the zone and prevent you from taking too many distracting breaks between calls. There's nothing more frustrating than coming out of a rhythm because you're skip tracing or misdialing phone numbers on your cell phone.

The longer you can stay on the phone, locked in and engaged, with an established rhythm, the sooner you will reach the number of contacts you need to achieve that all-important 25:1 conversion rate!

### Summary

Prospecting for expired listings has some of the best conversion ratios in the business. Experienced prospectors with good conversion rates typically contact between 20 and 25 expired-seller leads in order to get a single listing appointment.

Through time on task and with focus and discipline, the numbers will always average out to a 25:1 conversion rate. For every *No* you experience on a daily basis, that's a great deal of *Yes's* when you add it up over the course of a year.

Though there are several reasons why listings fail to sell and ultimately expire, again and again, the primary reasons for failure in any business are: pricing, communication, and a failure to understand the wants and needs of the client or consumer.

When prospecting for expired listings, you can learn from and capitalize on the failures of the *first agent* in order to differentiate yourself from the competition, communicate your value in a clear, concise, and compelling fashion, and assure the seller that the *second person is the best person* for the job.

When it comes to expired listings, the runner-up takes the prize—as long as you're able to secure an appointment!

It's very important that you do not make the mistake of trying to list the property over the phone. At the first stage of initial contact, the only thing you're trying to close is the appointment and persuading them to meet you in person.

Every time you're faced with an objection, handle it by using it as a *reason to meet in person*.

Closing appointments is awesome, but save yourself time conducting listing appointments that you don't have a realistic chance of converting by prequalifying the prospect in advance!

Time's a wastin'! Prospecting expired listings is all about working the numbers. Your objective is to contact as many expired listings as quickly as humanly possible each and every day.

And remember, sellers *want* to sell their home. This isn't so much a cold-call as a very warm lead.

So what are you waiting for? Start memorizing and practicing the scripts we've provided for you below, and pick up the phone today!

# Module 4

# Appendix 4.1

## Expired Listing Call Log

Name: _____  Date: _____

| | Name | Day 1 | Day 2 | Day 3 | Day 4 | Day 5 | Day 6 | Day 7 | 40 Touch SOI Database | Notes |
|---|---|---|---|---|---|---|---|---|---|---|
| 1. | | | | | | | | | ☐ | |
| 2. | | | | | | | | | ☐ | |
| 3. | | | | | | | | | ☐ | |
| 4. | | | | | | | | | ☐ | |
| 5. | | | | | | | | | ☐ | |
| 6. | | | | | | | | | ☐ | |
| 7. | | | | | | | | | ☐ | |
| 8. | | | | | | | | | ☐ | |
| 9. | | | | | | | | | ☐ | |
| 10. | | | | | | | | | ☐ | |
| 11. | | | | | | | | | ☐ | |
| 12. | | | | | | | | | ☐ | |
| 13. | | | | | | | | | ☐ | |
| 14. | | | | | | | | | ☐ | |
| 15. | | | | | | | | | ☐ | |
| 16. | | | | | | | | | ☐ | |
| 17. | | | | | | | | | ☐ | |
| 18. | | | | | | | | | ☐ | |
| 19. | | | | | | | | | ☐ | |
| 20. | | | | | | | | | ☐ | |

TOTAL: ____0____

© Copyright Icenhower Coaching & Consulting, LLC. All rights reserved.

ICENHOWER
COACHING & CONSULTING

# Module 4 — Appendix 4.2

**Name:** _____     **Daily Contact Log**     **Date:** _____

| # | Type* | Name | Ask for Appt? | Appt? | Ask for Referral | Referral? | Follow Up/Notes |
|---|---|---|---|---|---|---|---|
| 1. | Select Type | | ☐ Y / ☐ N | ☐ | ☐ Y / ☐ N | ☐ | |
| 2. | Select Type | | ☐ Y / ☐ N | ☐ | ☐ Y / ☐ N | ☐ | |
| 3. | Select Type | | ☐ Y / ☐ N | ☐ | ☐ Y / ☐ N | ☐ | |
| 4. | Select Type | | ☐ Y / ☐ N | ☐ | ☐ Y / ☐ N | ☐ | |
| 5. | Select Type | | ☐ Y / ☐ N | ☐ | ☐ Y / ☐ N | ☐ | |
| 6. | Select Type | | ☐ Y / ☐ N | ☐ | ☐ Y / ☐ N | ☐ | |
| 7. | Select Type | | ☐ Y / ☐ N | ☐ | ☐ Y / ☐ N | ☐ | |
| 8. | Select Type | | ☐ Y / ☐ N | ☐ | ☐ Y / ☐ N | ☐ | |
| 9. | Select Type | | ☐ Y / ☐ N | ☐ | ☐ Y / ☐ N | ☐ | |
| 10. | Select Type | | ☐ Y / ☐ N | ☐ | ☐ Y / ☐ N | ☐ | |
| 11. | Select Type | | ☐ Y / ☐ N | ☐ | ☐ Y / ☐ N | ☐ | |
| 12. | Select Type | | ☐ Y / ☐ N | ☐ | ☐ Y / ☐ N | ☐ | |
| 13. | Select Type | | ☐ Y / ☐ N | ☐ | ☐ Y / ☐ N | ☐ | |
| 14. | Select Type | | ☐ Y / ☐ N | ☐ | ☐ Y / ☐ N | ☐ | |
| 15. | Select Type | | ☐ Y / ☐ N | ☐ | ☐ Y / ☐ N | ☐ | |
| 16. | Select Type | | ☐ Y / ☐ N | ☐ | ☐ Y / ☐ N | ☐ | |
| 17. | Select Type | | ☐ Y / ☐ N | ☐ | ☐ Y / ☐ N | ☐ | |
| 18. | Select Type | | ☐ Y / ☐ N | ☐ | ☐ Y / ☐ N | ☐ | |
| 19. | Select Type | | ☐ Y / ☐ N | ☐ | ☐ Y / ☐ N | ☐ | |
| 20. | Select Type | | ☐ Y / ☐ N | ☐ | ☐ Y / ☐ N | ☐ | |

**TOTALS:** 0          0

**\*Type:** SOI, FSBO, Expired/Cancelled, Circle Prospecting, etc.

**Total Contacts Made:** _____

**Total Appointments Made:** 0

© Copyright Icenhower Coaching & Consulting, LLC. All rights reserved.

# ORGANIZED SALES PROCESS PHASES FLOWCHART

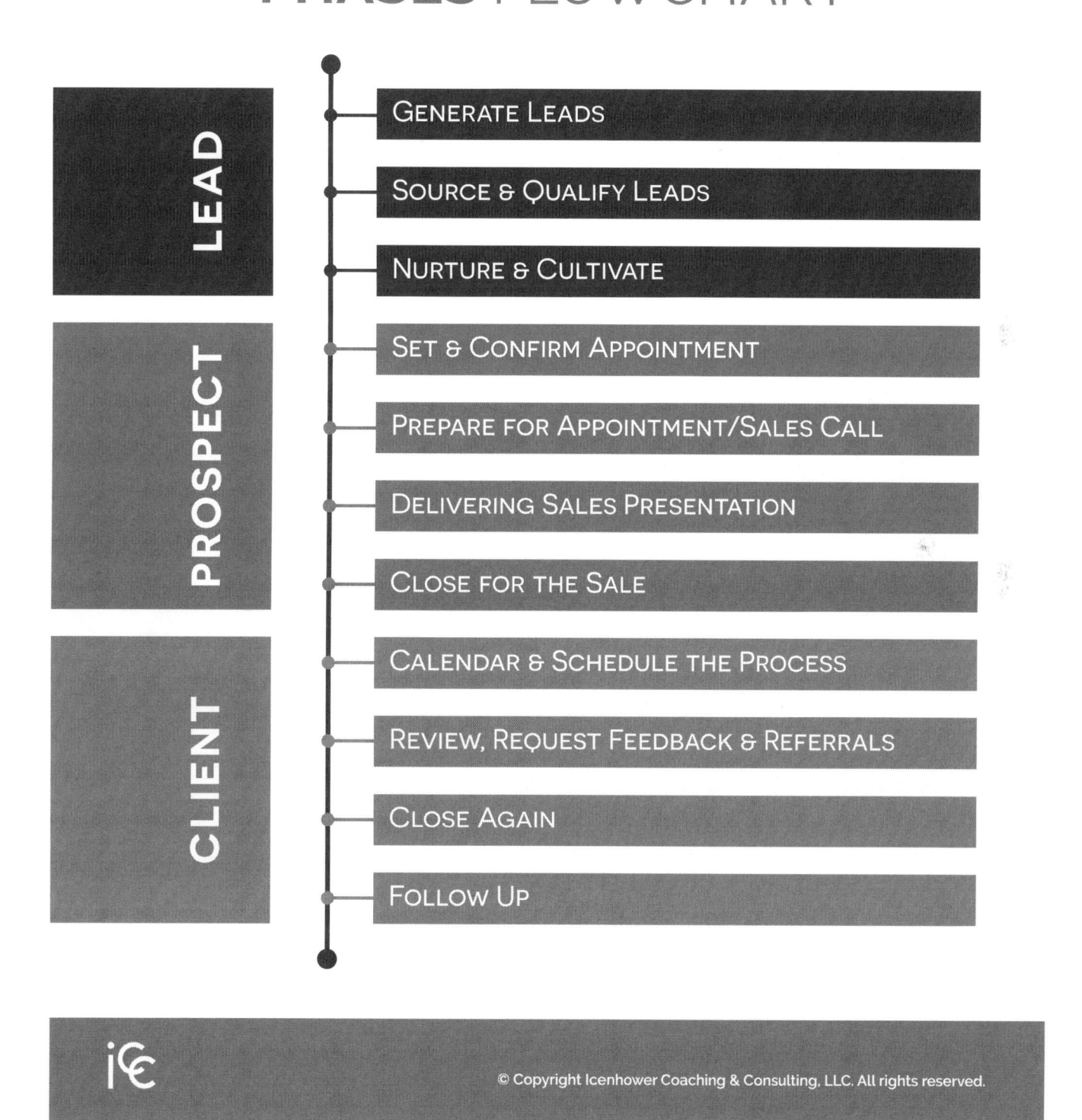

**LEAD**
- Generate Leads
- Source & Qualify Leads
- Nurture & Cultivate

**PROSPECT**
- Set & Confirm Appointment
- Prepare for Appointment/Sales Call
- Delivering Sales Presentation
- Close for the Sale

**CLIENT**
- Calendar & Schedule the Process
- Review, Request Feedback & Referrals
- Close Again
- Follow Up

© Copyright Icenhower Coaching & Consulting, LLC. All rights reserved.

# MODULE 4

# APPENDIX 4.4

## OBJECTION HANDLING & VALIDATION EMOTIONS

| Objection/Rejection | Validation | Handle & Close |
|---|---|---|
| We're leaving it off the market/taking a break. | That's an option; it's also taking a break from the plans you had when you did want to move. Where were you going? | What I'm excited to meet with you about is when you DO move to ____ , the net from your home sale is enough to buy down your next interest rate, pay for moving costs, if our program is a fit for you. Let's book time right now. |
| We're going to re-list with a friend/same agent. | What benefit do you expect to get by re-listing with the same agent? | What I'd like to do is walk you through how my system finds more options like the one I'm suggesting to you now; you can turn down all of them, if you like; I'm asking for 10 minutes to show them to you, and make it your choice. This evening is good for me. |
| We're going to sell ourselves, go FSBO. | Well, welcome to the industry! You're going to be represented in the market, maybe you'd be interested in a partnership and see what we bring to the table? | There are about 7 places you can concentrate on to avoid what happened last time; would you be open to working with me, to see if we can tackle 4 or 5 together in 15 minutes? Would you like to start tonight? |
| We're interviewing, but not dropping price. | Price is crucial; and we'll both talk about price. Let's be up front about it. | What we'll talk about first are a few key points that I'd like to show you in person… 10 minutes, and then you decide if I stay or if I go. And I can be there at 3. |

| Validation | Affirmation | Resolution |
|---|---|---|
| Having to cancel a listing is an awful feeling. | No one wants to be in a position of giving up. | I don't like to give up, either, so here's what I do for my listings… |
|  |  |  |
|  |  |  |
|  |  |  |
|  |  |  |
|  |  |  |

© Copyright Icenhower Coaching & Consulting, LLC. All rights reserved.

## LISTING CONSULTATION
### Pre-Qualification Script

1. I'd like to ask you a few quick questions to help me better prepare before our appointment. Would that be alright?

2. After you sell your home, where are you planning on moving?

3. How soon would you like to move there?

4. Do you know your current outstanding loan balance on the home?

5. At what price do you think your home should be listed for sale?

6. Could you tell me some of your home's best features and selling points?

7. Have you ever considered selling your home yourself?

8. If you are comfortable with me, are you planning on listing your home for sale when we meet?

9. Are you interviewing any other agents to sell your home?

> If "YES" then, "Are you meeting them before or after our scheduled appointment?"

10. I'll also be sending you an informational packet prior to our appointment. It will tell you a bit more about me and the services I provide, so could you look that over before we meet?

11. Do you have any questions for me at this time?

12. Great! I look forward to meeting with you on _____ at _____.

© Copyright Icenhower Coaching & Consulting, LLC. All rights reserved.

# Module 4

# Appendix 4.6

## Sample Weekly Calendar

| Time | Mon 3/13 | Tues 3/14 | Wed 3/15 | Thu 3/16 | Fri 3/17 |
|---|---|---|---|---|---|
| 6a | | | | | |
| 7a | | | | | |
| 8a | 8:30 - Prepare for Business | 8:30 - Prepare for Business | 8:30 - Prepare for Business | 8:30 - Prepare for Business | 8:30 - Prepare for Business |
| 9a | 9 — 11 Marketing/Business Generation | 9 — 11 Marketing/Business Generation | 9 — 11 Marketing/Business Generation | 9 — 11 Marketing/Business Generation | 9 — 11 Marketing/Business Generation |
| 10a | | | | | |
| 11a | 11 — 12p Business Servicing | 11 — 12p Business Servicing | 11 — 12p Business Servicing | 11 — 12p Business Servicing | 11 — 12p Business Servicing |
| 12p | 12p-1p Lunch | 12p-1p Lunch | 12p-1p Lunch | 12p-1p Lunch w/ Wife | 12p-1p Lunch |
| 1p | 1p — 2p Lead Conversion & Follow-Up | 1p — 2p Lead Conversion & Follow-Up | 1p — 2p Lead Conversion & Follow-Up | 1p — 2p Lead Conversion & Follow-Up | 1p — 2p Lead Conversion & Follow-Up |
| 2p | 2p — 3p Business Servicing | 2p — 3p Business Servicing | 2p — 3p Business Servicing | 2p — 3p Business Servicing | 2p — 3p Business Servicing |
| 3p | | | 3:30p — 6p Watch David's T-Ball Game | 3p — 4p Business Servicing | |
| 4p | 4p — 5:30p Listings Presentation - 123 Cottonwood Ct | 4p — 6p Show Homes to Johnsons | | 4:30p — 5:30p Buyer Consultation w/ Taylors | 4p — 6p Listings Presentation - 456 Spring Creek Way |
| 5p | | | | | |
| 6p | | 6:30p — 8p Family Dinner | | | 6:30p — 8:30p Family Birthday Party |
| 7p | | | | | |
| 8p | | | | | |
| 9p | | | | | |

152

© Icenhower Coaching & Consulting, LLC.

# EXPIRED LISTING
## When They Answer & Voice Message Scripts

## WHEN THEY ANSWER SCRIPTS

### SCRIPT 1:

"Hi, I'm looking for _____. This is John Smith with ABC Realty, and I'm calling because your home has come up as an expired listing. So I'm calling to see when you plan on hiring the right agent to sell your home?"

### SCRIPT 2:

"Hi, I'm John Smith with ABC Realty, and I'm calling about the house that was listed in the multiple listing service that expired. I wanted to interview for the job of getting your home back on the market and sold. Are you still interested in moving?"

### SCRIPT 3:

"Hi this is John Smith with ABC Realty, and I noticed that your listing on 123 Pepperwood Court is no longer active. I wanted to see if you are going to take this opportunity to interview a different agent. If so, I'd love to share my methods for getting homes sold quickly."

## VOICE MESSAGE SCRIPTS

### SCRIPT 1:

"I'm calling about the home for sale. My number is 555-123-4567."

### SCRIPT 2:

"Hi this is John Smith and I'm calling about the house you had listed in the multiple listing service, and I'd like to talk to you about the home. Would you please call me back as soon as possible at 555-123-4567?"

### SCRIPT 3:

"Hello this John Smith with ABC Realty, and I'm calling about your house listing that is no longer on the market. If you are interested in taking this opportunity to interview a different agent, please call me at 555-123-4567."

© Copyright Icenhower Coaching & Consulting, LLC. All rights reserved.

# MODULE 4

## APPENDIX 4.8

### EXPIRED LISTING Script

"Hello, is this Mr./Mrs. _____?"

*(Pause and continue with the script . . .)*

"The reason for my call today is because your home came up this morning as expired in the MLS. Is your home currently listed For Sale?"

**If "YES" then... "Great! Thank you for your time, and have a great day."**

**If "NO" then continue with the script...**

"Can I ask why you have not re-listed your home yet?"

*(Pause and continue with the script . . .)*

"Do you have any plans to put it back on the market?"

*(Pause and continue with the script . . .)*

"Well the reason for my call today is that I specialize in properties just like yours that didn't sell the first time around. I have a unique process for identifying and predicting the salability of a home and would be very excited to meet with you about the techniques I use to sell homes. Plus, I can help you identify exactly why your home did not sell. Does that sound like a good plan?"

*(Pause and continue with the script . . .)*

"Great, would 3:00pm today or 4:00pm tomorrow be better for you?"

© Copyright Icenhower Coaching & Consulting, LLC. All rights reserved.

# EXPIRED LISTING
## Script 2

"Hello, I'm looking for _____. This is (AGENT NAME) with (REAL ESTATE COMPANY). Of course, you know your home is no longer listed with your previous agent. So, I was wondering, when do you plan to hire an agent who will get your home sold?"

(OR)

"Hello, I'm looking for _____. This is (AGENT NAME) with (REAL ESTATE COMPANY). I noticed your home was no longer on the market for sale. I was calling to see if you still want to sell it?"

If they seem receptive, skip to the numbered questions below.
If they seem frustrated and are getting lots of calls, continue with the following questions first:

- "Are you just taking your home off the market?"
- "Do you no longer want to move?"
- "Are you getting a lot of calls?"
- "I bet you are wondering why these agents didn't show your home while it was for sale, don't you?... I totally understand. Curiously..." *(Continue below)*

1. "If you had sold this home... where would you be going?"
2. "What is your time frame to be moved?"
3. "Why do you think your home did not sell?"
4. "How did you pick your last agent?... What do you think went wrong?"
5. "Has anyone told you why they thought your home didn't sell?"
6. "Did you know that the primary reason homes don't sell is due to a lack of exposure?"
7. "If I can show you how to upgrade your exposure to get your home sold, would that be of any interest to you?"
8. "How about we meet for 20 to 30 minutes so you can see exactly what it will take to sell your home. Can I come by today at 4:00 or is 5:00 tomorrow better for you?"

© Copyright Icenhower Coaching & Consulting, LLC. All rights reserved.

# EXPIRED LISTING
## Objection Handlers

These expired listing objection handlers can be used to address the five most common objections that agents face when contacting expired listings by phone. Please review them all first since many of them can be used interchangeably as well.

### 1. OBJECTION: "We're Not Putting it Back on the Market"

1. "Really? Well if it sold, where were you moving to?"

2. "How soon did you want to be there?"

3. "What do you think stopped it from selling?"

4. "If I were to present you with a strong offer to purchase your home, would you be still be willing to at least take a look at it?"

5. "Well that's exactly what I would like to talk to you about. What would be the best time for me to quickly drop by, 4:00pm today or tomorrow?"

### 2. OBJECTION: "Waiting for the market to get better"

1. "Well I understand, this market has been challenging for some. Just out of curiosity, if you did sell, where were you moving to?"

2. "What's important to you about moving there?"

3. "You see, I specialize in selling houses that didn't sell the first time around. Many homes don't sell the first time they're on the market, and it just takes a different approach to get them sold. If I could show you a way to make that happen would you be interested?"

4. "Great! Would 4:00pm today or tomorrow work for you?"

### 3. OBJECTION: "I'm going to re-list with the same agent"

1. "I understand. It makes sense that you might feel obliged to allow your last agent another chance to sell your home. But what do you think they will do differently this time that they didn't do the last time?"

2. "Do you think that you're at least owed the opportunity to interview other agents to see what they can do differently to get homes sold at this time?"

3. "Well that's all I would like to do . . . apply for the job to get your home sold quickly and for the highest price possible. Would 4:00pm today or tomorrow work for you?"

© Copyright Icenhower Coaching & Consulting, LLC. All rights reserved.

# MODULE 4 — APPENDIX 4.10 CONTINUED

## 4. OBJECTION: "I'm going to sell it myself" (FSBO)

1. "After what you have been through I can certainly understand. What do you think went wrong the first time you had it up for sale?"

2. "Well I can certainly understand the need to make a change. But are you sure that you want to keep your home out of the multiple listing service when about 90% of all buyers use an agent to purchase homes?"

3. "You see, marketing homes to both the general public AND to other agents are crucial to getting homes sold quickly for the highest price possible. And many great houses don't sell the first time around. So don't you think it's at least worth 15 minutes to learn what I do differently to get homes sold before you make your decision?"

## 5. OBJECTION: "I've already found a different agent"

1. "I see, have you already filled out paperwork with them?" (If so, thank them and wish them good luck. If not, then continue with the script . . )

2. "Great. You know even the best houses don't sell the first time around. In fact, I specialize in selling homes that didn't sell the first time. Would you mind telling me what your next agent is planning on doing differently this time?"

3. "I see. Do you think you owe it to yourself to interview multiple agents for the job to ensure that the home sells for the highest price possible . . . at the very least for another opinion on your home's listing price?"

4. "It shouldn't take up too much of your time and I'd be happy to swing by at your convenience. Would 3:00 or 4:00pm today be good for you?"

© Copyright Icenhower Coaching & Consulting, LLC. All rights reserved.

# MODULE 4

# APPENDIX 4.11

## OLD EXPIRED LISTING
### Script

Hi, is this the owner of [Property Address]? Is this [Owner's Name]?

Great! This is [Your Name] with [Real Estate Company]. I noticed your home was recently up for sale, and we have buyers interested in your neighborhood. Because the value of your home has increased since being listed on the market, would you still consider selling your home for the right price?

[RESPONSE]

**IF YES . . .**

Great! Are you free [Day] at [Time] so I can stop by to take a quick look at your home and show you what it is now worth?

Great thanks. Looking forward to seeing you then!

**IF NO . . .**

Would it at least be of benefit to you to know what your home is worth now that the market has improved?

[RESPONSE]

OK great. Are you free [Day] at [Time] so I can stop by to take a quick look at your home and show you what it is now worth?

Great thanks. Looking forward to seeing you then!

**IF STILL NO . . .**

Ok I can certainly understand. You may have heard that real estate inventory is very low, and that there aren't enough homes for sale to keep up with buyer demand. This has caused home values to increase since your home was on the market. So can I ask why you were trying to sell your home before?

[RESPONSE]

That makes sense. We are really trying to do everything we can to find homes for our buyers. Would you even consider selling your home if you could sell it for more money than before?

[RESPONSE]

I tell you what . . . I would like to at least prepare a quick comparable sales report for you, similar to an appraisal, to show you what your home is worth now in case you do decide to sell at some point in the future. Would that be of benefit to you?

[RESPONSE]

Great. Are you free [Day] at [Time] so I can show it to you?

© Copyright Icenhower Coaching & Consulting, LLC. All rights reserved.

## Prospecting Through Open Houses

Once you've secured your listing, you will need to start thinking about marketing and showing the home that's for sale. It's time to host an Open House!

In the previous chapters, we talked about time-management and juggling business-generation along with servicing your existing clients. In this chapter, we will teach you *how to tie customer-service to lead-generation*, and show you that, regardless of their wants and needs, *everyone who walks through the door at an open house is a potential prospect.*

This chapter is divided into two distinct sections:

1. In the first section, we will put the cart before the horse somewhat and dive straight into your primary objectives and strategies while actually hosting an open house: generating leads and getting open house guests set up on an MLS Listing E-Alert email campaign. This will give you an upfront sense of one of your most important open house end-goals.

2. In the second section, we will take a step back in the timeline and discuss the preliminary logistics of hosting an open house, including scripts for scheduling an open house with your seller clients, how to market your open house and generate traffic, as well as practical considerations such as open house signage, parking, and registering visitors for security and insurance, as well as marketing, purposes.

## Learning Targets

In this chapter, you will:

- Learn how to use an open house for proactive marketing and prospecting.
- Discover tips and strategies for hosting an effective open house.
- Uncover ways to grow your SOI, convert Expired/FSBO clients, and set appointments with leads gained that day

Before we dive in, let's take a look at the rationale behind hosting an open house in the first place.

## WHY HOST AN OPEN HOUSE?

Most people have a basic understanding of the rationale for holding open houses, which tend to fall into the first two categories listed here:

**❶ Customer-Service: Open Houses Appease Sellers**

Though open houses have a statistically low chance of resulting in a sale, many sellers like and insist upon them. Oftentimes, sellers don't understand what's happening behind the scenes with their listing. If they don't see a lot of tangible, visual activity, they assume that nothing is happening and the agent isn't doing enough for their commission.

Sellers want a proactive agent that does everything within their power to market, showcase, and sell their home. Hosting an open house will satisfy their urge to be doing something tangible and concrete.

What's more, preparing a home for multiple private showings can be time-consuming and tiring. Sellers are often frustrated by the disruption and upheaval of having to keep their home constantly clean and tidy, not to mention having to leave the property to facilitate individual viewings.

Many sellers like the idea of holding an open house simply for the appeal of getting a large number of viewers through the door in a condensed period of time.

**❷ To Meet Buyers: Open Houses Attract Buyer Leads**

When you host an open house, you will meet many prospective homebuyers, but it's highly unlikely that any of them will be the ultimate buyer of the home you're showcasing. Some agents will host open houses their entire career and never once sell the home to someone who came to an open house event.

Buyers who visit open houses tend to be in the "just looking" stage. When hosting open houses, your goal is not to sell the listed house to every prospective buyer that walks in the door. Your goal is to connect with those prospects, build rapport, nurture the relationship, and help them to find a future home that they're ready, willing, and able to buy.

**❸ To Get New Listings: Open Houses Attract Seller Leads**

While the first two reasons are perfectly valid, the best reason to host an open house is not to sell this *current* listing, but to connect with sellers and get *new* listings. Holding an open house is a fantastic way to expand your sphere of influence and advertise your services to prospective sellers.

Like we said, sellers want an aggressive, proactive agent that does everything they can to market, showcase, and sell their home.

A lively, strategically organized, successful open house is the best way to show sellers how hard you will work to market and sell their home.

Listings are much more valuable than buyers. Listings generate more listings as well as more buyers. Listings take a lot less time to handle than buyers, and listings are an amazing way to get your name out there and market your brand.

Listing agents get more done in the same amount of time, using fewer resources such as fuel for commuting. In the 45 minutes it takes for a buyer's agent to show a prospect around a property that they may not even like, you can set two listing appointments from your desk during your morning prospecting phone calls. And while that buyer's agent is spending 30 minutes driving across town to another showing, you are busy converting at a listing presentation. Listing agents can also select when they want to work, but a buyer's agent is obligated to show property whenever the buyer has time—or let someone else make the sale.

Hosting an open house costs money, and so does listing a property. There's signage, lock boxes, and marketing to consider. But when you compare the totals against the expenses of being a buyer's agent, you come out ahead as a listing agent.

Listing agents are the powerhouses of the real estate industry and make most of the money. It only makes sense that you'd want to use an open house to help you get more listings—and if the listing sells from your open house, even better.

Top prospectors understand that pleasing and satisfying the seller of the home is a *byproduct* of holding an open house. Your primary motivation is to generate buyer leads and listing leads *as a result* of your great customer-service.

### ④ *Audit Your Systems: Open Houses Are A Great Way to Test Your Strategies*

In addition to the primary reasons above, open houses are a great way to audit your prospecting systems and strategies. The success of your open house will give you a feel for how you rank when it comes to marketing results, organization, and execution.

You can also audit your reach. Who showed up that was invited from each group you targeted? Were you able to get their contact information? How many open house guests are bona fide leads or prospects?

You can also gain insight about your interactions with prospects in a compressed timeline. How well do you convert an open house guest to an appointment, to a showing, to a listing presentation?

By the end of this chapter, you will have increased your skill set for all of these things.

# TRY BEFORE YOU BUY: THE PSYCHOLOGY BEHIND OPEN HOUSES

People love free experiences and—perhaps more importantly—risk-free experiences. Good prospectors understand the psychology of 'free' and 'risk-free' when it comes to hosting open houses. An open house is the real estate equivalent of a free sample or a product demonstration.

Internet marketers know that the word "FREE" draws a viewer's eyes to exactly where you want them to go on a website's page, and entices them to click on subsequent links or provide their contact information in exchange for something free and appealing to them.

In fact, it need not even appeal to them or have been something they were previously aware of or interested in. Psychologically, the human brain is hardwired to have an emotional charge when it is getting something in exchange for nothing.

> *Good prospectors understand the psychology of 'free' and 'risk-free' when it comes to hosting open houses. An open house is the real estate equivalent of a free sample or a product demonstration.*

At the same time, however, human beings are also generally hardwired to practice reciprocity: if someone does something for you, you will most likely feel obliged to do (or give) something for them in return—if not now then at some point in the future.

Studies repeatedly show a connection between increased sales and in-store samplings and product-demonstrations.

Samples and product-demonstrations allow consumers to taste a new craft beer, or visually experience how a kitchen appliance works, without having to buy it first. In certain cases, product-demonstrations enable people to temporarily experience an extremely expensive product for free—such as test-driving a luxury sports car or, in the case of an open house, experiencing a dream home.

Psychologically, the opportunity to "try before you buy" is very reassuring and instills a sense of trust and positive rapport in the consumer.

# WHAT DO PRODUCT DEMO'S DO?

### JUMPSTART

A potential client who takes time to watch a product demonstration is in the earliest stage of consideration. **An open house is a very robust way of raising someone's interest level.**

### IPO OFFER

People are paying for the demo; there may not be a cover charge at the door, they're still spending time and energy to be there. It's an initial investment.

### TRIGGER

A Product Demo serves two purposes: help the consumer make the decision to buy or sell and determine whom they want to buy or sell with. At an open house, your goal is to motivate them to buy or sell—and to choose you as their representative.

### HELP ME HELP YOU

People want to research in a no-pressure environment, but still have a specialist available to answer their questions; it's why auto shows are so popular. **At an open house, you're on hand to explain your services while allowing the guest to look and think with no obligation.**

### REFERRALS FOR HIRE

Product Demos are the birthplace of social proof. People may not be personally interested in a purchase or sale—they might just like the product or are fascinated by the process—**but they will, in turn, go back and tell family and friends what they saw, and initiate a referral, based off their recommendation.**

While it's true that not everyone who test-drives the latest Lamborghini has the means or even the desire to actually purchase one, studies show that most people who sample a free product do go on to purchase that product, if not right away then at some point in the near future.

People are curious about the lives of others. Wandering around an open house satisfies that curiosity and also allows people to imagine how different their life might be.

Even people who were not previously interested in buying or selling their home cannot help but be drawn into open houses just for the free experience of temporarily living a different life. Though they may not be in a position to buy right now, most people will appreciate this experience and return the favor by thinking of you at some point in the future.

*Human beings are hardwired to practice reciprocity: if someone does something for you, you will most likely feel obliged to do—or give—something for them in return, if not now then at some point in the future.*

At the same time, open houses allow you to showcase your product and services to more serious buyers and sellers. Seeing you in action at a successful open house allows sellers to experience firsthand what you would do for them as their representative. Effectively, they can try you out as their agent, risk-free, before signing on the dotted line and committing to you.

## PREPARE FOR CONVERSION

In real estate, an open house refers to an occasion when a property that is for sale can be viewed by prospective-buyers without a prior scheduled appointment. More generally, an open house simply refers to any place or situation in which all visitors are welcome.

When you host an open house, all visitors are welcome regardless of their current readiness, willingness, or ability to buy or sell a home. From drive-by traffic and curious neighbors, to prospective buyers and scrutinizing sellers, no matter who they are, everyone who walks through the front door of an open house is a welcome guest and a potential prospect.

Typically, when agents are thinking about hosting an open house, they will begin by focusing on how to generate traffic and getting people to come to the event itself. We'll get to the logistics of the event a little later in the chapter, but we're going to put the cart before the horse for a moment.

Before you think about *how* to get people to an open house, it's crucial that you develop your open house mindset in advance and understand *what you want to gain* from the event. You can prepare for conversion by setting goals for each of the different people that will eventually come by.

No matter their starting point, your goal is to take each individual to the next level in the process and incorporate them into a systematic contact plan. Here's an at-a-glance snapshot of your starting point and next level goals for each potential open house guest.

| STARTING POINT | NEXT LEVEL |
| --- | --- |
| Drive-By Traffic | • Open House Guest |
| Open House Guest | • Registered Visitor |
| Registered Visitor | • Nurture, lead, and prospect |
| Invited Buyer/Seller Lead | • Buyer/Seller Appointment<br>• Add to Listing E-Alert Email Drip Campaign |
| Buyer Lead | • Local Listing Showing Appointment<br>• Listing E-Alert Email Drip Campaign |

| Seller Lead | • Lead/Prospect<br>• Add to Listing E-Alert Email Drip Campaign |
|---|---|
| Neighbors | • SOI Member<br>• Add to Listing E-Alert Email Drip Campaign |
| Listing Client | • Satisfied Listing Client Willing to Refer Business<br>• Add to SOI Contact Plan |
| Expired Listing Lead | • Prospect for Listing Appointment<br>• Add to Listing E-Alert email drip campaign<br>• Subsequent SOI member. |
| FSBO listing | • Prospect for Listing Appointment<br>• Add to Listing E-Alert email drip campaign<br>• Subsequent SOI member |

As you can see, your primary goals at an open house are to register visitors and get their contact information, as well as getting them signed up to all-important MLS Listing E-Alerts.

We'll go over visitor registration when we discuss some of the logistics of holding an open house. For now, let's focus on MLS Listing E-Alerts, as this is a crucial component for converting open house contacts into clients. Preparing for conversion will involve practicing E-Alert scripts and talking points when interacting with the different people that come by.

## YOUR MLS LISTING EMAIL ALERT DRIP CAMPAIGN

Most MLS platforms provide a free tool that allows realtors to input the name, property address, and contact information of a client.

It also allows agents to set up their contacts on MLS Listing Alerts—an automated notification that alerts a contact to new listings or price changes for properties that match specific search criteria, such as ZIP code, list price, bed and bath count, as well as any number of features, specifications, and amenities.

When a home that matches their search criteria hits the MLS, clients get an email or even a text message that is branded to the agent.

MLS Listing Alerts are a wonderful engagement tool, and it's always a great idea to set up as many of your contacts on them as possible. At any open house, your goal is to get *at least 50% of all visitors* set up on an MLS Listing E-Alert Drip Campaign.

### PROCESS OVERVIEW

As you chat with guests at the open house, let them know that this one house is just a sample of what's available on the market.

- Ask about the visitor's specific needs, and run a quick MLS search to demonstrate

what's available in the area (remember the power of the product demo).
- Offer to set up appointments to go see the homes (for Buyers).
- You can also set up an appointment to meet at your office (for Buyers and Sellers).

You can collect their contact information and search-criteria using your Buyer & Seller Questionnaire & Lead Sheets (provided to you in chapter 2).

Or, better yet, you can *set up your laptop so that you can do a Listing Alert "product demonstration" in real-time*, explaining how the system works and its many features and benefits.

It's very important to sell your Listing E-Alert feature to *everyone* that comes through the open house. Whether they're a curious neighbor or a current member of your SOI, an invited buyer lead, or an expired seller lead, each type of visitor will have slightly different wants and needs.

But no matter who they are, just about everybody will fall into one of two categories: *they're either a prospective buyer or a prospective seller.*

Any visitor can be set up on one or other of these drip campaigns, so that you are sending them emails about either the kind of homes they're hoping to buy, or about their existing home and the local, neighborhood real estate seller's market.

In fact, *it's perfectly possible to set up prospective sellers on both types of searches.* Sellers are typically looking to buy another property after (or while) their current home is being sold, so you can keep the same person up-to-date on their local real estate market, as well as setting them up on a search for homes that they may want to purchase.

You can *prepare for conversion* by practicing different Listing Alert scripts and talking points for different types of guests. As always, it's a good idea to practice and internalize these scripts and talking points, so that your product demonstration is delivered smoothly and with the particular individual in mind.

---

### MLS & IDX

Many agents opt to purchase their own personal website and Customer Relationship Management (CRM) software tool that provides a similar E-Alert feature through an IDX feed with the local Multiple Listing Service.

Essentially, IDX enables members of an MLS to integrate real estate listings from the MLS database to their own personal website. It then feeds the data for all the same listings through the agent's website and CRM system to individuals that a real estate agent sets up on a similar home search auto-drip email campaign.

IDX is a fantastic tool and can draw viewers to your personal website.

However, IDX is not simply software. The term IDX also includes policies, rules, and standards for the display of listing information on websites. The National Association of Realtors (NAR) has a comprehensive list of rules and regulations pertaining to IDX. Examples include:

- Posting a seller's listing when a seller has not approved to have their home listed in IDX.
- Altering information included in IDX listings.
- Showing listings on a website that is not approved for display by the MLS or listing broker.

It's important that agents understand that these (and many more) regulations exist. Consult with your MLS about their particular policies and prohibitions around the use of their data on your personal website.

## Buyer Leads

There are not many realtors that would look for property by going to open houses. When agents are representing a buyer who is looking for a home, the first thing they do is look in the Multiple Listing Service (MLS). To be frank, buyer's agents very rarely look anywhere else.

Most buyers are more than willing to spend hours pouring over websites in search of their perfect home. Savvy real estate agents can facilitate the buyers' time investment by providing *insider online access* to homes.

This is the most traditional use of the Listing E-Alert tool. Agents have been using it for a decade or so, and it's a wonderful way to really drill down on the specifics that buyers are looking for—everything from a three-car garage to a swimming pool.

> *Savvy real estate agents can facilitate the buyers' time investment by providing insider online access to homes.*

Listing Alerts are a great way to offer value to prospective homebuyers as they provide a much more efficient way of looking for property, and the quality of property data on MLS listings is much higher than average search sites like Zillow.

Real estate agents can create bespoke browsing opportunities for interested buyers, but that's not all. You can also track buyer interest in real estate. The real estate agent provides a browsing service that buyers appreciate, and you can also collect valuable data on what buyers are looking for.

Agents can see when buyers are searching and how active they are in a couple of ways. If you have purchased a personal website and CRM system, you will be notified when buyers are actively looking on your website. Even with the free MLS Listing Alert tool, you can usually log in to see if they've saved any searches or are tracking particular properties.

> *Data helps you to better understand the wants and needs of each particular person. It also provides you with an opportunity to follow up and reach out to that person.*

This data helps you to better understand the wants and needs of each particular person. It also provides you with an opportunity to follow up and reach out to that person and continue to build relationship and rapport.

It might be a few months or even a year or two before buyers are actively searching. When setting up buyers on an E-Alert drip campaign, don't discriminate based on their buying timeframe. It costs nothing to set people up and start to create value for them today.

## Buyer MLS Listing Alert Script

The script below is designed to encourage buyers to search with *your tool* as opposed to the competing tools that are available to them when they just randomly go online looking for homes.

It's very important that you sell your tool to them because, often, people will just go online and search some of the many free, public websites out there, like Zillow, Redfin, and Trulia. Prospects need to be informed that those are *limited websites* where they don't get to see all the homes that are listed for sale, and not all the information contained on those sites is accurate.

What you are providing them is a direct feed into the Multiple Listing Service, allowing them to see *all the information that their real estate agent sees and in real time.* When a new listing comes up for sale, they're going to be alerted and see that property at the same time that real estate agents see it. They will be up-to-date and every listing will be Active.

It's very important to inform them that homes they see on secondary sites are typically *already sold* by the time they get to the public free websites. Often the best homes, in the best condition, and at the lowest prices go too fast for those sites.

This is a great selling point for your site. It is a constant source of frustration to real estate agents that their clients call them and say they were on Zillow and they want to see this or that specific house. The real estate agent says, "That house sold long ago" or "It sold two weeks ago," yet it's still showing up as an Active listing that just hit Zillow and other public sites. It really frustrates clients too, so you can provide value by giving them access. Use this frustration as an opportunity to set them up on your branded email drip campaign.

The script and talking points we provide will help you to clearly articulate the point: *that they won't miss out on homes that have already sold quickly and you're going to give them FREE realtor access.*

**Memorize and use the following script for open house guests that want to purchase a home, whether they are a first-time homebuyer or a repeat buyer:**

## Buyer MLS Listing Alert Script

"The most desirable homes listed at the lowest prices sell the fastest, so you don't ever get to see them on Zillow and other secondary websites. **Homes on those websites are actually the homes that most people did not want**. You see, all home listings are initially listed in the REALTOR®'s Multiple Listing Service (MLS) online database of homes for sale. Then the listing information is sent through digital feeds to other secondary sources, and then on to these other websites. This is why the information on these sites is often incorrect and a week or two old. That's why websites like Zillow do not have the same amount of listings as our MLS does. If you are looking for homes on Zillow, you're just seeing the leftovers that no one else wanted. Are you following me?"

"Plus, many offices, companies, and associations of REALTORS® do not allow digital feeds to go to secondary websites like Zillow. **Not only do you miss out on the homes that have already sold quickly, but there are many active listings that you can't see at all**. Does all that make sense?"

"If you want to **see all the listings the minute they go up for sale and get FULL REALTOR® ACCESS**, I can easily set you up on our buyer search tool. Then **you can see what the real estate agents see, as soon as they see it**. You can **look at the homes online in the privacy of your own home, on your own time, with absolutely no pressure** or obligation. I can even set the system up to send you email notifications the minute new homes hit the market that fit the specific criteria you are looking for in a home. If you happened to want to see the inside of one of them, you can just reply to the email or call me and we'll get you inside quickly. Would that be a benefit to you?"

"This way you'll also be able to learn about the prices of homes in different neighborhoods to **become a more informed buyer**. You'll start to **see what's a good deal and what's not, how quickly certain homes sell in different areas and price ranges**. Once you see what you can get for your dollar, you'll also be able to drive around on the weekends and check out some of the neighborhoods on your own time. Look at the school districts, nearby shopping, and other amenities. You can take your time with this if you want. How does that sound?"

## Seller Leads

When it comes to prospective sellers, your core message when signing them up to an automated email drip campaign is:

*"This tool will help you stay educated about your home's value and your neighborhood's conditions leading up to whenever you are ready to move."*

MLS Listing E-Alerts keep sellers up-to-date on their neighborhood's real estate market. Listing Alerts keep them apprised of how quickly homes are selling and the prices that they're selling for. Listing Alerts allow prospects to compare the local competition, so that they are educated when it comes time for them to sell.

Often, sellers will delay moving until they can get a certain price for their home. Listing Alerts (along with your guidance when following-up with them) can help them to make informed decisions about when to make their move. Watching other listings go from "For Sale" to "Pending" to "Sold" can motivate hesitant sellers to take the leap they've been waiting for.

> *Watching other listings go from "For Sale" to "Pending" to "Sold" can motivate hesitant sellers to take the leap they've been waiting for.*

All the while, this valuable tool has your name and branding attached to it, keeping you top of mind for when the time comes. It also gives you a great excuse to follow up and call them from time to time, building rapport through talking about the tool and gathering feedback about how well it's working for them. Once you have established a relationship and solid name-recognition, you can then add them to your 40-touch SOI database.

Oftentimes, sellers of Expired Listings or FSBO sellers will visit an open house to check out the local competition. It's very important to get these sellers started on an email drip campaign, because you know for certain that they definitely want to sell their home, or at least they recently did. Explain the above benefits of MLS Listing Alerts, and maintain a close follow-up relationship with these prospects in the following days and weeks.

> *Listing Alerts can be used for any prospect, no matter how soon they want to buy or sell.*

Having said that, Listing Alerts can be used for *any prospect*, no matter how soon they want to buy or sell, or even for curious neighbors who are happy where they are for the foreseeable future but popped into the open house out of simple curiosity.

Often, real estate agents will dismiss low-urgency or disinterested leads that are a long way out from selling. They don't make any effort and allow them to leave the open house, forgotten. Rather, you should take the long view and approach these leads from a place of value and contribution to get them ready for that future sale.

Any time you meet someone who says, "Oh, we're thinking about moving, yes, but not for another year or two," your prepared response should simply be:

> *"Well, we actually have something to help you in the meantime. We have a tool that'll help you stay educated and up-to-date on your housing market until you are ready to move."*

Tap into the neighbors' curiosity by explaining that any time one of their neighbor's homes goes up for sale, they will be automatically notified, and they'll be able to look through pictures of the home and see how much it's listing for, as well as any subsequent price-changes. This way, they can start to think about how that price will impact the price of their home, and keep track of the value of their property over time, with a view to selling down the road.

Listing Alerts provide an effortless way to track and follow up and slowly build rapport with each other. This tool adds value through information and education until they are ready to sell. It puts your name out in front of the pack.

Often, you'll find that people actually want to move sooner than they told you. In real estate, a good rule of thumb is to cut the time they tell you in half: if they tell you two years, it really means one, and if they tell you one year, it really means six months.

> *Setting prospects up on Listing Alerts is a subtle, risk-free way for you to give them something without them feeling obligated. They can 'shop' in the privacy of their own home, on their own time.*

People tend to push the timeline further on down the road, just like when you try to keep a clerk away from you in a store, by saying, "I'm just looking." Well, no, you're not just looking. You're buying very soon, or you wouldn't be in the store. Very few people just go to a store to browse. They ultimately want to buy, but they want to browse around and shop undisturbed on their own for a while.

That's what these prospective seller leads are really saying: "We're not ready just yet. We don't want to feel pressured or obligated." Setting prospects up on Listing Alerts is a subtle, risk-free way for you to give them something of value without them feeling obligated. They can 'shop' in the privacy of their own home, on their own time, with no pressure.

Ideally, you would set up as many prospective sellers as possible while at the open house itself. However, as long as you have their basic contact information, you can always set them up on a Listing Alert email drip campaign later that evening or in the following couple of days.

Use the following script/email template to notify prospective home sellers that you have set them up on the MLS Listing Alert/Neighborhood Update Tool. Explain or remind them about how the service works, and make sure to emphasize the value of staying educated and up-to-date in order to be better prepared for their eventual selling decision:

## SELLER LEAD AUTO EMAIL DRIP SCRIPT

Hi it's [AGENT NAME] with [REAL ESTATE COMPANY],

I wanted to give you a heads up that I've set you up on our new **Neighborhood Update Tool** and would love to hear your feedback on it. My clients really love it. This tool will really **help you stay educated about your home's value and your neighborhood's conditions leading up to whenever you are ready to move**. It might even help you decide when you want to put your home up for sale!

Here's how it works: when one of your neighbors puts their home up for sale, you'll immediately get an email with all the listing information and photos of the home. This way, you'll be able to:

1. Look through all the **photos of your neighbor's homes**;
2. Compare the **amenities, features & size** of the listings to your own home;
3. Know the **price of each new listing** to get a rough idea of the current value of your own home;
4. See **how quickly each home sells**, and the **prices that they ultimately sell for**;
5. This will give you a good idea of **how the value of your home is increasing** from month-to-month;
6. It will also **keep you up to date** on your local neighborhood's market conditions.

I really think you'll find this customer service tool useful since most of my clients already do. If for some reason you decide that you'd rather not receive these updates, you can unsubscribe yourself or just simply reply to an email and we'll discontinue it for you. However, I'd love to hear what you think about it first.

All that I need from you is to verify that I have the correct home address and email address for you. Sound good?

## YOUR NEIGHBORHOOD UPDATE TOOL AUTO-EMAIL DRIP SCRIPT

When presented as a 'Neighborhood Update Tool', just about anyone you know that owns a home can be set up on a seller lead auto-email drip campaign.

The above Seller Lead Auto-Email Drip Script should really go to *anyone* who is thinking about moving in the near future. In fact, like we said, it can even be used for someone who's not thinking about moving at all. Regardless of their desire to sell, people still like to be up-to-date on their neighborhood.

*When presented as a "Neighborhood Update Tool," just about anyone you know that owns a home can be set up on a seller lead auto-email drip campaign.*

That is why neighborhood homeowners stop into open houses down the street. They like to be informed about the place that they live, or they're quite simply nosy—there's no shame in that!

People like to know what the homes that come up for sale in their neighborhood are like. They like to know their prices. They like to compare their own home's condition and amenities to those other homes. They like to see how quickly homes are selling, and to look through photos of their neighbors' kitchens and living rooms. Listing E-Alerts allow them to do that from the privacy of their own home.

When members of your SOI come to one of your open houses, you can sell the "neighborhood update" aspect of the Listing E-Alert feature to them too (or at any other point in your relationship for that matter, it doesn't have to be at an open house).

> *By staying up-to-date with local listings, your friends, family, and acquaintances will be able to let their friends, family, and acquaintances know the minute a neighborhood home goes on the market.*

What's more, real-time E-Alerts can give members of your SOI first crack at picking their next neighbor. This is a fantastic selling point for valued members of your SOI. By staying up-to-date with local listings, your friends, family, and acquaintances will be able to let their friends, family, and acquaintances know the minute a neighborhood home goes on the market. And, naturally, you'll be the agent in first place position to help those people purchase!

The above Seller Lead/Neighborhood Update Tool scripting can be used to create a value proposition based on their own neighborhood information for members of your sphere of influence. It also creates a means for you to stay in contact with them, and to have your name at the top of their mind over time, both by email and phone. As you can see, the script contains 6 key value proposition points.

1. They can look through all the **photos of their neighbors' homes**.
2. They can compare the **amenities, features, and size** of the listings that come up for sale to their own homes.
3. They can know the **price** of each new listing to get a rough idea of the current value of their own home.
4. They can see **how quickly homes sell** and the final sale prices.
5. It will give them a good idea of how the **value of their home is increasing** over time.
6. It will keep them up-to-date on their local **neighborhood market conditions**.

These value proposition points should roll off your tongue every time you talk to an SOI member that you want to set up on a search.

Once you can get an SOI member set up on a search, your name will stay top-of-mind when they think of real estate, because they'll frequently be receiving emails from you

You can also present these value proposition points in a number of other ways:

- The six points could be stated quickly in a **purposeful phone call** made to each open house visitor/member of your SOI.

- Include the six points on a **mailer or postcard**, such as an invitation to "be on the lookout" because you've set them up on an automated search for their neighborhood as a customer-service that you provide to all your clients.

- Use the script in an **introductory email** before the drip campaign begins.

- Send the six points as a **digital image** that is sent as a personal message or as a **private message on Facebook** to every member of your SOI that is a Facebook friend.

Again, it's a game of touches. The more people that you have on these drip campaigns, the more contacts you will make, which will increase the likelihood that your SOI members will use you to sell their next home or refer business to you.

We'll round out this chapter with some additional ways that you can follow up and capitalize on the connections that you've made at the open house. For now, let's take a step back to before the open house has happened and look at the different ways you can generate traffic—and generate business—prior to the event itself.

## GENERATE TRAFFIC—GENERATE BUSINESS

Always maintain the mindset that the primary purpose of an open house is to *connect customer-service to lead-generation*. We cannot stress this enough.

When generating traffic and awareness of an upcoming open house, you are not only pleasing and appeasing the client, but you are also generating business and awareness of your name and services.

As you can see from the table below, there are numerous ways to generate business while generating traffic for an open house. Every activity you do around building interest for the open house will also generate more buyer and seller interest too.

### EXERCISE: Make Your Message

When the time comes for you to host your first open house, treat this table as a checklist or exercise of open house prospecting activities to complete.

- As you can see from the table, in addition to personally inviting people to visit the open house, you should also encourage them to invite their friends and family to come to the event too. The more the merrier!

- Keep the conversation going by asking questions about their plans to move and showing curiosity and a desire to help.

- You should also create an opportunity in the conversation to get their contact information and invite them into your SOI contact plan.

| Prospect/Target | Core Message | Details/ Calls to Action |
|---|---|---|
| Circle Prospecting 1 mile around open house | You're invited to see what's available in the market, and my service level. | Visit the home/invite who you know to the open house. |
| | | Tell me about your plans to move. |
| | | Join my SOI, learn about the market. |
| Neighbors on Same Street | You're invited to see what's available in the market, and my service level. | Visit the home/invite who you know to the open house. |
| | | Tell me about your plans to move. |
| | | Join my SOI, learn about the market. |
| Expired listing prospects | You're invited to test my systems, service, and what's on the market. | Visit the home/invite who you know to the open house. |
| | | Interview me through seeing what I do. |
| | | Join my SOI, learn about the market. |
| FSBO listing prospects | You're invited to test my systems, service, and what's on the market. | Visit the home/invite who you know to visit the Home. |
| | | Interview me through seeing what I do. |
| | | Join my SOI, learn about the market. |
| SOI members | You're invited to test my systems, service, and what's on the market. | Visit the home/invite who you know to visit the home. |
| | | Tell me about your plans to move. |
| | | Learn about the market. |
| Current Nurtures | You're invited to test my systems, service, and what's on the market. | Visit the home/invite who you know to visit the open house. |
| | | Tell me about your plans to move. |
| | | Join my SOI, learn about the market |
| Affiliates | You're invited to test my systems, service, and what's on the market. | Visit the home/invite who you know to visit the open house. |
| | | Showcase your service to potential clients. |
| | | Join my SOI as a preferred service member |

Bear in mind that we explore many of these business-generating activities in much greater detail in other chapters. We have already presented strategies for nurturing current prospects in chapter 1, and we discussed SOI and Expired Listing business-generation in chapters 3 and 4. Chapters 8 and 9 will teach you everything you need to know about FSBO Prospecting and Circle Prospecting.

For now, simply understand that, no matter what activity you engage in, your core message when prospecting around open houses is effectively the same: *"You're invited to see what's available on the market, and my service level."*

But, depending on the prospect, the details of that core message may be slightly different.

## NEIGHBORS

A week before the event, knock on the doors in the nearby area. Introduce yourself and explain the purpose of the open house and when/where it's located. When inviting nearby neighbors to the open house, your message will explain that the ultimate purchaser of a home is usually a friend, family member or acquaintance of somebody that already lives in the neighborhood, so you're dropping by to personally invite them and give them the inside scoop in case they know of someone who they'd love to be their new neighbor.

Keep this in mind: *You are inviting the neighbors to come and observe you in action.*

You want them to see how hard you are working to sell this home, and you'd do the same for them when they list their home with you.

Worried about being tongue-tied when it comes to talking to the neighbors? Not a problem. Use these open house scripts to help you say the right things and assure prospects that you're the right person for the job.

### Neighbor Invitation to Your Open House

*"Hi, I'm John Smith with ABC Realty. We have your neighbor's home at 123 Main Street up for sale and we are holding a special open house on Saturday from 11:00am to 3:00pm.*

*Since we know that the ultimate purchaser of a home is often a friend, family member or acquaintance of someone that already lives in the same neighborhood, we are inviting the entire neighborhood to come by to take a look.*

*So if you happen to know or meet someone looking to move into your community, this is a great way for you to hand-pick pick your own neighbors!*

*Do you think you can swing by?"*

Wait for response and proceed with . . .

If Yes: *"Great! And since we are doing everything we can to get your neighbor's home sold, I promised my seller that I'd ask: Do you know anyone looking to buy or sell a home in the area?"*

If No: *"No problem, I totally understand. And since we are doing everything we can to get your neighbor's home sold, I promised my seller that I'd ask: Do you know anyone looking to buy or sell a home in the near future?"*

But remember, not only are you extending an invitation, you are also trying to generate business and new listings. When talking to people in the neighborhood, it's a great idea to follow up by offering to help them with a pre-listing appointment.

As you can see from the following script, this isn't a hard sell but very much in keeping with the spirit of the no-pressure, no-obligation feeling of an open house.

## Script for Asking for a Pre-Listing Appointment

[Possible Follow Up Question]: "And by the way, it's my intent to specialize & focus my practice in this neighborhood. So I'm providing all of the homeowners a complimentary value of $500 with the hope that they might consider interviewing me when and if they ever decide to sell their home in the future. You see, an appraiser would typically charge you around $500 to appraise your home, and I'm attempting to help you alleviate that cost to determine what your home would be worth in this market. Would knowing your home's current value be of any benefit to you?"

If they are hesitant or otherwise object, proceed with . . .

[Objection Handler] "I see, and I want to assure you that there would be absolutely no obligation on your part. Again, this is a courtesy service that I am providing to all your neighbors with the hope that if you decided to sell 5, 10 or 20 years down the road, you would consider interviewing me for the job.

I would also never want you to straighten up your home just for me. I'm a REALTOR® and we're very used to viewing homes long before they're ready to show. I assure you it won't affect the value at all, and I'll be in and out in minutes. How does that sound?"

If they are interested proceed with . . .

[If Yes]: "Great! Would 3:00 or 5:00 tomorrow work better for you?"

Also be sure to obtain all of their contact information so that you can add them to your client database management system to stay in touch with them over time.

If No: "No problem, consider this a standing offer, so feel free to contact me if you are ever curious about your home's current value. In the meantime, can I count on you to let me know if you bump into anyone looking to move into the area so that we can get your neighbor's home sold?"

Wait for a response then "Great! I truly appreciate your time and help.

## CIRCLE PROSPECTING

When speaking with neighbors and circle prospecting around a neighborhood, make sure to show everyone that you're doing everything you can to get this home sold for the highest price possible to keep their property values going up. Not only are you selling their neighbor's home but you are also coming from a place of general neighborhood contribution.

The following script can be paired with the scripts above when circle prospecting around a neighborhood. This script illustrates how to maintain an open-ended, curiosity-driven conversation and create space in the dialog for obtaining their contact information.

## Open House Circle-Prospecting Script

**Real Estate Agent:** Hi (Home Owner), this is (Agent Name) with (Real Estate Company) and I just listed Emily and Joe's house around the corner from you. The sellers wanted me to invite you to our grand opening this weekend from eleven to one.

**Homeowner:** Oh okay.

**Real Estate Agent:** Yeah hopefully you can make it by. Tell me how long have you been in the neighborhood?

**Homeowner:** We lived here for about five years now.

**Real Estate Agent:** Five years, good for you! Well you know when a great property like this appears, when we list we generally expect to get two to four motivated buyers that will miss out on the property. Do you know of any other neighbors in the neighborhood that may be thinking about selling in this hot market?

**Homeowner:** Well…. You know I can't think of anybody right now. Every one that lives here loves it here.

**Real Estate Agent:** It is a great neighborhood. As for you (Home Owner) if you were to move where would you go next?

**Homeowner:** I don't know; we really like it here. I guess someday once the kids are gone we might move. I was thinking maybe in the country once the kids are out and out of the school district. I would go out to the country and become a country guy.

**Real Estate Agent:** A country guy! Good for you, so are your kids about to graduate? When do you plan on moving out there?

**Homeowner:** They will probably graduate in four years. Well they just started high school.

**Real Estate Agent:** Excellent, well hey, I'd love to follow up with you from time to time and see if anything changes. Just in case you want to talk before I call you back would it be ok if I send you my contact information?

**Homeowner:** Sure that's fine.

**Real Estate Agent:** Great what's the best email for you?

**Homeowner:** You could reach me at Homeowner@Emailaddress.com

**Real Estate Agent:** Perfect. Well come on out (Homeowner). We look forward to seeing you. Hopefully you can make it on Saturday. We'll be over at 123 Main St. and would love to meet you there.

### Expired Listing Leads & FSBO Prospects

Make sure to personally invite expired listing prospects and encourage them to come and see what you will do for them as their representative. Think of it as a less formal, more interactive job interview. Present the invitation as a risk-free product demonstration with no pressure or obligation.

The same applies for FSBO prospects—your message will encourage them to come and see what you will do for them if they decide to hire an agent to represent them.

You might also consider inviting nearby FSBO prospects to host a joint open house where you promise to send traffic from your open house their way if they agree to send traffic your way too. Present this message as a win-win and remind them that, typically, two open houses generate a lot more traffic than one. This is a great way to initiate contact and build rapport with a potential FBSO client.

## SOI Members

Remember that you're always looking for reasons to stay in front of your SOI and show them that you're successful as go the extra mile to market homes for sale. Invite your SOI to open houses with a variety of contact methods, from emails to phone calls. Remember that the purpose is not to sell them the property, but to keep your name top of mind with your SOI members.

## Affiliates

It's a great idea to invite your affiliates to an open house. Again, your purpose is not necessarily to sell them the listed property, but to stay top of mind. Additionally, affiliates can contribute to your open house marketing expenses, whether it's a Title & Escrow company, a preferred lender, or a home warranty company.

Your affiliates are in a position to refer you a lot of business, so getting them involved with open houses and co-marketing is a wise decision. Give your invited vendors an opportunity to showcase their work. If, for example, a carpet cleaning company has shampooed the carpets before the open house, ask for promotional materials. Encourage the landscaper to drop in to talk to prospects.

Remember that you're not only marketing the open house, you're generating business. Prospecting is a game of contacts, and the more contacts you can make around an open house, the better.

Above all, no matter what type of prospect you're talking to, or what type of business-generating activity you're performing, *your purpose is to show people how hard you work to sell your listed properties, and all the extra effort you put into generating interest, exposure, and traffic for an open house.*

Each of these activities presents an opportunity to *tie customer-service to lead-generation*, establish name-recognition, present your services, and demonstrate that you are an agent that will go above and beyond to get homes sold.

In the next section, we will show you some additional ways that you can market and advertise an open house for maximum traffic and exposure.

## Marketing & Advertising

When marketing an open house, guess again if you think it's simply a case of sticking a sign in the front yard!

There are many opportunities and communication channels you can use to market and advertise an open house event, not to mention marketing yourself.

In fact, most marketing activity is done for two reasons: (1) to appease and please your seller clients who want to see you doing everything you can to market their home, and (2) to generate business and branding for you as an agent.

When you market a listing for sale, or advertise an open house, you're not only marketing the property, you're also marketing yourself and weaving a variety of lead-generation opportunities into your customer-service obligations.

What's more, when marketing an open house, you're marketing to more people than you think you are.

How many times have you seen a property and thought: *"I know exactly who this house is perfect for"*?

The people who come to your open houses will do the same thing. A property might not have been what they were expecting, but they immediately think of someone else who should definitely see your listing.

- If potential buyers are not interested in the home, it's possible they'll tell someone who is.
- If neighbors who aren't interested in buying or selling, it's possible they'll tell someone who is.
- If a local expired or FSBO listing isn't interested, there's a chance they'll tell someone who is.

Especially if you encourage them to do so! Your marketing should offer a clear path for these referrals to make their way back to not just the listing, but to your prospecting funnel as well.

Marketing isn't just ads. It's a collaboration of all your pieces that place YOU as well as the home in the hands, or on the screens, of consumers in that market.

Utilize a blend of promotion strategies, the kind that generate multiple touches and come from a variety of outreach efforts, including:

- Emails
- Direct Mail
- Flyers
- Targeted social media posts and invitations
- Phone calls in the neighborhood and to your SOI
- Newspaper ads/traditional print advertising
- MLS listings online & other online ads
- Knocking on doors nearby
- Well-placed signs throughout the neighborhood

Your aim is to extend the open house invitation to as wide an audience as possible.

| Method | Projected Target Audience Size (Examples) |
|---|---|
| Newspaper Ads | 10,000 readers |
| Personal Invitations, through calls | 90 Calls |
| Personal Invitations, through door knocking | 100 Doors knocked |
| Flyers & Mailouts | 300 Flyers/mailouts |
| Emails to Your SOI Database | 600 member SOI emailed |
| Circle Prospecting, with Autodialer | 300 Local Homes |
| Social Media Posts to Personal Page | 1,000 Friends |
| Social Media Posts to Business Page | 500 Fans |
| MLS Open House Registration; Reverse Prospecting | To 50 Agents with Buyer Searches that match subject property |
| Syndication through Open House Sites | 1,000 searching for open houses |

## OPEN HOUSE FLYERS & MAILERS

Open House flyers can be emailed or mailed. Mailers are little more expensive, but sometimes it's worth the cost to send a personal invitation to a selection of immediate neighbors. Personal invites will make them feel welcome and increase local turnout.

Ask neighbors to come and get to know each other and talk about the benefits of living in the community. Create a memorable experience. The neighbors who come to the open house will remember you when they are ready to list their homes.

If distributing flyers is permitted in your area, flyers can also be hand-delivered to doorsteps. They really stand out and are less expensive and quicker than mailing. Make sure to hang them on a doorknob or tuck them under a doormat. You won't impress the neighbors if your flyers are blowing all over the neighborhood and creating an eyesore!

## PHONE CALLS & VOICE MAILS

It's a good idea to personally call neighbors, FSBOS, and expired listing leads to invite them to the open house. There are many online sources for obtaining phone numbers and other contact information. Again, the best sources change all the time, so talk with your ICC coach or a good circle-prospector for the most up-to-date recommendations.

As we discussed in a previous chapter, you can pay for Sly Dial or Sly Broadcast straight to voicemail services, and leave a personal, pre-recorded message with people in the neighborhood.

> *For Example:*
>
> *"Hi, this is Ann Johnson with ABC Realty. I'm holding your neighbor's open house on 1234 Main Street, and I wanted to let you know that all the neighbors in the Cotton Wood Glen neighborhood are invited this Saturday from 11 to 3. We ultimately find that the purchaser of a property is a friend, family member, or acquaintance. So, I'm reaching out to see if you know anyone or would like to join us as a guest. I'm doing my best to get this home sold at the highest price to keep your neighborhood's property values going up, up, up! I'd love to see you there, this Saturday from 11 to 3.*

## Social Media

Facebook is still one of the best social media platforms for real estate. You can post a shareable digital version of the open house flyer on your social media business pages, as well as on your personal page so that friends and family in your sphere of influence know about it.

You can also pay to target open house posts to hyper-local geographic areas and boost awareness to people in particular locations.

Facebook also has an "Events" feature that allows you to create a shareable invitation to the open house. People can RSVP or express that they are "interested" in attending, which can give you a rough estimate of the level of awareness and interest in the event.

Remember that social media is primarily a visual medium. People prefer pretty pictures to long descriptions and too much detail! Keep it short and sweet and stay visual when composing open house posts.

Lives-Streams are also increasingly popular on social media. During the event itself, you could consider recording the event on Facebook Live or Instagram Stories. This way, people who cannot attend the event in person can still be there.

And don't forget to post pictures of the open house on social media after the event. Don't go overboard. Only post the best pictures and those that showcase a lot of smiling, mingling, interested people. Your goal here is not so much to showcase the property but to showcase that you're an agent that knows how to throw one heck of a party!

## Design Tips

When designing your ad campaigns and marketing materials, don't forget the following:

- **Open House Address.** Digital ads should include a link with directions.
- **Bulleted points that build curiosity.** Digital ads should include a link to your full report.
- **Open House Times.** Digital ads should include a link to other open house times or a link to set up a private appointment.

- **Your Contact Information**: Digital ads should include a link to schedule an appointment.

- **Top 3 Photos**. Digital ads should include a link to your complete catalog of stunning photos.

- **How to Refer Listing**. Digital ads should include a share button. All ads should have a call to action to "spread the word" about the open house.

Whichever of the above marketing strategies you elect to do, your objective is to maximize the prospecting potential around each open house, and to use marketing as a means to generate business before the open house is even held.

Hosting an open house also proves to the seller that you are serious about marketing their home and finding a buyer for it. Explain what your prospecting activities and marketing efforts mean for the seller during your listing presentation. As you'll see, your goal of using the open house as a way to generate more business can actually be used as an advantage to secure the listing in the first place.

## SCHEDULING AN OPEN HOUSE

At the beginning of this chapter, we threw you immediately into the deep end to give you a sense of what you'll be doing when you're actually in the midst of hosting an open house—networking with all manner of guests and getting them signed up to those all-important MLS Listing E-Alerts.

From there, we took a step back and presented you with some scripts and strategies for generating traffic and generating business in the days prior to hosting the open house.

Our aim was to give you as much information upfront about what it's actually like to market and host an open house as well as get you excited and forward-looking about the process.

We also wanted to front-load the chapter with the most important takeaway first:

Pleasing and satisfying the seller of a home is a byproduct of holding an open house—your primary purpose is to tie customer-service to lead-generation and generate buyer and listing leads as a result of your great customer-service.

However, client satisfaction is obviously extremely important, so now it's time to take another step back in the timeline and discuss how to schedule an open house with the sellers of the property.

To begin with, you may have to explain the thought-process behind opening their home to the public at all.

Take a moment to read through the following script that tells your clients why it's in their best interests to schedule an open house.

## Script for Scheduling an Open House

"Mr/Mrs. SELLER, We find that the vast majority of homes that sell at a price close to our listing price sell within the **first few weeks** of putting the home up for sale in the market.

Accordingly, we have great success when we **generate multiple offers from different buyers at the same time**. More often than not, this occurs within the first couple weeks of putting a home up for sale. This is why we market so hard through mail, flyers, telephone calls, and open houses. **Right at the time of listing.**

We have also seen success at **generating prices above or at the asking price when we can create multiple offer situations**. Further, if your home does go under contract or at least generate an offer prior to holding the open house - **nothing is more effective at keeping the buyer honest than holding an open house as scheduled previously.**

For example, if we are negotiating back and forth with different offers - it often takes many days if not a week. If, during this process, we hold a pre-scheduled open house at the home, **we can create extreme urgency with the potential buyer that's in negotiations with us.**

When a home is under contract or at least being negotiated, buyers drive by the home to show it to friends and family members - as their future home. And **there is nothing worse than seeing people walk through it who may steal it away.** This strikes fear in the buyer and puts it in favor of you the seller.

Further, in situations where an offer has already been negotiated and accepted, **holding pre-set open houses helps show buyers that other people are interested in the home.** This way when it comes time to inspect and negotiate improvements in the home, later in the transaction process, the buyer will be less picky.

Which once again, **strengthens the buying and negotiating power of you, the seller.**"

As you can see, the thought process behind hosting an open house (or additional open houses) is to generate multiple and highly competitive offers on the home. If your client can get multiple offers on the home, you are in a great position to negotiate and increase your chance of getting an offer above asking price.

It's a good marketing strategy to schedule two open houses right off the bat. Try to schedule one for the very first weekend after listing, possibly followed with another the next weekend. Make sure your seller prospects and clients understand that their best chance of getting multiple, competitive offers is in the first week or two of listing.

And, before you even schedule a listing appointment with a prospective seller, make sure to practice and internalize this script so that you can deliver the message as powerfully and persuasively as possible during your listing presentation.

## SCHEDULE TO CONVERT: HOW SCHEDULING OPEN HOUSES CAN SECURE CLIENTS

The above script is a fantastic way to convert listing appointments. It's a great idea to incorporate it into your listing presentation business plan, especially in competitive listing situations where you're competing against other agents for the job.

Your goal is to paint a picture in the mind of the prospect of a veritable feeding frenzy around their house, while leaving them with the distinct impression that you will be the strategic mastermind behind it all.

When other agents are telling sellers that "open houses don't sell houses," it doesn't matter if those agents are more than likely correct—they're still going to come across as less motivated, less determined, less purposeful, and less persistent than the agent who is talking about multiple offers and offers above asking price.

When they hear the aggression, effort, and strategy that you bring to open houses, you will be much more attractive to a home seller who can see that you're not afraid to do the extra work and go to great lengths to market and sell their home.

Remember what we taught you in the very first chapter: sellers *want* an aggressive agent who will advocate hard on their behalf. This script will help you show them that that's precisely what you'll do.

What's more, you should now be able to see how you can merge the entire process together and connect all of your lead-generation and prospecting activities back to customer-service. Your primary goal of using the open house as a way to generate more business can actually be used as an advantage to secure the listing in the first place at the initial consultation appointment.

- You're the agent that's going to personally call every single one of their neighbors, not to mention your personal friends and acquaintances.
- You're the agent that's going to literally walk around the neighborhood and hand-deliver open house flyers door-to-door.

You can imagine the level of conversion for an agent that's willing to go to these marketing levels compared to other agents. The amount of listings (not to mention referrals) that you'll see from this type of effort and aggressive marketing is huge.

You can deliver all these things as a conversion message at listing presentation appointments, while knowing that doing these activities as promised will actually bring you more business!

# Final Logistics

Once the seller agrees to the open house in the initial marketing stages, you can begin organizing and implementing some of the practical considerations and logistics involved in holding the event.

## Length of Time

Decide on how long the open house will be. Usually, 2 to 5 hours is long enough to drive traffic to the listing, show the home, and generate more SOI contacts. The length you select will depend on your availability and the area in which you hold the open house.

For shorter open houses, you should focus on meeting prospects and getting their contact information. If you host a longer open house, expect lulls during the event, so take along thank-you cards, your SOI database, and your Expired and FSBO call sheets, so that you can maximize your time when no one's around. You can even door knock the neighbor's homes and 5 or 6 homes across the street.

You also should take a look at what's been successful in the past. If you know that open houses on Saturday mornings are good for families with kids, hold your open house then. If your target clients are hipsters who like late afternoon/early evening opportunities for viewing property, try to align your schedule to match their needs.

Don't stop there, however. Mix it up and offer a variety of dates and times for hosting your open houses.

Ask for an open house date from the seller when you list the property. It's too easy to procrastinate on an "after date"—after we pack the guest room, after we move the extra furniture to storage, after we repaint the hallway. Set the date and get things in motion.

## Signage

First, invest in professional signs that say you're serious about your business. For a few hundred dollars, you can get a stack of printed, weatherproof signs and wire stands. You'll need quite a few, too, because you'll be placing the signs internally in the neighborhood rather than externally.

## Placement

Traditionally, agents would place signs far away from the neighborhood to try to lure traffic to the open house. Unfortunately, data has shown that that rarely works. Most potential buyers are headed to the property anyway. All they need to find the home is their GPS. We like to see 8-10 signs within the existing neighborhood, not on busy external streets where people are driving by too fast to see them.

Placing signs outside the neighborhood isn't as helpful as placing them *inside* the neighborhood. Place signs on all the major entrances and exits of the neighborhood so that you catch everyone who leaves and comes in. Your target is not people who are just randomly driving by. Your attractive open house signs are a *brand awareness/recognition tool* for those already living in the area. Your goal is to attract the attention of parents on the way to soccer practice or coming back from church.

Your goal is for people to see your signs everywhere each time you hold an open house. They'll soon come to associate your name with hard work and as *the* listing agent in the neighborhood.

## Design

Too many open house signs miss the point of open houses entirely. They think of it as a functional item that points people in the right direction of the property in question. Remember, however, that your primary goal is lead-generation and marketing, which equals name-recognition and brand awareness. You're pointing people in the right direction by pointing them towards YOU.

To increase name and brand recognition, have your name/brand printed in LARGE letters with the words Open House printed in smaller letters below. At least 2/3rds of the sign should be occupied by your name only. There's no need to overly highlight your brokerage; that lettering should be as small as humanly possible. Agents switch companies all the time. You're not marketing your brokerage: you're marketing yourself.

Remember that marketing is a collaboration of all your advertising strategies and techniques working together. When someone drives by your open house sign, they should recognize that you're the same person whose flyer arrived through their door on Tuesday, or who left them a helpful voicemail the evening before. Maybe they've seen you on Facebook or received an email invitation.

When pieced together, they will see how very hard you work to get a home sold. Together, all of your prospecting activities and marketing strategies are a living, breathing testimony that points people towards you.

This is all they'll see and care about. The word 'Open House' can simply be placed inside a small arrow pointing to the home. There's no need to even put your phone number or email address on the sign. At this point, they should know when and where it is, and they're *going* to that open house.

## Parking

Once of the biggest challenges of hosting an open house can be finding a place for everyone's vehicle. Most neighbors will walk, but you may have to find space for as many as 5-10 vehicles. Some neighborhoods allow parking along the curb, and some do not. Become familiar with ordinances before you host the open house.

Again, this is simply a practical consideration that should take second place to open house marketing potential. Parking also offers a prime opportunity to evidence your success and market the open house.

When you arrive at the open house, don't park in the driveway, park out on the street. You should also ask your clients to park on the street, as well as every other guest who comes by. It sounds counterintuitive, but your goal is to show that this open house is so popular it's hard to find a place to park.

People are attracted to busy, lively places with lots of people. Perhaps it's the psychological fear of missing out, but more cars means more people! If you have four cars out there, you have an increased likelihood of getting eight. If you have no cars, it's very hard to even get one.

It's very important to evidence a large, successful open house in as many ways as possible. Make it hard to park!

## Sign-Ins and Contact Information

Every open house needs to register its guests. Make sure that you place a sign-in sheet near the front, in a very public place, so that you can stand near it and ask everyone who walks through the door to sign your guestbook.

But why should someone share their contact-information at an open house?

### Security & Insurance

Two critical reasons are for security and insurance purposes. Requiring names and contact information can prevent opportunities for burglary and reduce liability in the event of unforeseen accidents.

Be sure to address these factors with your seller during your brief on open houses. This is a great checklist item for your pre-listing packet!

Tell prospects that you are required to keep a record of everyone who comes through the house, and that you need the information for these important reasons.

---

**GUEST LIST SCRIPT**

**SCRIPT NO. 1: "SECURITY"**

"Please sign in for security purposes. I need to keep a record of everyone that comes through the house."

**SCRIPT NO. 2: "INSURANCE"**

"Please sign in for insurance purposes. I have to keep a log of every guest that walks through the home."

---

Be consistent with the script you use at each open house. Use the same one with all visitors so they know they are being treated equally.

In either case above, hold your open house flyer for the property as they complete the guest list, and then provide it to them once they are done.

It's very hard for people to argue with security and insurance reasons, and they will appreciate knowing that you are an agent who does their due diligence and will keep their safety in mind when they work with you too. Use the law of reciprocity here:

> "I'm sure if we listed your home, you'd want the same consideration, wouldn't you?"

If they are still concerned about leaving their information, assure them that you do not leave it out for others to see. Pick up sign-in sheets as soon as they are filled out. Some visitors may be cautious about their personal information if others can see it.

To prevent visitors from taking pictures of a sheet of guest names and contact information, you could also consider using individual index cards or sign-in flyers and pick them up immediately.

### DIGITAL SIGN-IN

Another option is to implement a digital sign-in. Save a copy of your open house flyer as an image on your mobile phone. When visitors arrive, simply ask them for their mobile phone number and/or email address so you can immediately send them the flyer in digital format and they can refer to the property information as they walk through the home. As a result, real estate agents are able to get the phone numbers and email addresses of each open house visitor. By also asking for each guest's name, agents can create a contact for every potential open house lead that walks in the door.

Remember, the primary function of gathering this information is for your SOI database input, and launching your 7x7 SOI introduction immediately following the open house. After all your hard work scheduling, organizing, and networking the event, don't forget to capitalize on your efforts by following up with your open house guests!

## DON'T FORGET TO FOLLOW UP!

By now it should be clear that real estate agents never host an open house simply for the sake of showing off a single piece of real estate. You cannot hold the event, pack up your things and wait until next week for things to happen. That open house was just the midpoint of your prospecting work. You miss the point of tying customer-service to lead-generation if you fail to follow up with guests and attendees.

*80% of all sales require 5 follow-up calls after the first meeting. 44% of sales reps give up after 1 follow-up.*

Each registered guest may fall into a different category and need different kinds of follow-up based off their long-term goals and needs. Yet most of the activities will be the same.

- It's a great idea to send everyone a "Thank You For Coming" card or email.
- Leads will require a follow-up call to set or confirm an appointment, and prequalification.
- SOI members will be put on a 7X7 (refer to Chapter 1)
- Nurtures will fall into a drip campaign you've designed.

## ACTIVITY PUNCH LIST

| Visitor/Category | Follow Up | Detail |
|---|---|---|
| Sam Johnson/ Lead | ☐ Call for Appt | Looking to buy in 3 mos.; liked home |
| Tammy Werner/SOI | ☐ Thank you note/ 7X7 | Neighbor, lived here 3 years, no plans to move |
| Luke Onus/Nurture | ☐ Thank you note/drip | Just started looking. Move in 2 years |
| Cybil Parker/SOI | ☐ Thank you note/ 7X7 | Neighbor, lived here 5 years, retiring from work in 5 years |
| Tony Bonnie/Lead | ☐ Call for Appt | FSBO in the area, curious about traffic, sales |

## LISTING E-ALERT FOLLOW-UP CALLS

At the beginning of this chapter, we focused on one of your primary goals while hosting an open house—getting as many guests as possible signed up to an MLS Listing E-Alert email drip campaign.

As you'll recall, open house guests can be signed up as prospective buyers to receive listing alerts that match the specific criteria they're looking for in a home. Or, they can be signed up as prospective sellers (or simply as informed neighbors) to receive listing alerts that help them to stay educated and up-to-date on their local, neighborhood real estate market.

These emails will automatically do a lot of the follow-up work for you. However, it's always wise to employ a variety of follow-up tactics and personal phone calls are far more effective than email alone.

### TOO MUCH OR TOO LITTLE?

Signing guests up to your tools and products gives you a reason to personally follow up with them over time. You can follow up as a customer service to see how they're enjoying the product, make sure they're not receiving too many or too few emails, and to see if there is any way you can help them.

As they begin to learn the different the price ranges of the different neighborhoods, they may say, "Nah, we don't like those houses, let's focus on a higher price range," or, "We really like that side of town, let's see more of those properties."

Now that they're getting emails, they're more alert, more aware. Their radar is up for different neighborhoods. Parents probably learned more about local school districts. You can start getting their feedback, following up, seeing if they want to further refine or modify their search.

You may find out that they're not getting enough emails, which may mean that their search criteria is too limited. You may need to expand into a larger geographic area or increase the price range. You could increase the home size, or the number of bedroom/baths, to expand the window of their search criteria to encompass more homes, etc.

## Softly, Softly

When making these follow-up calls, you never want to push too hard. Remember that most of these people are "just looking" and don't want to be pressured. The idea is to nurture, cultivate and probe just enough to ensure they are getting value and to make sure they're still in the market.

Rather than calling them to say, "Hey are you ready to buy or sell yet?" you are coming from a place of contribution and customer-service, which implies that you're working for them already. These kinds of calls are much better received than cold calling in the hope of converting a lead. It's almost as though you're already working on their behalf, which makes them much more inclined to work with you down the road.

## Getting Feedback

People love to be helpful. A great way to follow up is to tap into this willingness to help by reaching out to request feedback. You'll need to contact seller leads, the neighbors, guests and potential buyers. When you ask for feedback, always connect to the prospect's own experience with his or her home.

---

### Follow-Up Script & Dialog for Neighbors/ Seller Leads

"If you don't mind, it would greatly help me if I could get some marketing feedback from you. Did you happen to see the flyer I created for this home with the Comparative Market Analysis (CMA) on the back?

"Great! I'm curious if this was of any benefit to you. You see, I was attempting to show you the sizes and prices of other homes in the area so that you could use the neighborhood's average price per square foot to get a rough idea of what your house is worth in this market. Do you happen to know the square footage of your home?"

"Terrific! Thank you. Now oftentimes your home will have different amenities and features than the houses listed on the CMA, which can significantly alter the value of your home.

Since it is my intent to specialize & focus my practice in this neighborhood, I'd be more than happy to take a brief look through your home to give you a quick value with absolutely no obligation on your part. It's just something I do with the hopes that if you did sell sometime in the future you might consider my services."

You see, an appraiser would typically charge you around $500 to appraise your home, and I'm attempting to help you alleviate that cost.

I also wouldn't want you to straighten up your home just for me. I'm a Realtor and we're very used to viewing homes before they're ready to show. I assure you it won't affect the value at all."

Would this be of any benefit to you?

(PAUSE – Let silence do the heavy lifting)

Great! How about I swing by right after I lock-up here?"

## GIVING FEEDBACK

Any seller whose home has hosted an open house has one question: "How did it go?"

Let the seller know about the interest the home generated, and if there were any offers. If there were no offers, you could reveal what prospective buyers saw as advantages and if there were any concerns. Use the "sandwich method" of telling the sellers about their home:

- Say something positive
- Point out an area that may need correction (price reduction, tree trimming, etc.)
- Conclude with an affirmation that the home will sell to the right buyer

### EXERCISE:

Practice the Sandwich Method for giving feedback by writing several practice scripts. Begin with a positive, point out a need, and end with an affirmation.

**NEED**
They were, however, concerned that the asking price is too high.

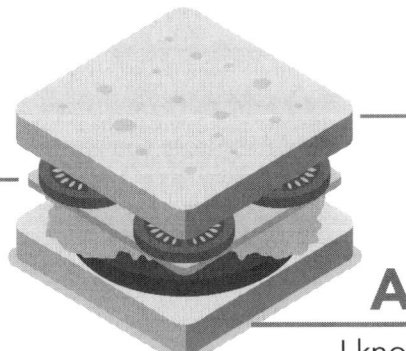

**POSITIVE**
Those who came to the open house loved your open floor plan.

**AFFIRMATION**
I know we will sell your home if we consider a reduction.

POSITVE: _____

NEED: _____

AFFIRMATION: _____

### WHERE WERE YOU?

You might also adapt the tactic of following up with "no-shows"—those who gave a verbal "yes," yet an actual "no" when it came time to game day. Be tactful, not accusatory, with this follow up: come from a place where you indicate that you know 'life happens', yet you noticed they weren't there, and they were missed.

The most important thing is that you remember to follow up and keep your name top of mind with everyone—from registered open house guests to the people who couldn't make it.

## Summary

Open Houses can form a major pillar of your prospecting business.

This chapter began right in the midst of an active open house with you signing guests up to MLS Listing Alerts, before going back in time to teach you how to market and prospect in the days prior to the event, then further back still to the very beginning when you first schedule the open house at the listing appointment.

Like we said, our aim was to give you as much information upfront about what it's actually like to market and host an open house as well as get you excited and forward-looking about the process.

In real-life, your Open House Timeline will look more like this:

# OPEN HOUSE TIMELINE

### SCHEDULE OPEN HOUSE
- Use an open house as a strategic selling point to convert the listing
- Confirm time & date and push for multiple open houses

### MARKET & PROSPECT
- Generate Traffic and Generate Business
- Invite as many people as posssible in as many possible ways.

### LOGISTICS, LOGISTICS
- Place signs strategically around the neighborhood
- Strategize parking, too. Make it hard to park!

### HOST AN OPEN HOUSE
- Register guests for security, insurance, and marketing purposes
- Set up as many people as possible for MLS Listing E-Alerts

### FOLLOW UP!
- Nurture. Cultivate. Get Feedback. Give Feedback. Follow Up!

chapter, however, our core message has been the same again and again:

Pleasing and satisfying the seller of a home is a byproduct of holding an open house—your primary purpose is to tie customer-service to lead-generation and generate buyer and listing leads as a result of your great customer-service.

Open houses offer endless opportunities for prospecting. Every open house guest is a potential prospect, and every prospect is a potential future client and SOI contact. By orchestrating everything regarding the open house, from invitations to signage and the follow-up afterward, you can combine and channel your ever-expanding skills into one spectacular event that the entire neighborhood will remember and talk about in the days and months that follow.

# NEXT LEVEL CONTACT PLAN

| STARTING POINT | NEXT LEVEL |
|---|---|
| Drive-By Traffic | • Open House Guest |
| Open House Guest | • Registered Visitor |
| Registered Visitor | • Nurture, lead, and prospect |
| Invited Buyer/Seller Lead | • Buyer/Seller Appointment<br>• Add to Listing E-Alert Email Drip Campaign |
| Buyer Lead | • Local Listing Showing Appointment<br>• Listing E-Alert Email Drip Campaign |
| Seller Lead | • Lead/Prospect<br>• Add to Listing E-Alert Email Drip Campaign |
| Neighbors | • SOI Member<br>• Add to Listing E-Alert Email Drip Campaign |
| Listing Client | • Satisfied Listing Client Willing to Refer Business<br>• Add to SOI Contact Plan |
| Expired Listing Lead | • Prospect for Listing Appointment<br>• Add to Listing E-Alert email drip campaign<br>• Subsequent SOI member. |
| FSBO listing | • Prospect for Listing Appointment<br>• Add to Listing E-Alert email drip campaign<br>• Subsequent SOI member |

© Copyright Icenhower Coaching & Consulting, LLC. All rights reserved.

# BUYER MLS LISTING ALERT
## Script

"The most desirable homes listed at the lowest prices sell the fastest, so you don't ever get to see them on Zillow and other secondary websites. Homes on those websites are actually the homes that most people did not want. You see, all home listings are initially listed in the REALTOR®'s Multiple Listing Service (MLS) online database of homes for sale. Then the listing information is sent through digital feeds to other secondary sources, and then on to these other websites. This is why the information on these sites is often incorrect and a week or two old. That's why websites like Zillow do not have the same amount of listings as our MLS does. If you are looking for homes on Zillow, you're just seeing the leftovers that no one else wanted. Are you following me?"

"Plus, many offices, companies, and associations of REALTORS® do not allow digital feeds to go to secondary websites like Zillow. Not only do you miss out on the homes that have already sold quickly, but there are many active listings that you can't see at all. Does all that make sense?"

"If you want to see all the listings the minute they go up for sale and get FULL REALTOR® ACCESS, I can easily set you up on our buyer search tool. Then you can see what the real estate agents see, as soon as they see it. You can look at the homes online in the privacy of your own home, on your own time, with absolutely no pressure or obligation. I can even set the system up to send you email notifications the minute new homes hit the market that fit the specific criteria you are looking for in a home. If you happened to want to see the inside of one of them, you can just reply to the email or call me and we'll get you inside quickly. Would that be a benefit to you?"

"This way you'll also be able to learn about the prices of homes in different neighborhoods to become a more informed buyer. You'll start to see what's a good deal and what's not, how quickly certain homes sell in different areas and price ranges. Once you see what you can get for your dollar, you'll also be able to drive around on the weekends and check out some of the neighborhoods on your own time. Look at the school districts, nearby shopping, and other amenities. You can take your time with this if you want. How does that sound?"

© Copyright Icenhower Coaching & Consulting, LLC. All rights reserved.

## SELLER LEAD AUTO EMAIL DRIP
### Script

Hi it's [AGENT NAME] with [REAL ESTATE COMPANY],

I wanted to give you a heads up that I've set you up on our new Neighborhood Update Tool and would love to hear your feedback on it. My clients really love it. This tool will really help you stay educated about your home's value and your neighborhood's conditions leading up to whenever you are ready to move. It might even help you decide when you want to put your home up for sale!

Here's how it works: when one of your neighbors puts their home up for sale, you'll immediately get an email with all the listing information and photos of the home. This way, you'll be able to:

1. Look through all the photos of your neighbor's homes;
2. Compare the amenities, features & size of the listings to your own home;
3. Know the price of each new listing to get a rough idea of the current value of your own home;
4. See how quickly each home sells, and the prices that they ultimately sell for;
5. This will give you a good idea of how the value of your home is increasing from month-to-month;
6. It will also keep you up to date on your local neighborhood's market conditions.

I really think you'll find this customer service tool useful since most of my clients already do. If for some reason you decide that you'd rather not receive these updates, you can unsubscribe yourself or just simply reply to an email and we'll discontinue it for you. However, I'd love to hear what you think about it first.

All that I need from you is to verify that I have the correct home address and email address for you. Sound good?

© Copyright Icenhower Coaching & Consulting, LLC. All rights reserved.

# MODULE 5

# APPENDIX 5.4

## OPEN HOUSE PROSPECTING ACTIVITIES

| Prospect/Target | Core Message | Details/ Calls to Action |
|---|---|---|
| Circle Prospecting 1 mile around open house | You're invited to see what's available in the market, and my service level. | Visit the home/invite who you know to the open house. |
| | | Tell me about your plans to move. |
| | | Join my SOI, learn about the market. |
| Neighbors on Same Street | You're invited to see what's available in the market, and my service level. | Visit the home/invite who you know to the open house. |
| | | Tell me about your plans to move. |
| | | Join my SOI, learn about the market. |
| Expired listing prospects | You're invited to test my systems, service, and what's on the market. | Visit the home/invite who you know to the open house. |
| | | Interview me through seeing what I do. |
| | | Join my SOI, learn about the market. |
| FSBO listing prospects | You're invited to test my systems, service, and what's on the market. | Visit the home/invite who you know to visit the Home. |
| | | Interview me through seeing what I do. |
| | | Join my SOI, learn about the market. |
| SOI members | You're invited to test my systems, service, and what's on the market. | Visit the home/invite who you know to visit the home. |
| | | Tell me about your plans to move. |
| | | Learn about the market. |
| Current Nurtures | You're invited to test my systems, service, and what's on the market. | Visit the home/invite who you know to visit the open house. |
| | | Tell me about your plans to move. |
| | | Join my SOI, learn about the market |
| Affiliates | You're invited to test my systems, service, and what's on the market. | Visit the home/invite who you know to visit the open house. |
| | | Showcase your service to potential clients. |
| | | Join my SOI as a preferred service member |

© Copyright Icenhower Coaching & Consulting, LLC. All rights reserved.

# MODULE 5

# APPENDIX 5.5

## OPEN HOUSE
### Neighbor Invitation

*"Hi, I'm John Smith with ABC Realty. We have your neighbor's home at 123 Main Street up for sale and we are holding a special open house on Saturday from 11:00am to 3:00pm.*

*Since we know that the ultimate purchaser of a home is often a friend, family member or acquaintance of someone that already lives in the same neighborhood, we are inviting the entire neighborhood to come by to take a look.*

*So if you happen to know or meet someone looking to move into your community, this is a great way for you to hand-pick pick your own neighbors!*

*Do you think you can swing by?"*

**Wait for response and proceed with...**

**If Yes:** *"Great! And since we are doing everything we can to get your neighbor's home sold, I promised my seller that I'd ask: Do you know anyone looking to buy or sell a home in the area?"*

**If No:**

*"No problem, I totally understand. And since we are doing everything we can to get your neighbor's home sold, I promised my seller that I'd ask: Do you know anyone looking to buy or sell a home in the near future?"*

© Copyright Icenhower Coaching & Consulting, LLC. All rights reserved.

# MODULE 5

# APPENDIX 5.6

**OPEN HOUSE**
**Asking for a Pre-Listing Appointment Script**

[Possible Follow Up Question]:

*"And by the way, it's my intent to specialize & focus my practice in this neighborhood. So I'm providing all of the homeowners a complimentary value of $500 with the hope that they might consider interviewing me when and if they ever decide to sell their home in the future. You see, an appraiser would typically charge you around $500 to appraise your home, and I'm attempting to help you alleviate that cost to determine what your home would be worth in this market. Would knowing your home's current value be of any benefit to you?"*

If they are hesitant or otherwise object, proceed with...

[Objection Handler]

*"I see, and I want to assure you that there would be absolutely no obligation on your part. Again, this is a courtesy service that I am providing to all your neighbors with the hope that if you decided to sell 5, 10 or 20 years down the road, you would consider interviewing me for the job.*

*I would also never want you to straighten up your home just for me. I'm a REALTOR® and we're very used to viewing homes long before they're ready to show. I assure you it won't affect the value at all, and I'll be in and out in minutes. How does that sound?"*

If they are interested proceed with...

**[If Yes]: *"Great! Would 3:00 or 5:00 tomorrow work better for you?"***

Also be sure to obtain all of their contact information so that you can add them to your client database management system to stay in touch with them over time.

If No:

*"No problem, consider this a standing offer, so feel free to contact me if you are ever curious about your home's current value. In the meantime, can I count on you to let me know if you bump into anyone looking to move into the area so that we can get your neighbor's home sold?"*

Wait for a response then

*"Great! I truly appreciate your time and help.*

© Copyright Icenhower Coaching & Consulting, LLC. All rights reserved.

# MODULE 5

## APPENDIX 5.7

**CIRCLE PROSPECTING**
**Open House Script**

**Agent:** Hi (Home Owner), this is (Agent Name) with (Real Estate Company) and I just listed Emily and Joe house around the corner from you. The sellers wanted me to invite you to our grand opening this weekend from eleven to one.

Home Owner: Oh okay.

**Agent:** Yeah hopefully you can make it by. Tell me how long have you been in the neighborhood?

Home Owner: We've lived here for about five years now.

**Agent:** Five years, good for you! Well you know when list a great property like this and we put it up for sale on the market, we generally expect to get two to four motivated buyers that will miss out on the property. Do you know of any other neighbors in the neighborhood that maybe thinking about selling in this hot market?

Home Owner: Well……. You know I can't think of anybody right now. Every one that lives here loves it here.

**Agent:** It is a great neighborhood. As for you (Home Owner) if you were to move, where would you go next?

Home Owner: I don't know, we really like it here. I guess someday once the kids are gone we might move. I was thinking maybe in the country once the kids are out and out of the school district. I would go out to the country and become a country guy.

**Agent:** A country guy! Good for you, so are your kids about to graduate? When do you plan on moving out there?

Home Owner: They will probably graduate in four years. Well they just started high school.

**Agent:** Excellent, well hey I love to follow up with you from time to time and see if anything changes. Just in case you want to talk before I call you back, would it be ok if I send you my contact information?

Home Owner: Sure, that's fine.

**Agent:** Great what's the best E-mail for you?

Home Owner: You could reach me at homeowner@emailaddress.com

**Agent:** Perfect. Well come on out (Home Owner) we look forward to seeing you. Hopefully you can make it on Saturday I'd love to meet you. We'll be over at 123 Main St. and would love to meet you there.

© Copyright Icenhower Coaching & Consulting, LLC. All rights reserved.

# OPEN HOUSE
## Scheduling an Open House Script

"Mr/Mrs. SELLER, we find that the vast majority of homes that sell at a price close to our listing price sell within the first few weeks of putting the home up for sale in the market.

Accordingly, we have great success when we generate multiple offers from different buyers at the same time. More often than not, this occurs within the first couple weeks of putting a home up for sale. This is why we market so hard through mail, flyers, telephone calls, and open houses. Right at the time of listing.

We have also seen success at generating prices above or at the asking price when we can create multiple offer situations. Further, if your home does go under contract or at least generate an offer prior to holding the open house - nothing is more effective at keeping the buyer honest than holding an open house as scheduled previously.

For example, if we are negotiating back and forth with different offers - it often takes many days if not a week. If, during this process, we hold a pre-scheduled open house at the home, we can create extreme urgency with the potential buyer that's in negotiations with us.

When a home is under contract or at least being negotiated, buyers drive by the home to show it to friends and family members - as their future home. And there is nothing worse than seeing people walk through it who may steal it away. This strikes fear in the buyer and puts it in favor of you the seller.

Further, in situations where an offer has already been negotiated and accepted, holding pre-set open houses helps show buyers that other people are interested in the home. This way when it comes time to inspect and negotiate improvements in the home, later in the transaction process, the buyer will be less picky.

Which once again, strengthens the buying and negotiating power of you, the seller."

# OPEN HOUSE
## Guest List Scripts

### GUEST LIST SCRIPT No. 1 – "Security"

"Please sign in for security purposes. I need to keep a record of everyone that comes through the house."

### GUEST LIST SCRIPT No. 2 – "Insurance"

"Please sign in for insurance purposes. I have to keep a log of every guest that walks through the home."

**NOTE:** In either case above, hold your open house flyer for the property as they complete the guest list, and then provide it to them once they are done.

### DIGITAL FLYER METHOD

Simply save a copy of your open house flyer as an image on your mobile phone. When visitors arrive, simply ask them for their mobile phone number and/or email address so you can immediately send them the flyer in digital format and they can refer to the property information as they walk through the home.

As a result, real estate agents are able to get the phone numbers and email addresses of each open house visitor. By also asking for each guest's name, agents can create a contact for every potential open house lead that walks in the door.

© Copyright Icenhower Coaching & Consulting, LLC. All rights reserved.

# MODULE 5

# APPENDIX 5.10

**FOLLOW-UP SCRIPT**
**Dialog for Neighbors/ Seller Leads**

"If you don't mind, it would greatly help me if I could get some marketing feedback from you. Did you happen to see the flyer I created for this home with the Comparative Market Analysis (CMA) on the back?

"Great! I'm curious if this was of any benefit to you. You see, I was attempting to show you the sizes and prices of other homes in the area so that you could use the neighborhood's average price per square foot to get a rough idea of what your house is worth in this market. Do you happen to know the square footage of your home?"

"Terrific! Thank you. Now oftentimes your home will have different amenities and features than the houses listed on the CMA, which can significantly alter the value of your home.

Since it is my intent to specialize & focus my practice in this neighborhood, I'd be more than happy to take a brief look through your home to give you a quick value with absolutely no obligation on your part. It's just something I do with the hopes that if you did sell sometime in the future you might consider my services."

You see, an appraiser would typically charge you around $500 to appraise your home, and I'm attempting to help you alleviate that cost.

I also wouldn't want you to straighten up your home just for me. I'm a Realtor and we're very used to viewing homes before they're ready to show. I assure you it won't affect the value at all."

Would this be of any benefit to you?

(PAUSE – Let silence do the heavy lifting)

Great! How about I swing by right after I lock-up here?"

© Copyright Icenhower Coaching & Consulting, LLC. All rights reserved.

# MODULE 5

# APPENDIX 5.11

**ICENHOWER**
COACHING & CONSULTING

# OPEN HOUSE
# Feedback Form

*Open House Feedback...*

| What do think of the house overall? |
|---|
| How's the price? |
| What do you recommend to make the home more saleable? |
| What's the home's best feature? |

*Thank You for Your Input!*

*Open House Feedback...*

| What do think of the house overall? |
|---|
| How's the price? |
| What do you recommend to make the home more saleable? |
| What's the home's best feature? |

*Thank You for Your Input!*

© Copyright Icenhower Coaching & Consulting, LLC. All rights reserved.

MODULE 5 APPENDIX 5.12

# POSITIVE NEED AFFIRMATION SANDWICH

**NEED**
They were, however, concerned that the asking price is too high.

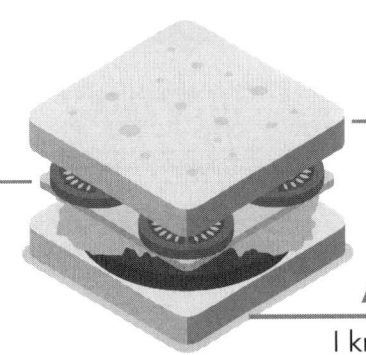

**POSITIVE**
Those who came to the open house loved your open floor plan.

**AFFIRMATION**
I know we will sell your home if we consider a reduction.

POSITVE: _____

NEED: _____

AFFIRMATION: _____


POSITVE: _____

NEED: _____

AFFIRMATION: _____


POSITVE: _____

NEED: _____

AFFIRMATION: _____

© Copyright Icenhower Coaching & Consulting, LLC. All rights reserved.

# OPEN HOUSE TIMELINE

## SCHEDULE OPEN HOUSE
- Use an open house as a strategic selling point to convert the listing
- Confirm time & date and push for multiple open houses

## MARKET & PROSPECT
- Generate Traffic and Generate Business
- Invite as many people as posssible in as many possible ways.

## LOGISTICS, LOGISTICS
- Place signs strategically around the neighborhood
- Strategize parking, too. Make it hard to park!

## HOST AN OPEN HOUSE
- Register guests for security, insurance, and marketing purposes
- Set up as many people as possible for MLS Listing E-Alerts

## FOLLOW UP!
- Nurture. Cultivate. Get Feedback. Give Feedback. Follow Up!

© Copyright Icenhower Coaching & Consulting, LLC. All rights reserved.

# Property Previews

*"There is a time when what is needed is not just rhetoric, but boots on the ground."* - Baldwin Spencer

In the last chapter, we showed you how open houses are a great way to tie customer-service to lead-generation and achieve two things at the same time. In this chapter, we will show you how property previews are a great way to tie lead-generation to learning the business and developing the skillsets that will, in turn, make you an even more powerful prospector.

For decades, previewing property has been an effective lead-generation method that real estate agents have systematically implemented to get new listings while also developing superior market knowledge and expertise.

Property previews solve many of the problems and issues that face new agents when they first get into the business. Although many top-producing agents make this activity a part of their regular routine, previewing property is a particularly good way for new agents who do not yet have a large client database to quickly *gain* business while *learning* the business.

Buyers need homes. Sellers need buyers. You are the one who can meet their needs, but only if you know what they really want. It's vital to engage with clients and contacts and find out more to really serve them, beyond what you read online or in training manuals.

Just as you need to thoroughly understand the wants and needs of your prospects, you should also know your existing and potential inventory at the highest level. Your goal is to master everything there is to know about the areas you want to focus your business in, and position yourself as *the* real estate expert in these communities and neighborhoods.

Previewing property isn't just a way for the novice real estate agent to casually "see what's out there." You must preview property systematically and with intention while building your own inventory of clients at the same time.

Fortunately, previewing property is a straightforward 4-part process that lends itself to systematic scheduling and efficient implementation.

Even better, the fact that previewing property costs absolutely no money makes it the most cost-effective lead-generation method for rapidly growing a real estate agent's business. There's no print marketing or targeted ads, there's no paying for phone numbers or contact information. All it takes is access to your Multiple Listing Service and some boots on the ground!

## Learning Targets

In this chapter, you will learn:

- The power of property previews
- The 4-part property preview process
- Understanding a neighborhood's characteristics
- How to formulate general descriptions of subdivisions/neighborhoods/communities
- Design a descriptive target area map

## THE POWER OF PROPERTY PREVIEWS

Have you ever walked into a store looking for help only to discover that you know more about the product or problem than the staff member that you asked for advice?

All too often, employees don't even know which aisle a particular product is on, let alone how it works, how it was made, what other customers have said or think about it, its advantages and disadvantages, not to mention whether there's a better option available on the market.

Knowing your product and market inside out is essential for success in sales. Extensive and exhaustive knowledge is the primary power of property previews.

### MARKET KNOWLEDGE

Agents who make previewing property a regular part of their business-generation routine develop a heightened and ongoing understanding of the local market and inventory.

Property previews are a wonderful way to learn about different neighborhoods and the features and amenities they offer. Previewing properties will help you learn about what's available in the local market, the value of regional real estate, how to price properties, and what type of home you can get within particular price-ranges.

By surveying homeowners and literally walking through and previewing their homes, you will gain first-person accounts of the condition and features of specific properties. Understanding the local inventory will help you to quickly find homes for buyers that may not even be listed on the Multiple Listing Service (i.e. pocket listings, recently expired listings, cancelled listings, and FSBOs).).

Your in-depth knowledge of the neighborhoods provides prospects with valuable "boots-on-the-ground" insight, making you the go-to reference point, and keeping your buyers loyal and listening.

Your goal is to develop supreme mastery of certain quadrants, sections, or zones of the town or city that you want to focus your business on. The level of confidence that an agent exudes after previewing property translates into instant local experience in the minds of prospective clients.

## Balance The Big 3

As you should know by now, prospecting success depends upon three things: Skill Level, Frequency, and Number of Contacts. Like a three-legged stool, when all three are in balance, they provide the structure and support that is essential for success.

However, most agents don't begin their prospecting journey with three legs of the same length. For new agents, a lack of contacts can create imbalance. Prospecting success hinges on making connections. You must have contact information and connect with a certain number of people so that you can prospect with high frequency and develop your skill level.

Luckily, a lack of contacts can be remedied through time on task. What you may lack in business, you make up for with a wealth of free time!

The less business you have, the less time you are spending on client customer-service and transactions under contract. New agents should take advantage of their disadvantages and load up their schedule with previewing properties and increasing their skill level by actively prospecting for business.

You cannot increase your skill level if you don't spend a substantial amount of time practicing and performing prospecting activities. Real estate is a numbers game. You must develop consistent habits and you must begin prospecting with high frequency to develop your skills and see steady and recurring results.

Consistently previewing properties allows agents to meet a great many homeowners on a daily basis and quickly develop large client databases that produce future business. Property previews are a wonderful way to increase contacts, get yourself in front of prospective buyers and sellers, and grow your SOI.

While previewing properties, and knocking on doors, you will also weave in expired listing and FSBO prospecting. Property previews are a great way to discover existing sellers you didn't know about as well as property owners who are waiting to sell in the future—not to mention picking the brains of prospects with their finger on the neighborhood pulse!

Property previews will also increase your skill level in every other area, from planning and scheduling to delivering effective scripts and practicing lead follow-up and implementing email drip campaigns.

Through frequency and time on task, previewing properties will help you to increase your contacts, increase your skillsets, and balance the Big 3!

## POWERFUL & PERSUASIVE LISTING PRESENTATIONS

When you're the supposed expert in the room, there's only one thing worse than being asked a question you don't know the answer to—it's when the person you're trying to sell something to knows more about it than you do!

When you're delivering a listing presentation and trying to convert a contact into a client, the last thing you want is to expose a gap in your knowledge or be in a position where the prospect knows something important or obvious that you have missed or failed to notice.

Previewing property and getting to know the neighborhood inside out will give you the confidence and self-assurance that's so crucial for delivering powerful and persuasive listing presentations. Previewing property will also enable you to handle any objections that arise with authority and certainty.

What's more, as your familiarity with and knowledge of the neighborhood grows, so will your affinity and affection for the local area. We're more likely to have positive feelings about things that we have a relationship with and know a lot about. Buyers and sellers will be drawn to your positivity and enthusiasm about the homes and neighborhoods you've developed a deep relationship with.

Previewing property not only establishes you as an expert with buyers and sellers, it also establishes you as an expert with your real estate peers. Your extensive and exhaustive neighborhood knowledge places you in a powerful position when negotiating offers, price-reductions, and repairs with agents who are not as clued into or well versed in the local market as you are.

## YOUR HOW-TO GUIDE TO PREVIEWING PROPERTY

Every endeavor requires a strategy, and previewing property requires not only intentional effort but also a strategy that will maximize your time and that of the people you are about to meet.

> *"Without strategy, execution is aimless. Without execution, strategy is useless."* – Morris Chang

Previewing property is a straightforward 4-part process or strategy. Essentially, you will prepare by first identifying and then scheduling properties to preview, and following that you will then door-knock and prospect around the homes that you have previously viewed.

Like we said, there is no marketing, hidden costs, or complicated logistics involved in previewing property. This is a very straightforward and easily achievable business-generation activity.

Below, we will examine each part of the process in turn.

- **STEP 01**: Search for clusters of active listings
- **STEP 02**: Note nearby Expired & FSBO properties
- **STEP 03**: Schedule showings to preview property
- **STEP 04**: Map out & prospect around previewed property

## Part 1: Search For Clusters Of Active Listings

Part 1 is relatively straightforward and simple. Search the Multiple Listing Service database for a group of 4 or 5 active listings located in a tight geographic area, preferably a cluster in the same neighborhood.

Not only is this more efficient from a drive-time perspective, it's better to learn market data information by targeting comparable homes in a single neighborhood or similar neighborhoods in nearby areas or communities.

## Part 2: Make Note Of Nearby Expired & FSBO Properties

Pull up the addresses of any expired or cancelled listings in the same neighborhood/surrounding area for the past 12 months.

As you'll recall from chapter 4, these are hot leads—people within the last year that you know for certain wanted to sell their home but either didn't or couldn't. When prospecting around the active listings that you have previewed, you will also weave in expired prospecting like we have already taught you.

At the same time, you should search online and make note of the addresses of any FSBO properties in the same area.

In chapter 8, we will explore FSBO prospecting in much more detail. For now, simply know that when previewing properties, you will also door-knock and prospect FSBO sellers who are trying to sell their home without the help of an agent.

While you *might* be able to list the property right away, typically FSBO prospecting is a waiting game where agents stay in touch over time, building relationship and rapport, and coming from a place of contribution until they ultimately decide to list with you.

When previewing properties, maximize your time by prospecting for FSBOs and expired listings in the same neighborhood or surrounding area.

When searching for active listings and identifying nearby FSBOs and expired listings, plan on time-blocking no more than an hour of your time for these preliminary preparation steps. The bulk of your time should be spent previewing properties and prospecting around those properties.

## PART 3: SCHEDULE & PREVIEW PROPERTIES

The idea behind previewing property is to develop an understanding of what's on the market and who is likely to buy it. Before previewing the properties, you will need to schedule appointments with the sellers of the active listings.

### SCHEDULING

When scheduling property previews, you need to consider how long and how often.

#### HOW LONG?

Set aside 2-3 hours in your calendar for previewing the active listing properties. Ideally, you would schedule previews for later that day or the following day.

Typically, this is an afternoon activity because you will generally be performing other business-generation activities first thing in the morning (such as systematically contacting your SOI).

Having said that, depending on your market, certain times may work better for the sellers to open their homes for a preview. Consider times during the day that you'll have more success connecting with neighbors.

#### HOW OFTEN?

The answer is several times a week, but property previews should never replace your other prospecting work. When there's an imbalance between previewing homes and finding people to buy or sell them, you will kill your business. If you're just beginning to focus on actively getting leads to fill your pipeline, use the time you have set aside to hold appointments to preview.

Make a target of 2-3 neighborhoods/afternoons per week, or set a goal to preview 8-10 homes a week. Typically, you will be alternating between previewing properties and prospecting around the previewed properties every other afternoon.

For example, you might preview properties on Mondays and Wednesdays and prospect around those previews on Tuesdays and Thursdays. When you factor in the preliminary prep work involved in steps 1 and 2, your schedule might look a little like this:

| Day 1 | Day 2 | Day 3 | Day 4 | Day 5 |
|---|---|---|---|---|
| Prep 10-11AM | | Prep 10-11AM | | Prep 10-11AM |
| Preview 2-5PM | Prospect 2-5PM | Preview 2-5PM | Prospect 2-5PM | Preview 2-5PM |

By month's end, previewing 40 or more homes will give you a great foundation as to what a particular area, price-range, and house style in your market looks like.

When you schedule your appointments, explain that you'd like to preview the home for prospective buyers. It's not necessary to have an actual buyer in mind. Most sellers will be more than amenable to this request as they are obviously highly motivated to sell their home and show it off in any way they can.

### PREVIEW PROPERTIES

When previewing properties, you are essentially surveying the owner and asking questions around the property itself as well as the neighborhood.

By previewing properties, you will start to learn a lot about the neighborhood and why different people like to live there. They'll tell you about the school district, the shopping, the amenities, as well as the downsides to living in the area.

When previewing properties, you'll get the good, the bad, and the ugly about living in the neighborhood! This information is invaluable for connecting with prospects and making powerful and persuasive listing presentations.

And, of course, prospective buyers will be highly interested in what you observed and noted when you previewed the home itself.

When previewing property, the notes you take will eventually serve as a reference script for describing the home to potential buyers. Essentially, your property preview is an advance walk-through that will get buyer leads curious and excited to see the home too.

When making your notes, think about how you will describe and talk about the property to potential buyers.

- Where did you start?
- Where were bathrooms located?
- What's the focal point of the living room?
- What's the privacy like in relation to the neighbors' homes?
- What one thing struck you the most about the home?

Your notes will cue your memory for future clientele. Think of your notes as building an MLS of your personal experience, which has a huge value to clients who haven't had the time to do it.

What's more, your notes and surveys will evidence your success and professionalism when you carry them with you and refer to them while prospecting.

The following Property Preview Checklist will assist you in taking notes and remembering to pay attention to every aspect and detail of the home, from the front yard to the entryway, through every single room, all the way through to the basement and the back garden.

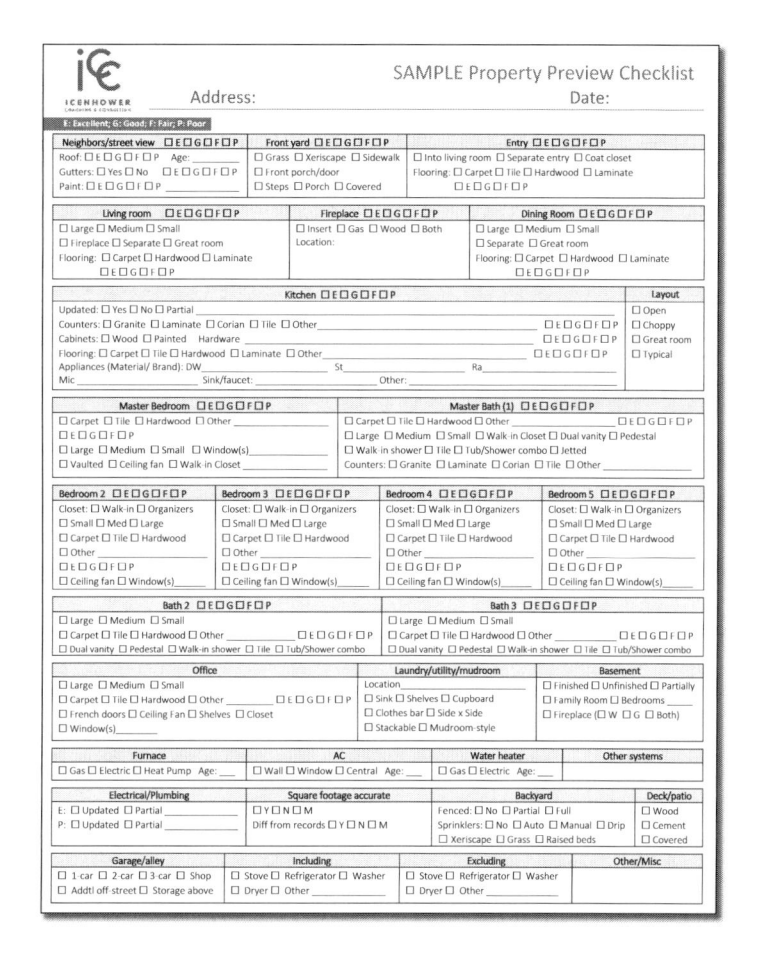

## 4. Map Out & Prospect Around Previewed Property

Part 4 in the process involves a couple of connected activities. Before you begin prospecting around previewed properties, you should have a plan in place. First you'll map out your properties, and then you'll start to prospect around the active listings as well as any FSBOs and expired listings you identified.

### Map It Out

After you have previewed the active listings and made detailed property notes, you should keep your records straight by printing agent reports for each of the active listings you previewed, as well as the nearby expired listings and FSBO properties.

After that, you will map out the properties in order to get a sense of where each home is in relation to the other. A simple online map such as Google Maps will do; don't spend unnecessary time making detailed, complicated maps. The idea is to simply give you a visual checklist and help you coordinate a logical and efficient prospecting route to maximize your time.

- FSBO
- Expired
- Preview
- Door Knock

## Prospect: 5 X 5 X 5

Once you've mapped out the properties, you will be ready to head out and prospect around each of the active listings that you previously previewed. We like to follow a 5 x 5 x 5 door-knock plan. Essentially, you will door-knock five houses to the left and five houses to the right of the active listing, and perhaps five houses across the street too.

Introduce yourself, give a quick overview of the property you previewed, and use the following script to initiate and develop a conversation with each of the neighbors who answers the door.

## Property Preview Door Knocking Script

"Hi! I'm John Smith with ABC Realty, and we're trying to find a buyer for your neighbor's home, which has 4 bedrooms, 2 baths and is priced at $220,000. Who do you know that would like to move into the area?"

[Obtain the contact information of any lead they may give you, proceed with the script below]

"I ask because, as a neighbor, you're the best marketing; you like the area so much, you live here, right?" (Pause)

"What caused you to choose here?" ["Great, let me write that down…"]

"How long have you lived in this home?" [Repeat back to client]

"Where did you move from?" ["Thank you for helping me!"]

"Where would you move to, if you were going to move?"

"While we're here, when do you plan on moving?" [If they plan to move in less than a year, proceed with the script.]

"Would it be of benefit to know what your home is currently worth and be able to start previewing homes online on your own?"

[Set an appointment to review comparison sales, set them up on MLS Listing E-Alert, and list the property for sale]

[**OR** if they say "We're not moving."]

"Great! I appreciate you taking time with me today, would you do me a favor? Be on the lookout for some of our invitations? Thanks again!"

As you can see, if the neighbor you talk to is not planning on moving, you can simply thank them for their time, explain that you're completing a survey and trying to learn more about the neighborhood so that you can help get their neighbor's home sold.

### NOTE:

It's important to understand that there is nothing manipulative about previewing properties. Though the property is another agent's listing, there is no reason why you cannot door-knock around it and prospect to find a buyer that will get it sold. Think of it as doing legwork that the listing agent would not typically want to do. Prospecting around previewed properties is a win-win situation for both of you. The whole idea around cooperating brokers is that you're cooperating and working for mutual benefit, after all.

## From One Script To Another

If you discover that the neighbor plans on moving in less than a year, you have a very hot lead and you will want to go slightly off-script and get them signed up on an MLS Listing

E-Alert email drip campaign using the scripts and talking points we shared with you in the previous chapter.

In order to make a smooth transition from one script to the other, make sure that you have thoroughly memorized the listing alert/neighborhood update talking points that we covered when discussing open houses. It's important to completely internalize different types of scripts and apply them to any occasion so that your conversations can flow naturally and seamlessly from one topic to another.

Remember, when presented as a 'Neighborhood Update Tool', just about anyone you know that owns a home can be set up on a seller lead auto-email drip campaign. The seller lead auto-email drip script should really go to *anyone* who is thinking about moving in the near future.

Here's a reminder of the talking points you can use when door-knocking around property previews and generating neighbor interest:

1. They can look through all the **photos of their neighbors' homes**.
2. They can compare the **amenities, features, and size** of the listings that come up for sale to their own homes.
3. They can know the **price** of each new listing to get a rough idea of the current value of their own home.
4. They can see **how quickly homes sell** and the final sale prices.
5. It will give them a good idea of how the **value of their home is increasing** over time.
6. It will keep them up-to-date on their local **neighborhood market conditions.**

These value proposition points should roll off your tongue every time you talk to someone who is thinking about selling their home in the near future.

As you can see, when previewing property, your end goals are the same as with any kind of prospecting: you are making contacts, expanding your network, and incorporating prospects into that all-important lead follow-up machine.

After prospecting 5 homes across and 5 homes side to side, you should have 15 people set up on MLS Listing E-Alerts within a very short time. The beauty of prospecting around closely grouped properties is that you can knock on more doors in less time while still generating a sizable number of leads.

Use the following Lead Tracking Sheet to track all of the conversations you have when previewing property. A copy of the tracking sheet is also included in the appendix. We will discuss this in more detail when we talk about accountability at the end of the book.

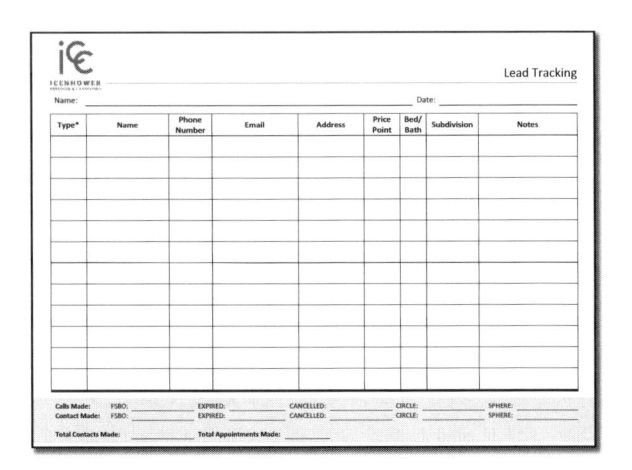

## Prospect Nearby FSBOs & Expireds

Don't forget to maximize your time and prospect expired listings and FSBO leads while you're in the neighborhood too.

It's a good tactic to approach these prospects *after* you've prospected around the active listings. At this stage, you will have learned so much about the neighborhood and can speak very intelligently and authoritatively to these homeowners.

Remember that these are much hotter leads. You know that they actively *want* to sell their home, or at least they very recently did, so it's important that you can communicate with them confidently and with valuable knowledge and insight.

By talking to them about what happened when you went through each of the active listings in the area, and the conversations you had with surrounding homeowners, you will establish yourself as a neighborhood expert in the minds of these prospects.

Remember to refer to your notes and property preview surveys/checklists. It may seem like a small thing to you, but this material offers visual evidence that you are conducting a survey and diligently researching the area—you're showing them that you're an agent that perfects their profession, hones their knowledge, and puts boots on the ground for your prospective buyers.

This will impress these prospects beyond belief. You will have so much more knowledge than other real estate agents who try to gain their business and make a much more impactful impression. Previewing properties and knowing the neighborhood can give you the edge you need over the competition, especially when you're just starting out and expanding your skillsets.

## The Results Are In

At the end of your property previewing, you will have covered a lot of ground. As well as getting your steps in, you will have made a whole lot of contacts!

If you preview 5 active listings and knock on 15 doors around each of those listing (5 across and 5 either side), that's 75 doors and 75 potential future clients.

When you consider the fact that you're also going to prospect around any nearby expired or FSBO listings too, for a no-cost activity, you can see how potentially lucrative this 2-3 hour period could be as you increase your contacts and hone your skills and efficiency.

Your neighborhood knowledge will increase exponentially with each connection you make. You will obtain a massive amount of leads in a short amount of time. You'll conquer the map and develop a great mastery of certain quadrants, sections, or zones of the city or community you're prospecting in.

The key with previewing property is to be efficient and systematic in your efforts. If you can remain diligent in previewing properties, you'll grow both your database and your referral business.

In one month's time spent previewing and prospecting around properties 2-3 times a week, you will have knocked on anywhere between 600 and 900 doors! If only 5% of the people you contacted decided to have you represent them in buying or selling their home, you will have increased your pipeline by 30-45 units in only 30 days while spending only a few hours a week doing it.

Considering you'll be previewing so many properties, you'll need a way to remember each of them. Be sure to take notes to trigger your 7x7 follow-up campaign with the people you'll now introduce to your database. Simplicity is key for your systems; your notes can look as simple as this:

## DOOR KNOCKING NOTE LOG EXAMPLE

| Preview/ Neighbor Property | First Name | Last Name | Moved Here From? When? | Net Move? When? | Invite Info? | Notes about Neighborhood? |
|---|---|---|---|---|---|---|
| 1212 Market St (PREVIEW) | Dave & Wendy | Foster | 1982, New York | Sold, San Fran | n/a | 3 Bd, 2 Ba, 1,900 sqft split level, unfinished basement, master bath opens to deck, gallery style kitchen, classic ford truck in garage |
| 1211 Market St | Tim | Donner | 1995, Baltimore | Not Sure | (555) 555-1212 | Likes Mtb Trails, peaceful, block party in summer |
| 1221 Market St | Linda & Bill | Witner | 1976, Downtown | 6 years, Florida | n/a | Updated house 5 years ago, lots of kids at Halloween, Local pub: sports |
| 1225 Market St | Heather & Ray | Thomas | 2004, San Fran | ??, Work | (555) 867-5309 | Work transfer, don't know neighbors, want sales prices |
| 1226 Market St | David | Castle | 1994, New Hampshire | ??, ??? | (555) 121-1212 | Daughter will be looking in may, call to follow up, Jamie 555-1212 |

# Your Master Plan

Now that you understand each part of the process, your next step is to think about which neighborhoods and target areas you want to master. The key is to be systematic, diligent, and hold yourself accountable to this powerful prospecting plan.

## Target Area Map Creation

As a real estate expert, you need to have facts at your fingertips. The most efficient way to do this is by generating a map of your target area and printing it out. You can find excellent maps from your county or parish, as well as other sources. Or, as we mentioned before, a simple Google Map will do.

1. Start with the neighborhood you live.
2. Check that you're using the map version instead of the satellite version.
3. Take a picture or a screenshot of the area on the screen.
4. Repeat the action until you have a good-sized map of the areas around you.
5. Include reference points where necessary to help you when referring to locations when you're consulting with clients

## How big should your map be?

That depends on how far you're willing to travel to show a property. Real estate agents working in smaller towns may find themselves driving 15 or 20 miles to show property in nearby cities. Real estate agents who work in large cities or metroplexes could drive 40 or 50 miles across town to show a single property.

As you prepare your previewing strategy, focus on the homes in a geographically close area to make the most efficient use of your time. Concentrate on one neighborhood at a time.

Gaining knowledge of the neighborhoods in your area helps you help your prospective clients. Each neighborhood can be identified by average lot size, home size, and price per square foot. They also will have a unique persona or vibe, and a neighborhood's characteristics or personality can matter greatly to prospects.

## EXERCISE: Map the Big Picture

The next activity will help you map your potential and existing inventory. For this exercise, you'll need your maps, some colored pens or pencils, and a computer.

When you have the map(s) printed out, **label the subdivisions or areas on each page.** We recommend beginning with the neighborhood in which you live. You'll have more intrinsic motivation to start here as it's always most interesting to look up what's going on in your own backyard. What's more, you will already have a head start on becoming the local expert, and you may already have some level of name-recognition in the area.

The Internet has made researching properties easier than ever. Your prospects are already researching homes this way, and you can use similar tools to get the information you need.

You can work with data from several websites, such as MLS, Realtor, Zillow, and Niche (i.e., https://www.niche.com/places-to-live/search/best-suburbs-to-buy-a-house/) from which to collect your data.

### Metrics to Learn About Buyers and Inventory

For each of the areas below, select a color and write the data you find in that color on your map or on a corresponding note card about the neighborhood.

- **Valuations**: Take a look at property values in the identified area. What's the average home price, and how does that translate to price per square foot? Write these two numbers down.

- **Lot Sizes**: How big are the lots? Some homes may be on a third or a quarter of an acre, and other subdivisions may have minimum lots sizes of one, five, or more acres. The amount of land can matter to homeowners who want little to do with maintaining a lawn or need space for big dogs.

- **Average Home Size**: What's the average size home in the area? You'll need to know the average square footage as well as how many bedrooms, baths, and spaces available for cars.

- **Builders**: For many buyers, quality matters. If a certain builder is renowned for his or her design work or construction, some buyers will be swayed by that knowledge. Likewise, buyers may wish to avoid certain contractors with poor reputations.

- **Typical Buyers:** Who lives in this neighborhood? Are they blue-collar or white-collar workers? Do you have young children, older children, or are they predominantly empty nesters? Is there a median income and education level? The demographics of a neighborhood will change over time, but potential buyers like to know what the area is like.

- **Schools**: Schools matter greatly to families with children. Does the neighborhood have good schools, and are they within walking distance? If not, is there bus service? How big are the schools, and have they earned any distinction? For example, A National Blue Ribbon Award certifies that a school has met rigorous standards. In addition, learn if there are any charter or private schools in the area, or if there are active homeschooling groups.

- **Amenities**: What amenities are available to buyers? Is there a park or children's playground? What about tennis courts, a golf course or a pool? You may also want to find out if the neighborhood has an HOA and what the fees are. The families in some neighborhoods routinely get together and hold special events, like an outdoor movie night or a BBQ. Sometimes you can learn about these happening if you're a member of a social media group like Facebook or Nextdoor.

- **The neighbors**: If you've been previewing property in the area, you have probably gotten to know the neighbors, and you can allay any fears about potential buyers not having anything in common with their neighbors.

## Branching Out to Surrounding Areas

Now that you've mapped out your immediate area, it's time to branch out and look at more areas in your potential inventory.

Each time you branch out, look for clusters of active listings in close proximity to each other. Focus on those that are tightly packed in neighborhoods to get the most "bang for your buck," which in this case is your time.

Once or twice a week, map out another area, each time moving a little farther from your sales area. Identify your clusters, and continue previewing property in each of these areas, too, because hands-on experience is the best way to learn about potential inventory.

It's also the best way to increase your contacts and list properties.

## Other Considerations: Turn Over Rates

Another way to identify which neighborhoods to target is to calculate property turnover rates.

Neighborhoods with lower turnover rates may be difficult for prospective buyers to get into, or prices could be prohibitive. By figuring out the turnover rate, you may be able to set yourself up as an expert in a particular area more quickly.

Determining the turnover rate is simple if you follow this formula:

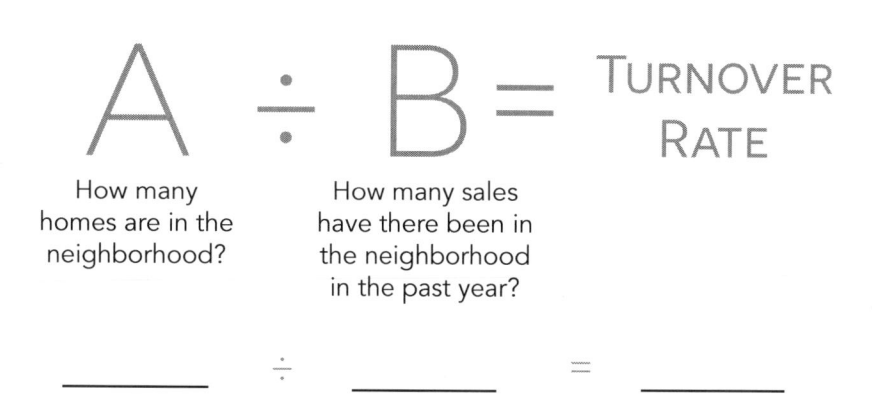

$$A \div B = \text{Turnover Rate}$$

A: How many homes are in the neighborhood?

B: How many sales have there been in the neighborhood in the past year?

_____ ÷ _____ = _____

Neighborhoods with high turnover rates will offer more opportunity for previewing property. Look for indicators that could be driving turnover, as well.

Used in conversation with your clients, you can establish your expertise and help them with options.

### Turnover Rate Script

> "Mr/Mrs. Buyer, I know that Templeton is the top on your list of favorites; what the market has shown me is in the last year, only 12 homes have sold, out of the 340, about 3.5%. With supply and demand driving your purchase price, I want to prepare you that the prices could be higher compared to Allentown, where there's higher turnover."

## Prepare For The Unexpected

After previewing property, agents can respond confidently to questions in listing presentations about FSBOs, expired listings and other homes currently listed for sale.

Agents can become adept at identifying options in available homes that weren't shared during the pre-qualification process, or that their buyers now realize are "must haves" as they walk through property. Other pitfalls that can be avoided include:

- Buyers love the photos of a home, yet didn't realize it was a split-level with multiple flights of stairs
- Seller compared their home to recent neighborhood sale, though unaware of the updates made that elicited a higher offer
- Home meets all needs, yet the surrounding homes are in disrepair
- Not enough "bedrooms" for needs listed, yet there is an office that could be used as a bedroom
- Unfinished basement space not accounted for in square footage
- Previous owner was a smoker, or had pets, and the smell is evident

By bringing a new fact to light, you are preparing your clients with first-hand information they might not have otherwise had. That alone is worth the effort, if not just for risk management!

## Consistency & Accountability

The idea behind previewing property is to develop an understanding of what's on the market and who is likely to buy it.

By previewing property, you are positioning yourself as *the* market expert and *the* real estate agent people turn to when it's time to list a property and purchase another one.

You will develop that expertise only if you do two things:

1. **Preview properties consistently.** That means that every week, you must schedule two hours for previewing. You should schedule 2-3 sets of previews a week, and follow through with knocking on the doors of the listed property and any expired listings or FSBOs and their neighbors.

2. **Hold yourself accountable.** There's no reason to beat your self up if you don't get your previews done, but you should spend time reflecting on what prevented you from

getting into the neighborhoods. You could have become ill or had another emergency in your life. It happens. Successful people find ways to get back on schedule afterward. Any time you don't get your previews in, take a few moments to ask yourself these questions:

### EXERCISE:

- What prevented you from previewing property this week?
- How can you prevent the distraction from happening again?

Develop a plan to make up the lost time and preview the properties. You'll soon find that you are getting to know what's currently available on the market, as well as what potential properties could become available. You also are generating more leads than you ever thought possible.

## Summary

Previewing property is a straightforward 4-part system.

1. Search the MLS for clusters of active listings in a tight geographic area.
2. Identify and note nearby FSBO and expired listing properties.
3. Schedule showings to preview properties later than afternoon.
4. Map out and prospect around the previewed properties the following day, making sure to hit up those local expired and FSBO leads to maximize your time and energy.

Property previews solve many of the problems and issues that face new agents when they first get into the business: lack of contacts, lack of business, and lack of skills. Previewing property is a great way for new agents who do not yet have a large client database to quickly *gain* business while *learning* the business, developing vital skillsets, and becoming the go-to neighborhood expert.

Your goal is to develop supreme mastery of certain quadrants, sections, or zones of the town or city that you want to focus your business on. The level of confidence that an agent exudes after previewing property translates into instant local experience in the minds of prospective clients.

Previewing property and getting to know the neighborhood inside out will give you the confidence and self-assurance that's so crucial for prospecting for leads, and delivering powerful and persuasive listing presentations.

Through frequency and time on task, previewing properties will help you to increase your contacts, increase your skillsets, and balance the Big 3!

So, don't wait. Identify your target area and schedule the time to start previewing properties today.

MODULE 6 APPENDIX 6.1

# 4 STEP PROPERTY PREVIEW STRATEGY

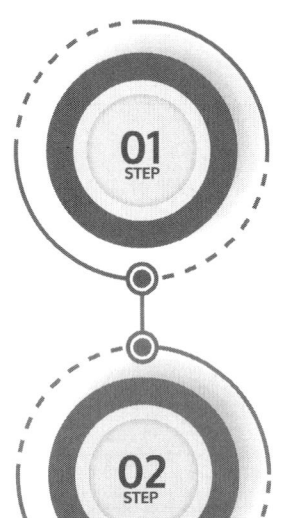

**01 STEP** — Search for clusters of active listings

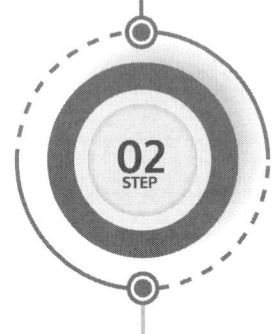

**02 STEP** — Note nearby Expired & FSBO properties

**03 STEP** — Schedule showings to preview property

**04 STEP** — Map out & prospect around previewed property

© Copyright Icenhower Coaching & Consulting, LLC. All rights reserved.

# MODULE 6                                        APPENDIX 6.2

## SAMPLE Property Preview Checklist

Address: _____    Date: _____

**E: Excellent; G: Good; F: Fair; P: Poor**

| Neighbors/street view ☐ E ☐ G ☐ F ☐ P | Front yard ☐ E ☐ G ☐ F ☐ P | Entry ☐ E ☐ G ☐ F ☐ P |
|---|---|---|
| Roof: ☐ E ☐ G ☐ F ☐ P  Age: _____<br>Gutters: ☐ Yes ☐ No  ☐ E ☐ G ☐ F ☐ P<br>Paint: ☐ E ☐ G ☐ F ☐ P _____ | ☐ Grass ☐ Xeriscape ☐ Sidewalk<br>☐ Front porch/door<br>☐ Steps ☐ Porch ☐ Covered | ☐ Into living room ☐ Separate entry ☐ Coat closet<br>Flooring: ☐ Carpet ☐ Tile ☐ Hardwood ☐ Laminate<br>☐ E ☐ G ☐ F ☐ P |

| Living room ☐ E ☐ G ☐ F ☐ P | Fireplace ☐ E ☐ G ☐ F ☐ P | Dining Room ☐ E ☐ G ☐ F ☐ P |
|---|---|---|
| ☐ Large ☐ Medium ☐ Small<br>☐ Fireplace ☐ Separate ☐ Great room<br>Flooring: ☐ Carpet ☐ Hardwood ☐ Laminate<br>☐ E ☐ G ☐ F ☐ P | ☐ Insert ☐ Gas ☐ Wood ☐ Both<br>Location: | ☐ Large ☐ Medium ☐ Small<br>☐ Separate ☐ Great room<br>Flooring: ☐ Carpet ☐ Hardwood ☐ Laminate<br>☐ E ☐ G ☐ F ☐ P |

| Kitchen ☐ E ☐ G ☐ F ☐ P | Layout |
|---|---|
| Updated: ☐ Yes ☐ No ☐ Partial _____<br>Counters: ☐ Granite ☐ Laminate ☐ Corian ☐ Tile ☐ Other_____ ☐ E ☐ G ☐ F ☐ P<br>Cabinets: ☐ Wood ☐ Painted  Hardware _____ ☐ E ☐ G ☐ F ☐ P<br>Flooring: ☐ Carpet ☐ Tile ☐ Hardwood ☐ Laminate ☐ Other_____ ☐ E ☐ G ☐ F ☐ P<br>Appliances (Material/ Brand): DW_____ St_____ Ra_____<br>Mic_____ Sink/faucet:_____ Other:_____ | ☐ Open<br>☐ Choppy<br>☐ Great room<br>☐ Typical |

| Master Bedroom ☐ E ☐ G ☐ F ☐ P | Master Bath (1) ☐ E ☐ G ☐ F ☐ P |
|---|---|
| ☐ Carpet ☐ Tile ☐ Hardwood ☐ Other _____<br>☐ E ☐ G ☐ F ☐ P<br>☐ Large ☐ Medium ☐ Small ☐ Window(s)_____<br>☐ Vaulted ☐ Ceiling fan ☐ Walk-in Closet _____ | ☐ Carpet ☐ Tile ☐ Hardwood ☐ Other _____ ☐ E ☐ G ☐ F ☐ P<br>☐ Large ☐ Medium ☐ Small ☐ Walk-in Closet ☐ Dual vanity ☐ Pedestal<br>☐ Walk-in shower ☐ Tile ☐ Tub/Shower combo ☐ Jetted<br>Counters: ☐ Granite ☐ Laminate ☐ Corian ☐ Tile ☐ Other _____ |

| Bedroom 2 ☐ E ☐ G ☐ F ☐ P | Bedroom 3 ☐ E ☐ G ☐ F ☐ P | Bedroom 4 ☐ E ☐ G ☐ F ☐ P | Bedroom 5 ☐ E ☐ G ☐ F ☐ P |
|---|---|---|---|
| Closet: ☐ Walk-in ☐ Organizers<br>☐ Small ☐ Med ☐ Large<br>☐ Carpet ☐ Tile ☐ Hardwood<br>☐ Other _____<br>☐ E ☐ G ☐ F ☐ P<br>☐ Ceiling fan ☐ Window(s)____ | Closet: ☐ Walk-in ☐ Organizers<br>☐ Small ☐ Med ☐ Large<br>☐ Carpet ☐ Tile ☐ Hardwood<br>☐ Other _____<br>☐ E ☐ G ☐ F ☐ P<br>☐ Ceiling fan ☐ Window(s)____ | Closet: ☐ Walk-in ☐ Organizers<br>☐ Small ☐ Med ☐ Large<br>☐ Carpet ☐ Tile ☐ Hardwood<br>☐ Other _____<br>☐ E ☐ G ☐ F ☐ P<br>☐ Ceiling fan ☐ Window(s)____ | Closet: ☐ Walk-in ☐ Organizers<br>☐ Small ☐ Med ☐ Large<br>☐ Carpet ☐ Tile ☐ Hardwood<br>☐ Other _____<br>☐ E ☐ G ☐ F ☐ P<br>☐ Ceiling fan ☐ Window(s)____ |

| Bath 2 ☐ E ☐ G ☐ F ☐ P | Bath 3 ☐ E ☐ G ☐ F ☐ P |
|---|---|
| ☐ Large ☐ Medium ☐ Small<br>☐ Carpet ☐ Tile ☐ Hardwood ☐ Other _____ ☐ E ☐ G ☐ F ☐ P<br>☐ Dual vanity ☐ Pedestal ☐ Walk-in shower ☐ Tile ☐ Tub/Shower combo | ☐ Large ☐ Medium ☐ Small<br>☐ Carpet ☐ Tile ☐ Hardwood ☐ Other _____ ☐ E ☐ G ☐ F ☐ P<br>☐ Dual vanity ☐ Pedestal ☐ Walk-in shower ☐ Tile ☐ Tub/Shower combo |

| Office | Laundry/utility/mudroom | Basement |
|---|---|---|
| ☐ Large ☐ Medium ☐ Small<br>☐ Carpet ☐ Tile ☐ Hardwood ☐ Other _____ ☐ E ☐ G ☐ F ☐ P<br>☐ French doors ☐ Ceiling Fan ☐ Shelves ☐ Closet<br>☐ Window(s)_____ | Location_____<br>☐ Sink ☐ Shelves ☐ Cupboard<br>☐ Clothes bar ☐ Side x Side<br>☐ Stackable ☐ Mudroom-style | ☐ Finished ☐ Unfinished ☐ Partially<br>☐ Family Room ☐ Bedrooms ____<br>☐ Fireplace (☐ W ☐ G ☐ Both) |

| Furnace | AC | Water heater | Other systems |
|---|---|---|---|
| ☐ Gas ☐ Electric ☐ Heat Pump  Age: ___ | ☐ Wall ☐ Window ☐ Central  Age: ___ | ☐ Gas ☐ Electric  Age: ___ | |

| Electrical/Plumbing | Square footage accurate | Backyard | Deck/patio |
|---|---|---|---|
| E: ☐ Updated ☐ Partial _____<br>P: ☐ Updated ☐ Partial _____ | ☐ Y ☐ N ☐ M<br>Diff from records ☐ Y ☐ N ☐ M | Fenced: ☐ No ☐ Partial ☐ Full<br>Sprinklers: ☐ No ☐ Auto ☐ Manual ☐ Drip<br>☐ Xeriscape ☐ Grass ☐ Raised beds | ☐ Wood<br>☐ Cement<br>☐ Covered |

| Garage/alley | Including | Excluding | Other/Misc |
|---|---|---|---|
| ☐ 1-car ☐ 2-car ☐ 3-car ☐ Shop<br>☐ Addtl off-street ☐ Storage above | ☐ Stove ☐ Refrigerator ☐ Washer<br>☐ Dryer ☐ Other _____ | ☐ Stove ☐ Refrigerator ☐ Washer<br>☐ Dryer ☐ Other _____ | |

© Copyright Icenhower Coaching & Consulting, LLC. All rights reserved.

# Property Preview Door Knocking Script

"Hi! I'm John Smith with ABC Realty, and we're trying to find a buyer for your neighbor's home, which has 4 bedrooms, 2 baths and is priced at $220,000. Who do you know that would like to move into the area?"

[Obtain the contact information of any lead they may give you, proceed with the script below]

"I ask because, as a neighbor, you're the best marketing; you like the area so much, you live here, right?"

(Pause)

"What caused you to choose here?"

["Great, let me write that down..."]

"How long have you lived in this home?"

[Repeat back to client]

"Where did you move from?"

["Thank you for helping me!"]

"Where would you move to, if you were going to move?"

"While we're here, when do you plan on moving?"

[If they plan to move in less than a year, proceed with the script.]

"Would it be of benefit to know what your home is currently worth and be able to start previewing homes online on your own?"

[Set an appointment to review comparison sales, set them up on MLS Listing E-Alert, and list the property for sale]

[OR if they say "We're not moving"]

"Great! I appreciate you taking time with me today, would you do me a favor? Be on the lookout for some of our invitations? Thanks again!"

© Copyright Icenhower Coaching & Consulting, LLC. All rights reserved.

# Module 6

# Appendix 6.4

## Lead Tracking

Name: _____  Date: _____

| Type* | Name | Phone Number | Email | Address | Price Point | Bed/Bath | Subdivision | Notes |
|---|---|---|---|---|---|---|---|---|
|  |  |  |  |  |  |  |  |  |
|  |  |  |  |  |  |  |  |  |
|  |  |  |  |  |  |  |  |  |
|  |  |  |  |  |  |  |  |  |
|  |  |  |  |  |  |  |  |  |
|  |  |  |  |  |  |  |  |  |
|  |  |  |  |  |  |  |  |  |
|  |  |  |  |  |  |  |  |  |
|  |  |  |  |  |  |  |  |  |
|  |  |  |  |  |  |  |  |  |
|  |  |  |  |  |  |  |  |  |

Calls Made: _____  FSBO: _____  EXPIRED: _____  CANCELLED: _____  CIRCLE: _____  SPHERE: _____
Contact Made: _____  FSBO: _____  EXPIRED: _____  CANCELLED: _____  CIRCLE: _____  SPHERE: _____

Total Contacts Made: _____  Total Appointments Made: _____

© Copyright Icenhower Coaching & Consulting, LLC. All rights reserved.

# Module 6
# Appendix 6.5

## Door Knocking Note Log

Name: _____  Date: _____

| Preview/ Neighbor Property | First Name | Last Name | Moved Here From? When? | Next Move? When? | Invite Info? | Notes about Neighborhood? |
|---|---|---|---|---|---|---|
|  |  |  |  |  |  |  |
|  |  |  |  |  |  |  |
|  |  |  |  |  |  |  |
|  |  |  |  |  |  |  |
|  |  |  |  |  |  |  |
|  |  |  |  |  |  |  |
|  |  |  |  |  |  |  |
|  |  |  |  |  |  |  |
|  |  |  |  |  |  |  |
|  |  |  |  |  |  |  |
|  |  |  |  |  |  |  |
|  |  |  |  |  |  |  |
|  |  |  |  |  |  |  |
|  |  |  |  |  |  |  |

© Copyright Icenhower Coaching & Consulting, LLC. All rights reserved.

## Turnover Rate Script

"Mr/Mrs. Buyer, I know that Templeton is the top on your list of favorites; what the market has shown me is in the last year, only 12 homes have sold, out of the 340, about 3.5%. With supply and demand driving your purchase price, I want to prepare you that the prices could be higher compared to Allentown, where there's higher turnover."

# THE BIG 3 OF PROSPECTING SUCCESS

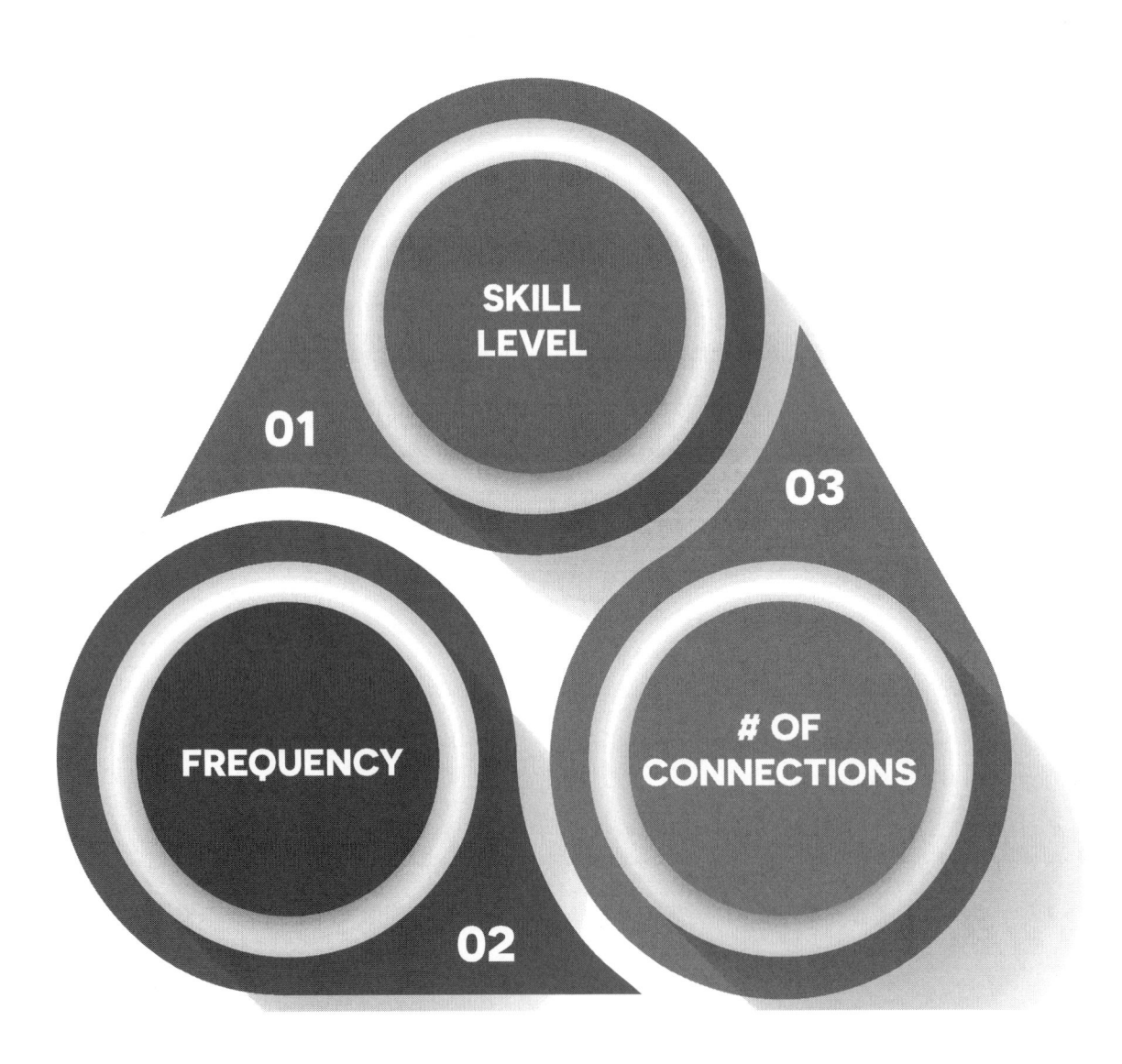

- 01 SKILL LEVEL
- 02 FREQUENCY
- 03 # OF CONNECTIONS

# Time-Management

*"Winning is habit. Unfortunately, so is losing."* – Vincent Lombardi

The National Association of Realtors (NAR) reports that 33% of all licensed agents don't make it to their second year in the business, and 87% of agents fail within the first five years. Whether it's in the first twelve months, or the first five years, the reason most agents quit is typically the same: "I just didn't make enough money."

However, if you ask those same agents, "How much time did you spend trying to get business?" it's usually a shockingly low percentage. Most of the time, we find that agents who struggle to succeed (a) don't have a plan (b) don't commit to a regular systematic schedule, and (c) don't prioritize lead-generation over customer-service.

Rather, they take a scattered, unsystematic approach to their business, and tend to get caught in an endless stop-and-start, up-and-down cycle.

They spend a little bit of time generating business and seem to be on the up and up, but as soon as they have a contract or a transaction in the pipeline, lead-generation grinds to a halt, and they devote all of their time to customer-service.

*Agents who struggle to succeed don't have a plan, don't commit to a regular systematic schedule, and don't prioritize lead-generation over customer-service.*

While they're running around, and filling their days with endless busy-work, their business is actually on the downturn. When the transaction closes, they cash their paycheck and begin the hustle for new business all over again, starting the steep climb back up from the bottom.

Month after month, they're riding the real estate roller coaster and playing the income guessing game. Once a habit has been established, it's very hard to break it—especially the bad ones! This is a very stressful, not to mention dangerous, way to work and live, but it need not be this way.

*Month after month, they're riding the real estate roller coaster and playing the income guessing game.*

Top-producing agents control how much money they make by controlling and religiously scheduling their time. They honor their commitments and they honor themselves by honoring their calendar.

As we've said before, what new agents lack in business, they make up for with a wealth of free time. It's crucial that inexperienced agents take advantage of this precious resource in their first few months in the business and devote all their possible time to skill development, making contacts, and generating leads.

Real estate is a numbers game. You must develop consistent habits and you must begin prospecting with high frequency to develop your skills and see steady, recurring, and sustainable results.

## Learning Targets

In this chapter, you'll learn how to:

- Maintain a healthy time-management mindset
- Tie your annual goals to daily and weekly time-management
- Schedule your first 30 days in the business
- Schedule your first 3 months in the business
- Track your contacts
- Hold yourself accountable

## TIME-MANAGEMENT MINDSET

Throughout this book we repeatedly stress the **fundamental importance of mindset, attitude, and perspective** when it comes to prospecting.

Numerous studies confirm a link between time-management and mindset.

LinkedIn influencer, Dr. Travis Bradberry, identifies a critical relationship between time-management and emotional intelligence. While your rational brain creates your schedule, it is your emotional brain that allows you to stick to it.

Our emotional intelligence is composed, in part, of Self-Management (the ability to care for self) and Relationship Management (the ability to care for others). These components must be balanced for effective time-management.

*While your rational brain creates your schedule, it is your emotional brain that allows you to stick to it.*

Most people understand the importance of adhering to the schedule they develop, but life happens. A family emergency needs your attention, a client email requires an immediate response, or you simply become distracted by a social media post.

You let your emotions get in the way of your motivation. Before you know it, the day has gone by, and you didn't accomplish what you had set out to do. Your ratio of relationship-management to self-management is out of balance.

Learning how to guard your time against interruptions from well-meaning family and friends will allow you the time you need during the day to prospect. You will also have to manage yourself, especially if you find yourself easily distracted. Real estate agents are particularly susceptible to this challenge at two times:

1. As you launch your real estate career, and
2. If you've become complacent in your real estate career

Often, we allow ourselves to procrastinate and become distracted when we have an underlying fear or worry. Though these emotions are very natural when you're just starting out or when your business is going through a bit of a slump, it's important to manage emotions and deal with low mood levels.

In researched published in *Proceedings of the National Academy of Sciences,* psychology professor, James Gross, discovered that people's moods play a decisive role in whether to spend time having fun or focusing on important but boring or tedious tasks.

Strangely enough, the study found that people tend to focus on unpleasant but essential activities (such as housework or doing their taxes) when they're in a *good mood.* When people are in a bad mood, they procrastinate on important tasks that are crucial for their long-term wellbeing, and choose fun or pleasurable activities to cheer themselves up in the short-term. However, once their mood improves they can then refocus on completing important tasks and goals.

---

*The more we can manage our emotions and mindset, and maintain a consistently positive perspective, the more time we can spend on activities that are vital for our future success.*

---

In short, people tend to use their positive mood as a resource that helps them achieve things that will be of benefit to them in the long run. The more we can manage our emotions and mindset, and maintain a consistently positive perspective, the more time we can spend on activities that are vital for our future success.

Scheduling your day isn't about being busy. Research is showing that it's about being healthy and smart.

A study in the *Journal of Occupational and Environmental Medicine,* linked irregular schedules to "diminished cognition and physical health." Workers exposed to such schedules for extended periods "showed decreases in their ability to reason, think, and recall information."

As you'll soon see, your first few weeks and months in the business will be loaded with lead-generation activities. Your days will be long and a working week will include many a weekend too. It's essential that you take the long view, focus on your end-goals, and maintain a positive attitude and mindset in those jam-packed days and weeks.

# **Manage Your Time, Manage Your Goals**

> *"How we spend our days is, of course, how we spend our lives."* – Annie Dillard, author

Time-management is more than scheduling monthly meetings or calendaring phone calls and appointments. Our calendars are a visual representation of our commitment to a larger plan or goal. Each day and week is a mini milestone on the path towards reaching your goals and living the life you want to live.

A long time ago, two Ivy League universities, Harvard and Yale, discovered something remarkable about the earning power of their graduates. Some of them were paid extremely well, and they reported being enormously satisfied with their lives.

Well, of course they were! Who wouldn't be happy making a considerable amount of money?

Not everyone, as it turns out. While money is necessary to live, true satisfaction in life comes from having *choices* and feeling *significant* in the lives of others. The same study showed that being rewarded with a lot of money was merely a *side effect* of setting—and reaching—meaningful goals.

Are you curious about the students who were able to reach their goals? So were the universities, and ten years later they followed up with the students.

Not all of the students in the study were highly successful. In fact, 84% of the students reported earning an average wage or feeling somewhat unsuccessful. These students never identified any goals.

In the meantime, while 10% of the students did have goals, they didn't write them down. They felt as though simply visualizing their goals would be enough and, maybe they were right, because those in the 10% category earned three times what those in the 84% category made.

That leaves 6% of the students, and here's where the study gets interesting. This small group of students had two things in common: they wrote down their goals, and they earned 10 times the salaries of their peers in the study.

> *Time-management is more than scheduling monthly meetings or calendaring phone calls and appointments. Our calendars are a visual representation of our commitment to a larger plan or goal.*

People who write down their goals are far more likely to achieve them. They will experience greater success and will earn more money. They will also have more satisfaction because they will be leading their lives rather than allowing life to direct them.

You can experience the same level of success if you write down your goals and create milestones that help you work towards them.

## GOALS & MILESTONES

Think of your goals as a destination far in the distance, much like a destination on a map. You have to formulate a plan for reaching these goals. You can't merely teleport yourself to them. Instead, you have to make your way step by step.

Along the way, there will be obstacles that could prevent you from being successful if you allowed them to get in your way. As you coordinate your journey towards the goal, you will find yourself picking a path. This path may take you across rivers, through forests, and over mountains. As you complete your journey in each region, you will have achieved a milestone.

Milestones are the stepping-stones that lead you to your goal.

According to Stephen Covey (*The 7 Habits of Highly Effective People*), the best way to identify your milestones and map them out is to work backward from your goal. If your goal is to create an SOI database of 300 contacts within three months (which can seem overwhelming), you will break down the steps like this:

### GOAL

*I will build an SOI database of 300 contacts by July 1.*

I.e. July 1: 300 SOI contacts in the database

### MILESTONE

*I will add 100 SOI contacts to the database every month.*

June 30: 100 SOI contacts
May 30: 100 SOI contacts
April 30: 100 SOI contacts

These milestones can be broken down even further, by week and by day.

**GOAL**
300 SOI contacts by July 1

*03* MILESTONE — I will add **100 SOI contacts** to the database **every month**.
- April 30: 100 SOI contacts
- May 30: 100 SOI contacts
- June 30: 100 SOI contacts

*02* MILESTONE — I will add **25 contacts** to the SOI database **weekly**.

*01* MILESTONE — I will add **5 SOI contacts daily**.

**MILESTONE**: *I will add 25 contacts to the SOI database weekly.*

**MILESTONE**: *I will add 5 SOI contacts daily.*

Note how these milestones can be broken down even further, by week and by day.

As you can see, milestones go hand in hand with time-management. In order to add 5 SOI contacts a day, you will need to block out time and schedule that activity.

Five SOI contacts a day seems much more manageable than the end goal of 300. If you create a daily schedule and a consistent habit of adding these contacts gradually, you may be surprised by how much your database grows. Often, by breaking large goals into smaller, manageable milestones, we wind up exceeding the original targets we set for ourselves.

*Milestones and goals go hand in hand with time-management*

What business plans or goals have you set for yourself? Perhaps you have a target Gross Commission Income (GCI) that you would like to achieve in your first year?

In Chapter 3, we introduced you to our 7:1 SOI ratio. An SOI contact plan with 40 annual touches (using a variety of contact methods) will result in 1 closed transaction for every 7 people in your SOI database. For example, if you have 300 SOI members in your database, a 7:1 conversion rate results in 43 closed transactions a year.

We then imagined that the average sales price in your area is $250,000, and assumed that you charge a 3% commission. This means you would earn $7,500 per closed transaction and have an annual GCI of $322,500.

- 43 Transactions x $7,500 GCI = $322,500 in annual gross commission income
- $322,500 in Annual Gross Commission Income simply by staying in contact with 300 people, 40 times a year

## EXERCISE: Set Your GCI Goals

Setting concrete goals is crucial. If you have not done so already, begin by setting a target GCI Goal:

*I will have an annual Gross Commission Income of*

$ _____.

To achieve this goal, you will first need to calculate the average sales price in your area and your average 3% commission figure.

- Average home price in your area: $ _____
- 3% per transaction side: $ _____

Then, divide your GOAL GCI by the average transaction commission amount in order to calculate how many transactions you must make in 12 months to reach that goal.

- $_____ ÷ _____ = _____

  Goal GCI      Average 3% Commission Figure      Transactions

Do you currently have enough SOI members to support those transaction conversion ratios? For example, 300 ÷ 7 = 43 transactions, but 200 divided by 7 = 28 or 29 transactions, and 100 ÷ 7 = just 14 transactions.

Depending on the average sales price in your area, you may need to add a lot more SOI members to achieve your annual GCI goals.

You will need to create monthly, weekly, and daily milestones to add enough SOI members to reach your desired income, and additional milestones for maintaining a 40-touch contact plan with each member.

These monthly, weekly, and daily milestones will not take care of themselves. You will need to schedule systematic and focused time on your calendar and develop the discipline and habits that will take you to where you want to be.

Now that you have a long-term goal in mind, it's time to take the first steps towards achieving your plan.

## THE FIRST 30 DAYS

*"The law of harvest is to reap more than you sow. Sow an act, and you reap a habit. Sow a habit, and you reap a character. Sow a character, and you reap a destiny."* – James Allen

The first thirty days are critical to your success in real estate. It is during these early weeks that you'll develop the habits that will help you achieve your goals.

From week to week, **your schedule will increasingly expand as you start to layer additional activities into your days**. The order of your schedule will also adjust slightly from week to week as you extend the time spent on certain activities and make room for other undertakings.

**The first 30 days are very aggressive**, particularly that all-important first week, where every minute of your day is spent on lead-generation, lead follow-up and skill-development. In the first 30 days, your working day will be extremely long and likely exhausting.

Of course, you are free to create whatever schedule you can. The schedules we suggest are for people who need to make income as quickly as possible to make ends meet, or for those of you who are highly driven to succeed.

In the first 30 days, you will face a lot of rejection and do a lot of activities that are completely new and out of your comfort zone. For this reason, one of your activities will be a constant from week to week.

**Each and every morning, you will start your day with a motivational recitation.** Whether it's a meditation, a prayer, an affirmation, or inspiration from your "success library" that we talked about in the first chapter, it's important that you take a few moments each morning to create a clear mind and a positive mindset.

As we said at the very beginning of this book, until you understand that your attitude and perspective is the fundamental bedrock of your business, it's unlikely that anything we teach you will stick or generate meaningful results in the long term. You might learn a few nifty tricks or techniques to get you started, but that can only take you so far. To truly succeed and go the distance in your prospecting career, you will need to adopt and maintain a positive mindset to fuel and reenergize you.

## WEEK 1

On this first important week, begin each day by looking at the **annual goals** you've set for yourself and visualizing what you want to achieve.

As we mentioned, if you have an inspirational quote or verse you like to recite, we recommend saying it at the beginning of your day. Beginning each day with a **motivational recitation** helps you shift your attitude toward the positive and get more done as a result. Spend no more than five minutes on your motivational recitation.

| Day 1 | Day 2 | Day 3 | Day 4 | Day 5 | Day 6 | Day 7 |
|---|---|---|---|---|---|---|
| Motivational Recitation AM | Motivational Recitation AM | Motivational Recitation AM | Motivational Recitation AM | Motivational Recitation AM | | |

The next part of your schedule is critical to your prospecting success.

Devote three hours a day to **memorizing scripts and practicing presentations**.

You do not want to practice on the fly when you're actually doing lead-generation. You will waste a lot of time and lose a lot of contacts that way. In these first crucial weeks, you want business and you want it fast, so make sure to practice, memorize, and internalize in order to master and refine these scripts.

Begin by practicing the following scripts. Your first week will primarily focus on growing your SOI, and expanding your knowledge through property previews.

1. SOI Scripts
2. Property Preview Scripts
3. MLS Listing E-Alert Scripts
4. Seller Pre-Qualification & Conversion
5. Objection Handling

However, make some time to practice scripts for expired listings, FSBOs, and other lead-generation strategies. Varying your practice will round out your scripts, while making sure you're not specializing to a point that you're ignoring other business-generating strategies.

When practicing scripts, don't forget the following tips:
- Practice Scripts in Parts.
- Positivity: Voice Inflection & Tonality.
- Posture: Stand Up, Chin Up!
- Partner Up: Work in Pairs.

As you'll recall from chapter 2, new agents often schedule practice with a partner first thing in the morning before they start making real calls. **Role-playing with a partner helps take the morning edge off**. That way, when you pick up the phone and start doing the real thing, you're already in the zone, you've hit your stride, and you won't miss out on some potentially great contacts because you're still warming up.

Three hours of script practice is a lot, so it's best if you break the time into a session in the morning and a session in the afternoon.

Practice SOI scripts in the morning before spending an hour on **SOI Prospecting** calls and making a minimum of **10 SOI Contacts each day**.

Your Week 1 schedule will expand like this:

| Day 1 | Day 2 | Day 3 | Day 4 | Day 5 | Day 6 | Day 7 |
|---|---|---|---|---|---|---|
| Motivational Recitation AM | Motivational Recitation AM | Motivational Recitation AM | Motivational Recitation AM | Motivational Recitation AM | | |
| 1.5 HR Scripted Presentation Practice AM | 1.5 HR Scripted Presentation Practice AM | 1.5 HR Scripted Presentation Practice AM | 1.5 HR Scripted Presentation Practice AM | 1.5 HR Scripted Presentation Practice AM | | |
| 1 HR Prospecting AM Call 10 SOI contacts & document on *Daily SOI Contact Form* to find out how soon they or someone they know will be selling a home. | 1 HR Prospecting AM Call 10 SOI contacts & document on *Daily SOI Contact Form* to find out how soon they or someone they know will be selling a home. | 1 HR Prospecting AM Call 10 SOI contacts & document on *Daily SOI Contact Form* to find out how soon they or someone they know will be selling a home. | 1 HR Prospecting AM Call 10 SOI contacts & document on *Daily SOI Contact Form* to find out how soon they or someone they know will be selling a home. | 1 HR Prospecting AM Call 10 SOI contacts & document on *Daily SOI Contact Form* to find out how soon they or someone they know will be selling a home. | | |
| 1.5 HR Scripted Presentation Practice PM | 1.5 HR Scripted Presentation Practice PM | 1.5 HR Scripted Presentation Practice PM | 1.5 HR Scripted Presentation Practice PM | 1.5 HR Scripted Presentation Practice PM | | |

Keep track of your daily SOI contacts with this form from ICC:

Between family, friends and acquaintances, you should have at least 100 names in your SOI database, but do not spend your working day writing down and inputting their names—that work is best done outside the regular business day.

Instead, you'll spend your time at work prospecting and making actual calls, because your ultimate goal for the month is to set up four appointments and complete two transactions.

To increase your chances of reaching this goal, your Week 1 schedule will also include another 2 hours a day **prospecting for other sources** (FSBOs, Expireds, Circle-Prospecting). As you can see from the schedule below, we suggest an hour in the AM and another hour in the evening.

And, as you know from the previous chapter, **new agents should take advantage of their wealth of free time and load up their schedule with previewing properties** and increasing their skill level by actively prospecting for business.

Typically, you will **alternate between previewing properties and prospecting around the previewed properties every other afternoon**. For example, you might preview properties on Mondays, Wednesdays, and Fridays and prospect around those previews on Tuesdays and Thursdays.

By now, your Week 1 schedule is incredibly full, but we're not quite done yet.

You should **devote your evenings to lead-generation follow-up** and making those crucial 7X7 touches.

It's also an excellent idea to **sit in on another agent's Open House**. Whenever possible, you should take advantage of any opportunity or opening to shadow more experienced agents and learn through real-life situations and scenarios.

| Day 1 | Day 2 | Day 3 | Day 4 | Day 5 | Day 6 | Day 7 |
|---|---|---|---|---|---|---|
| Motivational Recitation AM | Motivational Recitation AM | Motivational Recitation AM | Motivational Recitation AM | Motivational Recitation AM | | |
| 1.5 HR Scripted Presentation Practice AM | 1.5 HR Scripted Presentation Practice AM | 1.5 HR Scripted Presentation Practice AM | 1.5 HR Scripted Presentation Practice AM | 1.5 HR Scripted Presentation Practice AM | | |
| 1 HR Prospecting AM Call 10 SOI contacts & document on *Daily SOI Contact Form* to find out how soon they or someone they know will be selling a home. | 1 HR Prospecting AM Call 10 SOI contacts & document on *Daily SOI Contact Form* to find out how soon they or someone they know will be selling a home. | 1 HR Prospecting AM Call 10 SOI contacts & document on *Daily SOI Contact Form* to find out how soon they or someone they know will be selling a home. | 1 HR Prospecting AM Call 10 SOI contacts & document on *Daily SOI Contact Form* to find out how soon they or someone they know will be selling a home. | 1 HR Prospecting AM Call 10 SOI contacts & document on *Daily SOI Contact Form* to find out how soon they or someone they know will be selling a home. | | |
| 1 HR Propsecting AM - 20 Contacts from other sources | 1 HR Propsecting AM - 20 Contacts from other sources | 1 HR Propsecting AM - 20 Contacts from other sources | 1 HR Prospecting AM - 20 Contacts from other sources | 1 HR Prospecting AM - 20 Contacts from other sources | | OPEN HOUSE Sit another agent's Open House |
| 1.5 HR Scripted Presentation Practice PM | 1.5 HR Scripted Presentation Practice PM | 1.5 HR Scripted Presentation Practice PM | 1.5 HR Scripted Presentation Practice PM | 1.5 HR Scripted Presentation Practice PM | | |
| Preview 2-3 Properties PM | Lead Generation Follow-up (5-7) | Preview 2-3 Properties PM | Lead Generation Follow-up (5-7) | Preview 2-3 Properties PM | | |
| 1 HR Prospecting PM | 1 HR Prospecting PM | 1 HR Prospecting PM | 1 HR Prospecting PM | 1 HR Prospecting PM | | |
| Lead Generation Follow-up (5-7) | | Lead Generation Follow-up (5-7) | | Lead Generation Follow-up (5-7) | | |

Attending an open house in your first week will also help you adjust to the reality of working on the weekend. Like we said, this is an aggressive and intensive schedule, but in order to reap the rewards of running your own business, you will need to push yourself to go the extra mile in the first few weeks and months.

## EXERCISE: My Week 1 Schedule

Take a moment to complete your own Week 1 Schedule. Notice that the days are numbered so that you can choose which days of the week you will work. Your job is to fill in the days of the week, the activities, and the times you will do them. Include the times you plan to take lunch.

Blank schedules are available in the Appendix.

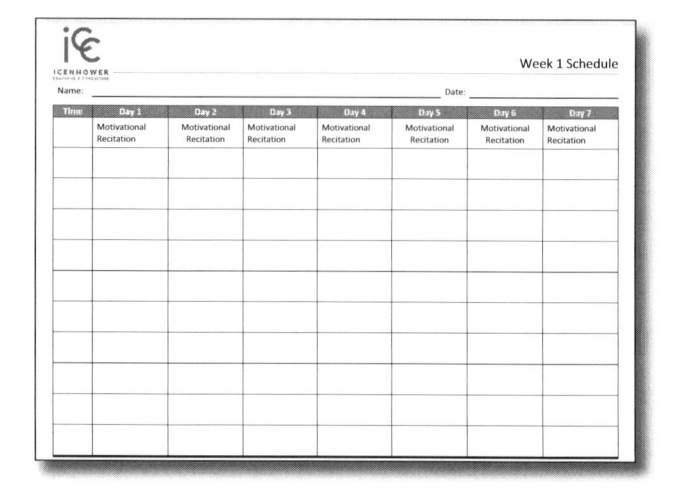

## EXERCISE: Debrief

At the end of each week, take a few moments to debrief and complete a reflection about how the week went. You can write your thoughts in your journal or on the included workbook page.

Write your honest responses to these questions:

- What percentage of the time were you able to follow the proposed schedule?
- What did you do that helped you to keep the schedule?
- What got in your way of keeping the schedule?
- What will you do to overcome scheduling obstacles in the future?

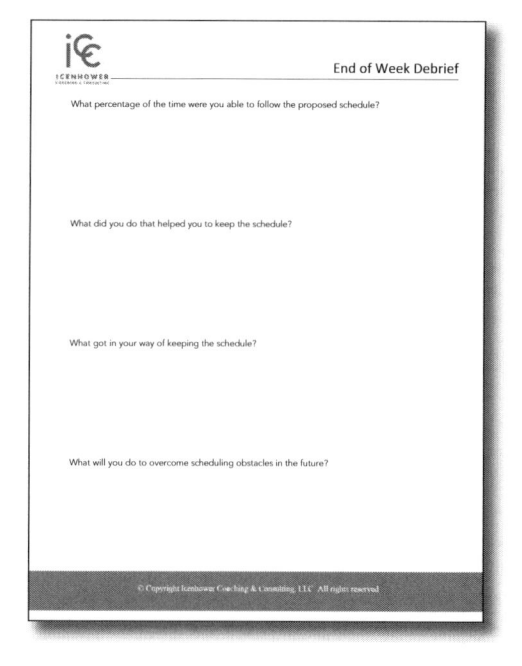

## WEEK 2

Repeat the key activities from Week 1's schedule. Begin each morning with a motivational recitation. Devote time in the morning to scripted presentation practice and systematically contacting your SOI for a minimum of 2 hours.

In week 2, you will also **add Expired and Cancelled Listing prospecting** phone calls to your schedule every single morning. Your schedule will now look something like this:

| Day 8 | Day 9 | Day 10 | Day 11 | Day 12 | Day 13 | Day 14 |
|---|---|---|---|---|---|---|
| Motivational Recitation AM | Motivational Recitation AM | Motivational Recitation AM | Motivational Recitation AM | Motivational Recitation AM | | |
| 1.5 HR Scripted Presentation Practice AM | 1.5 HR Scripted Presentation Practice AM | 1.5 HR Scripted Presentation Practice AM | 1.5 HR Scripted Presentation Practice AM | 1.5 HR Scripted Presentation Practice AM | | |
| 1 HR Prospecting AM Checkl MLS & contact Expired Listings & document on *One Day 20 Contacts Form.* | 1 HR Prospecting AM Checkl MLS & contact Expired Listings & document on *One Day 20 Contacts Form.* | 1 HR Prospecting AM Checkl MLS & contact Expired Listings & document on *One Day 20 Contacts Form.* | 1 HR Prospecting AM Checkl MLS & contact Expired Listings & document on *One Day 20 Contacts Form.* | 1 HR Prospecting AM Checkl MLS & contact Expired Listings & document on *One Day 20 Contacts Form.* | | |
| 1 HR Propsecting AM - Call 10 SOI contacts & document on *Daily SOI Contact Form* to find out how soon they or someone they know will be selling a home. | 1 HR Propsecting AM - Call 10 SOI contacts & document on *Daily SOI Contact Form* to find out how soon they or someone they know will be selling a home. | 1 HR Propsecting AM - Call 10 SOI contacts & document on *Daily SOI Contact Form* to find out how soon they or someone they know will be selling a home. | 1 HR Propsecting AM - Call 10 SOI contacts & document on *Daily SOI Contact Form* to find out how soon they or someone they know will be selling a home. | 1 HR Propsecting AM - Call 10 SOI contacts & document on *Daily SOI Contact Form* to find out how soon they or someone they know will be selling a home. | | |
| 1 HR Propsecting AM - Call 10 SOI contacts & document on *Daily SOI Contact Form* to find out how soon they or someone they know will be selling a home. | 1 HR Propsecting AM - Call 10 SOI contacts & document on *Daily SOI Contact Form* to find out how soon they or someone they know will be selling a home. | 1 HR Propsecting AM - Call 10 SOI contacts & document on *Daily SOI Contact Form* to find out how soon they or someone they know will be selling a home. | 1 HR Propsecting AM - Call 10 SOI contacts & document on *Daily SOI Contact Form* to find out how soon they or someone they know will be selling a home. | 1 HR Propsecting AM - Call 10 SOI contacts & document on *Daily SOI Contact Form* to find out how soon they or someone they know will be selling a home. | | |
| Preview 2-3 Properties PM | Lead Generation Follow-up (5-7) | Preview 2-3 Properties PM | Lead Generation Follow-up (5-7) | Preview 2-3 Properties PM | | |
| 1 HR Prospecting PM or Transaction Completion | 1 HR Prospecting PM or Transaction Completion | 1 HR Prospecting PM or Transaction Completion | 1 HR Prospecting PM or Transaction Completion | 1 HR Prospecting PM or Transaction Completion | | |
| Lead Generation Follow-up (5-7) | | Lead Generation Follow-up (5-7) | | Lead Generation Follow-up (5-7) | | |

Your goal is to make 20 to 25 contacts every day, 5 days a week.

If there aren't 20 expired listings in your area on any given morning, go back and call old expired listings as those people may still want to sell, and sometimes calling old expireds works just as well.

More importantly, you will be gaining valuable real-life experience handling objections and delivering your practiced presentations to a wide variety of people

Use the following form to hold yourself accountable and track your daily Expired Listing contacts.

> **NOTE:** A contact equals an actual conversation. When you make calls, not everyone is going to answer first time and you might merely be leaving a voice message. A conversation must take place to count the call as a contact.

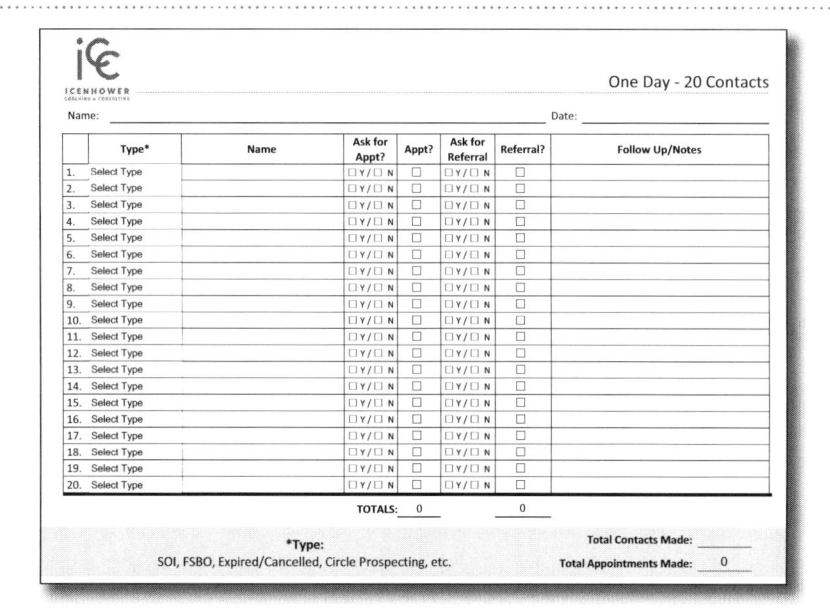

### EXERCISE: My Week 2 Schedule

As before, take a moment to review the sample schedule above and then complete your own Week 2 schedule.

## EXERCISE: Debrief

And, once again, at the end of your second week, write your honest responses to these accountability questions:

- What percentage of the time were you able to follow the proposed schedule?
- What did you do that aided you in keeping the schedule?
- What got in your way of keeping the schedule?
- What will you do to overcome scheduling obstacles in the future?

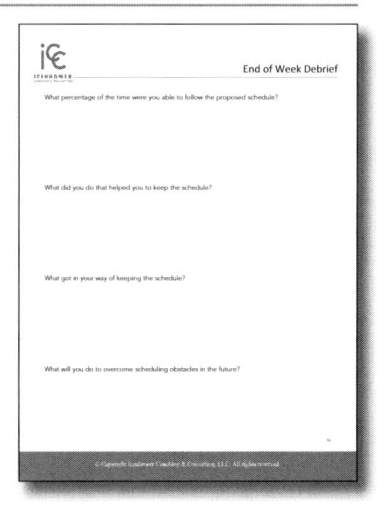

## WEEK 3

In your third week, your schedule will be quite similar to weeks 1 and 2. You will be previewing properties, prospecting, and contacting your SOI database in addition to practicing your presentation scripts.

At this stage, you may very well be seeing the first fruits of your labor and have a property under contract. For this reason, we have scheduled some time in the afternoon for **Transaction Coordination and Completion**. You will note that business-generation continues to take priority in the morning and the percentage of time spent on customer-service is quite low.

You must always prioritize business-generation over business servicing. Spend at least 80% of your time on tasks and activities that generate income, and spend 20% of your time (or less!) servicing the business that the 80% efforts created.

Your suggested schedule looks like this:

| Day 15 | Day 16 | Day 17 | Day 18 | Day 19 | Day 20 | Day 21 |
|---|---|---|---|---|---|---|
| Motivational Recitation AM | Motivational Recitation AM | Motivational Recitation AM | Motivational Recitation AM | Motivational Recitation AM | | |
| 1.5 HR Scripted Presentation Practice AM | 1.5 HR Scripted Presentation Practice AM | 1.5 HR Scripted Presentation Practice AM | 1.5 HR Scripted Presentation Practice AM | 1.5 HR Scripted Presentation Practice AM | | |
| 1 HR Prospecting AM Checkl MLS & contact Expired Listings & document on One Day 20 Contacts Form. | 1 HR Prospecting AM Checkl MLS & contact Expired Listings & document on One Day 20 Contacts Form. | 1 HR Prospecting AM Checkl MLS & contact Expired Listings & document on One Day 20 Contacts Form. | 1 HR Prospecting AM Checkl MLS & contact Expired Listings & document on One Day 20 Contacts Form. | 1 HR Prospecting AM Checkl MLS & contact Expired Listings & document on One Day 20 Contacts Form. | | |
| 1 HR Propsecting AM - Call 10 SOI contacts & document on *Daily SOI Contact Form*. | 1 HR Propsecting AM - Call 10 SOI contacts & document on *Daily SOI Contact Form*. | 1 HR Propsecting AM - Call 10 SOI contacts & document on *Daily SOI Contact Form*. | 1 HR Propsecting AM - Call 10 SOI contacts & document on *Daily SOI Contact Form*. | 1 HR Propsecting AM - Call 10 SOI contacts & document on *Daily SOI Contact Form*. | | |
| 1 HR Propsecting AM - Call 10 SOI contacts & document on *Daily SOI Contact Form*. | 1 HR Propsecting AM - Call 10 SOI contacts & document on *Daily SOI Contact Form*. | 1 HR Propsecting AM - Call 10 SOI contacts & document on *Daily SOI Contact Form*. | 1 HR Propsecting AM - Call 10 SOI contacts & document on *Daily SOI Contact Form*. | 1 HR Propsecting AM - Call 10 SOI contacts & document on *Daily SOI Contact Form*. | OPEN HOUSE Schedule & hold your own listed home or sit another agent's Open House | |
| Preview 2-3 Properties PM | Lead Generation Follow-up (5-7) | Preview 2-3 Properties PM | Lead Generation Follow-up (5-7) | Preview 2-3 Properties PM | | |
| 1 HR Prospecting PM or Transaction Completion | 1 HR Prospecting PM or Transaction Completion | 1 HR Prospecting PM or Transaction Completion | 1 HR Prospecting PM or Transaction Completion | 1 HR Prospecting PM or Transaction Completion | | |
| Lead Generation Follow-up (5-7) | Call backs | Lead Generation Follow-up (5-7) | Lead Generation Follow-up (5-7) | Accountability Meeting | | |

Notice that you have added **your own Open House** to your schedule. From this week forward, you will schedule at *least one* Open House per weekend.

You should also **schedule time to call back clients** and attend an **accountability meeting** that will help you develop a habit of holding yourself accountable to your goals and targets. We will discuss this in more detail in chapter 14.

### EXERCISE: My Week 3 Schedule

Once again, take a moment to review the suggested schedule above and complete your own Week 3 schedule.

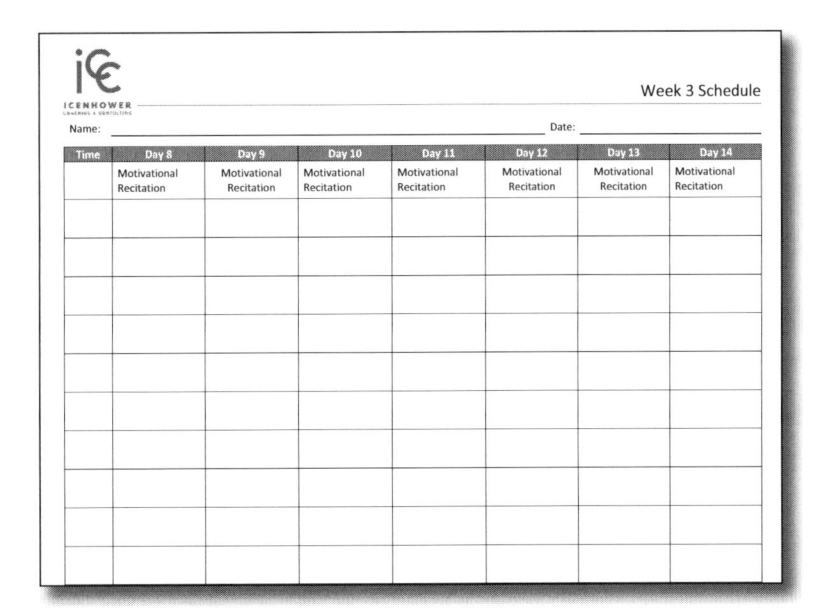

### EXERCISE: Debrief

At the end of your third week, write your responses to these questions:

- What percentage of the time were you able to follow the proposed schedule?
- What did you do that aided you in keeping the schedule?
- What got in your way of keeping the schedule?
- What will you do to overcome scheduling obstacles in the future?

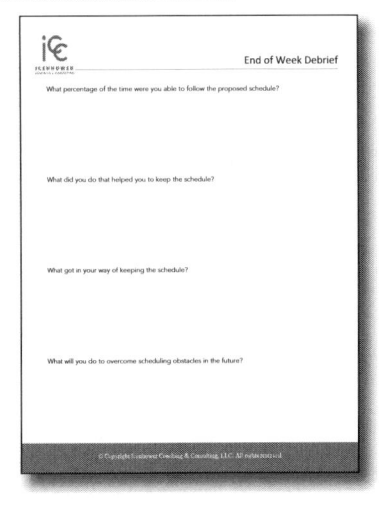

## WEEK 4

By now, some real estate agents begin to give up, after only a month of prospecting. Don't! The work is hard, but the results will be tremendous by the end of your first 90 days. Keep up your energy, maintain a positive outlook, and don't let up.

*"Character is the ability to carry out a good resolution long after the excitement of the moment has passed."* - Cavett Robert

Stay on schedule with the following strategies:

- Give your tasks undivided attention
- Create realistic deadlines or stopping points
- Train to avoid distractions by starting in small increments
- Glance at your schedule regularly
- Always add cushion time between tasks
- Schedule your hardest tasks in off hours
- Schedule play inside of work
- Look for ways to optimize time, or batch similar tasks together
- Develop and practice how to say "No" to new items that aren't in your schedule already

**By now you should have four appointments**—either you've already gone on them, or you are finishing them this week—**which should result in at least two transactions**. We will share our strategies for this in chapter 12 on the art of closing.

You will notice that we do not pre-schedule time for learning how to service customers and transactions. **Too many agents concentrate on learning customer-service before they even have a customer!** There will be plenty of time to learn this part of the process on the fly as you encounter various situations and scenarios. Believe us when we say that customer-service is the easy part—we have never met an agent who quit the business because they didn't know how to handle their clients!

**In the first few weeks, the key is to develop discipline, habits and skills around generating and converting business.** The rest will come in time. Continue with the schedule of previewing, prospecting, systematically contacting your SOI database, and organizing at least one open house each weekend.

| Day 22 | Day 23 | Day 24 | Day 25 | Day 26 | Day 27 | Day 28 |
|---|---|---|---|---|---|---|
| Motivational Recitation AM | Motivational Recitation AM | Motivational Recitation AM | Motivational Recitation AM | Motivational Recitation AM | | |
| 1.5 HR Scripted Presentation Practice AM | 1.5 HR Scripted Presentation Practice AM | 1.5 HR Scripted Presentation Practice AM | 1.5 HR Scripted Presentation Practice AM | 1.5 HR Scripted Presentation Practice AM | | |
| 1 HR Prospecting AM Contact Expired Listings & document on *One Day 20 Contacts Form*. | 1 HR Prospecting AM Contact Expired Listings & document on *One Day 20 Contacts Form*. | 1 HR Prospecting AM Call 10 SOI contacts & document on *Daily SOI Contact Form*. | 1 HR Prospecting AM Call 10 SOI contacts & document on *Daily SOI Contact Form*. | 1 HR Prospecting AM Call 10 SOI contacts & document on *Daily SOI Contact Form*. | | |
| 1 HR Propsecting AM - Call 10 SOI contacts & document on *Daily SOI Contact Form* to find out how soon they or someone they know will be selling a home. | 1 HR Propsecting AM - Call 10 SOI contacts & document on *Daily SOI Contact Form* to find out how soon they or someone they know will be selling a home. | 1 HR Propsecting AM - Call 10 SOI contacts & document on *Daily SOI Contact Form* to find out how soon they or someone they know will be selling a home. | 1 HR Propsecting AM - Call 10 SOI contacts & document on *Daily SOI Contact Form* to find out how soon they or someone they know will be selling a home. | 1 HR Propsecting AM - Call 10 SOI contacts & document on *Daily SOI Contact Form* to find out how soon they or someone they know will be selling a home. | | |
| 1 HR Propsecting AM - Call 10 SOI contacts & document on *Daily SOI Contact Form* to find out how soon they or someone they know will be selling a home. | 1 HR Propsecting AM - Call 10 SOI contacts & document on *Daily SOI Contact Form* to find out how soon they or someone they know will be selling a home. | 1 HR Propsecting AM - Call 10 SOI contacts & document on *Daily SOI Contact Form* to find out how soon they or someone they know will be selling a home. | 1 HR Propsecting AM - Call 10 SOI contacts & document on *Daily SOI Contact Form* to find out how soon they or someone they know will be selling a home. | 1 HR Propsecting AM - Call 10 SOI contacts & document on *Daily SOI Contact Form* to find out how soon they or someone they know will be selling a home. | | OPEN HOUSE Schedule & hold your own listed home or sit another agent's Open House. You will schedule one Open House every weekend going forward. |
| Preview 2-3 Properties PM | Lead Generation Follow-up (5-7) | Preview 2-3 Properties PM | Lead Generation Follow-up (5-7) | Preview 2-3 Properties PM | | |
| 1 HR Prospecting PM or Transaction Completion | 1 HR Prospecting PM or Transaction Completion | 1 HR Prospecting PM or Transaction Completion | 1 HR Prospecting PM or Transaction Completion | 1 HR Prospecting PM or Transaction Completion | | |
| Lead Generation Follow-up (5-7) | Call backs | Lead Generation Follow-up (5-7) | Lead Generation Follow-up (5-7) | Accountability Meeting | | |

## EXERCISE: My Week 4 Schedule

Again, it's your turn to take control of your week, personalizing the hours you will spend practicing and prospecting.

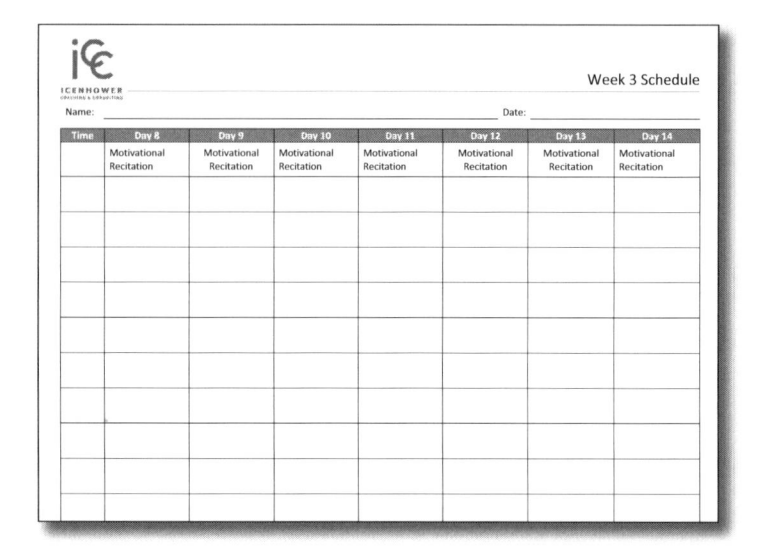

## EXERCISE: Debrief

And, again, it's very important that you debrief at the end of your week and write your responses to these questions:

- What percentage of the time were you able to follow the proposed schedule?
- What did you do that aided you in keeping the schedule?
- What got in your way of keeping the schedule?
- What will you do to overcome scheduling obstacles in the future?
- How will you keep your attitude and energy levels elevated?

## THE FIRST 3 MONTHS, DAYS 1-90

### MONTH 1

With the first month complete, you're on your way to developing the habits that will make you a real estate agent who gets results. You can't let up now, though, because if you do, you have to start the process over. Focus on the habits that will further your real estate career.

# WAYS TO MAKE HABITS STICK

1. Determine the real reason a habit hasn't stuck in the past.
2. Write it down.
3. Pick habits that reinforce each other.
4. Plan for yo\ur habits (create a schedule).
5. Be consistent.
6. Stay ahead, so you don't fall behind.
7. Track your habits regularly.
8. Anticipate challenges: people, places, events, things.
9. Remove temptations.
10. Get a buddy.
11. Place reminders in different places.
12. Visualize the rewards and results.
13. Start simple, and build on your wins.

**MONTH 2**

For the second month, days 31-60, aim to add a lot more presentations to your schedule. At this stage, you should be conducting buyer consultation appointments and listing presentations on a regular basis, converting buyers into signing buyer agency agreements and converting seller prospects into signing listing agreements.

You'll also need to maintain your prospecting schedule. You should be devoting four hours a day to this alone—two hours for previewing and two hours for prospecting, five days a week. You'll need to raise your number of SOI contacts, reaching out to 10 SOI contacts per day plus 20 contacts from these sources:

- FSBO
- Expired listings
- Just Listed
- Just Sold
- Previewing Properties (door knocking)

A good way to hold yourself accountable for making these additional contacts is with a tracking sheet like our One Day-20 Contacts form.

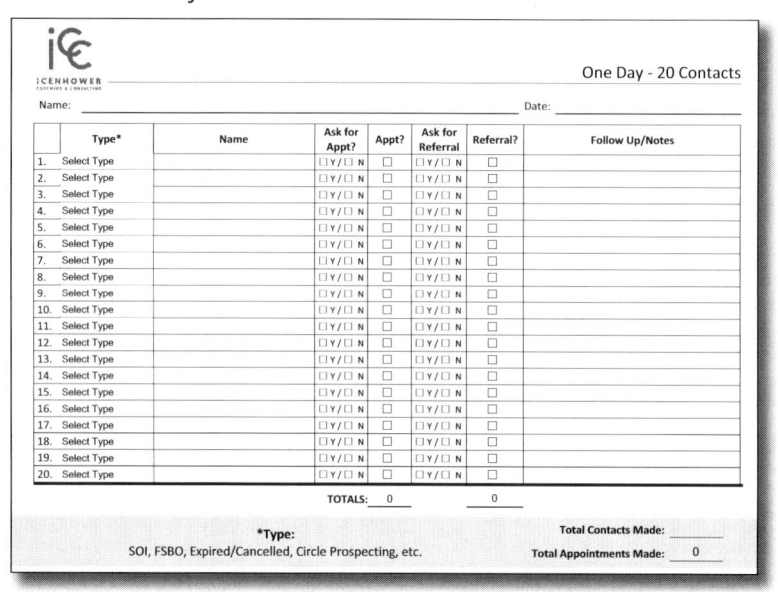

For the second month you spend prospecting, add an hour to your working day, so you can follow up with leads—a minimum of 5-7 people daily. Again, there's a form for this:

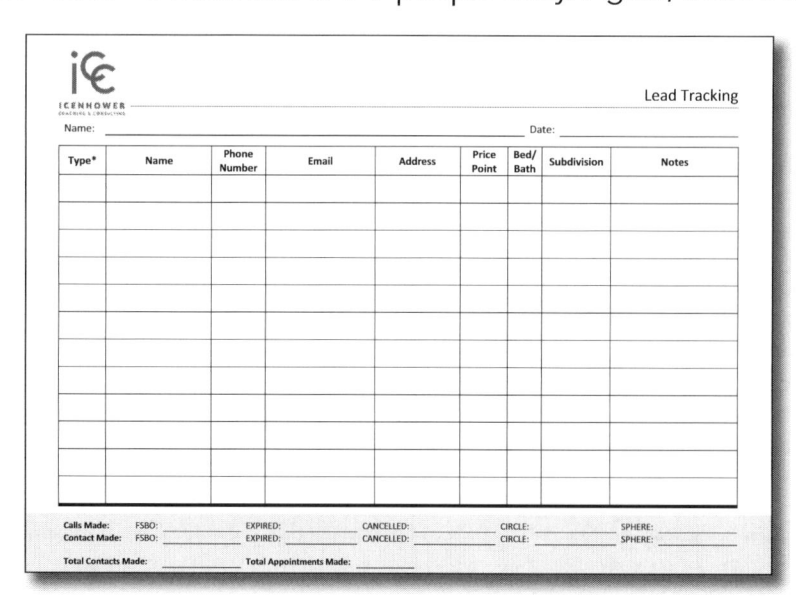

By the end of this month, you should have six appointments (which you can flex into your day) and three signed contracts.

Every week in your second month, plan your own personalized schedule based on your particular situation.

[Personalized Schedule blank form with Time column and Day 1–Day 7 columns, each with "Motivational Recitation" in the first row]

Continue your journals reflections every week. Look back at what you have written. Are there any trends or patterns that have emerged?

## MONTH 3

In your third month, days 61-90, the work will seem to get easier now. You're developing discipline and habits and starting to see results from your actions and activities.

The only way this month should be getting harder for you is because you're starting to generate so much business and customer-service is coming increasingly into play! This is a good problem to have. Converting clients is fantastic, but it's important to stick to your business-generation schedule and not veer too far away from that in any given day or week.

You should still be lead-generating a minimum of 4-5 hours a day. Maintain your schedule for making 10 SOI contacts each day, and add other prospecting methods to your calendar.

Don't get caught in a stop-and-start, rollercoaster cycle where you devote all your time to customer-service and have to start from scratch as soon as these transactions close.

Again, it's your turn. Every week in your third month, plan your own personalized schedule based on your particular situation.

## CHECK YOUR GAUGES

At the end of your initial 3-month prospecting period, you should take some time to review the data you've generated. These numbers include:

- Hours spent per month previewing

- Number of homes previewed
- Hours per month spent prospecting
- Number of SOI database contacts made
- Number of leads generated
- Number of appointments
- Numbers of transactions
- Open houses held

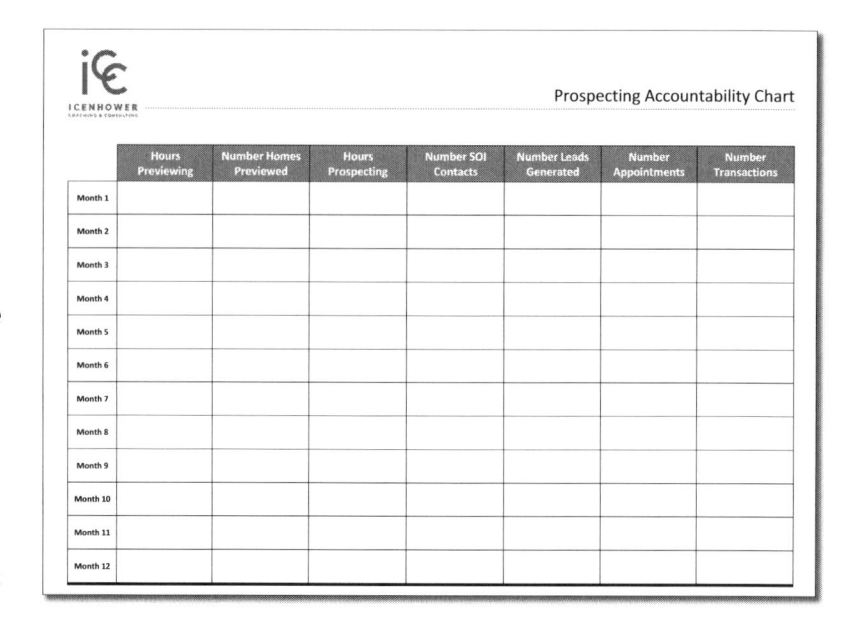

However, simply gathering the numbers isn't enough. Data is only useful when you commit to its analysis and use it to drive your next steps. We recommend completing our ICC Year-to-Date Data Check-Up Form to help you compare, track and analyze those numbers you've generated.

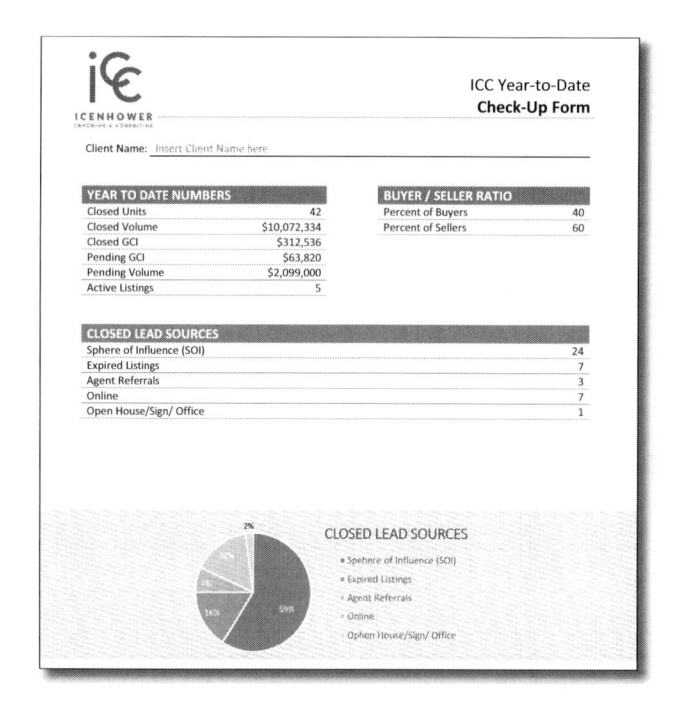

Now that you have some numbers to review, it's time to find two accountability partners who will help you stick to you schedule and meet your goals.

> **5 AGREEMENTS WITH YOUR ACCOUNTABILITY PARTNER(S)**
>
> The best accountability partners are willing to:
>
> 1. Own that tracking is part of doing business
> 2. Get your numbers together
> 3. Report real data in an agreed format
> 4. Discuss your data and answer the tough questions to help you find solution to what might not be working.
> 5. Accept their encouragement to continue what IS working.

When you agree to be accountable, you are obligated to track your activity, accept responsibility for your actions and report your results in a clear and accurate manner.

Of course, situations do sometimes arise that are genuinely urgent and more important than lead-generation. Sometimes, you will truly have to do something else during the time you had blocked off for income-producing activities.

However, don't develop a mindset that you had to something else *instead*. Rather, you have to do something else *as well*. You still need to hold yourself accountable for those hours of activity. When something comes up, you erase your time block for that day, but you extend your time blocks an hour each on the next two days. Never erase your tasks without replacing them somewhere else in your schedule.

We will discuss the importance of accountability in more detail in chapter 14.

## THE NEXT 3 MONTHS, DAYS 91-120

For Months 4-6, you will maintain your schedule from Month 3. By now, the habits of previewing, prospecting and contacting leads will feel natural because you've been doing it regularly and systematically.

Continue your motivational recitations every morning and your journal reflections every week. Look back at what you have written. Are there any trends or patterns that have emerged? Don't ignore potential problems and hope that they'll simply go away. Speak with your ICC coach about any stumbling blocks or perspectives that are preventing you from sticking to your schedule and achieving your goals.

Eventually, you will find ways to flex your calendar to meet your professional and personal needs. The first few months are exhausting but you will never again have this time in your career to lay the foundation you need for sustained success in the future.

Your goal is to increase your business and income to increase your personal freedom, work-life balance, and achieve the life you want.

In the first weeks and months, you'll have to work a little bit longer than you might want to, but understand that you are working towards a place where that will no longer happen, and you'll be able to tip the balance back in the other direction.

In time, your schedule will settle down and resemble something like this:

## SAMPLE WEEKLY CALENDAR

| Time | Mon 3/13 | Tues 3/14 | Wed 3/15 | Thu 3/16 | Fri 3/17 |
|---|---|---|---|---|---|
| 6a | | | | | |
| 7a | | | | | |
| 8a | | | | | |
| | 8:30 - Prepare for Business | 8:30 - Prepare for Business | 8:30 - Prepare for Business | 8:30 - Prepare for Business | 8:30 - Prepare for Business |
| 9a | 9 — 11 Marketing/Business Generation | 9 — 11 Marketing/Business Generation | 9 — 11 Marketing/Business Generation | 9 — 11 Marketing/Business Generation | 9 — 11 Marketing/Business Generation |
| 10a | | | | | |
| 11a | 11 — 12p Business Servicing | 11 — 12p Business Servicing | 11 — 12p Business Servicing | 11 — 12p Business Servicing | 11 — 12p Business Servicing |
| 12p | 12p-1p Lunch | 12p-1p Lunch | 12p-1p Lunch | 12p-1p Lunch w/ Wife | 12p-1p Lunch |
| 1p | 1p — 2p Lead Conversion & Follow-Up | 1p — 2p Lead Conversion & Follow-Up | 1p — 2p Lead Conversion & Follow-Up | | 1p — 2p Lead Conversion & Follow-Up |
| 2p | 2p — 3p Business Servicing | 2p — 3p Business Servicing | 2p — 3p Business Servicing | 2p — 3p Lead Conversion & Follow-Up | 2p — 3p Business Servicing |
| 3p | | | | 3p — 4p Business Servicing | |
| 4p | 4p — 5:30p Listings Presentation - 123 Cottonwood Ct | 4p — 6p Show Homes to Johnsons | 3:30p — 6p Watch David's T-Ball Game | | 4p — 6p Listings Presentation - 456 Spring Creek Way |
| 5p | | | | 4:30p — 5:30p Buyer Consultation w/ Taylors | |
| 6p | | | | | |
| 7p | | 6:30p — 8p Family Dinner | | | 6:30p — 8:30p Family Birthday Party |
| 8p | | | | | |
| 9p | | | | | |

## Summary

Real estate has a phenomenally high failure rate. 33% of all licensed agents don't make it to their second year in the business, and 87% of agents fail within the first five years.

These agents don't have a plan, don't commit to a regular systematic schedule, and don't prioritize lead-generation over customer-service.

Rather, they take a scattered, unsystematic approach to their business, and tend to get caught in an endless stop-and-start, up-and-down income cycle.

The first six months that you spend prospecting are for frontloading with lead-generation activities. This will be the *only* time in your career when you have this much time to generate leads since you have little or no pending transactions or clients to service. You will never again have this time in your career to lay the foundation you need for sustained success in the future. You *must* put in the time to produce income quickly.

The time you spend generating these leads will gradually decrease due to the necessity of handling the business that you generate. In fact, for the second half of the year, months

6-12, you will find that you have less time for prospecting because you will be routinely handling more closings. After all, that's your ultimate goal, right?

For now, however, you're forming the habits and developing the discipline that will build a strong foundation for a long and lucrative real estate career.

## BOOKS TO FUEL YOUR PLANNING

- *4 Disciplines of Execution*, Sean Covey
- *Make to Stick: Why some ideas Survive and Others Die*, Chip Heath
- *The Power of Habit: Why we do what we do in life and business*, Charles Duhigg
- *Million Dollar Habits: Proven Power Practices to Double and Triple your income*, Brian Tracy
- *Getting Things Done: The Art of Stress-Free Productivity*, David Allen
- *The Checklist Manifesto: How to Get Things Right*, Dr. Atul Gawande
- *168 Hours: You Have More Time Than You Think*
- *Becoming the 1%: How to Master Productivity and Rise to the Top in 7 Days: The New One Minute Manager*, Ken Blanchard and Spencer Johnson
- *The Effective Executive: The Definitive Guide to Getting The Right Things Done*

MODULE 7 — APPENDIX 7.1

# GOAL & MILESTONE

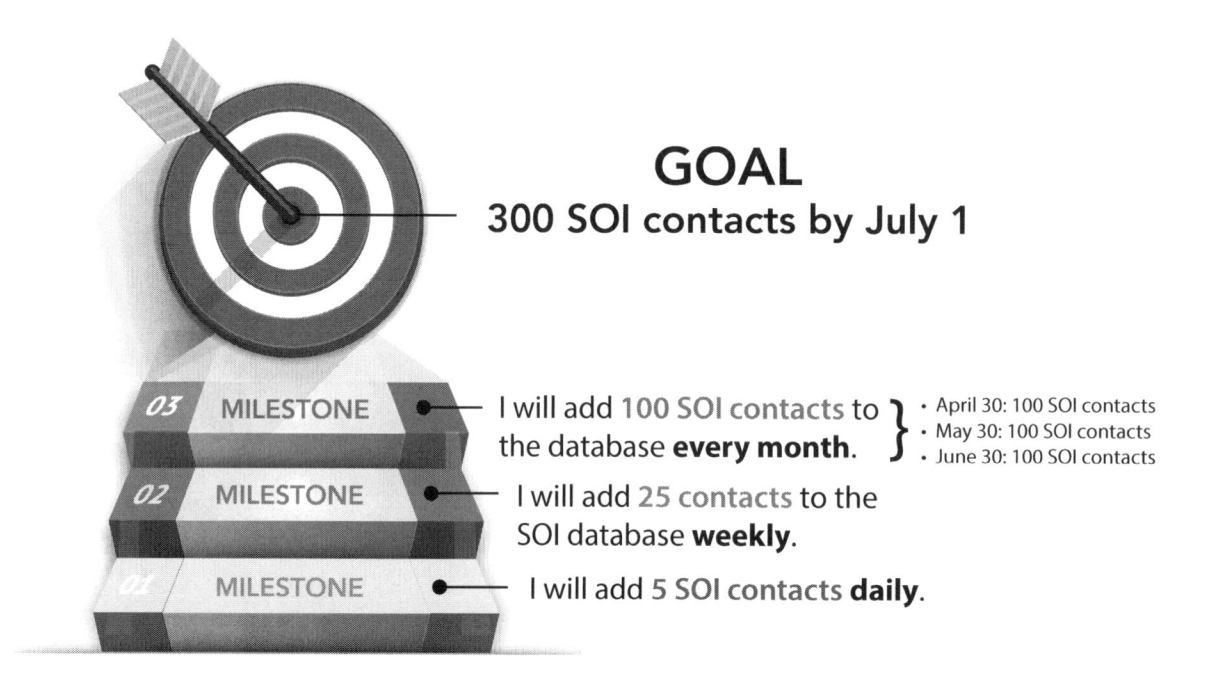

**GOAL**
300 SOI contacts by July 1

**03 MILESTONE** — I will add **100 SOI contacts** to the database **every month**.
- April 30: 100 SOI contacts
- May 30: 100 SOI contacts
- June 30: 100 SOI contacts

**02 MILESTONE** — I will add **25 contacts** to the SOI database **weekly**.

**01 MILESTONE** — I will add **5 SOI contacts daily**.

## GOAL

## MILESTONE

## MILESTONE BREAKDOWN

1.

2.

3.

© Copyright Icenhower Coaching & Consulting, LLC. All rights reserved.

# GOAL & MILESTONE TRACKER

## GOAL

## MILESTONE

### MILESTONE BREAKDOWN

1. 
2. 
3. 

## GOAL

## MILESTONE

### MILESTONE BREAKDOWN

1. 
2. 
3. 

© Copyright Icenhower Coaching & Consulting, LLC. All rights reserved.

# Module 7

# Appendix 7.3

## Daily SOI Contact Form

Name: _____  Date: _____

| # | Name | Ask for Appt? | Appt? | Ask for Referral | Referral? | Follow Up/Notes |
|---|------|---------------|-------|------------------|-----------|-----------------|
| 1. | | ☐Y/☐N | ☐ | ☐Y/☐N | ☐ | |
| 2. | | ☐Y/☐N | ☐ | ☐Y/☐N | ☐ | |
| 3. | | ☐Y/☐N | ☐ | ☐Y/☐N | ☐ | |
| 4. | | ☐Y/☐N | ☐ | ☐Y/☐N | ☐ | |
| 5. | | ☐Y/☐N | ☐ | ☐Y/☐N | ☐ | |
| 6. | | ☐Y/☐N | ☐ | ☐Y/☐N | ☐ | |
| 7. | | ☐Y/☐N | ☐ | ☐Y/☐N | ☐ | |
| 8. | | ☐Y/☐N | ☐ | ☐Y/☐N | ☐ | |
| 9. | | ☐Y/☐N | ☐ | ☐Y/☐N | ☐ | |
| 10. | | ☐Y/☐N | ☐ | ☐Y/☐N | ☐ | |
| 11. | | ☐Y/☐N | ☐ | ☐Y/☐N | ☐ | |
| 12. | | ☐Y/☐N | ☐ | ☐Y/☐N | ☐ | |
| 13. | | ☐Y/☐N | ☐ | ☐Y/☐N | ☐ | |
| 14. | | ☐Y/☐N | ☐ | ☐Y/☐N | ☐ | |
| 15. | | ☐Y/☐N | ☐ | ☐Y/☐N | ☐ | |
| 16. | | ☐Y/☐N | ☐ | ☐Y/☐N | ☐ | |
| 17. | | ☐Y/☐N | ☐ | ☐Y/☐N | ☐ | |
| 18. | | ☐Y/☐N | ☐ | ☐Y/☐N | ☐ | |
| 19. | | ☐Y/☐N | ☐ | ☐Y/☐N | ☐ | |
| 20. | | ☐Y/☐N | ☐ | ☐Y/☐N | ☐ | |

**TOTALS:** 0 0

**Total Contacts Made:** _____  **Total Referrals Received:** 0  **Total Appointments Made:** 0

© Copyright Icenhower Coaching & Consulting, LLC. All rights reserved.

# Module 7

## Appendix 7.4

## Week 1 Schedule

Name: _____  Date: _____

| Time | Day 1 | Day 2 | Day 3 | Day 4 | Day 5 | Day 6 | Day 7 |
|------|-------|-------|-------|-------|-------|-------|-------|
|      | Motivational Recitation | Motivational Recitation | Motivational Recitation | Motivational Recitation | Motivational Recitation | Motivational Recitation | Motivational Recitation |
|      |       |       |       |       |       |       |       |
|      |       |       |       |       |       |       |       |
|      |       |       |       |       |       |       |       |
|      |       |       |       |       |       |       |       |
|      |       |       |       |       |       |       |       |
|      |       |       |       |       |       |       |       |
|      |       |       |       |       |       |       |       |
|      |       |       |       |       |       |       |       |
|      |       |       |       |       |       |       |       |
|      |       |       |       |       |       |       |       |
|      |       |       |       |       |       |       |       |

© Copyright Icenhower Coaching & Consulting, LLC. All rights reserved.

# Module 7
# Appendix 7.5

## Week 2 Schedule

Name: _____ Date: _____

| Time | Day 8 | Day 9 | Day 10 | Day 11 | Day 12 | Day 13 | Day 14 |
|------|-------|-------|--------|--------|--------|--------|--------|
|      | Motivational Recitation | Motivational Recitation | Motivational Recitation | Motivational Recitation | Motivational Recitation | Motivational Recitation | Motivational Recitation |
|      |       |       |        |        |        |        |        |
|      |       |       |        |        |        |        |        |
|      |       |       |        |        |        |        |        |
|      |       |       |        |        |        |        |        |
|      |       |       |        |        |        |        |        |
|      |       |       |        |        |        |        |        |
|      |       |       |        |        |        |        |        |
|      |       |       |        |        |        |        |        |
|      |       |       |        |        |        |        |        |
|      |       |       |        |        |        |        |        |

© Copyright Icenhower Coaching & Consulting, LLC. All rights reserved.

# Module 7

# Appendix 7.6

## Week 3 Schedule

Name: _____  Date: _____

| Time | Day 8 | Day 9 | Day 10 | Day 11 | Day 12 | Day 13 | Day 14 |
|------|-------|-------|--------|--------|--------|--------|--------|
|      | Motivational Recitation | Motivational Recitation | Motivational Recitation | Motivational Recitation | Motivational Recitation | Motivational Recitation | Motivational Recitation |
|      |       |       |        |        |        |        |        |
|      |       |       |        |        |        |        |        |
|      |       |       |        |        |        |        |        |
|      |       |       |        |        |        |        |        |
|      |       |       |        |        |        |        |        |
|      |       |       |        |        |        |        |        |
|      |       |       |        |        |        |        |        |
|      |       |       |        |        |        |        |        |
|      |       |       |        |        |        |        |        |
|      |       |       |        |        |        |        |        |

© Copyright Icenhower Coaching & Consulting, LLC. All rights reserved.

# Module 7

## Appendix 7.7

## Week 4 Schedule

Name: _____  Date: _____

| Time | Day 8 | Day 9 | Day 10 | Day 11 | Day 12 | Day 13 | Day 14 |
|------|-------|-------|--------|--------|--------|--------|--------|
|      | Motivational Recitation | Motivational Recitation | Motivational Recitation | Motivational Recitation | Motivational Recitation | Motivational Recitation | Motivational Recitation |
|      |       |       |        |        |        |        |        |
|      |       |       |        |        |        |        |        |
|      |       |       |        |        |        |        |        |
|      |       |       |        |        |        |        |        |
|      |       |       |        |        |        |        |        |
|      |       |       |        |        |        |        |        |
|      |       |       |        |        |        |        |        |

© Copyright Icenhower Coaching & Consulting, LLC. All rights reserved.

# Module 7

# Appendix 7.8

## End of Week Debrief

What percentage of the time were you able to follow the proposed schedule?

What did you do that helped you to keep the schedule?

What got in your way of keeping the schedule?

What will you do to overcome scheduling obstacles in the future?

© Copyright Icenhower Coaching & Consulting, LLC. All rights reserved.

# Module 7

# Appendix 7.9

## One Day - 20 Contacts

Name: _____ Date: _____

| | Type* | Name | Ask for Appt? | Appt? | Ask for Referral | Referral? | Follow Up/Notes |
|---|---|---|---|---|---|---|---|
| 1. | Select Type | | ☐Y/☐N | ☐ | ☐Y/☐N | ☐ | |
| 2. | Select Type | | ☐Y/☐N | ☐ | ☐Y/☐N | ☐ | |
| 3. | Select Type | | ☐Y/☐N | ☐ | ☐Y/☐N | ☐ | |
| 4. | Select Type | | ☐Y/☐N | ☐ | ☐Y/☐N | ☐ | |
| 5. | Select Type | | ☐Y/☐N | ☐ | ☐Y/☐N | ☐ | |
| 6. | Select Type | | ☐Y/☐N | ☐ | ☐Y/☐N | ☐ | |
| 7. | Select Type | | ☐Y/☐N | ☐ | ☐Y/☐N | ☐ | |
| 8. | Select Type | | ☐Y/☐N | ☐ | ☐Y/☐N | ☐ | |
| 9. | Select Type | | ☐Y/☐N | ☐ | ☐Y/☐N | ☐ | |
| 10. | Select Type | | ☐Y/☐N | ☐ | ☐Y/☐N | ☐ | |
| 11. | Select Type | | ☐Y/☐N | ☐ | ☐Y/☐N | ☐ | |
| 12. | Select Type | | ☐Y/☐N | ☐ | ☐Y/☐N | ☐ | |
| 13. | Select Type | | ☐Y/☐N | ☐ | ☐Y/☐N | ☐ | |
| 14. | Select Type | | ☐Y/☐N | ☐ | ☐Y/☐N | ☐ | |
| 15. | Select Type | | ☐Y/☐N | ☐ | ☐Y/☐N | ☐ | |
| 16. | Select Type | | ☐Y/☐N | ☐ | ☐Y/☐N | ☐ | |
| 17. | Select Type | | ☐Y/☐N | ☐ | ☐Y/☐N | ☐ | |
| 18. | Select Type | | ☐Y/☐N | ☐ | ☐Y/☐N | ☐ | |
| 19. | Select Type | | ☐Y/☐N | ☐ | ☐Y/☐N | ☐ | |
| 20. | Select Type | | ☐Y/☐N | ☐ | ☐Y/☐N | ☐ | |

**TOTALS:** 0     0

**\*Type:** SOI, FSBO, Expired/Cancelled, Circle Prospecting, etc.

Total Contacts Made: _____

Total Appointments Made: 0

© Copyright Icenhower Coaching & Consulting, LLC. All rights reserved.

MODULE 7 APPENDIX 7.10

# WAYS TO MAKE HABITS STICK

1. Determine the real reason a habit hasn't stuck in the past.
2. Write it down.
3. Pick habits that reinforce each other.
4. Plan for yo\ur habits (create a schedule).
5. Be consistent.
6. Stay ahead, so you don't fall behind.
7. Track your habits regularly.
8. Anticipate challenges: people, places, events, things.
9. Remove temptations.
10. Get a buddy.
11. Place reminders in different places.
12. Visualize the rewards and results.
13. Start simple, and build on your wins.

© Copyright Icenhower Coaching & Consulting, LLC. All rights reserved.

# Module 7

## Appendix 7.11

## Lead Tracking

Name: _____ Date: _____

| Type* | Name | Phone Number | Email | Address | Price Point | Bed/Bath | Subdivision | Notes |
|---|---|---|---|---|---|---|---|---|
|  |  |  |  |  |  |  |  |  |
|  |  |  |  |  |  |  |  |  |
|  |  |  |  |  |  |  |  |  |
|  |  |  |  |  |  |  |  |  |
|  |  |  |  |  |  |  |  |  |
|  |  |  |  |  |  |  |  |  |
|  |  |  |  |  |  |  |  |  |
|  |  |  |  |  |  |  |  |  |
|  |  |  |  |  |  |  |  |  |
|  |  |  |  |  |  |  |  |  |
|  |  |  |  |  |  |  |  |  |

Calls Made: _____  FSBO: _____  EXPIRED: _____  CANCELLED: _____  CIRCLE: _____  SPHERE: _____
Contact Made: _____  FSBO: _____  EXPIRED: _____  CANCELLED: _____  CIRCLE: _____  SPHERE: _____
Total Contacts Made: _____  Total Appointments Made: _____

© Copyright Icenhower Coaching & Consulting, LLC. All rights reserved.

# Module 7 — Appendix 7.12

## Personalized Schedule

Name: _____  Date: _____

| Time | Day 1 | Day 2 | Day 3 | Day 4 | Day 5 | Day 6 | Day 7 |
|---|---|---|---|---|---|---|---|
| | Motivational Recitation | Motivational Recitation | Motivational Recitation | Motivational Recitation | Motivational Recitation | Motivational Recitation | Motivational Recitation |
| | | | | | | | |
| | | | | | | | |
| | | | | | | | |
| | | | | | | | |
| | | | | | | | |
| | | | | | | | |
| | | | | | | | |
| | | | | | | | |
| | | | | | | | |
| | | | | | | | |
| | | | | | | | |

© Copyright Icenhower Coaching & Consulting, LLC. All rights reserved.

# Module 7

## Appendix 7.13

### Prospecting Accountability Chart

| | Hours Previewing | Number Homes Previewed | Hours Prospecting | Number SOI Contacts | Number Leads Generated | Number Appointments | Number Transactions |
|---|---|---|---|---|---|---|---|
| Month 1 | | | | | | | |
| Month 2 | | | | | | | |
| Month 3 | | | | | | | |
| Month 4 | | | | | | | |
| Month 5 | | | | | | | |
| Month 6 | | | | | | | |
| Month 7 | | | | | | | |
| Month 8 | | | | | | | |
| Month 9 | | | | | | | |
| Month 10 | | | | | | | |
| Month 11 | | | | | | | |
| Month 12 | | | | | | | |

© Copyright Icenhower Coaching & Consulting, LLC. All rights reserved.

# Module 7

# Appendix 7.14

## ICC Year-to-Date
## Check-Up Form

**Client Name:** Insert Client Name here

### YEAR TO DATE NUMBERS

| | |
|---|---|
| Closed Units | 42 |
| Closed Volume | $10,072,334 |
| Closed GCI | $312,536 |
| Pending GCI | $63,820 |
| Pending Volume | $2,099,000 |
| Active Listings | 5 |

### BUYER / SELLER RATIO

| | |
|---|---|
| Percent of Buyers | 40 |
| Percent of Sellers | 60 |

### CLOSED LEAD SOURCES

| | |
|---|---|
| Sphere of Influence (SOI) | 24 |
| Expired Listings | 7 |
| Agent Referrals | 3 |
| Online | 7 |
| Open House/Sign/ Office | 1 |

### CLOSED LEAD SOURCES

- Sphere of Influence (SOI) — 59%
- Expired Listings — 16%
- Agent Referrals — 7%
- Online — 16%
- Open House/Sign/ Office — 2%

© Copyright Icenhower Coaching & Consulting, LLC. All rights reserved.

MODULE 7                                                                                                   APPENDIX 7.15

## SAMPLE WEEKLY CALENDAR

| Time | Mon 3/13 | Tues 3/14 | Wed 3/15 | Thu 3/16 | Fri 3/17 |
|---|---|---|---|---|---|
| 6a | | | | | |
| 7a | | | | | |
| 8a | 8:30 - Prepare for Business | 8:30 - Prepare for Business | 8:30 - Prepare for Business | 8:30 - Prepare for Business | 8:30 - Prepare for Business |
| 9a | 9 — 11 Marketing/Business Generation | 9 — 11 Marketing/Business Generation | 9 — 11 Marketing/Business Generation | 9 — 11 Marketing/Business Generation | 9 — 11 Marketing/Business Generation |
| 10a | | | | | |
| 11a | 11 — 12p Business Servicing | 11 — 12p Business Servicing | 11 — 12p Business Servicing | 11 — 12p Business Servicing | 11 — 12p Business Servicing |
| 12p | 12p-1p Lunch | 12p-1p Lunch | 12p-1p Lunch | 12p-1p Lunch w/ Wife | 12p-1p Lunch |
| 1p | 1p — 2p Lead Conversion & Follow-Up | 1p — 2p Lead Conversion & Follow-Up | 1p — 2p Lead Conversion & Follow-Up | | 1p — 2p Lead Conversion & Follow-Up |
| 2p | 2p — 3p Business Servicing | 2p — 3p Business Servicing | 2p — 3p Business Servicing | 2p — 3p Lead Conversion & Follow-Up | 2p — 3p Business Servicing |
| 3p | | | 3:30p — 6p Watch David's T-Ball Game | 3p — 4p Business Servicing | |
| 4p | 4p — 5:30p Listings Presentation - 123 Cottonwood Ct | 4p — 6p Show Homes to Johnsons | | 4:30p — 5:30p Buyer Consultation w/ Taylors | 4p — 6p Listings Presentation - 456 Spring Creek Way |
| 5p | | | | | |
| 6p | | 6:30p — 8p Family Dinner | | | 6:30p — 8:30p Family Birthday Party |
| 7p | | | | | |
| 8p | | | | | |
| 9p | | | | | |

© Copyright Icenhower Coaching & Consulting, LLC. All rights reserved.

© Icenhower Coaching & Consulting, LLC.

## Securing the FSBO Listing

Earning the business of a stubborn seller who wants to go it alone and sell their home by themselves is tough. 'For Sale By Owners' are motivated sellers—they want to sell their home—but they don't see the value in having a real estate agent.

FSBO prospecting can be a lucrative pillar in your lead-generation plan as long as you (a) don't take rejection personally and (b) are patient and can commit to following up, building relationship and rapport, and nurturing them to conversion over time.

In this chapter, we will teach you how to make the FSBO listing *your* listing.

### Learning Targets

In this chapter, you will learn:

- How to find FSBO leads.
- How to filter FSBO leads.
- How to follow-up with FSBO prospects and the best ways to build relationship and rapport.
- Scripts and Objection Handlers for every FSBO situation and scenario.

## Roll With Rejection

As you're well aware by now, prospecting involves reaching out to people that you do not know in an attempt to win their business, whether that's with a knock on the door or with a telephone call. Understandably, rejection is a considerable aspect of this lead-generation method, whether you're circle prospecting, or contacting expired listings or FSBO leads.

With circle prospecting, when you knock on that door or pick up the phone, you have no idea in advance if they want to sell or not, and oftentimes you'll find that they're not interested in selling their home right now. With expired listings, you at least know that they recently wanted to sell and probably still do: oftentimes they're unhappy with their existing agent and you can persuade them to at least meet with you for a listing-presentation.

In both cases, while you will certainly experience some rejection, the rejection is not overly personal—each of these prospects sees the fundamental value in having an agent, even if they don't ultimately choose you to represent them.

But when it comes to approaching For Sale By Owners (or FSBOs), real estate agents have their work doubly cut out for them. While you know in advance that they definitely *do* want to sell their home, it can be difficult to convince them that they need *any* agent at all, let alone you. FSBOs want to sell their home themselves. They don't want to pay the commission and they don't think they need professional help.

FSBOs think that selling a property is a piece of cake. They generally don't see the value in a real estate agent, and they can be standoffish, dismissive, and sometimes even demeaning. Naturally, this can be very off-putting for agents as nobody likes to feel undervalued or to have their entire profession looked down on.

> *Most FSBO sellers soon realize that selling a property is not at all as easy as it sounds. The National Association of Realtors (NAR) reports that a staggering 70% of FSBO sellers will eventually convert and sell their home with a real estate agent.*

Successful FSBO prospectors must develop a thick skin and an even temper. If you're a people person who defines themselves by social relationships, this can be tough, but you will need to roll with the punches and learn that a business rejection is not a personal rejection.

Likewise, if you're someone who is impatient and easily frustrated, you will need to learn how to slow down and spend a lot of time helping someone who won't necessarily want or appreciate your help at first.

> Most FSBO sellers soon realize that selling a property is not at all as easy as it sounds, and it can be very worthwhile to prospect FSBOs and stay the course in convincing them they need your help, not to mention the fact that they will be financially better off going with you than going it alone.

A staggering percentage of FSBOs ultimately do list with an agent when they are unsuccessful selling their home by themselves. The National Association of Realtors (NAR) reports that 70% of FSBO sellers will eventually convert and sell their home with a real estate agent.

It's crucial that you both push through the initial discomfort of feeling undervalued by your prospect and provide undeniable proof in your follow-up campaign that you are absolutely of value and always coming from a place of contribution for your clients.

## Finding FSBOs Fast

So where are all the FSBOs, anyway?

Marketing their properties isn't a skill most FSBOs have, so you have to know how to find them. They are there if you know where to look.

Prospecting for FSBOs can be worked in with a lot of other lead-generation activities. You will naturally come across them when you're previewing properties, circle prospecting around different neighborhoods or inviting neighbors to open house events.

You can also find FSBOs when you're driving around running errands, picking the kids up from school, and on your way to and from work. You just need to pay attention and notice the homes and neighborhoods you're passing through.

You can also ask your closest family members and friends to take photos of FSBO signs with phone numbers in front of homes and text them to you when they spot them

Make it worth it.

Set a goal of how many you'll discover each week. Don't take your keys out of your ignition until you do, if you're striving for being accountable. It will astound you how many FSBOs show up just by setting a goal.

| Activity | Previewing | Circle Prospecting | Showing | Off Hours |
|---|---|---|---|---|
| Goal | | | | |

But of course, there's a faster 'high-tech' method too.

## ONLINE SAVES TIME

Sellers who go the FSBO route take advantage of technology to market their home. Most homeowners do not have the time or the resources to run an active marketing campaign, so they turn to sites such as Craigslist, ListingDoor, and Zillow/Trulia to list and market their properties.

You can use the same sites to identify FSBOs in your area. Every site has a search tool, and Zillow also shows an area map that pinpoints each FSBO in the region of your choice. Harvest the property listings and get ready to prospect.

### EXERCISE: Search your area for FSBOs

Note the property location, owner's name, general description, asking price, number of days on the market, and the contact information. Use this chart to kick-start your FSBO prospecting.

| FSBO Contact Sheet |||||| 
|---|---|---|---|---|---|
| Location | Owner | Description | Asking Price | # Days on Market | Contact Information |
| | | | | | |
| | | | | | |
| | | | | | |

## FILTER YOUR FSBOS

As you'll recall from the first chapter, the word prospecting goes back to the Gold Rush of the 1800s, and the same principles of mining for gold apply to real estate prospecting methods.

Prospecting is the *first stage* of examining the lead landscape with a view to securing prospects and future clients. Prospecting is a repetitive, *exploratory* activity—you will have to *filter* through an enormous amount of leads to unearth your glimmers of gold.

Depending on where you live, you probably have a lot of FSBOs to call, but you'll likely face a lot of rejection too—you'll hear a great many NOs before you find that one YES.

*Save yourself time, stress, and frustration and filter your FSBOs!*

Spending a lot of time trying to convince FSBOs to meet with you can be taxing on your calendar, not to mention your mindset. So, once you have compiled your FSBO contact list, your first step is to explore the seller's receptiveness to being represented by an agent. To do this, you will ask 3 'filter' questions to get the lay of the land, and assess their openness to using the services of a real estate agent.

The 3 filtering questions are:

1. If I brought you a qualified buyer, would you be willing to pay me a 3% commission?
2. How long are you going to try to sell your home on your own before you explore other options?
3. If you don't sell your home by that time, what other options will you consider?

As you can see, with the first question, you're not even attempting to talk them into listing their home for sale with you or any agent. You're simply asking if they would pay you on the buyer's side.

If the answer to the first question is "Yes," you will proceed to the second question and ask how long they are going to go it alone before exploring other options. Remember that whatever time they tell you, you can cut in half. If they say, "Oh I'm good for awhile. I'll probably try for six months or till the end of the year," you can simply reply with an upbeat "Okay," but in your mind, you can shorten that time to three months. Most FSBOs get frustrated and will give up and look to list with an agent much sooner than they say or think.

*Most FSBOs get frustrated and will give up and look to list with an agent much sooner than they say or think.*

If the answer to the second question is "Six months or less," you can proceed to the third question. With both the second and third questions, you're planting the thought that their home might not sell any time soon, and getting them to think and talk about what they will do if they can't sell themselves.

If they tell you that they'll probably talk to a realtor if they can't sell in a few months, that's a great prospect, that's somebody that you can definitely follow up with.

However, if they tell you that they're going to list with their sister Janice if they can't sell it themselves, it's less likely that the FSBO will choose you as their agent over a friend or family member who might be willing to cut their commission in half.

As we said, there's a lot of rejection with FSBO prospecting and it's important to filter out the "Yes," "No," and "Maybe" prospects right up front. There's little point in pursuing a lead whose best friend is a real estate agent (though by all means give it your best shot), but if they exhibit any kind of openness to interviewing agents in the future, you can place them in your lead follow-up campaign and move onto filtering the next FSBO seller.

Again, the **FSBO Filtering Script** is efficient, clean and simple. Your goal is to sift and filter for yeses and explore their willingness and openness to using a real estate agent right off the bat:

> **FSBO Filtering Script**
>
> Hi, this is Anne Smith at ABC Real Estate and I noticed your home is for sale. I have a quick question for you: If were to bring you a qualified commission, would you be willing to pay me a 3% commission. *Answer: Yes.*
>
> Great! So how long are you going to try to sell your home on your own before you explore other options? *Answer: Six months or less.*
>
> Wonderful! I hope it works out for you. One last question, if you don't sell your home by that time, what other options will you consider? *Answer: I guess I might consider using an agent.*
>
> Fantastic! I wish you all the best, and I'd love to stay in touch and hear about how it goes.

FSBO leads may not be overly positive or effusive when answering these questions. Remember that they are wary of real estate agents and believe that they can sell the home by themselves. However, if you get something close to resembling three affirmative responses to the filter questions, this is a warm prospect that you should follow up with and nurture over time and perhaps even try to close for an appointment.

Towards the end of this chapter, we will explore a few more scripts that you can use when making initial contact with a FSBO lead. It's wise to memorize a variety of FSBO scripts that you can utilize and improvise with depending on the particular lead you're talking to. At least one of the scripts offers a slightly more aggressive approach where you can try to set an appointment to preview the home. Remember, though, with FSBO prospects it is generally *follow-up, nurture, and cultivation* that will seal the deal, rather than that first conversation, so we will now move swiftly on to that piece of the process.

However, no matter what script you use, you should always make sure to ask the filter questions first or very early on in the conversation. After weeks of following up and investing your time and energy, the last thing you want to discover is that the seller is unwilling to cooperate on commission. Save yourself a lot of time, stress, and frustration and filter your FSBOs!

## Follow Up With Your FSBO

After you make initial contact with a FSBO lead and have determined that they are a prospect worth pursuing, the key is to follow up and stay in touch with them from time to time, and slowly build a relationship built on partnership and trust.

At the end of your first phone call, it's a good idea set an expectation that you'd like to stay in touch and help them in any way you can. When nurturing and cultivating a FSBO prospect, you will always be coming from a place of contribution and showcasing your value to someone who may not immediately see your worth.

In all likelihood, you are not the first agent to contact them. There may have been several others before you who have told the sellers the very same things that you will:

- Listings with agent-representation sell for 20% more than FSBO listings
- Real estate professionals have insider data that helps them to market properties better
- Professional agents have the connections that can get a property seen by more potential buyers

While these things are true, that information alone will not convert a FSBO prospect. Set yourself apart from other agents by actively demonstrating that you can solve the FSBO seller's pain points and are more than worthy of your professional fee.

## The FSBO Follow-Up Campaign: Prove Your Worth

When we say that you should follow up with a FSBO prospect from time to time, it's a little more systematic than just randomly checking in now and then.

Make sure to add the FSBO contact to your CRM and set them on a 6-8 week follow-up campaign where you make contact with them a minimum of 5-6 times.

The best way to convert a FSBO listing to your listing is to prove that you are a problem-solver. Your services, tools, and strategies have value to homeowners looking to sell their property and those wanting to buy a home. With FSBOs, you're not looking to find fault with their efforts so much as exhibit a vast difference between your level of systems and theirs.

### Stay in Regular Communication

Remember that timeline you discovered during the filtering process? If a FSBO said they'd consider listing with a real estate agent within six months, you can safely cut that time to three months, which means *you have half that time to build a relationship* with the seller and earn his or her trust.

During those six or so weeks, you'll need to contact them at least 5 or 6 times, through email or by personally dropping off helpful information at the home. But the very best way to connect and establish rapport is with a personal phone call, and we highly suggest one phone call a week for every FSBO seller that you're beginning to build a relationship with.

When you call, ask if you can drop off a market analysis that you've done for other similar homes in the area, or just check in to see if you can be of service.

- Highlight and affirm the things they're doing right. Don't alienate the seller or put them off by pointing out what they're doing wrong.

- Empathize with any issues that they're having or problems they're encountering. Validate their emotions and how difficult and complicated it can be to sell a house.

- Add value by suggesting strategies or solutions to help them out. Providing them with several options will make them feel like they're still firmly in control of the selling process, while showcasing your superior knowledge and skillset.

Communicate what you're doing for them. Let the homeowner know that you've contacted their neighbors and your friends and family to see if they know of anyone looking for a home in the area (which you did while you were circle prospecting or contacting your SOI).

However, please don't employ any of the manipulative tactics that are, unfortunately, all too common with FSBO prospectors. Don't tell the seller that you have an interested buyer if one does not exist.

Remember that your goal is to build a relationship built on admiration and trust. You will only confirm their skepticism and prejudices and harden their resolve to avoid working with realtors. Be up front and honest about everything you're doing. Add genuine value and build trustworthy rapport until these people are ready to list with you.

In the meantime, draft a summary of your actions and time spent. You're applying for a job, and this is your previous experience, so-to-speak. If you're not tracking your prospecting efforts, it can be difficult to "manufacture" these logs; yet if you are, it's just a matter of making a copy.

## SEND UPDATES ON PROPERTY ACTION

If you haven't listed the property (yet), one of the most important things you can do is to set the FSBO seller up on MLS Listing E-Alert emails. If you have their email address, you can do this automatically and use one of the scripts we provided in the Open House chapter.

As you'll recall, any prospect can be set up on an MLS Listing email drip campaign. MLS Listing E-Alerts keep sellers up-to-date and educated on their neighborhood's real estate market. Listing Alerts keep them apprised of how quickly homes are selling and the prices that they're selling for. Listing Alerts allow prospects to compare the local competition and see how their home holds up when it comes to features and amenities.

MLS E-Alerts will keep the FSBO seller aware of how their home's value is continually changing and what the competition is doing in his market. This is of great value to them because they often don't know. They just see signs like the rest of the general public. They don't know when a property has gone pending or that it's sold or what price it sold for. More importantly, they don't know how these sales are impacting the appraised value and fair market value of their home over time.

Setting FSBO sellers up on MLS E-Alerts gives you a great excuse to call them every single week, not only to educate them and help them but also to keep your name continually top of mind.

## FSBO Quid Pro Quo

If you happen to have an open house nearby or anywhere in the neighborhood, it's a great idea to call your FSBO leads and offer them a favor for a favor. For example, hosting simultaneous open houses could be a quid pro quo scenario that benefits both of you.

An open house gives you another great excuse to follow up and add value at the same time.

*"Hey, if you want to coordinate open houses on the same day at the same times, I'll try to send all my buyers your way, and you can send me any buyers you have that aren't interested my way so we can get more traffic combined."*

You could even send them open house guest list forms by email or dropping by that they can use to collect contact information.

All of a sudden, you and the FSBO prospect are collaborating and working together and they will see that you do a lot more than most agents to drum up activity. You can even market their open house for them and include it in your ads, flyers, or phone calls when you're spreading the word about your own local listings.

Make sure to also show the FSBO's home as often as humanly possible to your prospective buyers, as long as the property reasonably matches their search criteria. It might not be exactly what they want, but it's a great way to stay in front of the FSBO prospect and show them how hard you're working to sell their home. Don't waste your buyer's time by showing them a home that you 100% absolutely know is not for them.

And don't waste your own time showing a property unless the FSBO has confirmed they're willing to at least consider providing a commission on the buyer side. Remember that you're following up and making the effort to build relationship with FSBOs that are firm prospects and that you have previously filtered.

While nothing is ever certain, there must be a reasonable expectation that the prospect will eventually return all the favors you've done for them by at least considering you for the job when the time comes to call it quits on trying to sell it themselves.

Sooner or later, the seller is likely to wear down and give up their attempt to sell themselves. Remember that 70% of FSBOs ultimately convert to using an agent. When that happens, you have established a relationship with them that is based on service, assistance, contribution, collaboration, and value. They will appreciate and trust you and your persistence will have paid off.

## Follow Through with Promises

Congratulations (finally!) on getting the FSBO listing!

Keep up the good work by following through with the promises you made. It's on you to show the property owner that you're willing to work just as hard as you said you would. That means:

- Returning phone calls quickly and leaving a detailed message if you only reach voicemail
- Using superior photos for the listing; blurry pictures are for amateurs
- Doing what you said you'd do, including hosting an open house or sending direct marketing mailers
- Calming the seller's anxiety
- Maintaining a positive attitude

In their mind, they've always got a back-up ready (themselves), so you're auditioning for your job every day. Don't allow that FSBO listing to turn into a Cancelled Listing.

Follow up and follow through with your FSBO every step of the way, from lead to prospect and from client to close.

## Additional FSBO First Contact Scripts

Now that you know how important it is to follow through with your FSBO prospects, here are a few other scripts, as promised, that you can use when making initial contact with a FSBO seller, whether it's in person or on the phone. Remember to save yourself time and frustration by asking important filtering questions, and that the real clincher with FSBO prospects is in the follow-up rather than the first contact.

Take a moment to read through each script. Then, you can either choose which approach you like best and implement it as part of your FSBO prospecting calendar, or if you're feeling very ambitious, you can memorize all of them and have a variety of scripts and talking points at your disposal no matter who you're talking to.

### FSBO Telephone Script

While FSBO sellers are less enthusiastic about listing pitches, they are generally very receptive to calls concerning the sale of their home. They are also often eager to get calls from agents that might have a buyer for their home and they might be willing to pay half the commission to an agent that brings them a buyer.

As you can see, in this first script, you begin by mentioning that you are calling to find out more about the home so that you can help serve the buyers you're working with. But remember—don't be manipulative or lie about having a buyer that wants to purchase this particular home.

This first script is similar to a property preview script. Not only are you gathering information and insights about the features of the home but you are also keeping the seller in continual conversation.

As you can see, in this script, you are also getting them to think about how hard it might be to sell the home themselves. They may not have adequately considered that their listing is in competition with many other listings and that they may need to do something different to sell their home besides putting up a "For Sale" sign in the front yard.

Though many first contact calls don't lead to an appointment, it's worth pushing for that if you have gained a sense that this FSBO lead is more receptive and open than most.

### FSBO Telephone Script

Hi, I'm looking for the owner of the home for sale.

This is (AGENT NAME) with (REAL ESTATE COMPANY). As an area specialist it's my goal is to know about all the homes for sale in the marketplace for the buyers I'm working with. Do you mind if I ask you a few questions about your property? Great thank you!

I know that when I saw your listing online it said your home had ____ bedrooms and ___ baths. Are the rooms a good size? How's the kitchen? Have the bathrooms been updated? Would you tell me about the yard? Is there anything else that is unique about your home that potential buyers would like to know?

Sounds like you have a great home, why are you selling?

Where are you moving?

How did you decide on that area?

So, do you have to your current home before buying your next one?

When did you want to be moved?

How did you determine your listing price?

You know, with so many other homes on the market right now, what are you doing differently to market yours…? What else…?

If there were an advantage to using me to market your home, would you consider it?

Normally at this point… I would say… let's get together for 20 minutes or so… so we can discuss how we can help you achieve your goal… I have some time (_____) or would (_____) be better for you?

## FSBO Prospecting Script

In the next script, please note that the use of the word "We" as used in the sentence "…*because we just sold another home…*" is intended to allow you to refer to any home you recently sold in the area, or any home sold by other agents in your entire real estate brokerage as well. Using "We" also conveys the message that you bring a team with you to sell their home.

Once again, it's very important to filter through your FSBO leads and ascertain their willingness to cooperate when it comes to a commission.

## FSBO Prospecting Script

"Hi, this is (AGENT NAME) with (REAL ESTATE COMPANY), and I'm calling because we just sold another home in the Johnson Meadows area, and I happened to notice that you are interested in selling your property, is that correct?"

"Is the property still available or do you currently have it under contract?"

"The home that sold recently had about 2,000 square feet with 4 bedrooms & 2 baths. How big is your home?"

"When your home does sell, where do you plan on moving?" (Ask more questions about why they are selling. Motivation is the key, so uncover all of their reasons.)

"Just curious, how long are you going to try and sell it on your own?"

"If I were to bring a buyer while you are trying to sell it, would you cooperate on commission?"

"Obviously, I cannot sell something without seeing it first. When would be a good time to preview the home? Would this afternoon around 3:00 p.m. be good, or would tomorrow at 4:00 p.m. be better?"

### FSBO 'Increased Net Profit' Phone Script

This next FSBO phone script is a little more assertive about pushing for an appointment to meet in person.

As you can see, your main selling point with this script is that using a realtor is likely to increase their net profit.

This is a fact. A National Association Realtor (NAR) survey of Home Sellers and Home Buyers found that the median FSBO property sold for approximately 16%-20% less than the median home listed with an agent.

If saving money on agent commissions is the primary goal of the FSBO, you can emphasize the significantly lower offer-numbers made to homeowners attempting to sell their own houses. In fact, the same report found that if the FSBO seller sells the home to a friend or relative, it typically sells at 39% less than the median home sold through a real estate agent.

### FSBO 'Increased Net Profit' Phone Script

Hello, I'm calling about the home for sale. Is this _____? Hi, this is (AGENT NAME) with (REAL ESTATE COMPANY) and I noticed that you have your home for sale and you're selling it yourself, is that correct?

I'm calling because I've helped a lot of For Sale By Owners sell their homes, and I decided to give you a call to see how things are going for you?

When you do sell this home, where will you be moving to?

In a perfect world, by when do you want to get there?

I'm curious, is having to pay a commission the main reason why you decided to sell the home yourself instead of using a real estate agent?

If I show you how I can sell your home and actually net you more money than trying to sell it yourself, even after paying my commission, would it be something you're interested in hearing about? *(If YES . . .)* I have an opening at 4:00 today or would 3:00 tomorrow, which would be better for you? *(If NO continue with the script . . .)*

I understand, if you believed an agent could do that you would've hired one already, right? But if you could net more money by listing your home for sale with me, rather than try to sell it on your own, you'd probably list your home with me wouldn't you?

That's exactly why we need to meet. I have an opening at 4:00 today or would 3:00 tomorrow, which would be better for you?

*(If you can't overcome their objections to meeting in person, ask for their mobile number and email address to follow up weekly and continue with ...)*

I tell you what, I will contact you with any new home sale activity that may impact the appraised value of your home. In the meantime, if you have any questions or if there is anything that I can help you with, please give me a call at (555) 799-2345. I'll be happy to assist you in any way that I can!

## FSBO 'Rolex Analogy' Script

Some FSBOs need to visualize what you're talking about when you tell them you can get them more money for their home than they can get trying to sell it on their own.

Also, some FSBOs will be skeptical about statistics that come from the National Association of Realtors, so the following analogy script is a way to level with them about the public perception of the value of a FSBO property.

Like the Rolex watch in the analogy where people expect a big discount because it's not being sold retail, people look at FSBO sales in the same way. When prospective buyers see a FSBO sign, they want a deal. Yes, the seller saves 3%-6% on commission, but they also lose 20% or more of the price because they're dealing with people who perceive their home differently simply because of the context in which it's being sold.

The analogy script is a wonderful way to make your point while building rapport when you meet with the prospect in person. It's generally not a great idea to tell longer stories when talking on the phone, so this script is more appropriate in a face-to-face scenario when you feel comfortable enough to level with the seller and say it straight.

> **FSBO 'ROLEX ANALOGY' SCRIPT**
>
> Mr. and Mrs. FSBO Seller, if I took a Rolex directly from the store, kept the packaging on it, and even left the original price tag on it, and I put that watch it a garage sale, do you think I could get the same amount of money for it than if it were in a store?
>
> You already know the answer. It's no, of course not, because there's a salesperson and a company involved in selling the watch. Just by having the expertise of a salesperson, the value of the watch goes up.
>
> Now, if I took that same watch and put it in an auction, could I get more money for it than if I put it in a garage sale? You're right, we definitely could.
>
> Now I can't promise you that you'll get more than one offer on your home, but I can tell you that putting it on the open market with an expert in your corner is more like selling it at an auction than listing it by yourselves -- which is more like the garage sale.
>
> And you do want a higher selling price, don't you…?

## OBJECTION HANDLERS WHEN WORKING WITH FSBOS

No matter what type of prospect you're interacting with you will always have to handle objections—that's the job of a real estate agent! FSBO objections can be particularly tough to overcome, but the following objection handlers have been tested and proven with our top FSBO prospectors and will work for you too.

Objections can arise at any point during your conversation with the contact. Therefore, our objection handlers are not so much scripted dialogs as *talking points* that you should memorize, internalize, and modify so that you are well prepared to provide an answer any time a FSBO raises an objection.

### FSBO OBJECTION #1: GOING FSBO WILL SAVE ME MONEY.

As we've previously discussed in-depth, this is patently untrue, but this will always be the #1 objection that you encounter when talking to FSBO sellers.

Time and again, FSBO properties sell for approximately 20% less than the median home listed with an agent. Whether you use NAR statistics or the Rolex Analogy Script, handle this objection by explaining in no uncertain terms that what they'll pay you in commission they will reap in net profit.

### FSBO Objection #2: Buyer demand is the same no matter how the home is being sold.

Buyer demand is technically the same in the sense that the same numbers of people want to purchase a home at any given point. However, the likelihood of an average buyer even knowing that a FSBO listing exists is very slim.

Most people think that real estate agents market a property to the masses, but agents know that their marketing is more intentional than that. 90% of homebuyers use an agent to find and purchase their new homes. Buyers don't look for FSBOs first, and neither do real estate agents who are helping buyers. FSBOs are often overlooked.

FSBO sellers often don't understand that if their home is not listed in the Multiple Listing Service (MLS), they are missing out on 90% of the homebuyers, which means there's going to be lower interest, which means the likelihood of them getting a higher price for their home goes down dramatically.

> *Increased exposure increases buyer-demand, which in turn can lead to a seller-demand for a higher price.*

Increased exposure increases buyer-demand, which in turn can lead to a seller-demand for a higher price.

Now, be aware that there are lots of online FSBO services popping up all over the country that will list a FSBO in the MLS. However, if a FSBO seller mentions this, you can handle the objection by telling them that the same principle applies—as a real estate agent, if you see a FSBO listed in the MLS, showing that home to your buyers is likely to be a last-case scenario.

Why? Because the FSBO seller doesn't have representation but in order to protect your buyers and ensure a smooth transaction, you as an agent are effectively going to have to represent the seller too (which actually triggers your Errors & Omissions liability insurance).

This last point leads us to another common FSBO objection.

### FSBO Objection #3: How hard can it be? I know what I'm doing? What could possibly go wrong?

Most FSBO sellers have no idea how complex, tenuous, and time-consuming a real estate transaction can be. You don't just print random paperwork off the Internet and hand it to buyers to sign.

Don't be condescending or demeaning to the FSBO seller, but explain that there are a lot of complicated state and federal required forms involved and that it's in everyone's best interests to protect themselves with organized and detailed paperwork.

As the buyer's representative, you will be drawing up a detailed purchase agreement that allows for inspections and contingencies and protects them should the home not appraise at the listed price.

Typically, FSBOs are not realistic about price and don't have the knowledge or skill level to research comparables and price the home competitively, but realistically, for their market. This can lead to stress and disappointment for all concerned when the home does not appraise. Your buyers run the risk of losing deposits and having to cancel moving companies, so as their agent you are more inclined to take the safe route and only show them homes that are listed with properly represented sellers.

Again, going the FSBO route reduces exposure but it also increases risks for both the buyers and the sellers themselves.

When handling this particular objection, it's also wise to emphasize that representation protects the seller as much as the buyer. Inexperienced and naïve FSBO sellers can be the victims of underhand, cut-throat tactics and could use the services of an agent who will protect and advocate hard on their behalf.

## Summary

Earning the business of a stubborn seller who wants to go it alone and sell their home by themselves is tough. For Sale By Owners are motivated sellers—they want to sell their home—but they don't see the value in having a real estate agent.

When making first contact with a FSBO lead, save yourself a ton of time, stress, and frustration and ask them these 3 crucial filtering questions:

1. If I brought you a qualified buyer, would you be willing to pay me a 3% commission?
2. How long are you going to try to sell your home on your own before you explore other options?
3. If you don't sell your home by that time, what other options will you consider?

With FSBO prospects, it's highly unlikely that you will secure a listing or even an appointment during initial contact. Rather, the key for successful FSBO prospecting lies in the *follow-up*.

FSBO prospecting can be a lucrative pillar in your lead-generation plan as long as you (a) don't take rejection personally and (b) are patient and can commit to following up, building relationship and rapport, and nurturing them to conversion over time.

70% of FSBO sellers will eventually convert and sell their home with a real estate agent. Keep the faith and focus on the value of FSBO prospecting, even when your prospects don't always value you.

# Module 8

# Appendix 8.1

## FSBO Contact Sheet

Name: _____  Date: _____

| Location | Owner | Description | Asking Price | # Days on Market | Contact Information |
|----------|-------|-------------|--------------|------------------|---------------------|
|          |       |             |              |                  |                     |
|          |       |             |              |                  |                     |
|          |       |             |              |                  |                     |
|          |       |             |              |                  |                     |
|          |       |             |              |                  |                     |
|          |       |             |              |                  |                     |
|          |       |             |              |                  |                     |
|          |       |             |              |                  |                     |
|          |       |             |              |                  |                     |
|          |       |             |              |                  |                     |
|          |       |             |              |                  |                     |

Total Contacts Made: _____  Total Referrals Received: _____  Total Appointments Made: _____

© Copyright Icenhower Coaching & Consulting, LLC. All rights reserved.

# MODULE 8 — APPENDIX 8.2

## FSBO "3 Questions" Filtering Script

1. **"If I brought you a qualified buyer, would you be willing to pay me a 3% commission?"**

   > If YES, continue on to the next question...

2. **"How long are you going to try to sell your home on your own before you explore other options?"**

   > Cut their answer in half for practical purposes. So, if they say 2 months, they will likely list in a month. If their answer is 6 months or less, continue on to the next question . . .

3. **"If you don't sell your home by that time, what other options will you consider?"**

   > This question is to ensure that an agent is not their relative or best friend and you don't waste too much time and effort. If they are open to the possibility of interviewing agents in the future, place them in your lead follow-up campaign and move on to contacting the next FSBO seller!

**Points to Consider:**

FSBO sellers are very receptive to calls concerning the sale of their home. They are also often eager to get calls from agents that might have a buyer for their home and they might be willing to pay half the commission to an agent that brings them a buyer.

Prospecting for FSBO listings is a numbers game, and even the most effective agents will list no more than 20% of the FSBO sellers they contact. Therefore, it is essential to filter through FSBO sellers quickly over the phone by asking the qualifying questions above. Don't always attempt to aggressively close an appointment on the first call or you might find yourself wasting a lot of evenings on fruitless appointments. They may never intend to us an agent or they might be obligated to use an agent that is a family member of friend if they ever do list their home.

© Copyright Icenhower Coaching & Consulting, LLC. All rights reserved.

# Module 8

## Appendix 8.3

## FSBO Telephone Script

1. Hi, I'm looking for the owner of the home for sale.

2. This is (AGENT NAME) with (REAL ESTATE COMPANY). As an area specialist it's my goal is to know about all the homes for sale in the marketplace for the buyers I'm working with. Do you mind if I ask you a few questions about your property? Great thank you!

3. I know that when I saw your listing online it said your home had ____bedrooms and ___ baths. Are the rooms a good size? How's the kitchen? Have the bathrooms been updated? Would you tell me about the yard? Is there anything else that is unique about your home that potential buyers would like to know?

4. Sounds like you have a great home, why are you selling?

5. Where are you moving?

6. How did you decide on that area?

7. So, do you have to your current home before buying your next one?

8. When did you want to be moved?

9. How did you determine your listing price?

10. You know, with so many other homes on the market right now, what are you doing differently to market yours…? What else…?

11. If there were an advantage to using me to market your home, would you consider it?

12. Normally at this point… I would say… let's get together for 20 minutes or so… so we can discuss how we can help you achieve your goal… I have some time (_____) or would (_____) be better for you?

© Copyright Icenhower Coaching & Consulting, LLC. All rights reserved.

# MODULE 8　　　　　　　　　　　　　　　　　　　　APPENDIX 8.4

**FSBO Prospecting Script**

1. "Hi, this is [AGENT NAME] with [REAL ESTATE COMPANY], and I'm calling because we just sold another home in the Johnson Meadows area, and I happened to notice that you are interested in selling your property, is that correct?"

2. "Is the property still available or do you currently have it under contract?"

3. "The home that sold recently had about 2,000 square feet with 4 bedrooms & 2 baths. How big is your home?"

4. "When your home does sell, where do you plan on moving?"

   *(Ask more questions about why they are selling. Motivation is the key, so uncover all of their reasons.)*

5. "Just curious, how long are you going to try and sell it on your own?"

6. "If I were to bring a buyer while you are trying to sell it, would you cooperate on commission?"

7. "Obviously, I cannot sell something without seeing it first. When would be a good time to preview the home? Would this afternoon around 3:00 p.m. be good, or would tomorrow at 4:00 p.m. be better?"

---

**Note to Consider:**

In paragraph No. 1, the use of the word *"we"* as used in the sentence *". . . because we just sold another home . . ."* is intended to allow you to refer to any home you recently sold in the area, or any home sold by other agents in your entire real estate brokerage as well.

© Copyright Icenhower Coaching & Consulting, LLC. All rights reserved.

# MODULE 8

## APPENDIX 8.5

**FSBO**
**Increased Net Proft Phone Script**

1. Hello, I'm calling about the home for sale. Is this _____? Hi, this is (AGENT NAME) with (REAL ESTATE COMPANY) and I noticed that you have your home for sale and you're selling it yourself, is that correct?

2. I'm calling because I've helped a lot of For Sale By Owners sell their homes, and I decided to give you a call to see how things are going for you?

3. When you do sell this home, where will you be moving to?

4. In a perfect world, by when do you want to get there?

5. I'm curious, is having to pay a commission the main reason why you decided to sell the home yourself instead of using a real estate agent?

6. If I show you how I can sell your home and actually net you more money than trying to sell it yourself, even after paying my commission, would it be something you're interested in hearing about? *(If YES . . .)* I have an opening at 4:00 today or would 3:00 tomorrow, which would be better for you? *(If NO continue with the script . . .)*

7. I understand, if you believed an agent could do that you would've hired one already, right? But if you could net more money by listing your home for sale with me, rather than try to sell it on your own, you'd probably list your home with me wouldn't you?

8. That's exactly why we need to meet. I have an opening at 4:00 today or would 3:00 tomorrow, which would be better for you?

9. *(If you can't overcome their objections to meeting in person, ask for their mobile number and email address to follow up weekly and continue with . . .)*

10. I tell you what, I will contact you with any new home sale activity that may impact the appraised value of your home. In the meantime, if you have any questions or if there is anything that I can help you with, please give me a call at (555) 799-2345. I'll be happy to assist you in any way that I can!

© Copyright Icenhower Coaching & Consulting, LLC. All rights reserved.

# FSBO Rolex Analogy Script

1. Mr. and Mrs. FSBO Seller, if I took a Rolex directly from the store, kept the packaging on it, and even left the original price tag on it, and I put that watch it a garage sale, do you think I could get the same amount of money for it than if it were in a store?

2. You already know the answer. It's no, of course not, because there's a salesperson and a company involved in selling the watch. Just by having the expertise of a salesperson, the value of the watch goes up.

3. Now, if I took that same watch and put it in an auction, could I get more money for it than if I put it in a garage sale? You're right, we definitely could.

4. Now I can't promise you that you'll get more than one offer on your home, but I can tell you that putting it on the open market with an expert in your corner is more like selling it at an auction than listing it by yourselves -- which is more like the garage sale.

5. And you do want a higher selling price, don't you...?

© Copyright Icenhower Coaching & Consulting, LLC. All rights reserved.

# Circle Prospecting

At the beginning of this book, we talked about some of the connotations that exist around prospecting. Agents that operate a purely SOI referral-based business are horrified at the idea of cold calling or reaching out to people that they don't know. Whereas, for many prospectors, the last thing they want to do is call up their friends and family to ask them for business or a referral. Instead, they would rather contact people that they definitely know *want* to sell their house, such as an expired listing or a FSBO. To a prospector, that's not a cold call at all—it's a very warm lead.

We're more than halfway through this book, and Circle Prospecting is the closest we've come to a true 'cold-call' prospecting method. Circle prospecting involves contacting people within a certain geographic area and asking them for business. With this method, you have no idea if the people want to buy or sell, and you will typically have no prior relationship with any of these contacts. For all intents and purposes, these people are pretty cold leads.

Circle prospecting has a somewhat lower conversion rate than working an SOI or prospecting around expired listings. However, circle prospecting is a very effective business-generation method and can serve a lot of crucial purposes that should not be overlooked or dismissed.

In the first part of this chapter, we will explain what circle prospecting is and the rationale and benefits behind it. In the second part of the chapter, we will get down to the nuts and bolts of circle prospecting and provide you with scripts and strategies for making contact with people you don't know.

## Learning Targets

In this chapter, you will learn:

- What circle prospecting is, and what circle prospecting is not.

- The many benefits of circle prospecting, from social proof to evidencing your success and swaying your SOI.

- The nuts and bolts of circle prospecting, from how to find contact information to the words you will need when making calls and knocking on doors.

# What is Circle Prospecting?

As its name implies, circle prospecting involves contacting homeowners in a radius—or circle—around a home that you have listed.

In fact, you need not prospect exclusively in a circle. Some people get a little too hung up on the name. If a particular neighborhood is square-shaped and all of the homes in that 'square' are the same price and size, and the neighborhood has a name, you could certainly prospect in that area. You don't need to create a circle on a map when it doesn't naturally exist. The main idea is that you're prospecting around one of your listings.

The listing might be active or it could be a listing that recently sold. One of the beauties of circle prospecting is that you can capitalize on the status of the listing at any point in the transaction—from 'For Sale' to 'Pending' to 'Just Sold'. As you've seen in previous chapters, you can also circle prospect around events like an Open House. You can even circle prospect around expired listings to get local feedback on why the home didn't sell. There are so many reasons to call around a listing and initiate a conversation with homeowners in the neighborhood.

However, an afternoon chitchat with Bob across the street isn't the primary goal of circle prospecting. This is an active prospecting method. You're not just marketing the listing—you're calling to search for prospective clients. There are many great reasons to circle prospect around a listing, but getting new listings and finding interested buyers is your number one goal.

Many agents or real estate teams will set specific goals for prospecting around a listing. A general rule of thumb is that for every one listing that you have in a neighborhood your circle prospecting activities should result in two buyers and one more listing.

| What Circle Prospecting IS | What Circle Prospecting Is NOT |
|---|---|
| Calling around 'Just Listed' properties to market the home, search for a Buyer, or find another home to list, either now or in the future. | Calling to alert neighbors to any of the events to the left, *without* searching for prospective clients! |
| Calling around 'Just Sold' or 'Pending' properties to pass along that homes are selling, find a Buyer, or find another home to list, either now or in the future. | |
| Calling around to tell neighbors you have a Buyer who'd like to buy in the neighborhood and do they know of any homes for sale. | |
| Calling around Expired Listings to ask for local feedback on what caused the home not to sell, search for a Buyer, or find another home to list, either now or in the future. | |
| Calling around a neighborhood to invite neighbors to an open house, find a Buyer, or find another home to list, either now or in the future. | |

## Why Circle Prospect?

There are many reasons to include circle prospecting in your repertoire of business-generation methods. Among many other benefits, circle prospecting can help you to:

- Impress & Influence Sellers
- Provide Social Proof
- Create Name Recognition
- Evidence Your Success
- Sway Your SOI
- Preview Your Prospects
- Grow Your GCI

### Impress and Influence Seller Sellers

Circle prospecting can impress and influence both your seller clients as well as prospective seller clients.

As we've said before, most real estate marketing activity is done for two reasons: (1) to generate business and branding for the agent and (2) to appease and please your seller clients who want to see you doing everything you can to market their home.

If sellers don't see a lot of high-profile activity, they assume that nothing is happening and the agent isn't doing enough for their commission. This can lead to a lot of frustrations and stress for everyone concerned.

It's common for circle prospectors to give a report to their seller clients at the end of the week, documenting all the people they've contacted, called, and left messages with within the neighborhood. Circle prospecting reports offer tangible, visual documentation of how hard you're working to market and sell their home.

> *Circle prospecting reports offer tangible, visual documentation of how hard you're working to market and sell their home.*

In fact, circle prospecting is a fantastic way to convert listing appointments in the first place. When delivering your listing presentation, you can speak to your highly proactive strategies and set yourself apart from the competition by incorporating circle prospecting into your marketing campaign for the home.

As with making the case for open houses in chapter 5, your goal at a listing presentation is to paint a picture in the mind of the prospective seller of a feeding frenzy around their home, and leaving them with the distinct impression that you will be the strategic mastermind behind it all.

> *When delivering your listing presentation, you can speak to your highly proactive strategies and set yourself apart from the competition by incorporating circle prospecting into your marketing campaign for the home.*

You're the agent that's going to personally call every single one of their neighbors, and you're the agent that's going to literally walk around the neighborhood and talk about their property with everyone you meet.

Ironically, though people might not ordinarily care for agents calling *their* number or knocking on *their* door, when it comes to selling *their* home, every seller wants to see this kind of activity. When every other agent is just putting a sign in the front yard and making a pretty flyer, you will set yourself apart by selling and pushing this level of proactive activity. Circle prospecting is a great way to convert clients in competitive listing situations.

What's more, you'll know you've really arrived in your real estate business when a client hires you because they've witnessed your prospecting efforts firsthand and admire how much you've worked to get their neighbor's home sold. When you walk into that listing appointment, you won't need to sell that prospect on your strategies, because they will have already experienced your strategies for themselves.

## Provide Social Proof

Studies in the psychology of sales show that the best way to sell something is to tell a person that their neighbor just purchased it.

For example:

> If a hailstorm damaged roofs in an area, a roofing company may call everyone in the neighborhood, saying something like this:
>
> > Hi, I'm Brad from ABC Roofing. As you know the hailstorm two weeks ago damaged a lot of homes in the area. We're repairing the roof at the house at 123 Apple Street, and wanted to see how your roof is doing. Eighty-five percent of the homes we've seen so far need at least a partial roof replacement; have you had a chance to check yours out yet?
> >
> > No?
> >
> > We'd be happy to set up an appointment…

Circle prospecting works the same way in real estate.

"Households make decisions by following what they see their neighbors doing," according to Qi Wang, associate professor of marketing at Binghamton University. "People learn from their peers what to buy."

Wang's study, which appeared in the *International Journal of Marketing Research*, credits this to observational learning—the process of learning through watching others and then replicating the observed behaviors. Observational learning is most commonly associated with babies and children but, in fact, this kind of social proof occurs throughout our entire lives.

Wang's study (which focused on online sales) also suggested that the number of sales did not overly influence the likelihood of future sales. As long as people could see, or were made aware, that some people were purchasing a particular product, the volume of sales was largely irrelevant.

When circle prospecting, it doesn't matter if you only have a single listing in the neighborhood. You're raising awareness and visibility so that neighbors can *see* that someone else saw value in your services.

According to a National Nielsen Harris survey, social proof is even more powerful when it comes from someone known to your prospect. 82% of Americans seek the advice and recommendations of friends and family before making a purchase decision.

If the neighbor is very familiar with the owner of the property you're calling about, the level of social proof is magnified even more. When a trusted friend or neighbor has your For Sale sign in their yard, they are visually acting as an influential spokesperson for your business.

## CREATE NAME RECOGNITION

When you are actively circle prospecting in person—calling people on the phone and knocking on doors—the majority of homeowners will likely tell you they aren't interested in selling their property anytime soon.

That's okay. Rejection is a normal part of the sales process and to be expected no matter what type of prospecting you're doing.

Simply getting your name out there and making a meaningful and positive impression is more valuable than you might realize in the moment. When talking to leads, coming from a place of contribution and remaining professional and positive in the face of rejection will cause neighbors to remember you favorably and they'll be more likely to reach out to you when they are ready to sell.

> *Getting your name out there and making a meaningful and positive impression is more valuable than you might realize*

What's more, when you have multiple types of contact information, you can diversify your circle prospecting touches and increase name recognition through different communication channels. From "Just Listed" mailers and flyers to "Open House" sly dial voicemails and social media posts to "Just Sold" emails and blog posts, there are innumerable ways for you to get your name out there and create positive, productive impressions.

## EVIDENCE YOUR SUCCESS

Circle prospecting around a listing isn't only about selling the listing (though that would certainly be a welcome byproduct). Circle prospecting is about selling your services, seeking business, and *evidencing your success*. When you market a listing, you're not only marketing the property, you're also marketing yourself and how successful and sought after you are.

> *Not only are you seeking business, but you are also telling people that you have business and are sought after.*

As we mentioned, with any given listing, every status-change presents an opportunity that should be leveraged. If you have a property that's going to be listed soon, you can circle prospect that a home is "Coming Soon." You can also advertise when the property is "Just Listed" or "Under Contract," as well as marketing "Open House" events (or multiple open house events). Every change along the way presents an opportunity, all the way through to "Sale Pending" and "Just Sold." You can even talk about a property *after* it's been sold, as a comparable in a Comparative Market Analysis.

At every stage in the process, you can find a way to circle prospect and talk about both the property and your success. Not only are you *seeking* business, but you are also telling people that you *have* business and are *sought after*. Circle prospecting is a wonderful way to say "Look what I'm doing" or "Look what I did" and, more importantly: "My strategies work and people know it."

## Sway Your SOI

Circle prospecting is also a great way to evidence your success to the people you already know. If you are a newly licensed agent, your friends and family will want you to succeed, but they may be a little reluctant to refer you to their friends and family due to your inexperience. They know you and they want to support you, but you're still an unknown entity in some ways.

When circle prospecting status-changes for a listing, make sure to include your SOI in that marketing campaign too. When your friends and acquaintances see dozens of "Just Listed," "Sale Pending," and "Just Sold" emails in their inbox, they will start to take you more seriously and see that you're successful.

Believe us, it won't matter that all of these emails refer to the same one or two listings. Your SOI won't notice that at all. All they'll notice is that they're receiving *frequent* emails in their inbox that show that you're on fire! They'll forget that you're new and inexperienced and start to associate you with success and expertise. This will remove any of their reluctance or concerns about referring you business and sway them towards recommending you and using you as their own agent too.

## Preview Your Prospects

Knowing your market inside out is essential for sales success. Just as you need to master your knowledge of neighborhood inventory and know everything there is to know about the areas you want to focus your business in, you should also thoroughly understand the wants and needs of your prospects that live in those neighborhoods.

The homeowner you're talking to on the phone had a reason for selecting the neighborhood they're in right now, and those reasons could keep them there for a long time. They include:

- Price
- Amenities
- Location
- Commute time
- Being near/far from family
- Schools

The appeal of these reasons for being in a particular area may fade over time as circumstances in life change. It's important that you stay up-to-date with what people need and want.

Previewing your prospects is the same idea as previewing properties.

Circle prospecting allows agents to meet a great many homeowners on a daily basis, and gather invaluable knowledge and information that helps to produce future business.

As you talk with prospects on the phone, ask authentically genuine questions to get them to open up about their rationale for living in their home and where they see themselves in the future.

Questions like these go a long way to opening the door of a business relationship:

- What drew you to this neighborhood?
- If you were to move, where would you like to live?
- How soon do you see that happening?

Listen carefully to the homeowner's answers. If they indicate they intend to sell their property within the next six months, ask for their business.

## Grow Your GCI

Circle prospecting can also help you take your established business in a new direction. If you've been selling a lot of homes in the $200,000 to $250,000 price-range, you may have discovered there's only so much time in the day to market properties and get them sold. The way to increase your GCI is to market and sell more expensive properties.

Identify the next price level in your area. Whether you decide to focus on homes in the $300,000 to $450,000 price range, or higher-priced luxury homes, begin your circle prospecting within that group of homes.

## The Nuts & Bolts of Circle Prospecting

Now that you know the rationale and many benefits behind circle prospecting, let's get down to the nuts and bolts so that you can incorporate this activity into your calendar as soon as possible. Below we will provide you with all of the words and scripts you will need to start circle prospecting, but first you should identify which area you're going to target.

Begin by completing the following exercise.

### EXERCISE: Where's my Circle?

The great thing about circle prospecting is that you get to decide where your target circle is.

- **Print a map** of your area.
- **Choose** which neighborhood you would like to sell homes in.
- **Draw a circle** around your target area—it doesn't have to be perfect or even a circle if that's not the natural shape of the neighborhood.
- **Research** the neighborhood. What homes have already sold in your area? What homes are on the market now? What homes expired? Plot them on the map, after compiling your list.
- **Compile** the stats so you can use them as examples in your circle prospecting scripts.

## Contacting Your Circle

Now that you've targeted your 'territory', how do you get in contact with the people in your circle?

- **Phone Number Data Service**: There are a number of online sources where you can either purchase lists, or a subscription to procure lists of names, addresses, and phone numbers. See your ICC coach for recommendations and ICC discounts, as the best sources are subject to frequent change.
- **Door Knocking**: Meeting prospects where they are can be extremely effective and, while it may take more time and energy, if the results are actually connecting with more people, and therefore more prospects, you're getting the feedback you're looking for.
- **Open House Registration**: If you hold an open house, you're going to get a number of the neighbors through; asking on your registration form 'how did you learn about this listing?' will usually prompt them to write in 'saw the sign' or 'neighbor.'
- **Homeowner Association Phone Book**: Planned neighborhoods and gated-communities will usually have some sort of phone list as a resource for homeowners: ask your sellers if they'd like to help you find their next buyer.
- **Online Websites**: Some directory sites, like whitepages.com will have a reverse address search option where you can not only learn the contact information for the owner of the home, you can also access a quick reference map should you want to pair calling with door knocking.
- **Your Website Registrations**: Usually an untapped resource, few agents make the connection that their buyers actually live in current homes in the areas they're prospecting through. Assume nothing, and connect with them! You're doing everything in your power to find their next place, including circle prospecting!

## Complete The Circle.... Prospecting

Circle prospecting involves contacting homeowners in a radius—or circle—around a home that you have listed. You can contact your prospects in a variety of ways.

## CALLING

With your list and your map (so you can reference their home in relation to the subject home you're calling about), you're ready to begin. Here's an example of the first part of one of the scripts (shared at the end of this chapter in its entirety). As you can see, you're basically introducing yourself and initiating a conversation around a specific property that you have listed. Remember that you can take advantage of every status change when calling around a listing.

> *Hi, I'm (John Smith) with (ABC Realty), and we just listed a home for sale in your neighborhood on (123 Main Street) for ($250,000), and we often find that the ultimate buyer of a home is a friend, family member or acquaintance of someone that lives in the same neighborhood. Since we are doing everything we can to sell your neighbor's home, I'd like to ask you if you know anyone looking to move into your community?*

Make sure to keep track of the people you're calling. Keep your Daily Contact Sheet in front of you to track your connections, and have a separate pad handy to take notes, and keep a log of the answers given. You can use a similar format to the log used when you learned about door knocking, as referenced in Chapter 4:

| Preview/ Neighbor Property | First Name | Last Name | Moved Here From? When? | Net Move? When? | Invite Info? | Notes about Neighborhood? |
|---|---|---|---|---|---|---|
| 1212 Market St (PREVIEW) | Dave & Wendy | Foster | 1982, New York | Sold, San Fran | n/a | 3 Bd, 2 Ba, 1,900 sqft split level, unfinished basement, master bath opens to deck, gallery style kitchen, classic ford truck in garage |
| 1211 Market St | Tim | Donner | 1995, Baltimore | Not Sure | (555) 555-1212 | Likes Mtb Trails, peaceful, block party in summer |
| 1221 Market St | Linda & Bill | Witner | 1976, Downtown | 6 years, Florida | n/a | Updated house 5 years ago, lots of kids at Halloween, Local pub: sports |
| 1225 Market St | Heather & Ray | Thomas | 2004, San Fran | ??, Work | (555) 867-5309 | Work transfer, don't know neighbors, want sales prices |
| 1226 Market St | David | Castle | 1994, New Hampshire | ??, ??? | (555) 121-1212 | Daughter will be looking in may, call to follow up, Jamie 555-1212 |

Remember that you'll use your time more efficiently if you write quick, concise notes and transcribe them into your CRM later: the risk of drift isn't worth the reward of focus.

1. Finish your scheduled time-block for circle prospecting
2. Highlight your "next action steps" for the prospective clients and referrals you've gained,
3. Check your next time-block to stay on schedule.

We'll discuss this further when we examine your ideal prospecting work-environment in chapter 10.

## DOOR KNOCKING

In the same amount of time that you can call 100 prospects on the phone, you can physically knock on approximately 20 doors. It would seem like a no-brainer to stay inside where it's warm and dry and stick to rocking out call after call.

However, though very slow compared to other circle prospecting methods, door knocking has a very high conversion rate compared to other methods and you should absolutely incorporate door knocking into your prospecting activities.

Though door knocking has a high conversion rate, don't replace calling with door knocking. You won't make quite enough contacts with this method. Rather, you should door knock in addition to calling and layer it into your prospecting activities, especially whenever the weather permits.

When door knocking, we recommend that you dress smart-casual, but sneakers are certainly permitted. Among its other benefits, door knocking is a great way to sneak some exercise and fresh air into your busy day!

When door knocking, you can use the very same scripts and follow-up processes that you would use for any other circle prospecting method.

## Call An Audible

A variation of the circle prospecting call is a *hot market call*, in which the real estate agent calls a homeowner to share information about the hot market they are currently in.

Typically, a hot market refers to a low-inventory situation where there are a lot of buyers but not enough homes for sale. Agents can call around and inquire whether the homeowner is looking to sell their home, or knows anyone else who is looking to sell their home.

The Hot Market Script can be used when you do not have an actual listing to market and work with. This can be one of the hardest times to generate leads. It's always better if you are circle prospecting around one of your own listings, but in hot market situations, you must continue to find ways to lead-generate when your business is low.

By telling the homeowner that when one home sells in a neighborhood, two more sell immediately afterwards, you can pique the homeowner's interest.

At that point, you can determine their willingness to enter that market. By doing so, you have the ability to place them in a position of selling their home faster than they ever thought possible. That's because you are helping them launch their sales campaign quicker and ahead of other similar properties in the neighborhood.

Making these calls is a lot easier when you think in terms of the service you can provide to people, even if you don't know them. You have something to offer to all homeowners, even if they weren't aware they needed it!

## The Words You Need

Cold-calling a prospect doesn't have to be difficult. In fact, if you can speak with confidence to a prospect over the phone, you stand a far better chance of sealing the deal.

To present yourself professionally over the phone, remember these tips for effective script delivery:

1. *Rehearse what you're going to say.* Practice your scripts so the phrases and questions flow as smoothly as if you were talking in person to a friend. Try recording yourself to see how natural you sound in delivering the scripts.

2. *Focus only on the call.* Avoid multi-tasking. Whatever else you are doing while you are prospecting will distract you enough for the person on the other end of the call to know. When you prospect on the phone, stayed focused on the call.

3. *Speak slower on the phone than you would in person.* Your words will be easier to understand in the event of poor reception.

4. *Be professional.* No matter how difficult the person on the other end might act, be positive and agreeable.

And finally, use the following tested and proven circle prospecting scripts.

## Your Circle Prospecting Scripts

You have four scripts to learn for circle prospecting: the "Just Listed" script, the "Just Sold/Sale Pending" script, the "Hot Real Estate Market" script, and the "Open House" script that we previously shared with you in chapter 5.

# "Just Listed" or "Coming Soon" Script

This script can be used for just listed homes or you can even use it for listings that are coming soon and get a head start with generating interest and leads. As you can see, when they tell you that they have no plans to move, you can preview your prospects and get to know them better by asking a lot of questions and keeping the conversation moving forward.

## Just Listed Circle Prospecting Script

Hi, I'm (John Smith) with (ABC Realty). We just listed a home for sale in your neighborhood on (123 Main Street) for ($250,000), and we often find that the ultimate buyer of a home is a friend, family member or acquaintance of someone that lives in the same neighborhood. Since we are doing everything we can to sell your neighbor's home, I'd like to ask you if you know anyone looking to move into your community? *Answer: "No."*

Great! I truly appreciate your taking the time to try and help. So tell me, when do you plan on moving? *Answer: "No plans."*

Fantastic! How long have you lived in your home? *Answer: "5 years."*

Terrific! Where did you live before that? *Answer: "Denver, Colorado."*

Excellent! How did you pick this community? *Answer: "To be near family."*

Wonderful! So if you *were* to move, where would you move next? *Answer: "To Florida."*

Exciting! And when would that most likely be?

**If their answer is "6 months or less," continue:**

Did you know that it can take up to 6 months to get a home prepared, marketed and sold in today's market? *Answer: "No."*

Great! So do you want your home sold in 6 months, or do you want to start the process of selling then? *Answer: "Sold."*

Perfect! All that we need to do to start you on your way to (Florida) is pick a time to get together. How does that sound? *Answer: "Great."*

Excellent! Would Wednesday or Thursday at 4:00 pm work better for you?

## "Just Sold" or "Sale Pending" Script

Essentially, with this script you are telling homeowners that your listing that just sold (or is about to close) has generated *a lot of interest from buyers* and that if they're looking to sell their home, *now is the time to do it* because you have a lot of eager buyers and, when one neighbor sells a home, typically two or three more homes in the neighborhood will sell right away.

### Just Sold Circle Prospecting Script

Hi, I'm (John Smith) with (ABC Realty), and we just sold a home for sale in your neighborhood on (123 Main Street) for ($250,000), and when one neighbor sells a home, typically 2 or 3 more homes in the same neighborhood sell right away. So I was curious as to when you plan on moving? *Answer: "No plans."*

Great! How long have you lived in your home? *Answer: "5 years."*

Terrific! Where did you live before that? *Answer: "Denver, Colorado."*

Excellent! How did you pick this community? *Answer: "To be near family."*

Wonderful! So if you were to move, where would you move next? *Answer: "To Florida."*

Exciting! And when would that most likely be?

**If their answer is "6 months or less," continue:**

Did you know that it can take up to 6 months to get a home prepared, marketed and sold in today's market? *Answer: "No."*

Great! So do you want your home sold in 6 months, or do you want to start the process of selling then? *Answer: "Sold."*

Perfect! All that we need to do to start you on your way to (Florida) is pick a time to get together. How does that sound? *Answer: "Great."*

Excellent! Would Wednesday or Thursday at 4:00 pm work better for you?

# HOT REAL ESTATE MARKET SCRIPT

As we mentioned, this script can be used when you do not have a listing to market or work with.

---

**HOT MARKET CIRCLE PROSPECTING SCRIPT**

Hi, I'm (John Smith) with (ABC Realty), I was calling to let you know that (85) homes have sold in your area in the last (30) days, and (63) of those sold at or above the marketed price! Did you know this? *Answer: "No."*

We know that when homes sell that fast, typically 2 or 3 more homes in the same neighborhood sell right away. So I was curious as to when you plan on moving? *Answer: "No plans."*

Great! How long have you lived in your home? *Answer: "5 years."*

Terrific! Where did you live before that? *Answer: "Denver, Colorado."*

Excellent! How did you pick this community? *Answer: "To be near family."*

Wonderful! So if you were to move, where would you move next? *Answer: "To Florida."*

Exciting! And when would that most likely be?

**If their answer is "6 months or less," continue:**

Did you know that it can take up to 6 months to get a home prepared, marketed and sold in today's market? *Answer: "No."*

Great! So do you want your home sold in 6 months, or do you want to start the process of selling then? *Answer: "Sold."*

Perfect! All that we need to do to start you on your way to (Florida) is pick a time to get together. How does that sound? *Answer: "Great."*

Excellent! Would Wednesday or Thursday at 4:00pm work better for you?

# OPEN HOUSE SCRIPT

An open house is a wonderful reason to circle prospect around a neighborhood.

## OPEN HOUSE CIRCLE PROSPECTING SCRIPT

**Real Estate Agent**: Hi (Home Owner), this is (Agent Name) with (Real Estate Company) and I just listed Emily and Joe's house around the corner from you. The sellers wanted me to invite you to our grand opening this weekend from eleven to one.

**Homeowner**: Oh okay.

**Real Estate Agent**: Yeah hopefully you can make it by. Tell me how long have you been in the neighborhood?

**Homeowner**: We lived here for about five years now.

**Real Estate Agent**: Five years, good for you! Well you know when a great property like this appears, when we list we generally expect to get two to four motivated buyers that will miss out on the property. Do you know of any other neighbors in the neighborhood that may be thinking about selling in this hot market?

**Homeowner**: Well…. You know I can't think of anybody right now. Every one that lives here loves it here.

**Real Estate Agent**: It is a great neighborhood. As for you (Home Owner) if you were to move where would you go next?

**Homeowner**: I don't know; we really like it here. I guess someday once the kids are gone we might move. I was thinking maybe in the country once the kids are out and out of the school district. I would go out to the country and become a country guy.

**Real Estate Agent**: A country guy! Good for you, so are your kids about to graduate? When do you plan on moving out there?

**Homeowner**: They will probably graduate in four years. Well they just started high school.

**Real Estate Agent**: Excellent, well hey, I'd love to follow up with you from time to time and see if anything changes. Just in case you want to talk before I call you back would it be ok if I send you my contact information?

**Homeowner**: Sure that's fine.

**Real Estate Agent**: Great what's the best email for you?

**Homeowner**: You could reach me at Homeowner@Emailaddress.com

**Real Estate Agent**: Perfect. Well come on out (Homeowner). We look forward to seeing you. Hopefully you can make it on Saturday. We'll be over at 123 Main St. and would love to meet you there.

## Summary

As its name implies, circle prospecting involves contacting homeowners in a radius—or circle—around a home that you have listed. Don't get hung up on the name, however. You do not need to prospect in an exact circle. The main idea is that you're prospecting around one of your listings.

The listing might be active or it could be a listing that recently sold. One of the beauties of circle prospecting is that you can capitalize on the status of the listing at any point in the transaction—from "Just Listed" to "Sale Pending" to 'Just Sold' and everything in between and beyond.

Circle prospecting is an active prospecting method. You're not just marketing the listing—you're calling to search for prospective clients. A general rule of thumb is that for every one listing that you have in a neighborhood your circle prospecting activities should result in two buyers and one more listing.

Circle Prospecting is the closest we've come to a true 'cold-call' prospecting method in this book. With this method, you have no idea if the people want to buy or sell, and you will typically have no prior relationship with any of these contacts. For all intents and purposes, these people are pretty cold leads.

However, there are many great reasons to include circle prospecting in your repertoire of business-generation methods. Among several benefits, circle prospecting can help you to impress and influence sellers, convert competitive listing presentations, provide social proof, create name recognition, evidence your success, sway your SOI, preview your prospects and, potentially, grow your gross commission income by targeting more affluent and expensive neighborhoods.

**You can even get some exercise and work on your tan while generating lots of leads and increasing your skillset! Don't dismiss or overlook this powerful prospecting method.**

# Module 9

# Appendix 9.1

## Daily Contact Log

Name: _____  Date: _____

| | Type* | Name | Ask for Appt? | Appt? | Ask for Referral | Referral? | Follow Up/Notes |
|---|---|---|---|---|---|---|---|
| 1. | Select Type | | ☐ Y/ ☐ N | ☐ | ☐ Y/ ☐ N | ☐ | |
| 2. | Select Type | | ☐ Y/ ☐ N | ☐ | ☐ Y/ ☐ N | ☐ | |
| 3. | Select Type | | ☐ Y/ ☐ N | ☐ | ☐ Y/ ☐ N | ☐ | |
| 4. | Select Type | | ☐ Y/ ☐ N | ☐ | ☐ Y/ ☐ N | ☐ | |
| 5. | Select Type | | ☐ Y/ ☐ N | ☐ | ☐ Y/ ☐ N | ☐ | |
| 6. | Select Type | | ☐ Y/ ☐ N | ☐ | ☐ Y/ ☐ N | ☐ | |
| 7. | Select Type | | ☐ Y/ ☐ N | ☐ | ☐ Y/ ☐ N | ☐ | |
| 8. | Select Type | | ☐ Y/ ☐ N | ☐ | ☐ Y/ ☐ N | ☐ | |
| 9. | Select Type | | ☐ Y/ ☐ N | ☐ | ☐ Y/ ☐ N | ☐ | |
| 10. | Select Type | | ☐ Y/ ☐ N | ☐ | ☐ Y/ ☐ N | ☐ | |
| 11. | Select Type | | ☐ Y/ ☐ N | ☐ | ☐ Y/ ☐ N | ☐ | |
| 12. | Select Type | | ☐ Y/ ☐ N | ☐ | ☐ Y/ ☐ N | ☐ | |
| 13. | Select Type | | ☐ Y/ ☐ N | ☐ | ☐ Y/ ☐ N | ☐ | |
| 14. | Select Type | | ☐ Y/ ☐ N | ☐ | ☐ Y/ ☐ N | ☐ | |
| 15. | Select Type | | ☐ Y/ ☐ N | ☐ | ☐ Y/ ☐ N | ☐ | |
| 16. | Select Type | | ☐ Y/ ☐ N | ☐ | ☐ Y/ ☐ N | ☐ | |
| 17. | Select Type | | ☐ Y/ ☐ N | ☐ | ☐ Y/ ☐ N | ☐ | |
| 18. | Select Type | | ☐ Y/ ☐ N | ☐ | ☐ Y/ ☐ N | ☐ | |
| 19. | Select Type | | ☐ Y/ ☐ N | ☐ | ☐ Y/ ☐ N | ☐ | |
| 20. | Select Type | | ☐ Y/ ☐ N | ☐ | ☐ Y/ ☐ N | ☐ | |

TOTALS: 0    0

**\*Type:** SOI, FSBO, Expired/Cancelled, Circle Prospecting, etc.

Total Contacts Made: _____
Total Appointments Made: 0

© Copyright Icenhower Coaching & Consulting, LLC. All rights reserved.

# CIRCLE PROSPECTING
## Just Listed Script

Hi, I'm (John Smith) with (ABC Realty), and we just listed a home for sale in your neighborhood on (123 Main Street) for ($250,000), and we often find that the ultimate buyer of a home is a friend, family member or acquaintance of someone that lives in the same neighborhood. Since we are doing everything we can to sell your neighbor's home, I'd like to ask you if you know anyone looking to move into your community?

Answer: "No".

Great! I truly appreciate your taking the time to try and help. So tell me, when do you plan on moving?

Answer: "No plans".

How long have you lived in your home?

Answer: "5 years".

Where did you live before that?

Answer: "Denver, Colorado".

Excellent! How did you pick this community?

Answer: "To be near family".

Great! So if you were to move, where would you move next?

Answer: "To Florida".

And when would that most likely be?

**If their answer is 6 months or less, continue:**

Did you know that it can take up to 6 months to get a home prepared, marketed and sold in today's market?

Answer: "No".

Great! So do you want your home sold in 6 months, or do you want to start the process of selling then?

Answer: "Sold".

Perfect! All that we need to do to start you on your way to (Florida) is pick a time to get together. How does that sound?

Answer: "Great".

Excellent! Would Wednesday or Thursday at 4:00pm work better for you?

© Copyright Icenhower Coaching & Consulting, LLC. All rights reserved.

# MODULE 9 — APPENDIX 9.3

## CIRCLE PROSPECTING
## Just Sold Script

Hi, I'm (John Smith) with (ABC Realty), and we just sold a home for sale in your neighborhood on (123 Main Street) for ($250,000), and when one neighbor sells a home, typically 2 or 3 more homes in the same neighborhood sell right away. So I was curious as to when you plan on moving?

Answer: "No plans".

Great! How long have you lived in your home?

Answer: "5 years".

Terrific! Where did you live before that?

Answer: "Denver, Colorado".

Excellent! How did you pick this community?

Answer: "To be near family".

Wonderful! So if you were to move, where would you move next?

Answer: "To Florida".

Exciting! And when would that most likely be?

**If their answer is 6 months or less, continue:**

Did you know that it can take up to 6 months to get a home prepared, marketed and sold in today's market?

Answer: "No".

Great! So do you want your home sold in 6 months, or do you want to start the process of selling then?

Answer: "Sold".

Perfect! All that we need to do to start you on your way to (Florida) is pick a time to get together. How does that sound?

Answer: "Great".

Excellent! Would Wednesday or Thursday at 4:00pm work better for you?

© Copyright Icenhower Coaching & Consulting, LLC. All rights reserved.

# MODULE 9 — APPENDIX 9.4

## CIRCLE PROSPECTING
### Hot Real Estate Market Script

Hi, I'm (John Smith) with (ABC Realty), I was calling to let you know that (85) homes have sold in your area in the last (30) days, and (63) of those sold at or above the marketed price! Did you know this?

Answer: "No".

We know that when homes sell that fast, typically 2 or 3 more homes in the same neighborhood sell right away. So I was curious as to when you plan on moving?

Answer: "No plans".

Great! How long have you lived in your home?

Answer: "5 years".

Terrific! Where did you live before that?

Answer: "Denver, Colorado".

Excellent! How did you pick this community?

Answer: "To be near family".

Wonderful! So if you were to move, where would you move next?

Answer: "To Florida".

Exciting! And when would that most likely be?

**If their answer is 6 months or less, continue:**

Did you know that it can take up to 6 months to get a home prepared, marketed and sold in today's market?

Answer: "No".

Great! So do you want your home sold in 6 months, or do you want to start the process of selling then?

Answer: "Sold".

Perfect! All that we need to do to start you on your way to (Florida) is pick a time to get together. How does that sound?

Answer: "Great".

Excellent! Would Wednesday or Thursday at 4:00pm work better for you?

© Copyright Icenhower Coaching & Consulting, LLC. All rights reserved.

# MODULE 9

# APPENDIX 9.5

## CIRCLE PROSPECTING
## Open House Script

**Agent:** Hi (Home Owner), this is (Agent Name) with (Real Estate Company) and I just listed Emily and Joe house around the corner from you. The sellers wanted me to invite you to our grand opening this weekend from eleven to one.

Home Owner: Oh okay.

**Agent:** Yeah hopefully you can make it by. Tell me how long have you been in the neighborhood?

Home Owner: We've lived here for about five years now.

**Agent:** Five years, good for you! Well you know when list a great property like this and we put it up for sale on the market, we generally expect to get two to four motivated buyers that will miss out on the property. Do you know of any other neighbors in the neighborhood that maybe thinking about selling in this hot market?

Home Owner: Well……. You know I can't think of anybody right now. Every one that lives here loves it here.

**Agent:** It is a great neighborhood. As for you (Home Owner) if you were to move, where would you go next?

Home Owner: I don't know, we really like it here. I guess someday once the kids are gone we might move. I was thinking maybe in the country once the kids are out and out of the school district. I would go out to the country and become a country guy.

**Agent:** A country guy! Good for you, so are your kids about to graduate? When do you plan on moving out there?

Home Owner: They will probably graduate in four years. Well they just started high school.

**Agent:** Excellent, well hey I love to follow up with you from time to time and see if anything changes. Just in case you want to talk before I call you back, would it be ok if I send you my contact information?

Home Owner: Sure, that's fine.

**Agent:** Great what's the best E-mail for you?

Home Owner: You could reach me at homeowner@emailaddress.com

**Agent:** Perfect. Well come on out (Home Owner) we look forward to seeing you. Hopefully you can make it on Saturday I'd love to meet you. We'll be over at 123 Main St. and would love to meet you there.

© Copyright Icenhower Coaching & Consulting, LLC. All rights reserved.

## Your Prospecting Arena

The impact that our workspace can have on our productivity and success is often overlooked. Prospecting is an activity that is straightforward and simple in its execution, but your environment and surroundings can augment and enhance it or complicate and impair it. Great energy and motivation can be harnessed by creating a comfortable, purposeful and accessible working-environment in which you can focus and use your precious time to its fullest potential. To get the most out of your workspace, take the advice that you give to your sellers and *stage your prospecting arena for success*, whether you generate business from the corner office on the top floor, your home office, or a cubicle.

### Learning Objectives

In this chapter you will learn:

- How to implement a prospecting space that is effective for you and the way that you personally work best.
- How to design and layout your prospecting workstation, and the technology and furniture that will increase your prospecting efficiency and productivity.
- How to use positive reinforcement and negative reinforcement to increase your prospecting behavior.
- How to guard against intruders and turn your distractions into your advocates.

*"It is important that you appreciate that the workplace must be a place of empowerment, but the empowerment must not only be connected to the job that you do." - Anthony Carmona*

## Map Your Prospecting Mindset

Although we have not touched on it too much in this book, at ICC we are firm believers in the power of behavior, and how our behavior profile impacts every single thing that we do.

We have written an entire book that explains the concept in much more detail (*Behavior: Improve Communication & Sales Performance in Real Estate*), but the basic premise is that everyone has a distinct behavior profile that influences what we do and how we act in our real, everyday lives. Depending on our behavior profile, each of us tends to do certain things in certain ways.

Behavior takes many different forms, from the way that we communicate when talking, writing, or even through our hand gestures, all the way down to what we wear, what we drive, or how we decorate our homes or organize our workspaces.

No behavior profile is better or worse than the other. There is no right way or wrong way to do certain things.

When creating your ideal workspace, therefore, it's important that you implement systems that are truly effective for you and the way that you personally work best. There are pros and cons to everything. The most productive workspace is one in which you feel comfortable and confident. When preparing your prospecting environment, you need to evaluate and implement systems that enable you to work in the most optimal and most efficient way for you.

No matter who you are, you can use these two 'Purpose & Access' questions as filters for what belongs in your particular prospecting workplace:

- **Purpose**: Does this serve my purpose for prospecting?
- **Access**: Does this give me access to prospects?

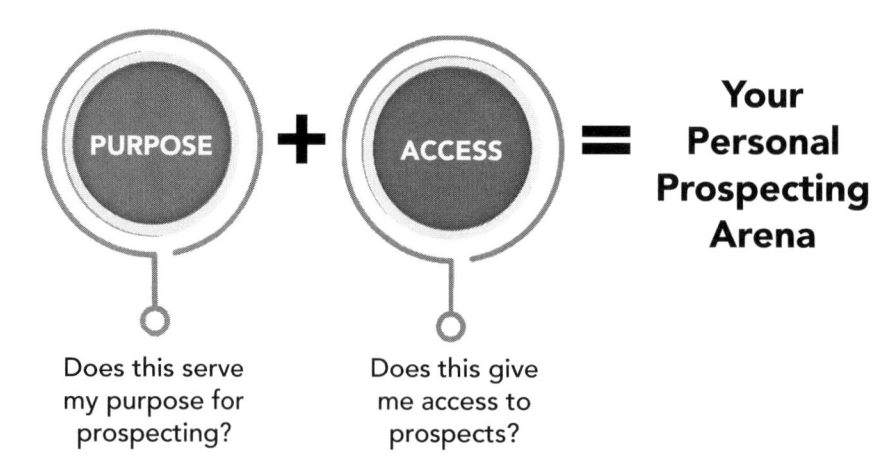

**PURPOSE** + **ACCESS** = **Your Personal Prospecting Arena**

Does this serve my purpose for prospecting?

Does this give me access to prospects?

As long as the answer to both of these questions is YES then you have the green light to proceed with your personalized prospecting arena plan. Our aim in this chapter is to provide you with a variety of options, suggestions, and factors to think about. Perfecting your personal prospecting arena is up to you.

However, the fact that you may not have an office or workspace that is 100% perfect for your particular personality or working-style can never be an excuse for not being able to generate business and meet your prospecting goals and targets.

## No Excuses

When William Marston developed his original DISC behavioral model, he argued that behavioral types come not only from people's sense of self but from their interaction with and response to their environment. He determined that two elements influence a person's emotional behavior:

1. The first factor is whether a person views his or her environment as favorable or unfavorable.
2. The second factor is whether a person perceives himself or herself as either having control or lack of control over that environment.

During moments of stress or frustration (that is, when our environment is *unfavorable* and we feel a *loss of control*), we tend to revert to instinctual behaviors that are familiar and feel most natural to us, even if they are behaviors and attitudes that are not in our best interests. This is true whether we're going through a difficult personal event or if we've simply had a bad night's sleep.

> *Oftentimes, we become stressed or frustrated when our office or work environment isn't exactly how we'd like it. We feel a loss of control and out of our comfort zone when our working conditions are unfavorable or less than perfect.*

Oftentimes, we can become extremely stressed or frustrated when our office or work environment isn't exactly how we'd like it. We feel a loss of control and out of our comfort zone when our working conditions are unfavorable or less than perfect.

In this chapter, we will give you a lot of suggestions about the ideal environment in which you should be prospecting and generating business. But the fact that you don't have some or all of these things available to you should never, ever, ever be an excuse to not lead-generate.

Some of the best lead-generators we know have generated business out of their car! Though, granted, that's not the norm, sometimes you may have to work from home and navigate the noise and distractions that come with sharing a space with your partner, children, or even your pets! Some of you will be sharing offices with three or four other people or prospecting in an open-plan cubicle environment.

> *Your workspace may not be 100% optimal but you can prospect to a very high level despite all those different distractions and inconveniences. Some of the best lead-generators we know have generated business out of their car!*

Your workspace may not be 100% optimal but you can still prospect to a very high level despite all those different distractions and inconveniences. You can lead-generate in any environment. There are no excuses.

Excuses are simply another distraction—a way for your mind to tell you that the reason you can't do something is because you don't have X, Y, or Z. Excuses are often covering a deeper issue—fear of failure or fear of the unknown. While these emotions are very normal, particularly when you first start prospecting, it's important to maintain a proactive and positive mindset no matter what environment you're working in.

This chapter is simply about carving out and creating the environment that you would choose in an ideal world. No matter what your current workspace is, there are ways that you can take control of that environment and make improvements and modifications that serve you best. However, the best way to take control of your environment is by controlling your perspective and mindset around the place that you work.

## MY OFFICE IS YOUR OFFICE

Though laptops and cell phones have made it extremely easy to work from anywhere, top-producing agents typically have some form of dedicated workspace from which to prospect and concentrate on business-generation.

As we said before, however, there is no 'right' or 'wrong' workspace: there are pros and cons to everything.

Many people idealize having their own office or isolated workspace. Some people work best in complete silence, while others find silence to be distracting and prefer a low level of background noise.

Again, much of this comes back to our personality or behavior profile, as well as our mindset. It's just as easy to be distracted in our own quiet company as it is in a room with twenty talking people.

In fact, when it comes to prospecting, it could be that being in a room with twenty talking people is actually more productive. There's a reason that telemarketing companies cram so many people into one room. The sound of other people converting leads and making sales creates a competitive and motivational energy that holds everyone accountable and driven to stay on task.

> *The sound of other people converting leads and making sales creates a competitive and motivational energy that holds everyone accountable and driven to stay on task.*

At ICC, we think it's a good thing when we see two or three people prospecting in the same space, as long as you have similar schedules. At first that might be difficult or distracting, but we find that it creates a stimulating and incentivizing atmosphere and keeps agents accountable.

When your office is also someone else's office, you will need to compromise to come up with a layout and workspace that works for everyone.

## Design & Layout

- Don't overcomplicate or overthink the layout. Your main concerns are efficiency and functionality.
- Don't block anyone into a corner they can't get out of. Create an accessible space where people can come and go without disturbing everyone else.
- Don't clutter a shared workspace with unnecessary items and furniture. You don't need a printer per person—learn to share. Likewise, minimize the amount of extra furniture in the space. Use a conference room for client appointments and consultations, and dedicate your workspace to generating new clients.

## Dual Desk Space

- Wall-mounted desks are legless and can save a lot of precious space in small places.
- Smaller desks can be placed facing each other or back-to-back, depending on your and your coworker's preferences.
- If privacy and concentration is a concern for someone, dividers can separate workstations while still providing the "sound of sales" and great energy of a shared workspace.

Again, your primary concerns are efficiency and functionality. When collaborating and designing a shared workspace with your coworkers, make sure that everyone is arranging the room around the following questions:

- **Purpose**: Does this serve my purpose for prospecting?
- **Access**: Does this give me access to prospects?

## Practically Perfect

Whether you share a workspace or are free to organize your very own office, a few websites to get ideas for design, décor, and layout might be:

- Pinterest
- Houzz
- Architectural Digest
- Dwell
- Dezeen
- Instagram

However, as a real estate agent you should remember that these photos are every bit as staged as the pictures of your client's bedrooms and kitchens!

Don't get caught up and carried away by perfect, pretty pictures. Keep *practicality*, *efficiency* and *utility* in the forefront of your mind—don't shop for convertibles when you need a truck.

One way to hone your choices might be to "tour" an actual agent's office whose business and production-levels you admire and aspire to. After all, your goal is to create a powerful prospecting space, not a Pinterest-worthy picture.

When you're inspired by something you see and want to replicate it in your own space, our advice is to document how it aids your purpose and access to prospects, and then build a budget and save for it if it's something you truly need.

*Keep practicality, efficiency and utility in the forefront of your mind—don't shop for convertibles when you need a truck.*

Remember that you're a business owner now. While you should by all means reward yourself for your successes, you should also be pragmatic, sensible, and forward thinking. One person will spring for a $1,500 desk that elevates with a remote control, while another will put a stack of phone books on top of an existing desk, and invest that same money back into their business! Obviously, we're kidding about the phone books (kinda), but our point is that your prospecting success does not depend on having fancy gadgets or the most expensive furniture and equipment.

## Tech Yourself, Don't Wreck Yourself

While you don't need fancy or expensive gadgets, we do highly encourage you to consider investing in an auto-dialer or power-dialer. As you'll recall from a previous chapter, these devices can help you to stay in the zone and prevent you from taking too many distracting breaks between calls. The longer you can stay on the phone, locked in and engaged, with an established rhythm, the sooner you will reach the number of contacts you need to achieve your conversion rates.

While they may seem like a luxury, they're actually relatively inexpensive and a very worthwhile investment. While dialing a phone number only takes about 5 seconds, if you're calling 30-40 leads a day, those seconds will soon add up. Three minutes lost to dialing each working day becomes two hours lost a month or twenty-fours a year. Reclaim a day of your life lost to dialing!

Headsets are another worthwhile expenditure. From clarity of sound to freedom of movement, headsets that connect to phones will always beat the "ear to shoulder" approach in the long run. Headsets free up your hands for taking notes and filing away lead-sheets, and they also allow for gesticulation (talking with your hands) that can help you get into a rhythm when delivering your message.

Whether corded, Bluetooth-enabled or USB-tethered, be willing to spend a little more money for better quality. Remember that replacing low-quality, cheap headsets 4-5 times a year will cost you financially in the long run, not to mention the cost of learning how to use them and the frustration when they fail.

Noise-cancelling headphones are a good investment if you are someone who does not work well with a lot of background noise. Like we said, there are pros and cons to everything. Some people thrive from the buzz of sales in the background, while others will find it distracting and counter-productive.

# To Stand, Or Not To Stand: That Is The Question

To stand, or not to stand: that is the question. We're pretty sure that's how the Hamlet quote goes right?

Again, there's no right or wrong when it comes to standing or sitting while you prospect. There is science supporting both options.

It's fairly obvious that sitting all day is not good for your health. Standing burns more calories than sitting. When you stand, you typically have better posture—you keep your chin up and your chest back a little bit more, which allows more oxygen to pump through your blood. This can help you sound more confident and assertive and provide you with the necessary energy to make call after call after call.

However, other studies have found that standing too much can compress the spine and lead to lower back problems over time. A recent study in the journal *Ergonomics* found that standing at a desk for prolonged periods of time can create "discomfort and deteriorating mental reactiveness." It's hard to be productive and focus on the task at hand when your feet are killing you or you're distracted with finding the perfect height adjustment.

> *There is no right or wrong when it comes to standing or sitting while you prospect. There is science supporting both options. As with all things in life, balance is key.*

Yet, in a different report, 167 employees in a Texas call center participated in a six-month standing-desk study, which showed that employees using standing-desks were more productive than their seated coworkers. In the first month, the standing group had 23% more successful sales calls than their seated colleagues, and by the end of the six-month period, they had 53% more successful calls.

As with all things in life, balance is key. You don't have to do one or the other exclusively.

Many agents use remote-controlled desks that can be heightened or lowered at the touch of a button. They stand up while making their prospecting calls and sit down when they're focusing on customer-service and administrative tasks. Others use a standing desk 'converter' that is placed on top of or attached to an existing desk. This is both an affordable option as well as a practical one when you work in a real estate office that already has furniture in place, or for those of you who work out of a home office.

Again, do what works for you and choose what's best for your health as well as your productivity. In everything you do, consider whether it's an aid to your prospecting or whether it's an unnecessary distraction that needs to be eliminated.

## Accentuate The Positive, Eliminate The Negative

In Applied Behavior Analysis, there are two types of 'Reinforcement': Positive Reinforcement and Negative Reinforcement.

**Both** types of reinforcement result in a desirable behavior *increasing* or occurring *more frequently in the future*.

"Negative Reinforcement" is one of the most misunderstood concepts when it comes to behavior. There's nothing negative about it at all, in fact it's good for you!

The best way to think about the word "negative" is in relation to math. When you see the negative or minus symbol in math, it means that something is being subtracted or *taken away*.

Negative reinforcement is not about punishment—it's about *removing* or terminating something undesirable or unpleasant in order to *increase* a favorable behavior.

| Negative Reinforcement | Unpleasant Stimulus | Desired Behavior |
|---|---|---|
| To stop his father's nagging, the boy does his chores | Nagging | Do chores |
| The girl can get up from the dinner table when she eats two bites of broccoli | Being stuck at the table | Eat broccoli |

"Positive Reinforcement" is about *adding* something pleasant to increase a favorable or desired behavior.

| Positive Reinforcement | Pleasant Stimulus | Desired Behavior |
|---|---|---|
| A father gives his son a treat for doing homework | Treat | Do Homework |
| A mother praises her daughter for practicing piano | Praise | Practice Piano |

In many ways, prospecting itself is easy and has extremely high success rates. The hardest part is being consistent and committing to frequency and time on task. Prospecting always works, as long as you work. It's essential that you focus and do not allow yourself to become distracted and diverted.

If you want to *increase your prospecting and prospect more frequently*, you have to *reinforce* or strengthen your behavior, by *adding and removing* things in order to achieve the desired behavior and enable it to occur more frequently and productively in the future.

## Take It Away

Below are some examples of unfavorable stimulus that stand in the way of your desired behavior and will need to be permanently or temporarily taken away. Understand that some of the things you'll be removing or taking away might feel pleasant or desirable in the moment, but they are in fact undesirable or unwanted when they get in the way of increasing the desired behavior of business-generation.

## EMAIL, PHONE & SOCIAL MEDIA

Needless to say, you should not be browsing Facebook or Instagram when you're calling expired listings or setting up property previews. However, agents are often surprised when we say that there is absolutely no need to have your email open either.

There is rarely such thing as a true "emergency" in real estate. Believe us, nothing is ever that urgent that it cannot wait a few hours. When generating leads, your laptop should be closed or your computer should be sleeping, and you should also turn your cell phone off, or at least to silent mode, so that you're not distracted by incoming calls or texts.

This is why most prospectors use an auto-dialer or call from a landline. It can be incredibly distracting for both you and the prospect on the other end of the line if there's a flurry of texts or calls coming through to your cell while you're on a call.

---

*You have an appointment with yourself and your future success.*

---

If you're in the middle of a listing presentation and you get a text from a seller already under contract, you would never dream of pausing the appointment to return a client call. Yet for some reason, the same agent will jump to respond to a call or text message when they're in the middle of their prospecting calls. They don't treat *making* contacts as seriously as converting contacts, but if you don't make contacts you won't have any appointments to convert.

In the hours that you have time-blocked to prospect, set up a recurring automated email response or voicemail that tells people you are at an appointment and will respond to their email or message as soon as possible.

Don't feel that you are not being truthful when you tell people you have an appointment. You do—you have an appointment with yourself and your future success. As long as you hold yourself accountable to actually performing income-generating activities during that time, there is absolutely nothing wrong with prioritizing and protecting this time of day.

## WINDOWS & DOORS

Everyone loves a beautiful view, but when you're prospecting, windows and doors are dangerous portals to daydreaming and distraction.

Prospecting requires you to get in the zone and stay there. You need to get locked in and maintain a certain rhythm. Sometimes, that might mean literally blocking yourself off and locking yourself in!

It's all too easy to get distracted by something that's happening on the street below. And if your workspace has interior windows, you can be doubly distracted—not only is your attention diverted by what's happening over at the water-cooler, but other people feel free to walk on in and say hi simply because they can see you.

---

*Prospecting requires you to get in the zone and stay there. You need to get locked in and maintain a certain rhythm.*

---

An exposed window is an unwanted, unfavorable stimulus. If you have an interior window, consider adding curtains or blinds in order to remove distraction and increase your prospecting focus.

Likewise, when you're prospecting, your door should always be closed. At other times of the day, it's okay to have an open door policy and make yourself available for people who might need your help or to consult on something. But when you're lead generating, your blinds should be down and your door should be shut.

## It All Adds Up

There are many more examples of unfavorable stimulus that stand in the way of your desired behavior and need to be taken away or removed from your line of sight. But what are some of the good things to have out and about around your workspace to enhance or increase your prospecting behavior? Remember that only the things that *add value* to your prospecting should remain visible and in front of you.

## Call Lists

On the morning that a listing expires, every agent in town is trying to be the first person to get through to the seller on the phone. If you wait until 9AM or 10AM to start searching the MLS and preparing your call-lists the competition is already hours ahead of you.

Prepare your call-lists and prospecting lists ahead of time, either the day before if possible or as early in the morning as you can. Preparation is good, but preparation is also one of the biggest causes of procrastination. Too many people get stuck in preparation mode and start the actual task too late or fail to start at all.

Don't allow preparation to creep into your prospecting time-blocks. Soon you'll be distracted by other administrative tasks or grabbing one more cup of coffee. If you have scheduled business-generation between 8:30AM and 11:30AM, that means you're behind your desk at 8:29AM, with your call-lists in front of you, ready to dial the first number.

## Scripts

In time, you will have completely memorized and internalized all of your various scripts. However, many agents will pin their scripts permanently on the wall or place them on a rotating podium or similar platform so that they can pull up whichever script they need in the moment—from SOI scripts to FSBOS to expired listing scripts, etc.

Depending on the length of the script, some agents break them into sections on smaller index cards. It's also a good idea to have scripts for handling typical objections that arise for the type of prospecting call you're making (FSBO, expired etc.).

You could have your scripts up on your computer screen, but remember that your computer should ideally be closed or, if it is open, then a minimal amount of items should be on your screen at any one time. If your computer is open, its main purpose should be entering information, taking notes on the lead you're calling, and setting appointments on your calendar.

## Calendar

Your calendar can also be used to keep you on track as well as scheduling new listing appointments.

Many agents will lead generate in a 3-hour block, dedicating an hour for expired listings first thing in the morning, followed immediately by an hour of SOI calls, and another hour of property preview calls or lead follow-up calls.

It's important to stay on track and make sure that you're transitioning from one prospecting category to another so that you're hitting all of the targets you've set yourself.

Some people swear by a timer, while others simply keep an occasional eye on their clock and calendar. While it's important to stay on track, you don't want to be distracted by continually checking to see what time it is.

Like we said, everything can have its pros and cons. Your mindset will be the biggest determining factor between focus and failure.

## Mr. In Between

Some of you might be just about old enough to know the song, "Accentuate the positive, eliminate the negative, and don't mess with Mr. In-Between."

Some things are not necessarily a positive that *definitely* needs to be added, or a negative that should be *completely* taken away, but rather fall into a debatable "in-between" category that is fine under certain circumstances, but poses potential risks.

## CRM

For example, many agents will tell you that you should not have your CRM up in front of you while you're making prospecting calls. You're supposed to be on the phone making call after call after call, not spending half your time typing detailed notes into your CRM.

If you do choose to have your CRM in front of you, learn to type while you're on the phone, and don't allow yourself to continue typing for too long in between calls. That's why auto-dialers and power-dialers can be so beneficial—they automatically start dialing the next number as soon as you hang up, so you will soon learn how to write clear, concise and, most importantly, *quick* notes.

Your prospecting arena is all about efficiency, functionality, productivity, and focus. Again, everything comes back to purpose and access.

- **Purpose**: Does this serve my purpose for prospecting?
- **Access**: Does this give me access to prospects?

## Drinks & Snacks

Another debatable in-between issue is drinks and snacks.

If you're lead generating for an hour in the morning, then we're pretty sure you can survive 60 minutes without food or water, but if you're prospecting in a continuous 3-hour block, or standing up for long periods of time, then it's understandable that you might need some refreshment to keep your energy up.

If you do need drinks or snacks while you're prospecting, don't allow them to become a distraction while you're talking on the phone or in between calls. Limit salty snacks that will increase your thirst (and need to go to the bathroom!) and choose something refreshing and energizing instead.

And, like your call-lists and your scripts, prepare in advance so that you're not walking across the office every thirty minutes to fill up a glass of water or grab something from the fridge. You risk running into someone and one minute away from your desk will soon turn into fifteen.

Bring everything you need in advance before you close your door behind you, and don't allow these potential time sucks to become a negative stimulus. If these things are impacting you negatively then you need to remove them. On the other hand, if the promise of a treat as a reward for hitting an hourly target works to increase your contact rate, then by all means use this as a positive reinforcement.

Whatever you include or don't include in your prospecting environment, it is not a true 'reinforcement' unless it results in your business-generation increasing or occurring more frequently in the future.

## Your Working Windshield

A visual way to think about all of this is to consider everything you see in your immediate prospecting workstation as your "Windshield" that helps you to navigate where you're going, avoid accidents, and pay attention to signs when there's a change in direction. Your Dashboard gives you an idea of where your important gauges are: fuel, mileage, speed, etc.

Compared side by side, how does the size of your windshield compare to your dashboard? Exactly.

Focusing on what doesn't matter in any given moment can become a potentially distracting and dangerous issue. Your focus and attention should be on the person you're calling and successfully navigating the conversation.

Your windshield is an eye-level left to right progression, and your dashboard is simply a reference checkpoint.

Your windshield includes scripts for prospecting and objection handling as well as your calendar and whatever system you choose for taking notes while on the phone.

Below your windshield is your dashboard. You'll be checking this regularly, but not to the extent that you aren't focusing on what lies immediately ahead.

Still important to support your prospecting efforts, these are your gauges for *where you are* with the client, with your activity, with your schedule, and possibly with the market.

Contact/Call List: A list of your contact targets for the day, showing names, phone numbers, possibly address and referring contact. This is solely for giving you a quick glance of who's in your sights for the time-block you have set aside.

Time Clock: Whether you're motivated by time on task, or time left on the clock, this can be the ultimate watchdog to keep you on track: decide for yourself if an audible "ticking" will be a hindrance or a help.

Market Report: A straightforward ticker report of what's available, selling, sold, expired, listing price vs. sales price, and average days on market, for quick reference with everyone.

Client Notes: Last conversations, important people in the lives of your contact, and potential questions you're answering with this follow-up call. This is mostly for SOI calls and follow-ups with prospects that you've previously made contact with.

Daily Contact Sheet: Your tally of activity, whether it be contacts, how many referrals you've asked for, or asking for the appointments.

Next Action Filter File: Depending on your systems, this can be a single file folder, accordion file, or outbox; it's the place to put the contact file, buyer or seller lead sheet, pre-qualification sheet, or appointment confirmation form. You'll work on these later, outside of prospecting time, yet it's a great "landing pad" that houses the necessary client work in a single place that you won't lose or forget about later.

## EXERCISE: Where Are You Now?

Take a moment to think about and answer the following questions.

Compared to what you're currently using, what are two benefits you can immediately see from this type of workstation?

1.
2.

What could be the biggest hurdle for you?

Where does your system save you time? Preparation? What about during the process? After the process? During leverage? Be specific where you can.

Would a repeated process help your efforts? How so?

Where would it hinder your efforts?

## WHERE TO NEXT, KIT BUDDY?

Let's step away from business-generation for a brief moment. Once you've made contact with new prospects, you will need to follow up with them.

As we mentioned, your prospecting dashboard should include a Next Action Filter File—a "landing pad" that houses the necessary client-work in a single place for future follow-up after you've finished making your phone calls.

Oftentimes, the Next Action Filter File tends to become a chaotic, disorganized "catch all" or prospecting cemetery if there's no subsequent system in place. You can avoid this by creating categorized kits so that you can quickly move documents from the Next Action

Filter File into appropriate sub-folders or packets.

For example, after a morning of circle prospecting calls, your Next Action Filter File might contain several different follow-up categories:

- 8 agreed to accept your open house invitation
- 2 were FSBO listings
- 1 was an expired listing

At the end of prospecting that day, you simply pair the contact sheet with the corresponding kit, to be mailed or delivered by the deadline you promised to the client.

Here are some of the kits you might create at the beginning of the week, month, or quarterly, depending on how much you change the look and content of the items.

- Open House Door Knocking Kits
- Expired Listing Kits
- FSBO Listing Kits
- Buyer Consultation Showing Kits
- Pre-listing Kits
- Listing Presentation Kits
- Preview Kits
- Call Day Kits

Now, you could wait and print these up "as needed" but it's far more efficient to have these to hand exactly when you want them and the contact is top of mind.

## EXERCISE: Where are you now?

The idea of using kits is taking your process, procedures, or systems, and creating a physical "baton" to move the client to a next action.

What are some of the systems that you currently use to keep your materials organized?

What are the activities that seem to take the most time, done "as needed" that you could build a kit for?

Do you currently have kits set up for the following prospect types?

| | |
|---|---|
| Open House Guests | ☐ Yes / ☐ No |
| Pre-Listing Prospects | ☐ Yes / ☐ No |
| FSBO Listings | ☐ Yes / ☐ No |
| Expired Listings | ☐ Yes / ☐ No |
| Listing Appointments | ☐ Yes / ☐ No |
| Buyer Presentations | ☐ Yes / ☐ No |
| Other | ☐ Yes / ☐ No |

What are some reoccurring documents that might show up in each kit, no matter the specialty? Put a Check or an X on those you use.   Circle those you need.

| Pre-Appointment Checklist | Business Biography | Testimonials |
|---|---|---|
| "How did you hear about us?" questionnaire<br><br>☐ Yes / ☐ No | Workflow of a Transaction<br><br>☐ Yes / ☐ No | Introduction to the People you Work With<br><br>☐ Yes / ☐ No |
| Market Snapshot<br><br>☐ Yes / ☐ No | What We Do For You<br><br>☐ Yes / ☐ No | Your Resume<br><br>☐ Yes / ☐ No |
| Other: | Other: | Other: |

## **DISTRACTED AND DESPERATE**

*I need your advice. I have a coworker that is constantly distracting me when I'm trying to work. I've tried closing my door, pulling down the blinds, and turning my back away from the window, but they haven't taken the hint. I've even tried locking the door but they just kept knocking and knocking until I answer, or they'll call or message me until I pick up. The same thing happens when I'm at home. I love my partner and my kids and I wish I could spend every second with them, but I'm trying to focus so that I can get more business and support us. I don't want to hurt anyone's feelings or be the office jerk, but I don't know what else to do.*

*Yours Sincerely, Distracted and Desperate!*

You don't need to be a psychologist or an advice columnist to know that some people either genuinely do not notice or simply don't respect 'subtle' signs and boundaries, such as a closed door or the fact that your window blinds are pulled down.

Oftentimes, even a locked door won't do it. Some people have an overly heightened sense of their own job's importance or the urgency of a situation and will knock down your door and insist upon getting your attention no matter what.

## Don't Reinforce Bad Behavior

People will continue to repeat their behavior if it gets them the desired result. Positive reinforcement doesn't mean that the *behavior* is positive; it simply means that you're adding or giving somebody something pleasant that increases that behavior.

The first step is to stop rewarding their behavior. Each time you give in and answer the door or pick up the phone, you're signaling that you're okay with being interrupted and that their problem or question is more important than your prospecting and business-generation.

They're happy because they've been given the reward that they want—your time and attention. By refusing to answer their call, you're taking away your attention, which will hopefully decrease their tendency to interrupt you in the first place.

Sometimes, however, you will have to take extra steps to guard against intruders and spell out your wishes in no uncertain terms.

## Guard Against Intruders

It might seem simple but a printed sign can work wonders. Believe it or not, a closed door is too subtle and understated for some people: they won't get the message unless they read it in black and white.

Put a sign on your door that says:

**DO NOT DISTURB**
Propsecting until 11:30 am.
Please feel free to come by after that time.

OR

**STOP!**
Lead-Generation in progress.
Call me back afer 12pm

A smiley face can go a long way to prevent you from being seen as the unapproachable office jerk! For this same reason, you should also make sure to take the sign down after you're prospecting, so people will know that it's okay to disturb you again.

Another good reason to remember to take the sign down is that it's less effective if people see it up there all the time. There's no way you could possibly be lead generating from 8AM to 5PM every single day, so it's more believable when colleagues and coworkers see the sign during specific, regular, and consistent times.

## Turn Your Distractors Into Your Advocates

Oftentimes, your biggest distractors are the people closest to you. They're well intentioned but a little oblivious. What's more, when you answer their every call, they may not even realize that they're disrupting you in the middle of your most important work.

It's one thing if a colleague or professional partner is knocking down your door. But if your family is not familiar with your schedule or how important this time is to you, then you can hardly blame them for what they don't know.

You need to explicitly ask people to be your advocates and your gatekeepers when it comes to protecting your prospecting time.

Make sure that your family knows exactly which times you're unavailable and why it's so important for you to focus during that period.

### For example:

> *"Hey honey, I'm going to be lead generating between 8:30 and 11:30 every single morning and I need your help. Can you do me a favor and not call me during that time unless it's an emergency? You've no idea how hard it is to focus during that time. I love you and I want to do everything I can to get business and support our family financially, so your support and help in this will mean the world to me."*

If you work from home, it can be even harder to stay on task and concentrate. Your spouse, partner, and even your children can be your support network by holding you accountable. Tell them:

> *"Make sure I stay on task. If you see me milling around in the kitchen or doing anything at all besides making my important calls, please let me know. Give me hell and get me back in my workspace!"*

Whether it's a family member or an assistant, explicitly ask and empower them to hold you accountable to prospecting during pre-determined times each day. You can even ask your fellow agents, since a true prospector is all too aware of how difficult it is to do it alone. Ask your coworkers to act as gatekeepers and allow nobody to gain access to you during prospecting time-blocks.

Depending on who they are, you can use combinations of the following scripts:

> *"Hey (coworker), I need your help and I'm serious. I'm trying to lead generate between 8:30 and 11:30 every morning. Can you make sure I stay in my office or I stay in my cubicle? The only time I'm allowed to get up is if I absolutely have to go to the bathroom and make sure I'm back in five minutes. If you see me talking to someone, yell at me and grab me, and get me back here!"*
>
> *"Hey (coworker). If you see anybody coming to interrupt me, can you please do me a favor and help me steer them away. Don't let them knock on my door. Say, 'Hey, go back to him after 11:00, he'll be free after 11:30.' And just try to keep them blocked off. I'll even do the same for you if you want me to. You just let me know and I'll help you out if you're interested in time blocking your time to lead generate and stay focused on your activities as well. It would really, really help me if you could a) keep me on task so I'm not distracted and b) block out anyone else."*

Whether intentionally or absentmindedly, other people can certainly be distracting it's true. But, at same time, there can be no excuses—all of this comes back to you. By asking people to change their behavior and tendency to interrupt you, you are also creating conditions to improve your own behavior.

When you ask people to be your advocate and hold you accountable, they have to live up to their promise to help you out, but you have to live up to your request for diligent and focused prospecting time. The last thing you want to do is disappoint them by failing to follow through on the very thing you said you were going to do.

We'll explore additional accountability strategies in chapter 14. But, at the end of the day, lead-generation generally accounts for a mere quarter of your working week, so it should be well within your reach to guard and protect your daily prospecting commitments.

## SUMMARY

Your prospecting workspace can enhance your business-generation goals or it can be a source of distraction and chaos.

When creating your ideal workspace, it's important that you implement systems that are truly effective for you and the way that you work best. Experiment with our recommendations and suggestions and give them a reasonable amount of time to take effect, but don't continue with anything that does not result in increased focus, increased efficiency, and increased prospecting productivity.

When creating and organizing your prospecting arena, remember to accentuate the positive and eliminate the negative. If you want to increase your prospecting and prospect more frequently, you should both include and remove elements that reinforce your desired behavior.

At all times, ask yourself the following questions: Does this serve my purpose for prospecting? Does this give me access to prospects?

In time, you will fashion and perfect your ideal prospecting environment. However, the fact that you may not have an office or workspace that is 100% perfect is not a reason for not being able to generate business. You can guard against intruders and turn your distractors into your advocates. But, when it comes down to it, you can prospect in any environment—no excuses!

## Mindset – Maintaining a Proper Perspective

Back at the very beginning of this book, we told you that mindset, attitude, and perspective is *the* most important factor for real estate success. Though we knew you were eager to dive right in and get going on the practical aspects of prospecting, we knew that mindset must form the fundamental bedrock of this book, because we know that mindset will form the fundamental bedrock of your business.

To truly succeed and go the distance in your prospecting career, you will need to adopt and *maintain* a positive mindset to fuel and reenergize you through the failures, setbacks, and rejections that lay before you.

Maintenance is key. In the initial excitement of a new experience or endeavor, it's easy to be positive and have a good attitude, but maintaining it over time is another thing altogether.

As you'll see in this chapter, the real estate industry goes through up and down periods. In your career, you will need to navigate the good and the bad when it comes to the market. And you will need to navigate your days and months and make sure that your personal life is in balance with your professional business responsibilities. It's important that you take the long view and approach each day with a positive attitude and your future goals and success in mind.

### Learning Targets

In this chapter, you will learn:

- How to maintain a positive and steady mindset despite the ups and downs of the real estate market.

- How to conduct a SWOT analysis to assess your Strengths, Weaknesses, Opportunities, and Threats.

- How to create SMART Goals that are Specific, Measurable, Achievable, Relevant, and Time-Bound.

## FREE YOUR MIND

Throughout this book, we've stressed the importance of time-management, time-blocking, and honoring your schedule and calendar. At this stage, there should be no need to repeat ourselves but, again and again, we find that even the most experienced and skilled agents struggle with this aspect of the business.

On a daily basis, it can be very difficult to stay on task and make sure that you perform a certain level of prospecting activities each day at the appointed time.

Oftentimes, people have a negative perspective about their calendar. They view it as a constraining, controlling force that keeps them caged in. If this describes your mindset, then we would ask you to instead see your schedule and your calendar as a tool for freedom that gives you the gift of more golden minutes and moments.

> *Your calendar is a tool for freedom that gives you the gift of more golden minutes and moments.*

Studies show that it takes 23 minutes to refocus after a distraction. Every time you check your email or, worse, your social media accounts, it takes almost a half an hour to get back on task. How many minutes are you throwing away each day?

"It's okay," you might say, "I make the time back up by multitasking." Well, guess again. Multitasking actually *reduces* your productivity by up to 40%. You might think you're being fabulously productive, but busyness is not a good indicator of productivity. Instead, you're wasting precious minutes that could be more effectively used by focusing on a single task.

The minutes that you fritter away are gone forever. Distractions and diversions are not only damaging your business, but they can hurt your life and steal precious minutes and moments from you and your friends and family.

Sticking to a strict schedule saves you time and, during the ups and downs of the real estate business, it might just save your sanity and your relationships. As we said at the beginning of this book, your goal is to increase your business and income to increase your personal freedom.

> *"Never get so busy making a living that you forget to make a life."* – Dolly Parton

Your calendar should not just include business activities. It should include your personal life outside of work, too. From spending time with friends and family to exercising and pursuing hobbies and pursuits that are important to you, if you don't make space in your schedule for the things that bring you joy and meaning, you will lose them to mundane distractions and meaningless drift.

When you rigorously honor your business schedule, you are not a slave to your calendar—you are storing up freedom and honoring yourself and the people in your life. Your calendar is what creates freedom and life-balance. It's crucial that you maintain this mindset as you navigate the vagaries and variables of the rollercoaster that is the real estate market.

## TOTAL MARKET MINDSET OVERHAUL

One of your responsibilities as a real estate agent is to educate and coach your clients through the buying and selling process. The vagaries of cyclical real estate markets can be confusing for regular people and, oftentimes, you will need to explain to a frustrated seller why their home isn't selling at asking price.

Many agents will use a 'Total Market Overview' to present objective data to their clients, and to educate sellers on pricing their home correctly to ensure a quick sale at the best possible price for their particular market.

For those of you who aren't familiar, TMO reports resemble something like this:

| Price Range | Active | Pending | Exp/Can | Sold/last 6 mos. | Avg Sold Price | Avg % of Listing Price | Avg Days on Market |
|---|---|---|---|---|---|---|---|
| Under $300K | 100 | 25 | 15 | 80 | $245K | 95% | 35 |
| $300K-$600K | 80 | 10 | 11 | 24 | $450K | 94% | 75 |
| Above %600K | 45 | 6 | 9 | 18 | $780K | 98% | 140 |

Total Market Overview reports are designed to set expectations about the selling process and *remove the assumptions* your clients have about the market.

We all make assumptions that are not always accurate, factual or true. Even prospectors are not immune to making their own assumptions about the real estate market.

> *We all make assumptions that are not always accurate, factual or true. Even prospectors are not immune to making their own assumptions about the real estate market.*

By and large, for motivated and persistent prospectors, market conditions are mostly irrelevant. The only thing that prevents prospectors from generating business is their good versus bad mindset. Negative perspectives and false assumptions create limiting beliefs that have sunk entire careers. It's crucial that you perform a total market mindset overhaul, examining and repairing dangerous mindsets before it's too late.

## SELLER'S MARKET

A seller's market comes into formation when demand exceeds supply for a product or service. In real estate, a seller's market describes a shortage of properties in the face of strong buyer demand. In a seller's market, homes sell quickly and often above asking price, as the seller holds the upper hand when it comes to negotiating.

When pondering business strategies, some agents will research turnover rate and see how many homes are selling in a particular neighborhood. The data itself is accurate, objective, and neutral, but depending on the agent's perspective, they might interpret the same data very differently.

In a hot seller's market, for example, one agent might take a look at turnover data and say:

> "Wow, a lot of homes are selling in that neighborhood, so I'm going to prospect in that area."

While another agent might say:

> "Hmm, you know what? Maybe that's not a good neighborhood to prospect in. If turnover rate is so high, that means all the homes have sold in that neighborhood and the likelihood that more homes are going to sell in the near future is going down."

If so, that agent might take the following course of action:

> "I'm going to prospect in an area with a low turnover rate that hasn't had a lot of homes sales because those homes are due. If I can get a few sales in that neighborhood, that will trigger and increase prices, and other homeowners will see that they can get more equity out of their home and decide to sell and move upwards, too."

Now, understand: neither of these perspectives are 100% right or 100% wrong. Both can be true, and either approach can work at different times, but both perspectives carry an element of chance that agents will have to allow for. The same numbers can conjure different impressions for different agents and can be looked at in a variety of contexts.

*Whether the real estate market is "good" or "bad" doesn't stop motivated and successful prospectors from generating business. The only thing that prevents prospectors from generating business is their black and white, good versus bad mindset.*

However, despite our right to have differing opinions and perspectives, whether the real estate market is "good" or "bad" doesn't stop motivated and successful prospectors from generating business.

The only thing that prevents prospectors from generating business is their black and white, good versus bad mindset. Real estate is inherently cyclical, but your mindset should be steady, consistent and positive through the inevitable ups and downs.

### For example:

Let's say we come out of a buyer's market into a seller's market where there's a very low amount of housing inventory and a very high buyer demand. During that time, a lot of agents will say:

"I'm not going to prospect for expired listings because no listings are expiring! Homes are selling too quickly. Prospecting for expired listings is a waste of time."

Quite frankly, that's simply untrue. At ICC we have coached and trained expired prospectors through every single real estate market, and we have found that the market doesn't really impact them.

While it's true that there are fewer expired phone numbers to call in a seller's market, it's also true that agents with the above assumptions will abandon expired prospecting as a potential source of income, with a result that there are far fewer agents competing for the same listing. Savvy expired prospectors will continue to prospect right through that market cycle. They have fewer numbers to call but there is far less competition.

Then, later on, when the market shifts and changes again, as it always will, homes start taking longer to sell, or not selling at all and, suddenly, there is a flood of expired listings on the market. And, along with the flood of expired listings comes a flood of expired prospectors once again. There is more competition, but there are also more potential prospects and more numbers to call, so the very same conversion rates will work out as before. Or, there will be so much competition that agents with a negative mindset will talk themselves out of trying and the competition will decrease again.

> *At ICC we have coached and trained prospectors through every single real estate market, and we have found that the market doesn't really impact them.*

The same thing happens with FSBO prospectors. They'll look at the turnover numbers and say:

> "Wow, it's a really good seller's market. I don't want to prospect for FSBOs because homes are selling like hotcakes. Inventory is so low that anyone could put up a home for sale and sell it right now."

Yet, once again—and for the same reasons as before—good FSBO prospectors continue to prospect and generate the same amount of business in that market. There are less FSBO prospects to contact, but half your competition has run for the hills!

Later, when the market cycles through in the favor of buyers again, the competition will return but so too will the number of FSBO prospects. When homeowners see their neighbors' "For Sale" signs sitting out on the lawn forever, they will be less motivated to attempt to sell their home by themselves, and there will be a higher number of FSBO leads to make connections with.

## Buyer's Market

A buyer's market is, admittedly, tougher for real estate agents. In a buyer's market, there are a lot more homes for sale so agents will have to spend a lot of time showing property. In a buyer's market, the buyer has the upper hand in negotiating and, oftentimes, they will back out of deals and simply move onto another property, which can be incredibly time-consuming and frustrating.

In a buyer's market, there is high inventory but lower demand, which can often result in sellers having to come down on price to attract a smaller number of buyers to purchase their home.

In the industry, we call this a "bad" market, but understand that it is so-called because of *price*, not because there is a lack of business-generation potential. A bad real estate market does not prevent people from selling their homes, and it should not prevent motivated prospectors from being the agent to help them sell it.

> *A bad real estate market does not prevent people from selling their homes, and it should not prevent motivated prospectors from being the agent to help them sell it.*

People still need to move, no matter what's happening in the wider world. People have babies and need bigger homes for their growing family and changing needs. People need to relocate for employment purposes or a myriad of circumstantial reasons. Life goes on and the total sales volume and commission paid does not change much at all. The same amount of commission dollar earned is out there for the taking in a buyer's market.

It all comes down to mindset and the way you look at things.

### You Are What You Think

While it's true that the real estate market goes through up-and-down cycles that are more or less favorable for buyers or sellers at any given time, from an agent's perspective there is no good or bad market—there is only your mindset and your tendency to look at the market in a certain way.

As Shakespeare said: "There is nothing either good or bad, but thinking makes it so."

A shockingly small number of real estate agents actively and consistently make an effort to get new business.

Agents who do not consistently lead-generate and create business by their own design are more likely to see a bad pricing market as a bad personal market. They are accustomed to business simply coming to them in a "good" market and, quite frankly, they become dangerously complacent.

They say:

> "Expired prospecting won't work in this market. Calling FSBOs won't work in this market. There's no point in even using the phone at all when everything's going online."

Meanwhile, agents that frequently and consistently lead-generate for new business pick up more market-share in a so-called bad market. They know that the above thought-process is not only a negative perspective but it's simply bad information.

> *"There is nothing either good or bad, but thinking makes it so."* – William Shakespeare

The Internet has actually created a higher need for telemarketing. Telemarketing call centers are opening up all over the world at a very rapid rate. Anyone that works online-leads knows that a big part of it is working the phone. You still have to prospect. Trust us, prospects don't just call you! You have to call them and you have to do lead follow-up and nurture them over time as with any other prospective client.

This is simply a fact, but different agents will see things in very different ways. Be assured, however, that as long as you do something actively and regularly to generate business, the techniques and strategies we teach you *will work* as long as you commit to diligently applying them.

## Who's Your Hero?

Now, please understand that we are not passing judgment. There are many talented and naturally skilled agents that do not succeed. They're not necessarily bad agents, and they're certainly not bad people.

Oftentimes, these agents will have other jobs and are less motivated. Or, they haven't learned successful strategies for mastering their mindset and mastering time-management, or they haven't been taught any sound business-generation techniques. This creates a very negative experience for them, which results in a negative mindset that they might share and pass on to other people in the business.

While they're not bad people and perfectly well-intentioned, if you allow yourself to listen to them, and be persuaded by their perspective, you're closing a big door behind you and shutting yourself off from your potential success.

> *Your mentors and role models should have what you want—a lot of clients and a lot of business—so make sure you choose them wisely.*

Even agents with lots of experience and are very knowledgeable do not always lead-generate at an extremely high level, so their advice is not useful or relevant for agents that are highly motivated and disciplined, which we are assuming you are.

Please ensure to follow the mentors and role models that you aspire to be like. Just because another agent is willing to help you, or is very knowledgeable about how to process a transaction, doesn't mean that you should be incorporating all of their ideas about how to lead-generate and build your business.

Your mentors and role models should *have* what you *want*—a lot of clients and a lot of business—so make sure you choose them wisely. We have seen false assumptions, negative mindsets, and bad information spread like a virus.

A very tiny percent of agents consistently reach out and contact their SOI or do any type of prospecting technique with a high level of consistency or discipline. The fact that you are going to be doing it, or are already doing it, is a huge testament to you and really stacks the odds in your favor of being one of the top agents in your local area. As long as you have the right mindset, you will learn how to do this. We've seen it work for everyone, as long as they *try*.

## AFFIRMATIONS & GOALS

Back at the very beginning of this book, we challenged you to build and nurture a library filled with evidence of success that would motivate, renew, and empower you in as many different areas you could think of, from health and wellness, to relationships and career. Our hope was that something that began as an exercise in a book would evolve into a lifelong ritual that you can continually draw from for inspiration and affirmation.

Later, in our module covering your weekly and monthly prospecting schedule, we stressed that each and every day should begin with a motivational recitation. Whether it's a meditation, a prayer or an affirmation, it's crucial that you take a few moments each morning to create a clear mind and a positive mindset.

And now, as we begin to approach the final chapters in this book, we are going to ask you to be honest about where you are with this:

- Have you been practicing a daily affirmation or morning motivational recitation?

- Have you taken the time to document your successes or the successes of others that you aspire to achieve one day?

- Did you do it for the first few days and then slowly stop? Did you stop because it felt corny or pointless or uncomfortable?

It's very important that you do not assess whether something is comfortable or effective when you first start doing it. In order to become better at anything, we have to repeatedly practice it and do things that are initially uncomfortable, time and time again, until it ultimately becomes comfortable, natural, and effective. If we assess whether we like something upfront when it's uncomfortable, we don't really know if we're going to like it once it eventually becomes ingrained and natural to us.

The ability and willingness to push through discomfort is what makes people great in their careers and in life. We just have to have the faith that we're doing something that has been *tested and proven* and will eventually reap incredible rewards.

Being positive isn't about denying reality or pretending that everything will always be great or that every technique you apply will generate instant and wild success. Sometimes it can take a while before we start seeing successful results from our daily practices and activities. The key is to focus on the activities and not on the results.

### FOCUS ON THE ACTIVITIES

Imagine you're at a bar and one of your buddies proposes the following bet. He's going to flip a coin ten times. If it comes up *heads* more often than tails, he'll pay *you* $50, but if it comes up *tails* more often than heads, you'll pay *him* $50.

It's a fair bet—there are no hidden tricks—so each flip has a statistically equal 50/50 chance of coming up heads or tails.

Your friend starts to flip. The first flip comes up tails then the second flip comes up tails too. He hands the coin to you to try, but your flips come up tails also. In fact, every single flip of the coin comes up tails, and this time you lose the bet.

Now, some people might be bitter and accuse their buddy of rigging the wager somehow or calling the entire game into question.

However, while it admittedly stings a little, you hand him your $50 because you know it's a fair bet and that every time he flipped that coin there was a statistical 50% chance it would flip in your favor. It just so happened that those first ten flips didn't go your way.

You also know, however, that if you and your friend had continued to flip the coin, it simply had to come up heads at some point. The laws of probability would eventually pan out. If the coin were tossed a thousand times, statistically it would come up tails 500 times and it would come up heads 500 times overall too.

Every real estate agent goes through dry spells where they don't get a lot of results even though they're doing all of the required and recommended activities.

> **For example:**
>
> They might be diligently making their 25 expired listing contacts each and every morning, week in week out, but they're just not getting the expected results.
>
> Their mindset turns to a negative, discouraged place and they start thinking:
>
> > *This isn't working. The market has turned and there aren't enough expired listings. There are too many other agents calling expired listings. Maybe I should start using the Internet—the telephone clearly doesn't work in this day and age. Or maybe it's me…. Maybe I'm just not good at this.*

At ICC, we've seen agents use all of these excuses and more. Their focus is too much on the daily results and not enough on the activities. They've heard that a good expired prospector will get 1 listing appointment for every 25 contacts they make, and they take that ratio extremely literally.

While the 25:1 ratio is statistically true and accurate—there are no hidden tricks—that doesn't necessarily mean you're going to make 25 calls on a Monday morning and have 1 listing appointment by noon. It doesn't even mean that if you make 100 phone calls by Thursday that you'll have 4 listing appointments as you head towards the end of the week.

Sometimes you'll make 200 expired listing calls and get *nothing*. We know this is hard to hear, but it's important that you develop the right mindset around this fact early on, because after 200 phone calls you may well want to give up. But if you stay the course and stay focused on the tested and proven activity then, eventually, the numbers will catch up, and the metaphorical coin will begin to flip in your favor.

In the following two weeks you'll set 8 listing appointments. You'll secure a listing with a seller who has 4 rental properties, or you'll contact a few people in a row who are finally ready to list their home. When you look back over the *total* time and do the math on the *total* number of contacts made and the *total* number of appointments set, it works out to a 25:1 ratio.

All of the methods and prospecting activities in this book have been tested and proven over decades. They've survived through every real estate market, and they've survived the rise of the Internet age and the advent of searching for homes online—in fact, many of these methods have thrived and performed better in this period of time.

It's essential that you maintain the proper mindset when performing your daily prospecting activities. Don't worry so much about the daily results. Instead, focus on and celebrate the success of completing your daily activities. Take the long view and have faith that the ratios will work out with increased activity and time on task. Don't despair when you experience dry spells. The laws of probability are stacked in your favor.

## SWOT's Up?

Maintaining a positive mindset is about keeping things in perspective and learning from our struggles and challenges, while constantly pushing through discomfort and continually seeking out areas for development and improvement and ways to become the very best version of ourselves.

In the business world, a SWOT analysis is a strategic planning technique used to help an organization identify strengths, weaknesses, opportunities and threats related to their entire business or a particular project.

Performing a SWOT analysis provides organizations with an objective perspective on what the business does well, what its challenges and struggles are, as well as opportunities and avenues it should take advantage of in the pursuit of improvement and excellence.

A personal SWOT analysis can do the same for you.

As you can see, a SWOT analysis is divided into four distinct categories:

- **S**trengths
- **W**eaknesses
- **O**pportunities
- **T**hreats

Furthermore, a SWOT analysis aims to identify both the *internal* and *external* factors that will play a part in achieving your goals or objectives.

In a personal SWOT analysis, strengths and weakness are typically internal or related to you personally as an individual, while the identification of opportunities and threats are typically focused on the external environment.

**STRENGTHS**
(Internal)

**WEAKNESSES**
(Internal)

**THREATS**
(Internal)

**OPPORTUNITIES**
(Internal)

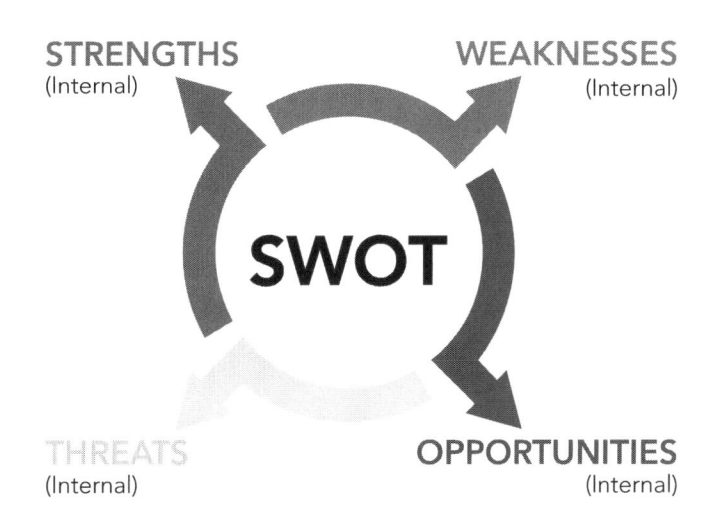

### EXERCISE: Conduct a Personal SWOT Analysis

Completing a SWOT analysis takes thoughtful introspection and self-examination. Honesty is crucial if you want to gain meaningful insights and results. Allow yourself at least 30 minutes to reflect on each quadrant of the chart. You may even find that you need to spread the analysis out over a couple of days and sleep on some of the questions. To be of true value, complete the analysis with care and thought, rather than an item to check off a list. You're not in school anymore; this isn't homework, it's your career and your life.

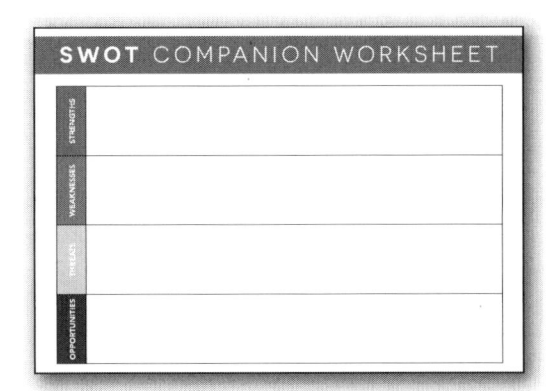

Use the *SWOT Companion Worksheet* in the Appendix so that you have a larger area to write your answers, or write out your responses on blank paper.

No two people will answer the questions in the same way. Take a look at possible answers below to help explore ways in which you could respond.

## STRENGTHS

Begin by identifying your strengths—the things that make you unique or set you apart from everyone else.

When answering the 'Strength' questions, don't be shy or modest. Humility is an admirable trait, but it's important that you don't understate or undermine your strengths because you're worried about bragging. It's important to acknowledge the positive and valuable things you bring to the world and affirm your abilities and your worth.

Possible answers might include:

- I'm very patient. People often tell me that I'm good at explaining difficult financial or real estate market concepts.
- I love people. I'm good at striking up conversations and enjoy talking to people from all walks of life.

- I'm even-tempered. I'm good at diffusing conflict and helping to calm situations.
- People tell me I'm a great team player. I'm competitive and motivated, but I want everyone on my team to be successful too.

## Weaknesses

When answering the 'Weakness' questions, the point is not to put you down, but to acknowledge personal areas that need improvement or that could set you back in your career (remember that, in a SWOT analysis, weaknesses are *internal* and relate to you as an individual, not the external world).

No one likes to talk about weaknesses or imperfections, but a SWOT analysis is a proactive, forward-looking exercise. By identifying your weaknesses, you can then decide how to deal with them and become better.

- I'm constantly running late for appointments.
- I'm great with people in informal situations but I get nervous and clam up as soon as I start delivering a listing presentation.
- I hate having to work on weekends. I avoid organizing open houses.
- I spend too much time on social media. I struggle with this area of marketing because I get sucked in and waste hours browsing Facebook each week.

## Opportunities

When reflecting on the 'Opportunities' questions, remember to focus on external factors that you can take advantage of to further your career and increase your skills.

Finding opportunity in any situation can breathe life back into your work. The ability to pay attention and notice the world around you is crucial. Opportunities are everywhere if we remember to look. Our internal strengths and abilities can also present external opportunities.

For example:

- My daughter's teacher asked me to talk to their class about different jobs that grown-ups do. This could be a no-pressure way to get comfortable talking to people about what I do. I can also add the teacher and possibly some other parents to my SOI.
- I'm fluent in Spanish. This presents an opportunity to tap into different neighborhoods in my city.

## Threats

Anything that holds you back or prevents you from being abundantly successful is a threat. Again, a SWOT analysis is designed to be a proactive, forward-looking exercise. When answering the 'Threat' questions, don't dwell on your answers or get sucked into a negative thought spiral. Rather, acknowledge that these threats exist while thinking of what you can do to remove or minimize the threats or obstacles.

## STRENGTHS
(Internal)

- What skills and talents do you have?
- What advantages do you have that others don't?
- What achievements are you most proud of?
- What makes you unique?
- What do other people like about you?

## WEAKNESSES
(Internal)

- What areas need improvement?
- What's your greatest weakness?
- What do you try to avoid doing?
- What are your negative work habits?
- What would others suggest you improve?

## SWOT

## THREATS
(External)

- What obstacles do you face at your company or as a solo agent in real estate?
- Who are your strongest competitors?
- How are your finances? How long can you go without earning your commission?
- What extranal factors prevent you from prospecting?
- What is the biggest external danger that would prevent you from reaching your goals?

## OPPORTUNITIES
(External)

- What new technology can help you?
- Do you have an overlooked network of contacts that you can tap into?
- What trends do you see at your real estate company, and how can you benefit from that?
- Is there a need in your company or community that nobody is filling? How can you contribute or help?

When answering 'Threat' questions, remember to be objective and stick to the facts. Sometimes our fears are unfounded and we perceive things as a threat when they actually aren't. This is particularly the case for new prospectors who lack experience and are going through discomfort while learning new things.

While it's important to acknowledge and deal with external threats, the tendency to see threats everywhere can create limiting beliefs that hold you back from success and achieving your goals.

Once your personal SWOT analysis is complete, it's time to *take action* and *follow through* on what you've discovered about your strengths, weakness, threats and opportunities.

It's time to get SMART and set your goals.

## Get SMART

When thinking about the future and what you want to achieve, it can be hard to know quite where to begin, especially when you feel so far from where you want to be.

SMART is an acronym that provides structure and guidance to your goal setting.

Consider the two statements:

| *I'd love to figure out prospecting and sell some more homes this year so I can get out of debt and have some fun!* | VS | *My goal is to list and sell 25 properties and close 20 buyers in Anytown. In the next 12 months, I'll hold 12 listing appointment and 24 buyer appointments a month through prospecting my SOI, Expired listings, FSBO listings, and circle prospecting target areas.* |

Which statement seems more likely to occur? Both statements have the same general goal, but the second statement is amped up with concrete descriptors that lead to a next step and incites specific actions at particular times.

To make sure your goals are clear and realizable, they must be SMART:

- **S**pecific
- **M**easurable
- **A**chievable
- **R**elevant
- **T**ime-bound

### Specific

Your goal should be clear and specific. If it's too general or vague, you will struggle to find concrete efforts to focus on or motivate yourself to take action. When formulating your goals, the following five W questions can help kick-start your plan:

- **What** specifically do you want to accomplish?
- **Who** is involved?
- **Where** is the goal located?
- **Why** is this goal important to you?
- **Which** opportunities or obstacles are involved?

You can also ask yourself **How?** you will achieve your goal, as long as your answer is specific.

> For example:
>
> *I want to sell $50 million in real estate in the desirable Anytown neighborhood to create a better life for myself and for my family. In order to do so I will need to increase my SOI by 200 people, as my current number of contacts is a potential obstacle. One way I will do this is by taking advantage of a recent invitation to sit on the board of a local nonprofit with several other prominent community members.*

## MEASURABLE

For a goal to be effective, it must be measurable. That means you'll need concrete numbers—like that $50 million in real estate we identified in the previous section.

You can break the goal down even further. How much will you need to earn each month to meet your yearly goal?

What other metrics can you use to determine if you're on track to achieving your goal? Scoreboards? Tracking sheets? If you don't apply metrics to your goal, you won't know when you're following through or falling short.

## ACHIEVABLE

Of course, your goal should also be achievable. If $50 million in real estate sales seems too ambitious, what number is more achievable for you this year? $25 million? $10 million? Perhaps it's even less. That's okay.

Setting your course for an impossible goal is a sure-fire way to doom yourself to failure. If, however, you run the numbers and it seems doable, then run with it. Be confident and optimistic about what is and isn't achievable. Be realistic but don't allow a negative mindset to creep in and convince you that can't do something big or important.

## RELEVANT

Is your goal actually relevant to you? For a goal to be relevant it must make sense and align with other goals you've set for yourself. If another goal is to go back to school or start a family this year, then your real estate goals will have to take your broader life and objectives into account.

## TIME-BOUND

Is your goal to make $50 million in real estate sales a 1-year plan or a 5-year plan?

Every goal needs a target date, so that you have a concrete deadline to focus on and something to work towards on a daily or monthly basis.

Your target dates should be realistic. Anyone can set goals, but if you're not realistic about timing, your likelihood of success is slim.

When formulating your goals, think about the end date and all of the dates in between.

- When do I want to achieve my goal by?
- What can I do 6 months from now?
- What can I do 6 weeks from now?
- What can I do 6 hours from now?
- What can I do *right now*?

The answer to that last question is obvious. You can get SMART and start to visualize and define your very own goals.

## EXERCISE: Get SMART

**Create your SMART Action Plan** by using the worksheet to think about your goal using the different criteria we discussed. If you need more space, develop and write down your goals in your journal using the same SMART criteria. Then, write your goal, or goals, in a single sentence at the bottom of the page.

Just like everything else in real estate, things can change—including your SMART goals.

Real estate is cyclical and change is an inevitable and normal part of life. When life or business changes, your steady, positive, and consistent mindset will be your biggest strength.

When life happens, simply **Evaluate** where you are and **Re-Do** your SMART goals to create a SMARTER goal.

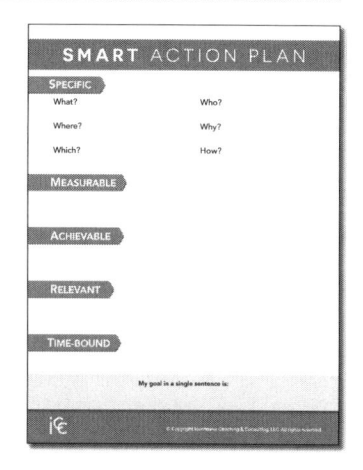

## Summary

Mindset will make or break an agent's business.

The real estate market goes through up-and-down cycles that are more or less favorable for buyers or sellers at any given time, but from an agent's perspective there is no "good" or "bad" market. The only thing that prevents prospectors from generating business is their mindset and their tendency to look at the market in a certain way.

Negative perspectives and false assumptions create limiting beliefs that have sunk entire careers. It's crucial that you perform a total market mindset overhaul, examining and repairing dangerous mindsets before it's too late.

Make sure that you follow only those mentors and role models that you aspire to be like. Just because another agent is willing to help you doesn't mean that you should be incorporating all of their ideas about how to lead-generate and build your business.

Your mentors and role models should *have* what you *want*—a lot of clients and a lot of business—so make sure you choose them wisely.

Hopefully your mentors have a great deal of life-balance, too. Your role models should understand that the purpose of a calendar is not to cage you in but is a tool for freedom that gives you the gift of more golden minutes and moments in life.

Finally, remember that it's very important that you do not assess whether something is comfortable or effective when you first start doing it. The ability and willingness to push through discomfort is what makes people great in their careers and in life. If you are not already doing a daily affirmation or motivational recitation it's never too late to start!

# MODULE 11

# APPENDIX 11.1

# SWOT

## STRENGTHS
(Internal)

- What skills and talents do you have?
- What advantages do you have that others don't?
- What achievements are you most proud of?
- What makes you unique?
- What do other people like about you?

## WEAKNESSES
(Internal)

- What areas need improvement?
- What's your greatest weakness?
- What do you try to avoid doing?
- What are your negative work habits?
- What would others suggest you improve?

## THREATS
(External)

- What obstacles do you face at your company or as a solo agent in real estate?
- Who are your strongest competitors?
- How are your finances? How long can you go without earning your commission?
- What extranal factors prevent you from prospecting?
- What is the biggest external danger that would prevent you from reaching your goals?

## OPPORTUNITIES
(External)

- What new technology can help you?
- Do you have an overlooked network of contacts that you can tap into?
- What trends do you see at your real estate company, and how can you benefit from that?
- Is there a need in your company or community that nobody is filling? How can you contribute or help?

© Copyright Icenhower Coaching & Consulting, LLC. All rights reserved.

354

© Icenhower Coaching & Consulting, LLC.

# MODULE 11

## APPENDIX 11.1 CONTINUED

### SWOT COMPANION WORKSHEET

| STRENGTHS | WEAKNESSES | THREATS | OPPORTUNITIES |
|-----------|------------|---------|---------------|
|           |            |         |               |

© Copyright Icenhower Coaching & Consulting, LLC. All rights reserved.

# SMART ACTION PLAN

## SPECIFIC

What?                   Who?

Where?                  Why?

Which?                  How?

## MEASURABLE

## ACHIEVABLE

## RELEVANT

## TIME-BOUND

My goal in a single sentence is:

# THE ART OF CLOSING

In the previous chapter, we talked about how mindset can make or break a business and how the only thing that prevents prospectors from generating business is their perspective.

But no matter how much business you generate, or how wonderful you are at striking up conversations and making initial contact, if you can't close then all your prospecting efforts will have been in vain.

Among other things, the art of closing is having the right words at the right time, and we promise that this chapter will make your head spin with scripts and a multitude of closing styles and models to choose from. Closing hinges on the ability to handle the objections that prevent people from moving forward in the sales process, and this chapter is chock-a-block with every objection handler under the sun—and then some!

## Learning Targets

In this chapter you will learn:

- How closing is the application of everything we have taught you so far, and that closing occurs at every stage of an organized sales process.
- The kind of confidence necessary to Assume the Sale.
- An abundance of closing styles and models, from 'Choice-Effect-Choice' to 'Best-Case, Worst-Case, Most-Likely' and many more.
- Dozens of scripts for common objections, and how to handle any objection using the 'Clarify, Qualify, Close' method.
- The importance of a 'Trial Close' before asking for final commitment.

This is our largest and longest chapter yet and there's a lot to learn, but before we dive right in, allow us to make a very brief recap and relate where we are right now to where we've come from. As you'll soon see, it's all connected—closing is a continual process, from contact to contract.

## FROM THERE TO HERE: A BRIEF RECAP

Closing is not a separate, isolated activity or skill. Closing is a collection of skills that results in a deeply embedded competency.

Closing is the application of *everything* we have taught you so far, from preparation to practicing prospecting scripts, to understanding perspectives and recognizing behavioral styles. When done in concert, it looks like a single, fluid motion.

As we begin to approach the final stages of this book, let's take a brief look back at where we started and tie some of our foundational concepts to the art of closing. In particular, let's look at the relationship between Closing and the following ideas:

- The Organized Sales Process
- Misconceptions & Negative Connotations
- Wants & Needs

### THE ORGANIZED SALES PROCESS

As you'll recall from the first chapter, prospecting is a three-step organized sales process where we take an individual from 'Lead' to 'Prospect' to 'Client' or, in other words, from 'Contact' to 'Appointment' to 'Contract'.

The idea is that you are *always moving the lead or prospect forward to the next stage in the sales process*, taking them in the right direction from contact to appointment to contract.

Closing happens when we *stop talking about what we will do or would do* and *ask them if they're ready to start doing it.*

> *The art of closing is the art of transitioning an individual from one stage to the next.*

Closing, therefore, is not a one-time event. *Closing happens at every stage in the process*, whether you're trying to close an appointment, a contract or agreement, a price-reduction, a counter-offer, and every other event where you present a scenario, vision or option to an individual and ask them if they're ready to make a decision and move forward.

For example:

### CLOSING FOR THE APPOINTMENT

*"Based on these factors, here's what I suggest we do: Let's meet, outline your options, and take the first two or three steps together for about 15 minutes. Does this make sense? Let's get you booked…"*

## CLOSING FOR THE LISTING

*"You've agreed that the marketing and launch plan looks solid, and our price point is established. Would you like to work with me, starting tonight? Let's make it official with paperwork, okay?"*

## CLOSING FOR WRITING OR ACCEPTING THE CONTRACT

*"This is over the net proceeds you wanted, and we've reviewed the other terms and liked them.... We can accept this now with your agreement. Are you on board?"*

The art of closing is the art of transitioning an individual from one stage to the next in the organized sales process.

## MISCONCEPTIONS & NEGATIVE CONNOTATIONS

As you also know, throughout this book we have continually challenged some of the common misconceptions, perceptions, and connotations about prospecting and selling. For example, oftentimes an agent's fear of being perceived as the stereotypical slick and seedy "used car salesman" can hold them back from doing their job.

But making sales *is* your job, and it's a job you can—and should—be proud of, so please heed our advice and rid yourself of any of the negative connotations and perceptions you have about prospecting and being an aggressive, pushy salesperson.

**ORGANIZED SALES PROCESS PHASES FLOWCHART**

- CONTACT
  - Generate Leads
  - Source & Qualify Leads
  - Nurture & Cultivate
- APPOINTMENT
  - Set & Confirm Appointment
  - Prepare for Appointment/Sales Call
  - Delivering Sales Presentation
  - Close for the Sale
- CONTRACT
  - Calendar & Schedule the Process
  - Review, Request Feedback & Referrals
  - Close Again
  - Follow Up

> *The art of closing is the art of having pride and confidence in your professional services.*

Buyers and sellers care mainly about their pain points and what you can do to help them solve their problems. Your job is to identify the needs of the seller or buyer so that you can serve them best and secure their business.

Many agents are afraid of *securing* business and asking people for a *commitment*. For example, the vast majority of agents don't secure some sort of exclusive Buyer Agency Agreement with prospective buyers. They don't like the perception that they're "locking in a client."

However, the same agents get mad and upset when a prospect that they've been nurturing, cultivating, and bending over backwards for—showing houses on evenings and weekends, and driving all over town—puts in an offer with somebody else or buys directly from a home builder.

The agent's perception is that the prospect has been disloyal or deceptive, but quite frankly an agent that refuses to make a Buyer Agency Agreement a requirement of their normal sales process has a lot to own in these situations.

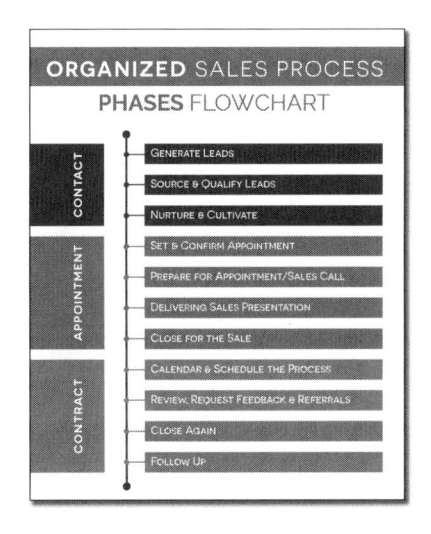

*The art of closing is establishing clear expectations and explicitly asking people for commitment.*

Oftentimes, agents are operating under the assumption that they have an implied agreement or understanding with prospects, which can make them *feel* as though they've closed the sale. However, if you have not explicitly asked for and received an actual commitment, then you have not closed, and you're operating under dangerously ambiguous assumptions.

You really have no right to get mad and call people disloyal if you haven't had the courage to ask someone to sign an agreement and clearly explain the obligations between you both. You may feel frustrated and hard done by, but thinking the blame lies completely with the prospect is a misconception. All top-producing agents and high-producing teams require Buyer Agency Agreements as part of their regular sales process.

The art of closing is the art of having pride and confidence in your professional services. And, the art of closing is establishing clear expectations and explicitly asking people for commitment.

### Scripts for Presenting the Buyer Agency Agreement

SCRIPT 1 – "It is our policy to have you consent to me representing you as your agent before we start looking at homes. By signing this you are just agreeing to that."

SCRIPT 2 – "I'm required to have an agreement between us to be able to act as your agent and show you homes. I just need your signature to get started."

SCRIPT 3 – "By signing this agreement you are authorizing me to represent you and look out for your best interests throughout the home buying process."

SCRIPT 4 – "In order for me to help you without possible conflicts of interest, protect your confidentiality, and operate in your best interests, I am required to have you sign this agreement to represent you as an agent."

SCRIPT 5 – "My broker requires that I have my buyers sign this agreement so I can get to work for you and be on your side."

### Handling Objections to Signing the Buyer Agency Agreement

SCRIPT 1 – "Often times I find that if a buyer is uncertain about signing this agreement, it usually means I haven't answered all of your questions or there is something you haven't told me. Was there something you wanted to cover today that I forgot to ask you?"

SCRIPT 2 – "What is it that concerns you? Would it help if I stepped out of the room for a bit so that you two can chat privately?"

SCRIPT 3 – "Signing this agreement is actually our policy since I can't be 100% committed to you unless your 100% committed to me representing your best interests."

SCRIPT 4 – "I sense a little apprehension. I tell you what, if we get to a point in the process where you don't like working with me, then I won't have a problem ending our agreement. I just ask that you let me know as soon as possible. How does that sound?"

SCRIPT 5 – "I tell you what, how about we look at a few homes to make sure you're comfortable working with me, then we can worry about signing it?"

## Wants & Needs

On the face of it, your prospective clients' wants and needs are seemingly simple. Fundamentally, what every seller wants and needs is to list and sell their home, and what every buyer wants and needs is to find and purchase a new home.

Of course it's a little more detailed and complicated than that, and one of the reasons it can be so complicated is because humans beings themselves are quite complicated. The real estate transaction itself is relatively straightforward, but people are emotional animals and, oftentimes, your clients and prospects become overwhelmed with fear and caution, and paralyzed by indecision.

Just because people want and need something doesn't mean that they're not nervous or daunted by it.

Change can be scary. Buying a home is a huge financial decision, and people can become overwhelmed by the thought of so much debt and obligation. Sellers, meanwhile, can feel a strong sense of sadness and regret about leaving a home that they loved and invested a lot of money and labor in. While they may want a new home in a new neighborhood with a new lifestyle, sellers can still grapple with uncertainty about the unknown and will sometimes wonder if they're making a mistake.

*Just because people want and need something doesn't mean that they're not nervous or daunted by it.*

Now, understand: your job is to *help* people, not to *please or pander* to people. If you are a "people pleaser" who wants everyone to like them, and will do anything to make someone feel better in the moment, that can be very dangerous.

Your job is to determine the actual wants and needs of the buyer and hold true to those wants and needs. While you must certainly sympathize with and validate their emotions, it's not in people's best interests if you allow or enable them to stay stuck in their emotions and inaction because you're worried about being perceived as uncaring.

The art of closing is the art of redirecting the prospect's focus and guiding them forward through various emotional states that are holding them back from what they really want.

## Tying It Together

In short, while an individual may want and need to buy or sell a home, they can become frozen with fear and paralyzed by indecision, which prevents them from transitioning to the next stage in the process.

Real estate agents who truly understand the art of closing know that it is not a macho, ego-driven event where a salesman overpowers someone in a single dramatic scene like we see in the movies.

Rather, closing is a continual process, with commitment points along each step of the way, and closing is very much focused on serving and helping the client or prospect. Closing is about getting buy-in at each stage so that there are no surprises at the end of the negotiation process. The art lies in knowing which closes will work for particular prospects and which ones won't.

- A good closer recognizes the individual's emotional reality while focusing on the ultimate wants and needs of the client or prospect.
- A good closer helps the individual to remember, realize, and self-discover those needs and what's in their own best interests.
- A good closer helps to alleviate the stress caused by fear and indecision by motivating and empowering the prospect to take a step closer to achieving their goals—whether they're at the initial appointment stage, signing a contract, or making or accepting an offer.
- A good closer guides the client or prospect out of a paralyzed state of inaction into the place that they ultimately want to be, and a good closer helps them to get there quicker than if they were left alone to find the determination and courage themselves.

## Which Closer Are You?

Being a great closer is within your power. The right tactics will get the right results.

## WHICH CLOSER ARE YOU?

| I'M A GREAT CLOSER | I'M A NOT SO GREAT CLOSER |
|---|---|
| I get incredibly clear and honest answers because I ask great, clear questions. | I get vague remarks and incomplete answers, because I ask vague and ambiguous questions. |
| I offer a great service based off real client's real concerns. | I mysteriously infer or hint at what I failed or forgot to research. |
| I get great time-value from clients because I get to the point and cut out unneeded or unwanted parts. | I overspend my time, thinking that the more words I use, the more value I bring. |
| My client's time value goes up because I move through the process they truly need at the pace they understand and respect. | I wander through my presentations, rushing because I'm lost, or stalling because I've given everything I've got and they seem bored and disinterested. |
| My clients are educated and trained on what's what, what's happened, and what's coming next. | My clients call me a miracle worker—not because they're impressed, but because it's a miracle they made it out alive. |
| Not only do my people feel heard, they feel empowered because I communicate in a way that they know they are making a decision based on the best information available for their specific needs. | My clients probably feel that they just watched a presentation that they didn't necessarily need to be present for. |
| People trust and respect me sooner, because I'm confident to ask the tough questions and elicit the real answer. | My clients are wondering if they're in big trouble financially and organizationally, and are thinking of just doing it themselves. |
| People trust and respect me sooner, because I'm confident to ask the tough questions and elicit the real answer. | My clients are wondering if they're in big trouble financially and organizationally, and are thinking of just doing it themselves. |
| People are willing to take more risks with me because I've presented great options with clear results and I avoid overdramatic repercussions. | I scare my clients with terrible scenarios. They're suspicious of me and are exploring other options without me at the helm. |
| My schedule is full of appointments because I've set an expectation that I'll be asking for business if it's a great fit for everyone involved. | I'm booked to the gills with meetings with people who are happy to catch up during business hours without giving me any business, now or ever. |
| People tell me "No" sooner, because my offer is clear, doesn't fit, and they don't want to waste my time. | People are unsure about what exactly I'm offering and say, "We'll see..." just to get me off the phone or their doorstep. |

## ASSUMING THE SALE

Before you *ask* for the sale, have the confidence to *assume* it's in the bag.

With an assumptive sales approach, you act as if the prospect has already made a decision, and you begin to describe:

- Transactional next steps
- Unforeseen benefits of the decision
- Scenarios that allow the client to visualize points in the future
- Using phrases that remind clients of progress already made, like "Since we've agreed…" or "When you've committed…"

If you learn only one closing technique today, it should be the assumptive sales technique.

## CONFIDENCE NOT COCKINESS

The dangers of making false assumptions have been well documented in this book. The difference here is that your confidence is not the cockiness associated with winging it or making things up on the fly. Rather, your assumptive confidence stems from a high level of advance preparation that creates a situation in which there is nothing left to discuss.

For example, let's say you're going into a listing appointment. After touring the home, rather than sitting down and applying for the job with a formal presentation, a better idea is to deliver a Pre-Listing Packet in advance, either by email or hand-delivery.

A Pre-Listing Packet contains your Agent Bio, a comprehensive list of Frequently Asked Questions, and other essential information that prospective sellers will typically need to know about the seller side of the process.

By delivering the informational packet in advance of the presentation, you have effectively already given them your presentation and told them everything that another agent will waste time telling them in person.

> *Your assumptive confidence stems from a high level of advance preparation that creates a situation in which there is nothing left to discuss.*

After you've finished touring the home and focusing your energy on further building relationship and rapport, you can simply say:

*"Did you receive my information packet? Do you have any questions or would you prefer if we just sit down and start talking about what price to list your home?"*

As you can see, in everything you're saying and doing, you're assuming that the prospect has been educated and informed and is comfortable and good to go with you. Your actions and your words display a level of comfort and confidence in your abilities and services.

While you will certainly offer a space for them to ask questions or clarify an issue, by transitioning the conversation in the direction of price, you're subtly but swiftly moving the prospect forward to the next stage in the process.

Assuming the sale exudes professionalism and confidence, but it is not cocky or overly presumptuous. In fact, the assumptive close often utilizes 'permission-based' statements that gently guide prospects in a forward moving direction.

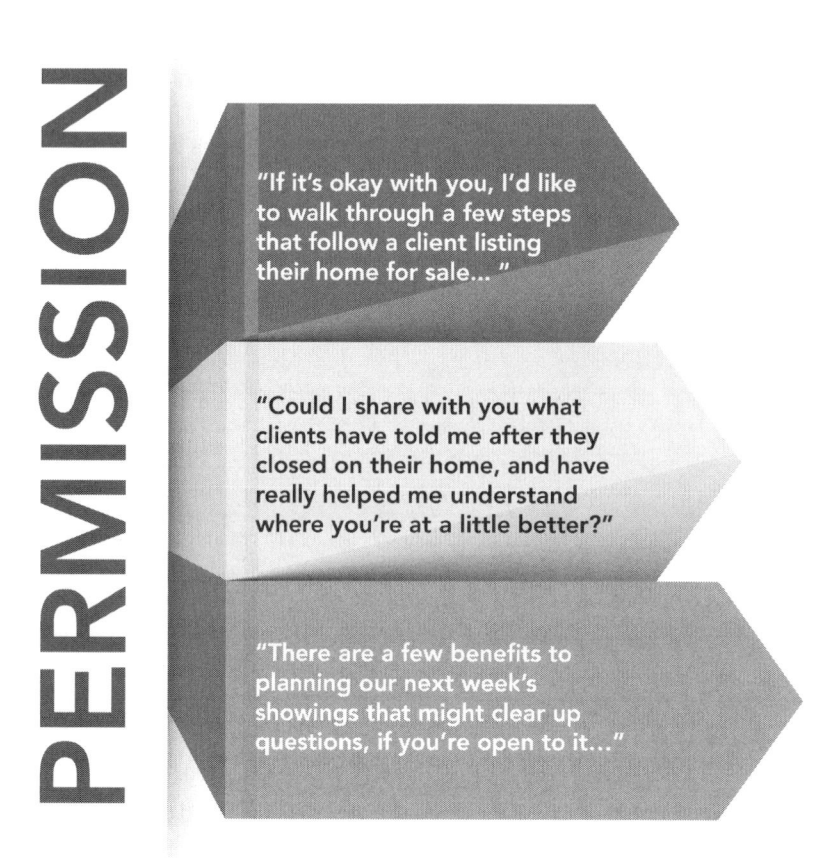

## PERMISSION

- *"If it's okay with you, I'd like to walk through a few steps that follow a client listing their home for sale..."*

- *"Could I share with you what clients have told me after they closed on their home, and have really helped me understand where you're at a little better?"*

- *"There are a few benefits to planning our next week's showings that might clear up questions, if you're open to it..."*

## Assuming The Sale Does Not Replace Asking For The Sale

Assuming the sale does not *replace* asking for the sale. Each of the above questions is simply transitioning the prospect to the next stage or step in the process. You can end a conversation, agreement, or appointment and be the only person who's still standing there when the smoke clears.

At some point, you will have to be far more explicit and assertive about asking them to sign on the dotted line or making a concrete decision. We will look at this in detail when we discuss the importance of a Trial Close at the end of the chapter.

While it's important to be confident and assume that your research and preparation will pay off, nothing is ever in the bag until the transaction closes and the keys are exchanged. Don't be so cocky and assumptive that you neglect to secure commitments each step of the way.

The assumptive close is the most important closing style that an agent can master. We'll take a look at several more closing models a little later in the chapter. For now, let's take an in-depth look at converting Buyer and Seller leads.

## Do Buyers Really Know What They Want?

As we've said before, the art of closing is keeping your clients and prospects focused on their wants and needs so that you are always guiding them forward towards their goals.

But do your prospects always know what they want and need? What do buyers typically want from you when they make first contact?

Buyers initially want to either see a specific property or obtain information about the property. They generally don't want to take the time to meet for an in-person buyer consultation.

Many homebuyers erroneously believe they don't need to tell an agent their needs prior to looking at houses. They don't think about what happens if they see a well priced home they want to buy. Are they pre-qualified? Is their existing home up for sale?

They often put the cart before the horse and miss out on homes they want to buy because they aren't in a position to make an offer that will actually be accepted.

In order to keep your prospects *focused* on their wants and needs, you will have to convince them to begin the formal process of *identifying* their wants and needs.

## Initial Conversation With a Buyer Lead: Take Control And Come From Curiosity

Confident professionals are not just "people pleasers," which is why it's crucial for agents to take control of these initial conversations with buyers to conduct a proper diagnosis with the confidence of a good doctor. A good doctor would not prescribe a patient with painkillers just because the patient wanted them. Instead, they would first ask a series of questions to determine the patient's needs and then prescribe what is in the patient's best interests.

Top agents also act on their clients' best interests by validating that they have heard buyer requests by repeating the subject matter of each request back to the buyer in their answers. Agents should then ask a follow-up question to tie down each validation statement and further ascertain more of the buyer's situation and needs.

Agents use a Buyer Lead Sheet to maintain curiosity by asking a series of questions and filling out all of the blanks on the lead sheet. In the sample dialog below, notice how the agent validates each request and then proceeds with a question in each exchange.

> *Buyer*: "Could you tell me the price of the home located at 123 Main Street?"
>
> *Agent*: "Yes, 123 Main Street, that' a great house. Are you're looking to buy sometime soon?"
>
> *Buyer*: "Yes we're thinking of moving to this side of town and that house looks really nice. How much is it?"
>
> *Agent*: "It's beautiful home for sure. Tell me, are you renting right now? Or do you own a home?"
>
> *Buyer*: "We're renting until we can find a home to buy near my parent's house."
>
> *Agent*: "Yes being close to family is important for sure. How soon are you looking to move?"

## SELL YOUR PRODUCT TO GET THE APPOINTMENT

Once control of the conversation has been established, a good closer will then explain that the buyer's current method of looking for homes is not the most effective.

Buyers typically look for homes on secondary websites (Zillow, etc.), or by visiting open houses, looking at advertisements, or simply by driving around and calling numbers on yard signs. Though the buyer may tell you what they want and seem happy with their process, it's not necessarily what they need.

It is important to educate buyers that a Multiple Listing Service (MLS) auto-prospecting search will enable them to see all homes listed on the market by all agents the minute they come up for sale.

Marketing this feature to potential clients is an important part of the conversion process.

What's more, agents should use this auto-prospecting service as the reason to meet in person for an initial buyer consultation appointment.

Remember that the art of closing is the art of moving a lead or prospect forward in any particular part of the process. In longer presentations, a good sales script will include several closing moments that gradually guide the prospect forward towards where you want them to go.

Notice how the following script contains several transitioning moments. In particular, notice that at the end of the script, the offer to give the lead some time to think is immediately followed with a firmer close for an actual appointment date and time, followed by another close for completing the Buyer Lead Sheet.

## MLS CONVERSION SCRIPT

"The most desirable homes listed at the lowest prices sell the fastest, so you don't ever get to see them on Zillow and other secondary websites. Homes on those types of sites are actually the homes that most people did not want.

You see all home listings are initially listed in the REALTORS® Multiple Listing Service (MLS) online database of homes for sale. Then the listing information is sent through digital feeds to other secondary sources, and then on to these other websites. This is why the information on these sites is often incorrect and a week or two old. That's why websites like Zillow do not have the same number of listings as our MLS does.

**(Closing/Guiding Moment)** If you are looking for home on Zillow you're just seeing the leftovers that no one else wanted. Are you following me?"

"Plus, many offices, companies, and associations of REALTORS® do not allow digital feeds to go to secondary websites like Zillow. So not only do you miss out on the homes that have already sold quickly, but there are many active listings that you can't see at all. Does all that make sense?"

"If you want to see all the listings the minute they go up for sale and get FULL REALTOR® ACCESS, I can easily set you up on our online platform. Then you can see what the real estate agents see, as soon as they see it. You can look at the homes online in the privacy of your own home, on your own time, with absolutely no pressure or obligation. I can even set the system up to send you email notifications the minute new homes hit the market that fits the specific criteria you are looking for in a home.

**(Closing/Guiding Moment)** If you happened to want to see the inside of one of them, you can just reply to the email or call me and we'll get you inside quickly. Would that be a benefit to you?"

"This way you'll also be able to learn about the prices of homes in different neighborhoods to become a more informed buyer. You'll start to see what's a good deal, what's not, how quickly certain homes sell in different areas and price ranges. Once you see what you can get for your dollar, you'll be able to drive around on the weekends and check out some of the neighborhoods on your own time. Look at the school districts, nearby shopping, and other amenities.

**(Closing/Guiding Moment):** You can take your time with this if you want. How does that sound?"

**Closing/Guiding Moment**: "Great, all that I need to do is briefly meet with you in person to set you up on our system and then you can leisurely browse for homes on your own time. Would 4:00 pm today or 2:00 pm tomorrow work for you?"

**(Closing Moment)** "Thank you! I just need to ask you a few more quick questions before we meet. This will help me get you set up on our online platform ahead of time so you can be in, out, and on your way faster when we meet in person. Is that OK?" (At this point, you complete the Buyer Lead Sheet to further determine their wants and needs)

## SET THE LENDER APPOINTMENT

Next you will set the buyer on course for committing to a lender appointment. To be clear, at this initial stage, we're not asking the prospect to set a lender appointment in the traditional sense of getting pre-approved for a home loan. That will certainly come in time, and is yet another conversation you will have to close on!

Rather, at this stage, you should encourage interested buyers to talk to a lender in the context of their upcoming, prospective home-search. Explain that meeting with a lender could actually help them find their new home. For example:

---

### LENDER APPOINTMENT SCRIPT

"When you search for homes online, would it be a benefit to know what your down payment and monthly payments would be based upon each home's asking price?"

"To most people, it's more important to know what their monthly payments would be when initially selecting home search criteria, not to mention later on while they are comparing homes that they are actively searching for online. Does that make sense to you?"

"Depending on the type of loan program you select the down payment and monthly payment amounts can vary significantly. I can have my lender give you a call before we meet to help you get a rough idea of what each of these amounts will be based upon the loan programs you might select. There will be absolutely no cost or obligation on your part, it will just help you get more clarity about the homes you actually want to see in your online search. How does that sound?"

"Not to mention, if you do see a home that's priced well, it will likely sell quickly. So, having your financial ducks in a row with a lender pre-qualification letter to provide to the sellers to increase the likelihood of your offer being accepted. Make sense?"

"Great! Here's my lender's name and number. I will provide your contact information to her as well. This way you can both start trying to get in touch with one another prior to our meeting. Then we will be able to further refine your online home search based upon what you learn from her. Sound good?"

"Wonderful. I'm looking forward to meeting you in person!"

---

Now, contact the lender to ensure that they speak with the buyer prior to your buyer consultation appointment. Ensure that the lender knows to proactively contact you if they are unable to reach the buyer so that you can help follow up.

This is how you take a prospective buyer from someone who *thinks* they know what they want to someone who actually knows—and tells you—what they need.

By identifying and determining what the prospect wants and needs, you're on track to moving the buyer continually forward in the sales process—and *that* is the art of closing.

# Converting Seller Leads into Listing Appointments

One of the major differences in skill between top-producing listing agents and the rest of the agent population is the ability to convert seller leads into listing appointments. Don't get ahead of yourself in this process!

Far too many agents get ahead of themselves by trying to close the contract over the phone rather than closing the appointment.

> **For example**
>
> During the initial telephone call sellers will often raise objections to listing like the following:
>
> - "We still need to do a lot of work to our home before we're ready to sell."
> - "We need to find a home to buy before we're going to sell."
> - "We don't really need to sell now."
> - "We're planning on moving later on in the year, we're not quite ready yet."
> - "We need to wait to be able to get a little bit more equity out of our home."
> - "We can't afford to pay a full commission. How much will you charge us?"

All of the seller objections listed above are actually objections to listing the property for sale now. In other words, they are objections to signing a listing contract. They are not objections to meeting for an appointment at all. Agents that get stuck in telephone conversations by these types of objections are getting ahead of themselves by trying to close the contract instead of the appointment.

## Right Back at You

Instead, top listing agents use these objections as a reason to set the appointment. They turn the seller objections back against the sellers by using them as a reason to meet to discuss the issues the sellers are having.

Here are some ways the top-producers do it and you can too:

- **A seller that needs to find a home before they list** should meet with you so that you can set them up on a Multiple Listings Service (MLS) auto prospecting home search to get "full REALTOR® access" of all the homes that are listed by all agents that meet their specific criteria as soon as they hit the market.

- **Homeowners that still need to "fix up a lot of things" in their home before selling** could use your advice on what things to fix and what to leave as is. You can also suggest cheaper methods and products to make improvements, or even have some of your preferred vendors take care of some issues for them.

- **Sellers that need to get more out of their home or are otherwise waiting to sell** might benefit from a Comparative Market Analysis (CMA) to be able to see what their home would sell or appraiser for in this market. You could also show them comparison listings that are active and pending to give them a rough idea of what their home will be worth later in the year.

- **Concerns about commission** are better explained in person than discussed over the phone. It's much easier to show them than tell them all of the potential costs associated with the sale in order to determine the amount of net proceeds sellers will have at closing.

Agents too frequently will lose listings to competing agents because they are unable to set appointments when they first speak with a lead. They assume that the seller isn't ready, and they don't want to be pushy by pressuring them to list now.

They wait with the hope that they will later be able to *close the seller from contact directly to contract, skipping the appointment step in between.* These very same agents are severely upset when they later learn that home was listed by another agent that was able to set the appointment and help the sellers much earlier in the process.

The key is to remember that you can in fact help sellers more by meeting with them sooner rather than later. Then all you have to do is communicate this point to them.

## Take Control with a Seller Lead Sheet

As was the case with converting buyer leads by using a Buyer Lead Sheet, it's equally important to control the conversation with sellers by coming from curiosity. Asking a series of questions pertaining to seller needs and circumstances by utilizing a Seller Lead Sheet (provided in chapter 2) shows confidence, organization and professionalism.

It also demonstrates that you care about their needs. Therefore, it is important that you end every sentence with a question mark and avoid statements that end with periods. Moving down through the questions contained on a Seller Lead Sheet keeps the conversation focused and purposeful.

Another benefit of the Seller Lead sheet is that it helps to unearth possible objections that you will likely need to overcome during the in person listing consultation later. Some most common examples of the questions on a lead sheet and the objections they will uncover include:

- "Have you spoken with any other agents yet?" (Any Competitors?)
- "Have you thought about selling the home yourself?" (Commission Objections)
- "Do you have an idea of what price you want to sell it for?" (Price Objections)
- "What price did you pay for your home? Have you made any improvements to it?" (Price Objections)
- "How much do you owe on the property?" (Price Objections)
- "When do you want to move?" (Lack of Seller Urgency Objections)
- "What do you think you still need to do to the home before putting it on the market?" (Condition Objections)
- "Why do you want to move? What happens if you don't?" (Lack of Seller Motivation)

## Get in the Door

Oftentimes sellers need to be assured that by meeting with you they won't be obligated to list their home now or with you.

Remember, the key during the initial contact stage is just to get the appointment, so don't start worrying about getting the listing contract yet. Your odds of getting the listing will go up significantly the minute you meet with them face to face. In the meantime, it's important to try to disarm them about the purpose of your meeting.

Here's how that might look:

> *Seller:* "We're just not ready to even think about it until the kids are out of school in a few months."
>
> *Agent:* "I can understand that. It's much easier to move when you don't have to work around a school schedule. Let me ask you, if I were to be able to show you how much your home is currently worth, and how much it will likely sell for over the summer, would it be of any benefit to you?"
>
> *Seller:* "I suppose, maybe . . . but I think it's better if we just wait till the kids are out of school."
>
> *Agent:* "Sure. In the meantime, what if I set you up on our system to give you "full REALTOR® access" to all the homes that are listed by all agents that meet their specific criteria as soon as they hit the market? This way you could look at homes without any pressure or obligation in the privacy of your own home? This way whenever you are ready to sell you have a good idea of what you might be able to purchase. Would that help?"
>
> *Seller:* "That would be great, yes!"
>
> *Agent:* "Excellent, when would be a good time for me to swing by? Would 4:00 pm tomorrow of 3:00pm Wednesday work better?"
>
> *Seller:* "Wednesday is better fora me."
>
> *Agent:* "Great! Just so that I can do a bit more homework and save us a little time on Wednesday, would you mind if I asked you just a few more questions?" (Proceed with Seller Lead Sheet questions)

This is how you take a prospective seller from someone who has a hundred and one objections to someone who feels comfortable closing with you precisely because they know they're not obligated to.

By turning the seller objections back on the seller, you're on track to moving the prospect continually forward in the sales process and meeting you in person—and *that* is the art of closing.

## ABC: Always Be Closing

As we've said, closing is not a dramatic, climactic moment at the end of the entire sales process, nor is it separate from your other prospecting activities. Closing is a series of smaller and larger culminations involving a steady progression of choices and directions. Closing happens at every stage of a seamless organized sales process.

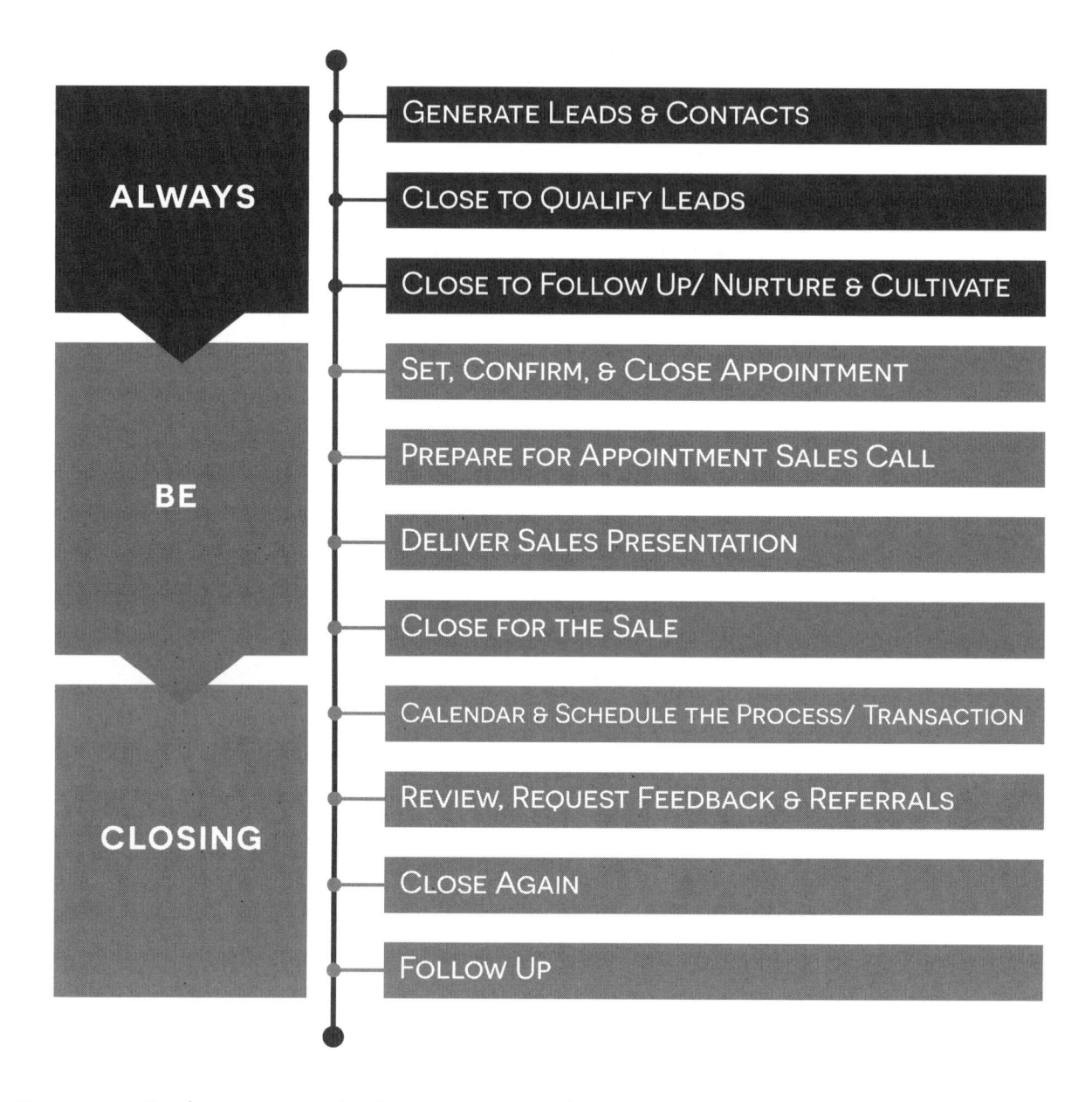

**ALWAYS**
- Generate Leads & Contacts
- Close to Qualify Leads
- Close to Follow Up/ Nurture & Cultivate

**BE**
- Set, Confirm, & Close Appointment
- Prepare for Appointment Sales Call
- Deliver Sales Presentation
- Close for the Sale

**CLOSING**
- Calendar & Schedule the Process/ Transaction
- Review, Request Feedback & Referrals
- Close Again
- Follow Up

Every step in the organized sales process involves a presentation at some level, and to move forward to the next stage, a close is vital.

Let's focus on stage one (generating leads, closing to qualify leads and closing to follow-up) and a portion of stage two (set & confirm appointment, and closing tactics embedded in the presentation).

## Stage 1: Closing to Qualify Leads & Follow-Up

You might have someone's contact information, yet until you discover their 'willingness, ability, or readiness' to either purchase or sell, they're not a true lead—just a contact to be added to your database.

After continuous communication and follow up you can figure out these factors. In this stage, you are *closing* to follow up and you are *closing* to prequalify.

Prequalifying has a number of closing points built into it:

1. As you work your way through the questions together, you're exhibiting the type of behavior a skilled consultant has when preparing a client to make a move in the market.

2. You'll write down their answers on your Buyer or Seller Prequalification Sheet.

3. Summarize their needs and wants, and then

4. CLOSE on what happens next: lender approval, property preview, outlining a timeline of what's to happen next, and then invite them to an appointment for the next stage.

## STAGE 2: CLOSING TO CONFIRM THE APPOINTMENT AND CLOSE THE PRESENTATION

Most agents will set the in-person appointment at the end of their prequalification, then quickly confirm by email, text, or voicemail. That's acceptable. Yet if you find that you have a high percentage of "no-shows" for your appointments, maybe you've moved without getting real buy-in, or you've lost them along the way somewhere.

Life happens and schedules shift. Build value into the time you've booked, and then refresh that value during your confirmation. You're actually tapping into a couple of psychological triggers. The first is that of *reciprocity*: if you're booking time with them, they're booking time with you. Phrase it accordingly:

> *"Tom and Sandy, I wanted to **confirm that you've booked time with me** tomorrow at 3:00PM, so I've prepared two sets of your property profiles, and I'm excited to walk you through what we've **researched**!"*

The second trigger is that of *commitment* by revisiting the small commitments they've made already and emphasizing that this is just one in a series of successes:

> *"Tom and Sandy, I wanted to **call and confirm** for today. **So far**, you've looked at property online, you've both shared your insight on what your wants and needs are, **and** you took additional time to explain what your timeline is, **and how I can help**."*
>
> ***This next step puts you right in line*** *with selling your place in the time you wanted, for the most amount of money. I'm excited to meet you at your house **at 4 today**!"*

As you can see, you *closing* on what's been prepared for them, *closing* on what they've accomplished so far, and you're *closing* on their earlier commitment to keep the process going.

Whether a buyer, seller, or investor presentation, you close before you even meet the client through practice and preparation. You've probably organized your presentation to include periodic reviews and recap major points.

| Presentation Section | Close? | Their Commitment |
|---|---|---|
| What's happened up until now | YES | YES, then… |
| What their goals are | YES | YES, then… |
| What your goals are for the presentation, and the relationship | YES | YES, then… |
| What the risks are, and plans to avoid them | YES | YES, then… |
| Your process, systems, and team | YES | YES, then… |
| The prices and terms | YES | YES, then… |
| The entire plan, and "closing remarks" | YES | YES, then… |

Your closes occur at the end of every section of your presentation. To paraphrase:

"If *this* occurs under *these conditions* how I describe them, *are you okay with me being your partner through this*?"

The reason you close this often—either by directly saying or indirectly inferring it—is that most people are linear thinkers. Gaining a series of commitments, or small "yeses" makes the final "yes" justified. You've built your case, and they've been the character witness for each victory, so to speak.

## CLOSING STYLES & MODELS

Behavior modeling (a component of social learning theory) is the act of showing someone how to do something and guiding them through the process of imitating the modeled behavior. This happens between parents and their children, as well as in the workplace, or any other environment where you're guiding someone to where you need them to go.

Closing models are the same. Each of the following models will guide your clients and prospects in the direction that both of you want and need to go.

After you review the four models, we will summarize with the building blocks you can use to build your own closing model. And after that, we'll explore who your target audience is, and which model might work the best while you're prospecting in different scenarios.

### LEAD-LEAD-LEAD-CLOSE

This is the model of small commitments and validations. You state three 'leads'—statements the prospect has agreed to be true or valid, and your 'close' is stating the logical next step:

*Lead:* You've explored homes for sale online,
    *Lead*: There are so many choices—you're not sure what's a great fit,
*Lead*: The time it would take me to explore them for you is time you'd save,
*Close*: Let's agree to meet Tuesday, so I can report what I've found.

With the Lead-Lead-Lead-Close model, you essentially validate, validate, validate and then close based upon that validation.

## Choice-Effect-Choice

At the end of the day, when there's a decision to make, the choice belongs to the client or prospect. With the Choice-Effect-Choice closing style, the agent weighs in with a few benefits or effects of the prospect making this choice, and then invites them to commit and make a final decision.

*Choice*: What do you say you let me preview the property, and have you walk me through it?

*Effect*: I'll gain perspective through the eyes of a buyer, and share what we'd do if we listed it, as well as some tactics you can use no matter who you list with.

*Choice*: I'll be in your area around 5 tonight, and will finish with what I've promised to do by 5:30, okay?

## Best Case, Worst Case, Most Likely Scenario

This closing style offers three options that run the spectrum of what could occur. When using this closing model, always present realistic scenarios. Don't swing for the fences or overly dramatize the possible outcomes, or you'll create suspicion and distrust.

"MR/MRS PROSPECT, Here's what I suggest:

*Best Case Scenario*: We explore how I can help, you love most of what I have to say, and I answer your concerns to where you'll want to work with us.

*Worst Case Scenario*: After the first 10 minutes, should you decide this is NOT a good fit and you'd like to look elsewhere, we will part as friends.

*Most Likely Scenario*: We explore together, and what you don't like, we find a way through to a mutual understanding where you win on all fronts. Is this acceptable?"

## Feel-Felt-Found

The Feel-Felt-Found closing style uses tried and true empathy:

"I completely understand how you feel. I can appreciate it because some of my other clients have felt the same way when they _____. What they found later was that _____ . Would this last factor change your mind about making a decision, at the risk of feeling _____ in the beginning?"

## Basic Closing Components

Each of the above models shows a few of the same 'reflections' of what high level consultation is really about:

6 Reflections You'll See in Closing Models

1. You've exhibited active listening
2. You've either experienced or researched what helps people in similar situations
3. You've offered clear description of benefits

④ You've stressed the choice lies with the client

⑤ You've outlined that there's a process that leads to success, or at least clarity

⑥ You know this process

Words are powerful. You'll come to understand what emotions or drives your words pull or push on when you experiment with different types of closes. Yet it really boils down to choice, clarity, earning and then gaining commitment.

## EXERCISE: Who Are You Talking To?

Let's experiment with what you've learned so far with a few prospecting audiences you may come in contact with. Choose a closing style that you would use in each scenario and make a note of points you would highlight when using that style or model on the prospect.

**CLOSING SCENARIOS**

| Scenario | Model or Style | What Points You'll Highlight |
|---|---|---|
| Close for a Referral with a SOI member | | |
| Close with an SOI member for an Appointment | | |
| Close with a Prospect for a Buyer Consultation | | |
| Close with a Prospect for a Buyer Representation Agreement | | |
| Close for a Listing Presentation | | |
| Close for a FSBO Property Preview | | |
| Close for an Expired Listing Appointment | | |
| Close for a Follow Up call with details about an Unlisted Home | | |

## CLOSING STYLE GALLERY

Just when you thought you've tried every closing possible, here's a list of closing styles to keep you on your toes and get you back on your game. Remember: these are just themes—you will need to piece together the components to make them work.

**Adjournment Close**: Take an adjournment or break and give them time to think.
**Affordable Close**: Ensuring people can afford what you are selling.
**Alternative Choice Close:** Offering a limited set of choices.
**Assumptive Close:** Acting as if they are ready to decide.
**Balance Sheet Close:** Adding up the pros and the cons.
**Best Time Close:** Emphasize how now is the best time to buy.
**Bonus Close:** Offer something extra not discussed to clinch the deal.
**Bracket Close:** Make three offers, with the target in the middle.
**Calculator Close:** Use calculator to do a time or money discount.
**Calendar Close:** Schedule the next steps in a calendar to set the pace.
**Companion Close:** Sell to the person with them.
**Concession Close:** Give them a concession in exchange for the close.
**Conditional Close:** Link closure to resolving objections.
**Cost of Ownership Close:** Compare cost over time with competitors or cost of not doing anything.
**Daily Cost Close:** Reduce cost to daily amount.
**Demonstration Close:** Show them the goods.
**Diagram Close**: Draw a picture that draws them in.
**Doubt Close**: Show you doubt the product and let them disagree.
**Economic Close**: Help them pay less for what they get.
**Emotion Close:** Trigger identified emotions.
**Empathy Close:** Empathize. Share a similar personal experience. And then close.
**Exclusivity Close**: Not everyone can buy this.

**Extra Information Close**: Give them more info to tip them into closure.
**Future Close**: Close on a future date.
**Give-Take Close:** Give something, then take it away.
**Golden Bridge Close**: Make the only option attractive.
**Handover Close:** Someone else does the final close.
**Handshake Close:** Offer handshake to trigger automatic reciprocation.
**Humor Close:** Relax them with humor.
**IQ Close**: Say how this is for intelligent people.
**Minor Points Close**: Close first on the small things.
**Never The Best Time Close:** For prospects who are stalling and procrastinating.
**No Hassle Close:** Make it as easy as possible.
**Now Or Never Close:** To hurry things up.
**Opportunity Cost Close:** Show cost of not buying.
**Ownership Close:** Act as if they own what you are selling.
**Price Promise Close:** Promise to meet any other price.
**Quality Close:** Sell on quality, not on price.
**Rational Close:** Use logic and reason.
**Repetition Close:** Repeat a closing action several times.
**Requirements Close:** Write down what they want as a formal requirement.
**Retrial Close:** Go back to square one.
**Selective Deafness Close:** Respond only to what you want to hear.
**Shopping List Close:** Tick off list of their needs.
**Similarity Close:** Bond them to a person in a story.
**Standing Room Only Close:** Show how others are queuing up to buy.
**Summary Close:** Tell them all the things they are going to receive.
**Testimonial Close**: Use a happy customer to convince the new customer.
**Treat Close**: Persuade them to 'give themselves a treat'.
**Trial Close**: See if they are ready for a close.
**Ultimatum Close**: Show negative consequences of not buying.
**Valuable Customer Close**: Offer them a special 'valued customer' deal.
**Yes, Set, Close**: Get them saying 'yes' and they'll keep saying 'yes'.

## HANDLING OBJECTIONS: CLARIFY, QUALIFY, CLOSE

It would be incredible if every call to a prospect were met with 100% readiness, willingness, and ability (not to mention a warm reception by the fire), but the reality is that half of a real estate agent's job-description is handling the innumerable objections that come your way each and every day.

While objections vary, because people and their situations vary, we've got the benefit of thousands and thousands of case studies from previous leads that reveal this:

People usually have the same concerns at the same stages in the process. If you practice how to handle it, prospecting will be a success.

Here's a formula for response when you hear someone objecting to moving to the next step, whether it be working with you, meeting with you, or staying on the phone for another few moments:

**01 CLARIFY**   **02 QUALIFY**   **03 CLOSE**

1. Clarify the objection, concern, or question by parroting or repeating their words back to them.

   *Eg. "So it sounds to me like you don't want to list your home for sale until you find a property you want to buy? Is this the only thing you're unsure about, or are there other issues we can address here, too?"*

2. Qualify the objection, concern, or question by confirming that if you can solve the issue then they will definitely move forward.

   *Eg. "So, if we are able to find you a home you want to buy, you will then be ready to list your property for sale? Once we get clear on this, will you be ready to move forward?"*

3. Close by stating the action you need them to take to move to the next step.

   *Eg. "How about we meet so we can sit down and help you get full realtor access to better help you find a property to buy, so we can ultimately list your property for sale?"*

## COMMON OBJECTIONS & HOW TO HANDLE THEM

Here is a selection of common objections with a large variety of responses for you to practice—either to learn word-for-word, or to break down and adapt into what feels comfortable and best for you.

### COMMON OBJECTION #1: I'M JUST LOOKING

*"I'm just looking..."*

"I understand MR/MRS Prospect: A lot of people just like you are coming to our website are just looking at homes, but have some interest in the homes they are looking at. In fact, we took a look and found most people are between 9 and 18 months away from purchasing their home. So, I'm just curious, if we could wave a magic wand here, when would you like to be in your next home?

*"I'm just looking..."*

"Of course, MR/MRS Prospect. I understand. I want to assist you in any way I can. May I ask you a few quick questions so that I can help as much as possible in your search?"

*"I'm just looking..."*

"Got it, and thank you so much for looking here MR/MRS Prospect. I want to make this as painless for you as possible. If I can ask you just a couple of quick questions I can make this very easy on you."

*"I'm just looking..."*

MR/MRS Prospect, as you can see, there are a lot of choices on the market. Is there a particular area or neighborhood I can direct you to so you can look? There are a few different ways to search for property—you've probably seen a few already! This way you can at least look at the things you want to look at. So tell me, what are a few of the areas you're curious about looking at?

## COMMON OBJECTION #2: WE'RE ALL SET

*"We're all set."*

"I can appreciate that! MR/MRS Prospect. Most people I speak with are 'all set' and that's why I'm reaching out to you now. I want to give you an option for the next time you're in need of any help. Let me ask you…"

*"We're all set."*

"MR/MRS Prospect No problem, in fact it's great to hear that you're on your way already! Let me ask you: the next time you're in need of help or information, what's number one on your wish list?"

*"We're all set."*

"I understand – I didn't expect to catch you in the market right now. MR/MRS Prospect. Instead, let me get an idea of your perfect home. Then I'll send you some choices you can keep on while next time you're searching. In fact, if you'd like, I can tailor an automatic search to give you a head start! So, tell me…"

*"We're all set."*

"I can appreciate that MR/MRS Prospect. Our best-prepped clients are usually 9-12 months away for a firmer relationship. Let me ask you: When is your next buying season for this?"

*"We're all set."*

"That's fine; MR/MRS Prospect I totally understand. Let me ask you, the next time you're in the market for this, how many agents are you going to reach out to, or is this the first step you've taken?"

## Common Objection #3: Let Me Think About It

*"Let me think about it…."*

"MR/MRS Prospect, whenever I tell someone I need to think about it, I usually mean one of three things: (1) I'm not going to be a deal for whatever reason and I just want to get them off the phone, (2) I kind of like the idea but I'm going to have to win the money or talk to my partner, or something else is holding me back, and (3) I really like the idea and I just have to move something around before I say yes. Be honest with me: which one of those things is it for you right now?"

*"Let me think about it…."*

MR/MRS Prospect, I've heard the only thing costlier than making a bad decision is not making one at all. If you don't change things then things won't get better for you. You've mentioned that you're in the beginning stages of a very important process…

Then do what my other clients do and put me and my company to work for you. Once you see the positive results, we both know are possible here, you'll be saving time, money, AND energy. That's going to be a win/win for us both, isn't it? Then here's what we need to do….

*"Let me think about it…."*

"MR/MRS Prospect, since we both agree this has a great chance to work for you, let me do this: while we're on the phone right now, I'm going to email you three customer testimonials, clients who just like you were hesitant as well. Once you see for yourself how successful they were with us and how it works, then we can talk about further involvement, is that fair?"

## Common Objection #4: It's Not A Good Time/We're Not Ready Yet

*"It's not a good time…"*

"I can appreciate that, MR/MRS Prospect, let's quickly find 5 minutes when it's better for you, or do you have 5 minutes now? GREAT! One last thing, what can I research for you in the meantime, to make it worth it for you to pick up the phone when I call back?"

*"It's not a good time…"*

**Agent:** I completely understand, can we set a 30-minute window next week to talk more?

**Prospect:** Send me an email. I'll take a look at my calendar to see if it's possible

**Agent:** Not a problem. What's the best email to send that to in the next 5 minutes?

**Prospect:** 123abc@client.com

Agent:  Great, I'll send you an email and include some possible times. Just so I propose some reasonable times, is there a day that works better for you?

Prospect: Tuesdays or Wednesdays.

Agent:  Mornings or afternoons?

Prospect: Afternoon Tuesday.

Agent: Great, 3pm Tuesday works for me. I'll send you a calendar invite as a placeholder. Look for that in the next 5 minutes. Is there a hurdle you're having that I can solve to make our time together worth it for you?

*"It's not a good time…"*

Understood, MR/MRS Prospect. There is a lot to get in order before buying a new home, preparing your current home for sale, meeting with a lender, insurance, inspectors, repairs, finding a new home, etc. Would you like some help with all of that?

## COMMON OBJECTION #5: WE'RE ALREADY WORKING WITH SOMEONE

*"We're already working with someone…"*

"MR/MRS Prospect, I'm sure a motivated person like you is already working with another firm to handle your home search needs. The reason I contacted you is because you'd registered on our site and we move quickly the way you do. Based on my experience working with clients searching online, when searching for homes online happens, it usually creates immediate questions or the need for help right at that moment. So, how can I help you?"

*"We're already working with someone…"*

"MR/MRS Prospect, almost every person interested in the housing market is searching in a few different places. How many sites have you searched on already? Doesn't it make sense to have a backup to make you feel more secure?"

*"We're already working with someone…"*

That's great, MR/MRS Prospect. Since you've already begun the process of searching, would you mind if I asked what they're doing great? We're always looking for great tips. Thank you for that. Now, if there were one place they could improve, where would that be? Could we put our name in as a backup? What can we do to earn that place in the next few days/weeks?"

## COMMON OBJECTION #7: WE WANT TO FIND ANOTHER HOME FIRST

*"We want to find another home before we put ours on the market…"*

"I agree, MR/MRS Prospect. Finding your new home is important. Can I share a thought with you? It may take as long as two to four months for your home to sell. Then it will take another 30-45 days to get the closing done. By that time, another buyer may have seen the quality you saw—someone who could act quickly without a home to sell. That can be heartbreaking, and I am definitely not in the heart-breaking business. Let's start the process to get your home on the market right now and get to work on getting your home sold so you don't have to wait any longer than is necessary to get moved into your new home. Does this plan work for you?"

## Common Objection #8: You Have The Wrong Number

*"You have the wrong number...."*

"I'm sorry! Well, now I have a problem. Maybe you can help me solve it. My name is X and I work for X and we've got at least Y buyers looking for their next home. The market doesn't have enough to offer them. Have you ever considered taking a look at homes like yours online to see what they're being offered for?"

As you can see, there really is a response for everything someone might possibly say to you!

# The Trial Close

A recent survey found that 94% of couples discussed getting engaged in the 6 months before the actual proposal happened, and 30% of those had talked about marriage at least once a week before their engagement was 'Facebook Official'.

It might not seem as romantic as the elaborate surprise proposals we see in the movies, but when you're asking someone to make one of the biggest decisions of their life, you want to be fairly certain that they're likely to say yes.

While you may be more than ready to tie the knot, your partner might be thinking that it's early days in your relationship and are a long way off from making a marriage decision. Likewise, just because you're ready for the prospect to sign on the dotted line, or move forward to the next stage in the sales process, your prospects might not be completely committed to making the biggest financial decision of their lives, or committing to work with you as their agent.

## Is a Trial Close Crucial?

A Trial Close serves several important purposes:

- A Trial Close *plants the idea of closing or commitment in the mind of the prospective client*—a trial close describes or sets an expectation of what commitment will look like without quite asking them to commit just yet.
- A Trial Close *tells you where you are in the sales process*—sometimes you're further behind or further along than you think you are.
- A Trial Close is a 'light close' or a 'soft close' that *allows you to test the waters without risking a firm rejection*—if you're not 100% confident that their answer will be a definite Yes, a trial close will gauge their reaction while saving the relationship if they're not quite ready.

- A Trial Close *tells you when the right moment is to ask for the sale*—the response you get from your trial close will confirm one way or another what you should do next.

## What's So Different About a Trial Close?

There's a big difference between a trial close and the moment when you actually ask for the sale or the commitment. Like we said, it's the difference between asking your partner how they feel about marriage and getting down on one knee and popping the question.

For example, let's look at the difference between asking for the sale and a trial closing when it comes to discussing an exclusive buyer agreement.

### Asking for the Sale

*"I'm required to have an agreement between us to be able to act as your agent and show you homes. I just need your signature to get started. Are you ready for me to be your official partner through this?"*

Asking for the sale presents a straightforward, bottom-line **Yes or No** proposal to the prospect. As such, you want to be pretty secure in your relationship when asking for the sale—it can be tricky for an agent to rebound from a definitive No.

### Trial Closing:

*"Just to let you know, I'm required to have an agreement between us to be able to act as your agent and show you homes. But if we get to a point in the process where you don't like working with me, then I won't have a problem ending our agreement. I just ask that you let me know as soon as possible? How does that sound?"*

Like most sales scripts, a trial closing uses **open-ended or exploratory questions** that keeps the prospect in continual conversation and, in this case, allows you to assess and evaluate their likely response to a request for commitment.

With a trial close, you can set an expectation for what the next level of commitment entails, while providing the prospect with ample space and breathing room to think about it.

## Always Be (Trial) Closing

As we mentioned, closing the sale is not a one-time-at-the-end-of-the-presentation strategy. Here are some examples of trial close questions that you can use at different stages in the process. Partner these trial closes in your scripts or presentations.

Covering introduction of benefits, ask:

- *Are you with me so far?*
- *How does that sound?*
- *Do you see what I mean?*
- *Does that make sense?*

Giving an idea of something of value:

- *How would you use that?*
- *How could you use that?*
- *How do you think that would work for you?*
- *How would that be of benefit in your situation?*

Use this next line of questions sparingly; if we overuse this, it can feel condescending:

- *Do you have any questions so far?*

It's one of the least-used, and most effective, because it leaves the presenter (the salesperson) vulnerable. Be confident.

Some trial closes will begin to feel natural once you've adapted this frame of thinking:

- *Does this seem to be the kind of solution you are looking for?*
- *How is this sounding so far?*
- *Am I getting close to having a new client yet?* (Humor can go a long way; yet it's cologne in the customer service field; use just a little bit.)

The Finish, or when your Close is right around the corner:

- *What haven't I covered yet that is important to you?*
- *Is there anything I should have covered, and didn't?*
- *When we started, you had questions…which ones did we miss that we can cover now?*

## Summary

No matter how much business you generate, or how wonderful you are at striking up conversations and making initial contact, if you can't close then all your prospecting efforts will have been in vain.

- The art of closing is the art of having pride and confidence in your professional services.
- The art of closing is establishing clear expectations and explicitly asking people for commitment.
- The art of closing is the art of transitioning an individual from one stage to the next in the organized sales process.
- The art of closing is the art of redirecting the prospect's focus and guiding them forward through various emotional states that are holding them back from what they really want.

While an individual may want and need to buy or sell a home, they can become frozen with fear and paralyzed by indecision, which prevents them from transitioning to the next stage in the process.

Real estate agents who truly understand the art of closing know that closing is a continual process, with commitment points along each step of the way, and that closing is very much focused on serving and helping the client or prospect.

Lastly, the art of closing is having the right words at the right time, and closing hinges on the ability to handle the objections that prevent people from moving forward in the sales process.

Like success, closing is where preparation and opportunity meet, so start practicing and memorizing the closing scripts, styles, and models we have armed you to the teeth with.

Don't be overwhelmed! We know there's a lot to digest in this beast of a chapter, and that's because closing itself is the beast that will test you again and again in your prospecting career. Choose the closing style that's best for you and remember that the best closing model must include confidence and the authentic desire to help and serve.

MODULE 12　　　　　　　　　　　　　　　　　　　　　　　APPENDIX 12.1

# ORGANIZED SALES PROCESS
## PHASES FLOWCHART

**CONTACT**
- Generate Leads
- Source & Qualify Leads
- Nurture & Cultivate

**APPOINTMENT**
- Set & Confirm Appointment
- Prepare for Appointment/Sales Call
- Delivering Sales Presentation
- Close for the Sale

**CONTRACT**
- Calendar & Schedule the Process
- Review, Request Feedback & Referrals
- Close Again
- Follow Up

© Copyright Icenhower Coaching & Consulting, LLC. All rights reserved.

## Exclusive Buyer Agency Agreement Scripts

**SCRIPT 1** – "It is our policy to have you consent to me representing you as your agent before we start looking at homes. By signing this you are just agreeing to that."

**SCRIPT 2** – "I'm required to have an agreement between us to be able to act as your agent and show you homes. I just need your signature to get started."

**SCRIPT 3** – "By signing this agreement you are authorizing me to represent you and look out for your best interests throughout the home buying process."

**SCRIPT 4** – "In order for me to help you without possible conflicts of interest, protect your confidentiality, and operate in your best interests, I am required to have you sign this agreement to represent you as an agent."

**SCRIPT 5** – "My broker requires that I have my buyers sign this agreement so I can get to work for you and be on your side."

### Handling Objections to Signing the Buyer Agency Agreement

**SCRIPT 1** – "Often times I find that if a buyer is uncertain about signing this agreement, it usually means I haven't answered all of your questions or there is something you haven't told me. Was there something you wanted to cover today that I forgot to ask you?"

**SCRIPT 2** – "What is it that concerns you? Would it help if I stepped out of the room for a bit so that you two can chat privately?"

**SCRIPT 3** – "Signing this agreement is actually our policy since I can't be 100% committed to you unless your 100% committed to me representing your best interests."

**SCRIPT 4** – "I sense a little apprehension. I tell you what, if we get to a point in the process where you don't like working with me, then I won't have a problem ending our agreement. I just ask that you let me know as soon as possible. How does that sound?"

**SCRIPT 5** – "I tell you what, how about we look at a few homes to make sure you're comfortable working with me, then we can worry about signing it?"

© Copyright Icenhower Coaching & Consulting, LLC. All rights reserved.

# WHICH CLOSER ARE YOU?

| I'M A GREAT CLOSER | I'M A NOT SO GREAT CLOSER |
|---|---|
| I get incredibly clear and honest answers because I ask great, clear questions. | I get vague remarks and incomplete answers, because I ask vague and ambiguous questions. |
| I offer a great service based off real client's real concerns. | I mysteriously infer or hint at what I failed or forgot to research. |
| I get great time-value from clients because I get to the point and cut out unneeded or unwanted parts. | I overspend my time, thinking that the more words I use, the more value I bring. |
| My client's time value goes up because I move through the process they truly need at the pace they understand and respect. | I wander through my presentations, rushing because I'm lost, or stalling because I've given everything I've got and they seem bored and disinterested. |
| My clients are educated and trained on what's what, what's happened, and what's coming next. | My clients call me a miracle worker—not because they're impressed, but because it's a miracle they made it out alive. |
| Not only do my people feel heard, they feel empowered because I communicate in a way that they know they are making a decision based on the best information available for their specific needs. | My clients probably feel that they just watched a presentation that they didn't necessarily need to be present for. |
| People trust and respect me sooner, because I'm confident to ask the tough questions and elicit the real answer. | My clients are wondering if they're in big trouble financially and organizationally, and are thinking of just doing it themselves. |
| People trust and respect me sooner, because I'm confident to ask the tough questions and elicit the real answer. | My clients are wondering if they're in big trouble financially and organizationally, and are thinking of just doing it themselves. |
| People are willing to take more risks with me because I've presented great options with clear results and I avoid overdramatic repercussions. | I scare my clients with terrible scenarios. They're suspicious of me and are exploring other options without me at the helm. |
| My schedule is full of appointments because I've set an expectation that I'll be asking for business if it's a great fit for everyone involved. | I'm booked to the gills with meetings with people who are happy to catch up during business hours without giving me any business, now or ever. |
| People tell me "No" sooner, because my offer is clear, doesn't fit, and they don't want to waste my time. | People are unsure about what exactly I'm offering and say, "We'll see..." just to get me off the phone or their doorstep. |

© Copyright Icenhower Coaching & Consulting, LLC. All rights reserved.

# MODULE 12

# APPENDIX 12.4

## MLS CONVERSION
### Script

"The most desirable homes listed at the lowest prices sell the fastest, so you don't ever get to see them on Zillow and other secondary websites. Homes on those types of sites are actually the homes that most people did not want.

You see all home listings are initially listed in the REALTORS® Multiple Listing Service (MLS) online database of homes for sale. Then the listing information is sent through digital feeds to other secondary sources, and then on to these other websites. This is why the information on these sites is often incorrect and a week or two old. That's why websites like Zillow do not have the same number of listings as our MLS does.

**(Closing/Guiding Moment)** If you are looking for home on Zillow you're just seeing the leftovers that no one else wanted. Are you following me?"

"Plus, many offices, companies, and associations of REALTORS® do not allow digital feeds to go to secondary websites like Zillow. So not only do you miss out on the homes that have already sold quickly, but there are many active listings that you can't see at all. Does all that make sense?"

"If you want to see all the listings the minute they go up for sale and get FULL REALTOR® ACCESS, I can easily set you up on our online platform. Then you can see what the real estate agents see, as soon as they see it. You can look at the homes online in the privacy of your own home, on your own time, with absolutely no pressure or obligation. I can even set the system up to send you email notifications the minute new homes hit the market that fits the specific criteria you are looking for in a home.

**(Closing/Guiding Moment)** If you happened to want to see the inside of one of them, you can just reply to the email or call me and we'll get you inside quickly. Would that be a benefit to you?"

"This way you'll also be able to learn about the prices of homes in different neighborhoods to become a more informed buyer. You'll start to see what's a good deal, what's not, how quickly certain homes sell in different areas and price ranges. Once you see what you can get for your dollar, you'll be able to drive around on the weekends and check out some of the neighborhoods on your own time. Look at the school districts, nearby shopping, and other amenities.

**(Closing/Guiding Moment):** You can take your time with this if you want. How does that sound?"

**Closing/Guiding Moment**: "Great, all that I need to do is briefly meet with you in person to set you up on our system and then you can leisurely browse for homes on your own time. Would 4:00 pm today or 2:00 pm tomorrow work for you?"

**(Closing Moment)** "Thank you! I just need to ask you a few more quick questions before we meet. This will help me get you set up on our online platform ahead of time so you can be in, out, and on your way faster when we meet in person. Is that OK?" (At this point, you complete the Buyer Lead Sheet to further determine their wants and needs)

© Copyright Icenhower Coaching & Consulting, LLC. All rights reserved.

# LENDER APPOINTMENT
## Script

"When you search for homes online, would it be a benefit to know what your down payment and monthly payments would be based upon each home's asking price?"

"To most people, it's more important to know what their monthly payments would be when initially selecting home search criteria, not to mention later on while they are comparing homes that they are actively searching for online. Does that make sense to you?"

"Depending on the type of loan program you select the down payment and monthly payment amounts can vary significantly. I can have my lender give you a call before we meet to help you get a rough idea of what each of these amounts will be based upon the loan programs you might select. There will be absolutely no cost or obligation on your part, it will just help you get more clarity about the homes you actually want to see in your online search. How does that sound?"

"Not to mention, if you do see a home that's priced well, it will likely sell quickly. So, having your financial ducks in a row with a lender pre-qualification letter to provide to the sellers to increase the likelihood of your offer being accepted. Make sense?"

"Great! Here's my lender's name and number. I will provide your contact information to her as well. This way you can both start trying to get in touch with one another prior to our meeting. Then we will be able to further refine your online home search based upon what you learn from her. Sound good?"

"Wonderful. I'm looking forward to meeting you in person!"

© Copyright Icenhower Coaching & Consulting, LLC. All rights reserved.

MODULE 12  —  APPENDIX 12.6

# ALWAYS BE CLOSING
## PHASES FLOWCHART

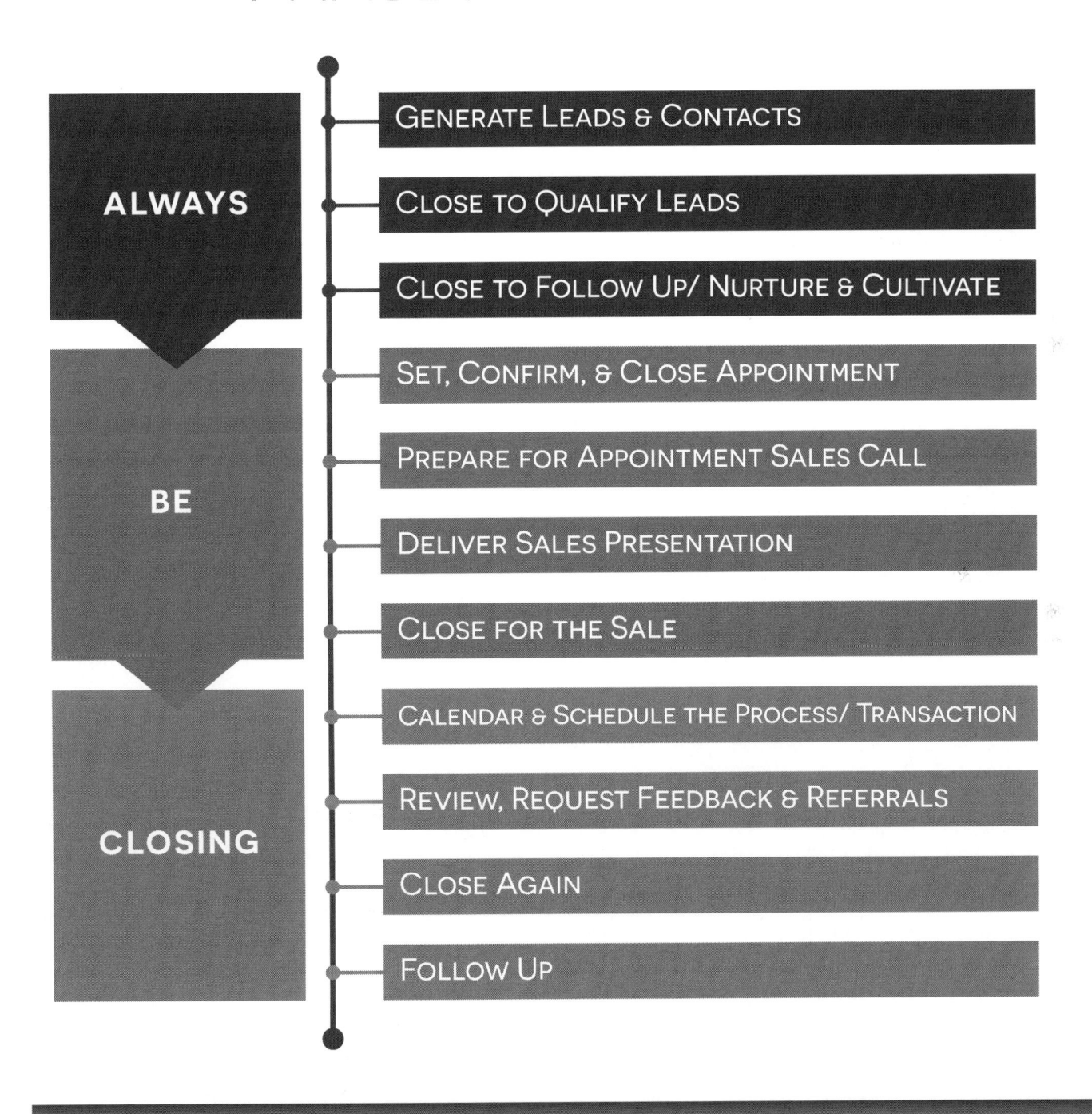

**ALWAYS**
- Generate Leads & Contacts
- Close to Qualify Leads
- Close to Follow Up/ Nurture & Cultivate

**BE**
- Set, Confirm, & Close Appointment
- Prepare for Appointment Sales Call
- Deliver Sales Presentation
- Close for the Sale

**CLOSING**
- Calendar & Schedule the Process/ Transaction
- Review, Request Feedback & Referrals
- Close Again
- Follow Up

© Copyright Icenhower Coaching & Consulting, LLC. All rights reserved.

# MODULE 12 — APPENDIX 12.7

## CLOSING SCENARIOS

| Scenario | Model or Style | What Points You'll Highlight |
|---|---|---|
| Close for a Referral with a SOI member | | |
| Close with an SOI member for an Appointment | | |
| Close with a Prospect for a Buyer Consultation | | |
| Close with a Prospect for a Buyer Representation Agreement | | |
| Close for a Listing Presentation | | |
| Close for a FSBO Property Preview | | |
| Close for an Expired Listing Appointment | | |
| Close for a Follow Up call with details about an Unlisted Home | | |

# MODULE 12  APPENDIX 12.8

# CLOSING STYLE GALLERY

| | |
|---|---|
| **Adjournment Close** - give them time to think. | **Handover Close** - someone else does the final close. |
| **Affordable Close** - ensuring people can afford what you are selling. | **Handshake Close** - offer handshake to trigger automatic reciprocation. |
| **Alternative Choice Close** - offering a limited set of choices. | **Humor Close** - relax them with humor. |
| **Artisan Close** - show the skill of the designer. | **IQ Close** - say how this is for intelligent people. |
| **Ask-the-Manager Close** - use manager as authority. | **Minor points Close** - close first on the small things. |
| **Assumptive Close** - acting as if they are ready to decide. | **Never-the-best-time Close** - for customers who are delaying. |
| **Balance-sheet Close** - adding up the pros and the cons. | **No-hassle Close** - make it as easy as possible. |
| **Best-time Close** - emphasize how now is the best time to buy. | **Now-or-never Close** - to hurry things up. |
| **Bonus Close** - offer something extra not discussed to clinch the deal. | **Opportunity Cost Close** - show cost of not buying. |
| **Bracket Close** - make three offers - with the target in the middle. | **Ownership Close** - act as if they own what you are selling. |
| **Calculator Close** - use calculator to do a time or money discount. | **Price-promise Close** - promise to meet any other price. |
| **Calendar Close** - schedule the next steps in a calendar to set the pace. | **Quality Close** - sell on quality, not on price. |
| **Companion Close** - sell to the person with them. | **Rational Close** - use logic and reason. |
| **Compliment Close** - flatter them into submission. | **Repetition Close** - repeat a closing action several times. |
| **Concession Close** - give them a concession in exchange for the close. | **Requirements Close** - write down what they want as a formal requirement. |
| **Conditional Close** - link closure to resolving objections. | **Retrial Close** - go back to square one. |

© Copyright Icenhower Coaching & Consulting, LLC. All rights reserved.

# CLOSING STYLE GALLERY

| | |
|---|---|
| **Cost of Ownership Close** - compare cost over time with competitors, or cost of not doing anything. | **Selective-deafness Close** - respond only to what you want to hear. |
| **Customer-care Close** - the Customer Care Manager calls later and re-opens the conversation. | **Shopping List Close** - tick off list of their needs. |
| **Daily Cost Close** - reduce cost to daily amount. | **Similarity Close** - bond them to a person in a story. |
| **Demonstration Close** - show them the goods. | **Standing-room-only Close** - show how others are queuing up to buy. |
| **Diagram Close** - Draw a picture that draws them in. | **Summary Close** - tell them all the things they are going to receive. |
| **Doubt Close** - show you doubt the product and let them disagree. | **Testimonial Close** - use a happy customer to convince the new customer. |
| **Economic Close** - help them pay less for what they get. | **Thermometer Close** - they score out of ten, you close gap. |
| **Emotion Close** - trigger identified emotions. | **Treat Close** - persuade them to 'give themselves a treat.' |
| **Empathy Close** - empathize with them, share a similar personal experience then close. | **Trial Close** - see if they are ready for a close. |
| **Exclusivity Close** - not everyone can buy this. | **Ultimatum Close** - show negative consequences of not buying. |
| **Extra Information Close** - give them more info to tip them into closure. | **Valuable Customer Close** - offer them a special 'valued customer' deal. |
| **Extra Information Close** - give them more info to tip them into closure. | **Yes-set Close** - get them saying 'yes' and they'll keep saying 'yes'. |
| **Future Close** - close on a future date. | **Trial Close** - see if they are ready for a close. |
| **Give-Take Close** - give something, then take it away. | **Ultimatum Close** - show negative consequences of not buying. |
| **Golden Bridge Close** - make the only option attractive. | **Valuable Customer Close** - offer them a special 'valued customer deal. |

© Copyright Icenhower Coaching & Consulting, LLC. All rights reserved.

MODULE 12　　　　　　　　　　　　　　　　　　　　　　　　　APPENDIX 12.9

# CLARIFY QUALIFY CLOSE

**01 CLARIFY**　　**02 QUALIFY**　　**03 CLOSE**

① Clarify the objection, concern, or question by parroting or repeating their words back to them.

*Eg. "So it sounds to me like you don't want to list your home for sale until you find a property you want to buy? Is this the only thing you're unsure about, or are there other issues we can address here, too?"*

② Qualify the objection, concern, or question by confirming that if you can solve the issue then they will definitely move forward.

*Eg. "So, if we are able to find you a home you want to buy, you will then be ready to list your property for sale? Once we get clear on this, will you be ready to move forward?"*

③ Close by stating the action you need them to take to move to the next step.

*Eg. "How about we meet so we can sit down and help you get full realtor access to better help you find a property to buy, so we can ultimately list your property for sale?"*

© Copyright Icenhower Coaching & Consulting, LLC. All rights reserved.

# MODULE 12 — APPENDIX 12.10

# OBJECTION HANDLERS

Objection: "I'm just looking…"

Handler:

- I understand MR/MRS Prospect, A lot of people, just like you, are coming to our website just looking at homes, but also have some interest in the homes they are looking at.
- In fact, we took a look and found most people are between 9 and 18 months away from purchasing their home. So, I'm just curious, if we could wave a magic wand here, when would you like to be in your next home?

Objection: "I'm just looking…"

Handler:

- "Of course, MR/MRS Prospect. I understand. I want to assist you in any way I can. May I ask you a few quick questions so that I can help as much as possible in your search"?

Objection: "I'm just looking…"

Handler:

- "Got it, and thank you so much for looking here MR/MRS Prospect. I want to make this as painless for you as possible. If I can ask you just a couple of quick questions, I can make this very easy on you."

Objection: "I'm just looking…"

Handler:

- MR/MRS Prospect, as you can see, there are a lot of choices on the market. Is there a particular area or neighborhood I can direct you to, so you can look?
- There are a few different ways to search for property, you've probably seen a few already! This way you can at least look at the things you want to look at. So tell me, what are a few of the areas you're curious about looking at?

Objection: "We're all set"

Handler:

- "I can appreciate that MR/MRS Prospect! Most of the people I speak with are 'all set' and that's why I'm reaching out to you now – I want to give you an option for the next time you're in need of any help. Let me ask you…"

Objection: "We're all set"

Handler:

- "MR/MRS Prospect, no problem; in fact it's great to hear that you're on your way already! Let me ask you, the next time you're in need of help or information, what's number one on your wish list?"

# MODULE 12

## APPENDIX 12.10 CONTINUED

Objection: "We're all set"

Handler:

- "I understand – I didn't expect to catch you in the market right now. MR/MRS Prospect, instead, let me get an idea of your perfect home, and then I'll send you some choices you can keep on file for the next time you're searching. In fact, if you'd like, I can tailor an automatic search to give you a head start! So, tell me…"

Objection: "We're all set"

Handler:

- "I can appreciate that MR/MRS Prospect, our best prepped clients are usually 9-12 months away for a firmer relationship. Let me ask you, when is your next buying season for this?"

Objection: "We're all set"

Handler:

- "That's fine, MR/MRS Prospect I totally understand. And let me ask you – the next time you're in the market for this, how many agents are you going to reach out to, or is this the first step you've taken?"

Objection: "Let me think about it…"

Handler:

- MR/MRS Prospect, whenever I tell someone I need to think about it, I usually mean one of three things: 1 - I'm not going to be a deal for whatever reason and I just want to get them off the phone, 2 - I kind of like the idea but I'm going to have to find the money or talk to my partner, or something else is holding me back, or 3 - I really like the idea and I just have to move something around before I say yes. Be honest with me; which one of those things is it for you right now?"

Objection: "Let me think about it…"

Handler:

- MR/MRS Prospect, I've heard the only thing costlier than making a bad decision is not making one at all. If you don't change things, then things won't get better for you. You've mentioned that you're in the beginning stages of a very important process…
- Then do what my other clients do, and put me and my company to work for you. Once you see the positive results that we both know are possible here, you'll be saving time, money, AND energy… and that's going to be a win/win for us both, isn't it? Then here's what we need to do…"

Objection: "Let me think about it…"

Handler:

- MR/MRS Prospect, since we both agree this has a great chance to work for you, let me do this:
- While we're on the phone right now, I'm going to email you three customer testimonials from clients just like you, who were hesitant as well.

# Module 12

## Appendix 12.10 continued

- And, when you read about how successful they were with us, you'll have peace of mind to take a step further. Once you see for yourself how this works, then we can talk about further involvement, is that fair?"

Objection: "We're not ready yet... or Not a good time"
Handler:

- I completely understand, can we find a 30-minute window next week to talk more?
  - Prospect: Send me an email. I'll take a look at my calendar to see if it's possible.
- Not a problem. What's the best email to send that to within the next 5 minutes?
  - Prospect: 123abc@client.com
- Great, I'll send you an email and include some possible times. Just so I propose some reasonable times, is there a day that works better for you?
  - Prospect: Tuesdays or Wednesdays.
- Mornings or afternoons?
  - Prospect: Afternoon Tuesday.
- Great, 3pm Tuesday works for me. I'll send you a calendar invite as a placeholder. Look for that in the next 5 mins. Is there a hurdle you're having that I can solve to make our time together worth it for you?

Objection: "We're not ready yet... or Not a good time"
Handler:

- I can appreciate that, MR/MRS Prospect, let's very quickly schedule 5 mins when it's better for you, or do you have 5 mins now? GREAT! One last thing, what can I research for you in the meantime, to make it worth it for you to pick up the phone when I call back?

Objection: "We're not ready yet... or Not a good time"
Handler:

- Understood, MR/MRS Prospect. There is a lot to get in order before buying a new home: preparing your current home for sale, meeting with a lender, insurance, inspectors, repairs, finding a home, etc. Would you like some help with all of that?

Objection: "You have the wrong number..."
Handler:

- I'm sorry! Well, now I have a problem, and maybe you can help me solve it.... My name is X and I work for Y, and we've got at least Z buyers looking for their next home; the market doesn't have enough to offer them. Have you ever considered taking a look at homes like yours online to see what they're being offered for?

Objection: "We are already working with someone"

Handler:

- MR/MRS Prospect, I'm sure a motivated person like you is already working with another firm to handle your home search needs. The reason I contacted you is because you'd registered on our site and we move quickly the way you do. Based on my experience working with clients who are searching online, online searches usually create immediate questions or the need for help right at that moment. So, how can I help you?

Objection: "We are already working with someone"

Handler:

- MR/MRS Prospect, almost every person interested in the housing market is searching in a few different places… how many sites have you searched on already? Doesn't it make sense to have a backup to make you feel more secure?

Objection: "We are already working with someone"

Handler:

- That's great, MR/MRS Prospect. Since you've already begun the process of searching, would you mind if I asked what they're doing great? We're always looking for great tips. Thank you for that… now, if there was one place they could improve, where would that be? Could we put our name in as a back-up? What can we do to earn that place in the next few days/weeks?

Objection: "We want to find another home before we put ours on the market"

Handler:

- "I agree, MR/MRS Prospect, finding your new home is important… can I share a thought with you? It may take as long as 2 to 4 months for your home to sell.
- Then it will take another 30-45 days to get the closing done; and in that time, another buyer may have seen the quality you saw, someone who could act quickly without a home to sell first; that can be heartbreaking, and I am definitely not in the heart-breaking business.
- Let's start the process to get your home on the market right now and get to work on getting your home sold, so you don't have to wait any longer than necessary to get moved into your new home… does this plan work for you?

## TRACKING TRUTH IN NUMBERS

In the past year, the Fitbit community grew to more than 25 million users, and that number is surely growing every day. The wearable, electronic activity-tracker measures steps taken, distance traveled, calories burned, and even a number of metrics that make up sleep-quality.

By reviewing previously untracked numbers, users reported that they saw their Fitbit as a "friend to help them reach their target goals."

The device gets a lot of use: more than 84% of wearers check their Fitbit at least twice a day. Active users report that Fitbit gives them a sense of happiness, satisfaction, and motivation to reach their goals and improve on their daily achievements.

> "There are two types of claims; those based on hard numbers and those based on slippery numbers." Simon Sinek

Conversely, when users forgot to use their activity-tracker, the activities they completed felt wasted somehow. Although they technically did perform the activities, they did not experience the same levels of motivation and achievement that come with tracking metrics and viewing hard data.

As with fitness tracking, analyzing your real estate numbers can be as sobering as it is motivating, but you must commit to doing it if you want to be healthy and have a long and lucrative business life.

As you work your way through each month of our prospecting program, you will begin to generate a lot of data. All of the numbers you collect are a valuable predictor of your success in meeting your milestones and achieving your annual goal. This data gives you an objective view of the actual time you put into prospecting, and it will also reveal how effective your efforts have been.

## Learning Targets

In this chapter, you will learn how to:

- Assemble and analyze prospecting data
- Inspect data for patterns and trends
- Create various Inventory Pipelines to maximize lead follow-up
- Design new goals based on interpretations of numbers

## WHY TRACK MY PROSPECTING ACTIVITIES?

The three primary reasons that you should track your business-generation activities are:

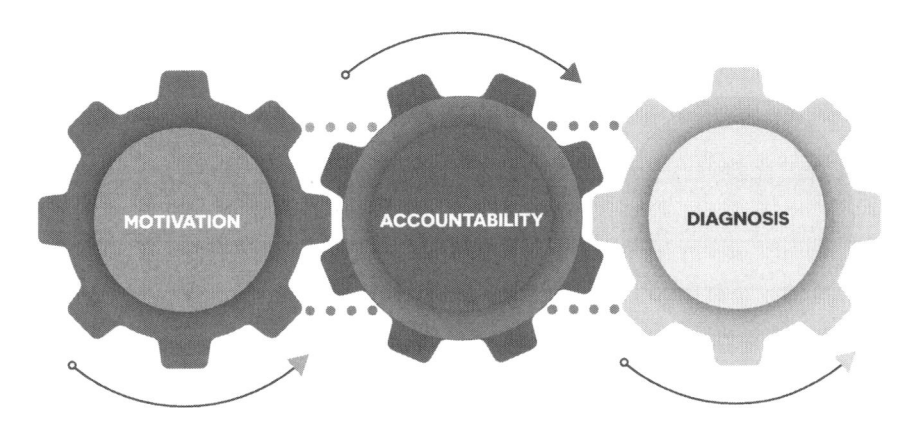

**MOTIVATION — ACCOUNTABILITY — DIAGNOSIS**

### MOTIVATION

Tracking your prospecting activities helps you to see what you're actually achieving in real time.

For example, if your goal is to call 10 members of your SOI database every day, there's a sense of motivation and accomplishment that comes with visually seeing your progress advance call by call.

On a Monday morning or a Friday afternoon, 10 SOI phone calls might seem overwhelming, but tracking your progress will provide periodic motivation boosts. When you reach the quarter mark, you're almost at the halfway mark, and when you reach the halfway point, you're practically done!

### ACCOUNTABILITY

Motivation and accountability are intrinsically linked. You can be highly motivated to complete your 10 SOI calls, but if you don't hold yourself accountable then you might not reach your goals.

No matter how motivated you are, there will always be interruptions to contend with and calls that don't work out how we'd hoped. On those tough days, it will be all too easy to do a little bit of business-generation and then tell yourself, "That's good enough for today, let's call it quits."

If you've had a particularly slow, difficult morning, then reaching the halfway point might seem pretty darn good. However, your goal is to make 10 calls and inside of those few extra contacts could be a couple of extra listing referrals that you miss out on because you didn't make the target number of contacts.

If you don't hold yourself accountable to reaching your stated targets each and every day, it becomes easier and easier to tell yourself, "That's good enough for today," "That's good enough for today," "That's good enough for today."

Soon 10 phone calls turn into 8 calls, which turn into 5 and then 2 or 3, and at that point you're in pretty big trouble! Believe us: it's far easier to track your activity and hold yourself accountable on a daily basis than it is to build your business back up from scratch.

## Diagnosis

The third reason that you should track your prospecting activities is so that you can troubleshoot and diagnose potential problems before it's too late.

In addition to making your 10 daily SOI phone calls, if you start tracking additional metrics related to those 10 daily contacts, you will soon begin to gather a lot of useful diagnostic data.

For example, you might track the following data points:

- How many referral leads you're receiving from those 10 contacts
- How many appointments you generate from those referral leads
- How many contracts you write
- How many closings you ultimately get from those 10 contacts,

If you get 15 referral leads and, from those 15 referral leads, you only set five appointments, and from those 5 appointments, you're not getting any contracts signed, then you should be examining what's happening here.

For starters, 15 leads and only five appointments is a pretty big drop off. Followed by 5 appointments with no resulting contracts? Your conversion rates are looking pretty bad, and the data suggests that you need to improve your listing presentation appointments.

Or, perhaps the reason you went from 15 leads to only five appointments is that you're not closing early enough for the appointment, and you're just sitting back and waiting on your clients to call you when they're ready, which is a really common but really bad idea in real estate.

Whatever the ultimate problem is, tracking your activities and the results you get from those activities will prevent you from becoming complacent and presumptuous about your business-generation techniques and strategies. Tracking and monitoring helps you to identify weaknesses and possible pitfalls in your sales process, and can set you on the path to recovery before the diagnosis becomes fatal.

## Activity Tracking Methods

There are a variety of ways to track and monitor your prospecting activities. Some forms will be familiar to you already, while others are brand new. To assist you, and to provide a mental recap, we have assembled each of our tracking forms here in one place for you to refer and return to.

Let's look at the following types of activity tracking:

- Daily SOI Contacts
- Daily Prospecting Contacts
- Appointment Tracking
- Inventory Pipelines

## Track Your SOI Contacts

As you'll recall, your primary prospecting goal is to make contact with the people in your Sphere of Influence. Remember that prospecting is a numbers game. You must contact a person 40 time times over the course of a year to stay top of mind and see highly successful conversion rates.

However, maintaining contact with your SOI isn't a simple case of calling up your friends and family for a casual conversation. Your daily SOI calls need to be more purposeful than that. Make sure to ask for appointments, make sure to ask for referrals, and make sure to keep track of any information that might prove useful now or in the future.

In Chapter 3, we introduced you to the Daily SOI Contact Form, so you should already have some familiarity with it. This form allows you to check off the numbers quickly every time you make a contact, and it also allows you to tally the total number of contacts and appointments you make as well the total number of referrals received.

Some people prefer writing in a notebook when making SOI calls, or you may be using Customer Relationship Management software where you can type directly into the system, and that is fine too.

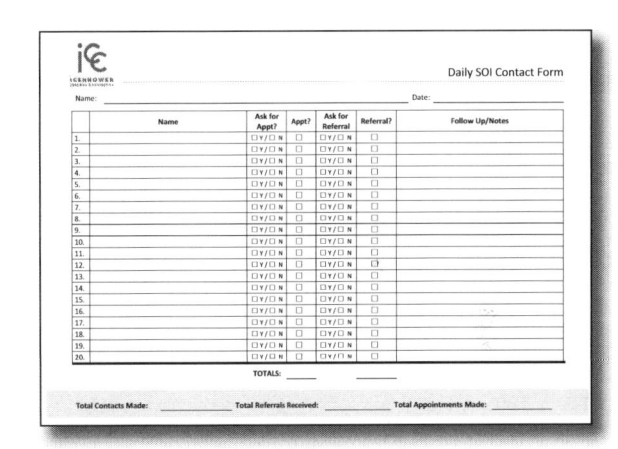

Either way, it's important that you track and document your contacts, as you develop and deepen your relationships over time. As the weeks, months, and years pass, your SOI will grow and grow. Soon you will have a large number of relationships to maintain, and it's crucial that you take notes and not just rely on memory.

When you follow up with SOI members or meet with them in person, the information that you have documented will demonstrate that you have been listening and paying attention. Your Daily SOI Contact Form is an important tool for building rapport over time and establishing people's trust in you to refer business to the people they know.

## Track Your Prospecting Contacts

Of course, in addition to tracking your SOI contacts, you should also be tracking all of your other prospecting activities, from FSBO contacts to Expired Listing contacts and everyone you connect with during your Circle-Prospecting and Property Preview activities.

Use the following lead tracking and contact forms to hold yourself accountable and track your daily prospecting activities.

**Remember:** A contact equals an actual conversation. When you make calls, not everyone is going to answer first time and you might merely be leaving a voice message. A conversation must take place to count the call as a contact. Fudging the numbers might make you feel better in the moment, but it's not good data.

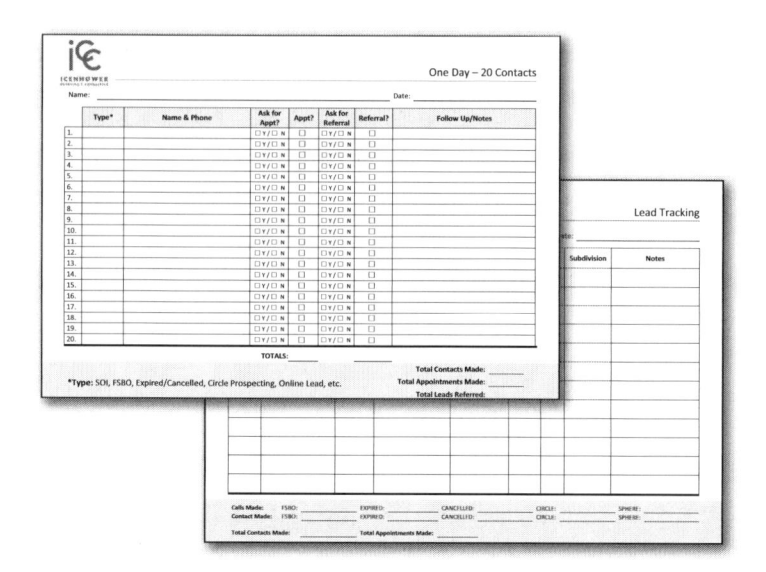

## Track Your Appointments

In addition to tracking your daily SOI contact calls, you should also track the appointments you get as a result of any and all of your prospecting activities.

The purpose of tracking your appointments is to analyze how many contacts resulted in an appointment, and how many appointments result in contracts.

*"I met with my best friend for lunch and we talked about real estate: is that an appointment?"*

If there was no preparation, presentation, or asking for business, you may decide not to mark this as an appointment. The connection still has value, yet you might chalk it up to a "meeting," or a "get-together," and both are vital to *sales development*.

*An appointment serves a specific purpose and has a concrete end goal in mind.*

However, generally speaking, an appointment serves a specific purpose and has a concrete end goal in mind. Naturally, the appointments you track will typically fall into one of two categories:

- **Listing Presentation Appointments** where you meet with a prospective seller for the purposes of securing a **Listing Agreement**
- **Buyer Consultation Appointments** where you meet with a prospective buyer with a goal of securing an exclusive **Buyer Agency Agreement**

As we discussed at length in the previous chapter, the art of closing is establishing clear expectations and explicitly asking people for commitment.

The purpose of a Listing Presentation appointment is to set expectations about the selling process and have the prospect commit to listing their home for sale with you. And, all top-producing agents and high-producing teams ask prospective buyers to demonstrate their commitment by signing a Buyer Agency Agreements.

If you have not explicitly asked for and received an actual commitment, then you have not closed, and you're operating under dangerously ambiguous assumptions.

Remember that the reason for tracking your activities is to provide you with motivation, accountability, and diagnosis opportunities. By tracking your appointments and monitoring your outcomes, you will stay on target and quickly identify weaknesses in your sales process if the data shows a high level of appointments but a low level of signed agreements or contracts.

## Track Your Buyer & Seller Leads

Prior to a Listing Presentation appointment or a Buyer Consultation appointment, you will also need to evaluate your contacts and learn as much about them as humanly possible.

Again, we have discussed both the Buyer Questionnaire & Lead Sheet and the Seller Questionnaire & Lead Sheet in detail at previous points in this book. These forms will help you to engage the prospect, identify their needs, maintain an open dialog and systematic line of questioning, and ultimately convert them to sign a listing contract, exclusive buyer agency agreement, or possibly an offer to purchase a home.

The reason we bring them up again in the context of 'tracking' is because these questionnaires are potentially important *diagnostic tools*. Both of these forms provide quantitative data (ideal price-range, amount of down payment, ranking their motivation to buy or sell on a scale of 1-10) as well as qualitative data (unique, personal responses to the benefits and negatives of buying or selling).

*Lead Sheets generate meaningful quantitative data and qualitative information that allow you to anticipate, troubleshoot and diagnose potential problems with your prospects before they arise.*

As you work your way through the questions, the prospect's answers will generate meaningful quantitative data and qualitative information that will allow you to anticipate, troubleshoot and diagnose potential problems with your leads before they arise.

Tracking and qualifying your leads helps you to identify weaknesses and possible pitfalls in their personal situation that could negatively impact the sales process. There is little point in gathering information if all you're going to do is file the form away and never look at it again. Data is supposed to be examined and analyzed. Gathering this information upfront provides you with a checklist of future activities, and data points that will need to be further tracked, monitored, circled back to, and resolved along the way.

Take a moment to review the Buyer Lead Sheet and the Seller Lead Sheet below, and start thinking about these forms in the context of the ultimate purpose of tracking. Every number and nugget of information that you collect is a potentially valuable predictor of your success in meeting your milestones and achieving your annual goals. When completing a Buyer or Seller Questionnaire, you are not just "going through the administrative motions." You are generating data that is vital to your success.

## TRACK YOUR PIPELINES

The purpose of activity tracking is to provide you with diagnostic opportunities, a system of accountability, and a powerful *motivational* tool.

Too often, agents take a scattered, unsystematic approach to their business and tend to get caught in an endless stop-and-start, up-and-down cycle. They spend a little bit of time generating business, but as soon as they have a contract or a transaction in the pipeline, their lead-generation grinds to a halt, and they devote all of their time to customer-service.

Month after month, they're riding the real estate roller coaster and playing the income guessing game.

In Chapter 7, we discussed how top-producing agents control how much money they make by controlling and religiously scheduling their time. In addition to excellent time-management skills, systematically tracking, monitoring, and growing your pipelines will help you to keep consistent control of your business.

'Inventory Pipelines' are a wonderful tool for *motivating* you to go out and get more business, rather than resting on your laurels and settling for the business you already have.

Let's take a look at three essential inventory pipelines and their individual components:

- Buyer Inventory Pipeline
- Seller Inventory Pipeline
- Pending Contracts

### BUYER INVENTORY PIPELINE

Oftentimes, agents make the mistake of focusing all their efforts on three or four buyer clients—hustling to try to find them a house and close the transaction so they can get paid. Unfortunately, life happens and buyers lose interest or something comes up and they have to delay their search for a while.

If you only have a handful of 'buyer eggs' in your basket at any given time, you risk losing everything, as these numbers are too low to reliably count on converting.

On the buyer side, a better way to control your overall conversion ratios is, ironically, to spend less time focusing on finding property for your current prospects and spend more time on closing Buyer Consultation appointments and growing your committed buyer pipeline.

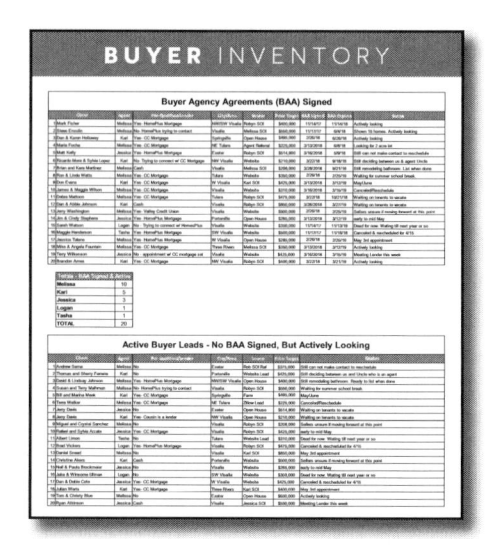

Depending on the market, if you have 20 signed Buyer Agency Agreements at any given moment you can almost always count on writing four purchase contracts a month. Because you have so many Buyer Agency Agreements, at least one of them is going to be Active, and at least one of them is going to be proactively finding a house that they want to buy.

Remember, real estate is a numbers game and the more committed buyers you have in your pipeline, the greater your odds are of converting and closing multiple transactions.

The 'Buyer Inventory Pipeline' is a list of buyers that have signed exclusive Buyer Agency Agreements and are actively looking for homes. This form also contains a second list of 'hot buyer' prospects that have yet to sign an agency agreement to exclusively work with you but are actively looking at properties.

This second list of Active Buyer Leads is where the majority of your time and effort should be focused. It's very important that you track and monitor who is and is not exclusively committed to you at any given moment. Your goal is to follow up with these active buyer leads as often as humanly possible, nurturing them to meet you for a Buyer Consultation with the purpose of converting them to sign a Buyer Agency Agreement.

Once the lead has signed a BAA, you can move them to the top of the buyer inventory pipeline. Once the prospect is a committed component of your pipeline, your likelihood of seeing them through to a closed transaction—and a definite paycheck—is exponentially higher.

## Seller Inventory Pipeline

The Seller Pipeline is very similar to the Buyer Pipeline.

Active Listings are on top: these are people with signed listing agreements that are active and up for sale.

Below that is a list of clients with signed Listing Agreements that are waiting to go active. For some reason they're waiting to officially put the home up for sale for a short period of time (perhaps they're fixing it up or maybe they're on vacation), but they are committed to sell.

These people are current clients and fall into the customer-service category. While customer-service is still important, it is not as important as *generating new business.*

The most important category in the Seller Pipeline is the **Listing Leads** section at the bottom. This is the section that you are tracking and monitoring most closely, and the section that should motivate you the most.

Listing Leads are your hottest targets, and you need to hold yourself accountable to converting these prospects on the bottom of the chart into committed clients that become part of your customer-service pipeline.

Yes, it's wonderful to have a pipeline full of Active Listings and a host of committed clients, but the purpose of tracking is to keep you focused, motivated, and accountable to what still needs to be done.

## Connect Your Inventory Pipelines

Top-producers don't get pigeonholed on one particular client. They utilize the pipeline method and focus on the business they don't *definitely* have more than the business they've already secured.

Top-producing teams also understand that the Buyer pipeline is not separate from the Seller pipeline. On most large real estate teams, some agents work listings while other agents work the buyer side. These teams make sure to share their pipelines in real estate meetings and strategize on how to connect pipelines for optimal conversion.

For example, a Listing Specialist might be trying to set appointments with a lot of Listing Leads who are delaying listing their home because they also need to purchase a new home. These individuals are both prospective buyers as well as prospective sellers.

Oftentimes, these prospects won't pull the trigger and start making offers on new homes until they settle on the price they're going to list their current home for sale for. Once their current home is listed, people start looking for homes with a lot of increased urgency and purpose, so the Listing Specialist will nurture and cultivate for a signed Listing Agreement, while the team's specialist Buyer Agents will motivate the prospect by showing them property and create an extra sense of urgency to list.

Solo agents can do this too. It's important to cross-reference both pipelines and push urgency both ways to improve the efficiency of your time, their time, and ensure that they get moving into their new home by listing their existing home as soon as possible.

## Pending Inventory Pipelines

The final pipeline you will use is the Pending Inventory Pipeline. This tool tracks properties that are currently under contract or in escrow, whether it's a buyer who's found a home and had an offer accepted, or a seller that has sold their home to a buyer.

The Pending Inventory Pipeline tracks the number of clients under contract and it also tracks upcoming commissions. It goes without saying that this type of tracking is hugely motivating when you can see how much commission income is coming to you in the next 30-60 days.

Your Buyer and Seller Pipelines can also give you a pretty good idea of how much you can expect to make over the next year. If your current pipelines show a ton of signed Buyer Agency Agreements and Listing Agreements, you can reasonably project what the rest of the year is going to look like. Pipelines can be a great motivational-tool and inspire you to move confidently forward in your business, as long as you hold yourself accountable to repeating the activities that resulted in these outcomes in the first place.

## How to Analyze the Data You Collect

At the end of your workweek, you will have a minimum of five daily tracking sheets (six, if you also worked on the weekend).

Gather the sheets you filled out then compile the numbers for each section and add them together. Compare the results to the numbers you need to meet your goals. How close are you to reaching them?

If you did not meet your goals for the week, it's time to ask yourself these four key accountability questions:

1. How do you think you did?
2. What got in the way?
3. What do you need to do differently next week?
4. What help do you need?

> *"The purpose of computing is insight, not numbers."* Richard Hamming

Next, it's time to complete a monthly analysis.

Once you have completed four weeks of business-generating activities, add the section totals for each week. How close did you come to meeting the goals for the month? Were you able to set four appointments resulting in two contracts?

> How many leads did you have? _____
>
> How many property previews did you conduct? _____
>
> How may SOI Database contacts did you make? _____
>
> What else did you do to make the month successful? _____

### Your Ratios are Relationships

You can also drill down into your data by taking a look at various sales ratios. Simply put, a ratio says how much of one thing there is compared to another thing. Performing a ratio analysis can help you understand sales results and identify trends over time, as well as pinpoint procedural strengths as well as weakness from which strategies can be created and implemented.

For ratios to be productive and meaningful, they must be:

- Calculated using accurate, precise, and valid information
- Calculated on a regular and consistent basis
- Analyzed in relation to specific targets, benchmarks, and goals
- Carefully and objectively interpreted—don't neglect to overlook other factors when assessing performance, especially in the initial stages of your prospecting career.

Performing a ratio analysis won't offer you a readymade solution to your prospecting challenges, but it can provide the support you need to decide how to adjust your business practices.

For example, this simple table shows how many hours an agent spent on business appointments in a single month. The ratio of hours spent at listing appointments to hours spent at buyer consultation appointment is 10:40.

| Activity | Hours |
| --- | --- |
| Buyer Consultation Appointments | 40 |
| Listing Presentation Appointments | 10 |

Of course, it's wonderful if you're securing a high number of Buyer Agency Agreements, but consider the fact that buyer clients take a lot more time to service than seller clients.

If you have a low Seller to Buyer ratio, you may decide to adjust your business practices to focus on improving your listing conversions if financials show that that type of client would be a more efficient and profitable use of your time and energy.

Your ICC coach can help you run the numbers and decide if and when to adjust your fundamental business practices.

You can also compare numbers for Closed Lead Source categories.

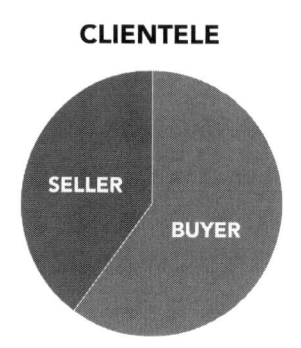

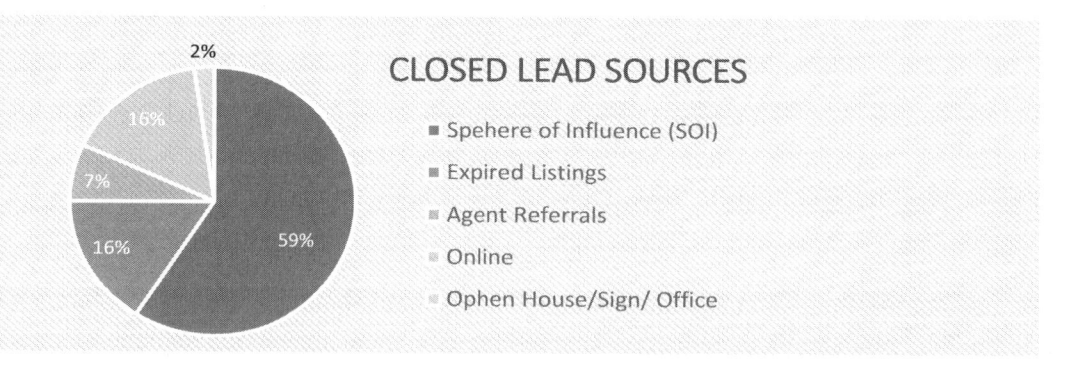

**CLIENTELE**
SELLER
BUYER

**CLOSED LEAD SOURCES**
- Sphere of Influence (SOI) — 59%
- Expired Listings — 16%
- Agent Referrals — 7%
- Online — 16%
- Ophen House/Sign/ Office — 2%

If your analysis shows that you made fewer recommended SOI Database contacts and property previews, or you generated fewer leads, but you still met your goals, you either got lucky this month or you are doing something right.

> "There is strength in numbers, but organizing those numbers is one of the greatest challenges." John C. Mather

If you did not meet your goals because your numbers are low, you'll have to increase your contacts, previews, and leads. You may also want to have your accountability coach help you identify what you need to improve and how to overcome any blocks you might have. The same is true if your numbers are there, but you're not getting the transactions and contracts you should be getting.

Some questions to consider include:

- Are you using the presentation scripts?
- Do you have the scripts memorized so that you can deliver your presentation naturally and authentically?
- When previewing property, how close to each other were the properties you saw?
- Did you contact listings with no showings in the last 30 days?
- How well did you make use of your time?
- Have you been honest about the numbers you've recorded?
- What's really holding you back?

For the month ahead, adjust your schedule to compensate for any areas of deficiency. For example, if you know you need to make more SOI Database contacts, add 30 minutes to your day or plan to work on a weekend day to reach your contacts.

Put your plan in writing.

By writing down your plan, you are more likely to implement and achieve it.

## When It's Time to Put on Your WIG (Wildly Important Goal)

Real estate prospecting is a game of numbers. The more people you contact, the more prospects you have. More prospects mean more leads, which will result in more appointments, more transactions, and more contracts.

Ultimately, that means more in sales for you.

Be careful that you don't become complacent about your sales. There's nothing wrong with making one sale a month—at $7500 GCI per sale on a $250,000 property, you'll earn $90,000 annually. That number, however, is your gross, so you'll still need to figure your expenses, including taxes, withholding, office space, advertising, fuel, etc.

If your per transaction GCI is $7,500, yet your net commission income is $3,500, wouldn't you agree that it's vital to include this as part of your calculations?

It can seem like most of what you earn is predestined for the necessities of life, with little left over for discretionary income. That's when it's time to put on your WIG and create some Wildly Important Goals.

### Your 2 Gas Pedals for Goals

If you're not successfully on track to meet you annual GCI goals, you have two options:

1. Increase your daily, weekly, and monthly prospecting contacts to increase your overall income

② Increase your GCI by previewing, listing and selling more expensive properties.

Some real estates agents find that a combination of these two strategies works best for them.

It's time to put on your WIG. In the book, *4 Disciplines of Execution*, the authors outline how a focusing priority can help you organize the onslaught of data points that come across your desk, and filter what's going to affect it and what's not. Imagine you're a general waging war to defend your territory (your business). Your WIG helps you pick your battles.

What is your Wildly Important Goal? If you knew you would be successful *regardless* of the goal you set, what number would you strive for?

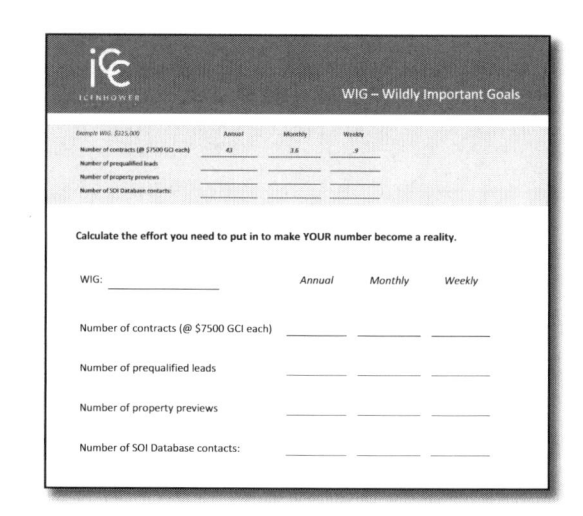

Write it here:  $_____

Complete the Wildly Important Goals worksheet and see what your numbers look like.

## Production Ratio Planner

Knowing your conversion ratios is essential for a variety of reasons. It helps your efficiency by providing focus on moving sequentially from contact to appointment to contract. It also provides daily motivation by tying your daily activities directly into alignment with your annual goals.

Take the time to fill out the Production Ratio Planner below.

As you can see, you will begin with a target Gross Commission Income goal and then break that goal down piece by piece until you arrive at the number of buyer consultation and listing appointments you will need to conduct on a monthly and weekly basis in order to hit your ideal GCI.

Completing (and regularly revisiting) a Production Ratio Planner will not only help you stay motivated and accountable, it will also assist you in diagnosing potential problems that could stand in the way of your long-term financial success.

At ICC, we don't know of any successful real estate business that survives and thrives with any type of longevity that does not do a good job of tracking and monitoring their key performance indicators.

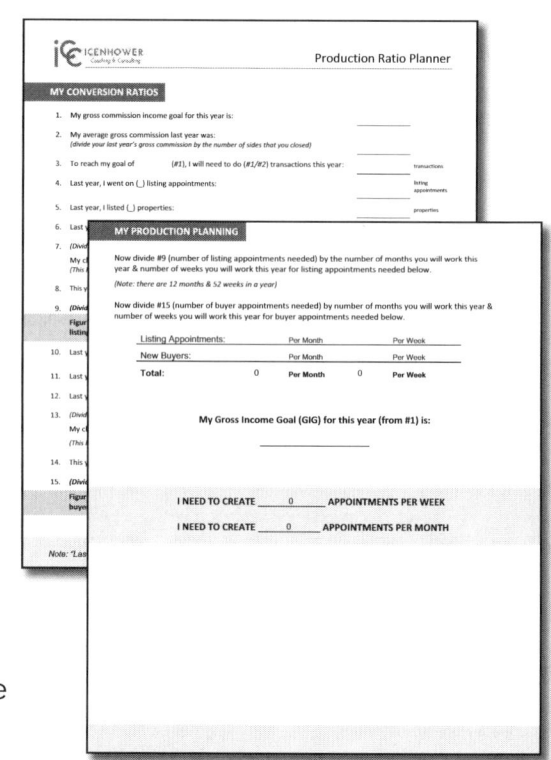

So make sure that you follow their lead and start tracking your activities and outcomes from Day 1.

## Summary

Tracking and monitoring your business-generation activities provides the motivation, accountability, and diagnostic data that are essential for lucrative and long-term prospecting success.

By tracking your daily contacts and appointments, and monitoring your outcomes, you will stay on target and quickly identify weaknesses and potential pitfalls in your sales processes.

Likewise, Buyer and Seller Lead Sheets are important diagnostic tools that generate meaningful quantitative and qualitative data that will allow you to anticipate, troubleshoot and resolve potential problems with your leads before they arise.

Systematically tracking, monitoring, and growing your pipelines will help you to keep consistent control of your business. 'Inventory Pipelines' are a wonderful tool for motivating you to go out and get more business, rather than expending a disproportionate amount of your energy and efforts servicing the business you already have.

Every number and nugget of information that you collect is a potentially valuable predictor of your success in meeting your milestones and achieving your annual goals.

Whatever your Wildly Important Goal is, you can make it happen. All you have to do is develop your plan, believe in your capabilities, and work the numbers.

# Module 13

## Appendix 13.1

### Daily SOI Contact Form

Name: _____

Date: _____

| | Name | Ask for Appt? | Appt? | Ask for Referral | Referral? | Follow Up/Notes |
|---|------|---------------|-------|------------------|-----------|-----------------|
| 1. | | ☐Y/☐N | ☐ | ☐Y/☐N | ☐ | |
| 2. | | ☐Y/☐N | ☐ | ☐Y/☐N | ☐ | |
| 3. | | ☐Y/☐N | ☐ | ☐Y/☐N | ☐ | |
| 4. | | ☐Y/☐N | ☐ | ☐Y/☐N | ☐ | |
| 5. | | ☐Y/☐N | ☐ | ☐Y/☐N | ☐ | |
| 6. | | ☐Y/☐N | ☐ | ☐Y/☐N | ☐ | |
| 7. | | ☐Y/☐N | ☐ | ☐Y/☐N | ☐ | |
| 8. | | ☐Y/☐N | ☐ | ☐Y/☐N | ☐ | |
| 9. | | ☐Y/☐N | ☐ | ☐Y/☐N | ☐ | |
| 10. | | ☐Y/☐N | ☐ | ☐Y/☐N | ☐ | |
| 11. | | ☐Y/☐N | ☐ | ☐Y/☐N | ☐ | |
| 12. | | ☐Y/☐N | ☐ | ☐Y/☐N | ☐ | |
| 13. | | ☐Y/☐N | ☐ | ☐Y/☐N | ☐ | |
| 14. | | ☐Y/☐N | ☐ | ☐Y/☐N | ☐ | |
| 15. | | ☐Y/☐N | ☐ | ☐Y/☐N | ☐ | |
| 16. | | ☐Y/☐N | ☐ | ☐Y/☐N | ☐ | |
| 17. | | ☐Y/☐N | ☐ | ☐Y/☐N | ☐ | |
| 18. | | ☐Y/☐N | ☐ | ☐Y/☐N | ☐ | |
| 19. | | ☐Y/☐N | ☐ | ☐Y/☐N | ☐ | |
| 20. | | ☐Y/☐N | ☐ | ☐Y/☐N | ☐ | |

**TOTALS:**

Total Contacts Made: _____  Total Referrals Received: _____  Total Appointments Made: _____

ICENHOWER COACHING & CONSULTING

© Copyright Icenhower Coaching & Consulting, LLC. All rights reserved.

# Module 13

## Appendix 13.2

**One Day – 20 Contacts**

Name: _____ , Date: _____

| Type* | Name & Phone | Ask for Appt? | Appt? | Ask for Referral | Referral? | Follow Up/Notes |
|---|---|---|---|---|---|---|
| 1. |  | ☐Y/☐N | ☐ | ☐Y/☐N | ☐ |  |
| 2. |  | ☐Y/☐N | ☐ | ☐Y/☐N | ☐ |  |
| 3. |  | ☐Y/☐N | ☐ | ☐Y/☐N | ☐ |  |
| 4. |  | ☐Y/☐N | ☐ | ☐Y/☐N | ☐ |  |
| 5. |  | ☐Y/☐N | ☐ | ☐Y/☐N | ☐ |  |
| 6. |  | ☐Y/☐N | ☐ | ☐Y/☐N | ☐ |  |
| 7. |  | ☐Y/☐N | ☐ | ☐Y/☐N | ☐ |  |
| 8. |  | ☐Y/☐N | ☐ | ☐Y/☐N | ☐ |  |
| 9. |  | ☐Y/☐N | ☐ | ☐Y/☐N | ☐ |  |
| 10. |  | ☐Y/☐N | ☐ | ☐Y/☐N | ☐ |  |
| 11. |  | ☐Y/☐N | ☐ | ☐Y/☐N | ☐ |  |
| 12. |  | ☐Y/☐N | ☐ | ☐Y/☐N | ☐ |  |
| 13. |  | ☐Y/☐N | ☐ | ☐Y/☐N | ☐ |  |
| 14. |  | ☐Y/☐N | ☐ | ☐Y/☐N | ☐ |  |
| 15. |  | ☐Y/☐N | ☐ | ☐Y/☐N | ☐ |  |
| 16. |  | ☐Y/☐N | ☐ | ☐Y/☐N | ☐ |  |
| 17. |  | ☐Y/☐N | ☐ | ☐Y/☐N | ☐ |  |
| 18. |  | ☐Y/☐N | ☐ | ☐Y/☐N | ☐ |  |
| 19. |  | ☐Y/☐N | ☐ | ☐Y/☐N | ☐ |  |
| 20. |  | ☐Y/☐N | ☐ | ☐Y/☐N | ☐ |  |

**TOTALS:** _____

**\*Type:** SOI, FSBO, Expired/Cancelled, Circle Prospecting, Online Lead, etc.

**Total Contacts Made:** _____
**Total Appointments Made:** _____
**Total Leads Referred:** _____

© Copyright Icenhower Coaching & Consulting, LLC. All rights reserved.

**ICENHOWER**
COACHING & CONSULTING

# Module 13

## Appendix 13.3

### Lead Tracking

Name: _____  Date: _____

| Type* | Name | Phone Number | Email | Address | Price Point | Bed/Bath | Subdivision | Notes |
|---|---|---|---|---|---|---|---|---|
|  |  |  |  |  |  |  |  |  |
|  |  |  |  |  |  |  |  |  |
|  |  |  |  |  |  |  |  |  |
|  |  |  |  |  |  |  |  |  |
|  |  |  |  |  |  |  |  |  |
|  |  |  |  |  |  |  |  |  |
|  |  |  |  |  |  |  |  |  |
|  |  |  |  |  |  |  |  |  |
|  |  |  |  |  |  |  |  |  |
|  |  |  |  |  |  |  |  |  |
|  |  |  |  |  |  |  |  |  |

**Calls Made:** _____  FSBO: _____  EXPIRED: _____  CANCELLED: _____  CIRCLE: _____  SPHERE: _____
**Contact Made:** _____  FSBO: _____  EXPIRED: _____  CANCELLED: _____  CIRCLE: _____  SPHERE: _____
**Total Contacts Made:** _____  **Total Appointments Made:** _____

© Copyright Icenhower Coaching & Consulting, LLC. All rights reserved.

MODULE 13　　　　　　　　　　　　　　　　　　　　　　　　　　　APPENDIX 13.4

**ICENHOWER**
COACHING & CONSULTING

## Buyer Questionnaire & Lead Sheet

Date: _____ Lead Source: _____

Name: _____ Spouse Name: _____

Property Address: _____ City: _____ State: _____ Zip: ____

Phone #s – Mobile: _____ Spouse Mobile: _____ Home: _____ Work: _____

Email: _____ Spouse Email: _____

Family / Children (include ages): _____

1. Have any other agents shown you homes?　☐ Yes　☐ No
   If Yes, do you have a signed agency agreement?　☐ Yes　☐ No
2. Is anyone buying the home with you? _____
3. Are you renting, or do you own a home?　☐ Homeowner　☐ Renter
   a) HOMEOWNER:
      - Do you need to sell your home before you buy?　☐ Yes　☐ No
      - Have you signed a listing agreement to sell your home?　☐ Yes　☐ No　**If "No" use Seller Lead Sheet.**
   b) RENTER:
      - When does your lease end? _____
4. What date do you want to be moved by? _____
5. Are there any negatives to not moving by then? (suggest lifestyle sacrifices, job, costs, schools, family, etc.)
   _____
6. Tell me all the benefits of buying a new home: (dig deep & find out WHY?)
   _____
7. On a scale of 1 to 10, how would you rank your motivation to move? With 10 meaning you must buy as quickly as possible, and 1 meaning you're not sure you'll really buy anything: _____
   - What's missing? What would it take to make you a 10? _____
8. Do you know where you want to move to? _____
9. Will you be paying cash or getting a mortgage?　☐ Cash　☐ Mortgage
10. Have you been pre-approved by a lender?　☐ Yes　☐ No
11. How much will your down payment be? _____
12. What price range are you looking in? _____
13. How many BR: ____ Baths: ____ SqFt: ____ Stories: ____ Other: _____
14. What else are you looking for in a home? _____
15. Will anyone else be involved in your home buying decision? _____
16. "Thank you! I'd love to help you find your perfect home. All that we need to do is to set an appointment so that I can help you find the home you're looking for. Does 4:30 tomorrow or 5:00 Wednesday work for you?"

Appointment Date/Time: _____

DISC Behavioral Profile: _____ Why: _____

© Copyright Icenhower Coaching & Consulting, LLC. All rights reserved.

417

MODULE 13　　　　　　　　　　　　　　　　　　　　　　　　　　　　APPENDIX 13.5

## Seller Questionnaire & Lead Form

Date: _____

Name: _____ Spouse Name: _____

Property Address: _____ City: _____ State: _____ Zip: _____

Phone #s – Mobile: _____ Spouse Mobile: _____ Home: _____ Work: _____

Email: _____ Spouse Email: _____

Family / Children (include ages): _____

1. Have you spoken with any other agents? ☐ Yes ☐ No _____
2. Have you considered selling the home yourself? ☐ Yes ☐ No _____
3. Why do you want to move? _____
4. Do you know where you want to move to? _____
5. What date do you want to be moved by? _____
6. Are there any negatives to not moving by then? (suggest lifestyle sacrifices, job, costs, schools, family, etc.) _____
7. Tell me all the negatives of not moving at all? (same suggestions above) _____
8. Tell me all the benefits of buying a new home: (dig deep & find out WHY?) _____
9. On a scale of 1 to 10, how would you rank your motivation to move? With 10 being highly motivated: _____
10. When did you buy your home? _____ What price did you pay? _____
11. Do you know how much you still owe on it? _____
12. Have you made any major improvements to the home since? ☐ Yes ☐ No _____
13. Do you happen to have an idea as to what you think it's worth, or should sell for? _____
14. Do you have a price you won't sell your home below? _____
15. Tell me about the positive & negative features of your home: _____
16. How many BR: ____ Baths: ____ SqFt: ____ Stories: ____ Other: ____
17. How did you hear about me/us? _____
18. Are you interviewing any other agents? ☐ Yes ☐ No Who? _____ When? _____
19. "Thank you! The next step is for me to take a quick look at your home and I can answer any other questions you may have. Then you can decide what we do next. How does that sound?" (pause)
    "Great! Does 4:30 tomorrow or 5:00 Wednesday work for you?"

Appointment Date/Time: _____

DISC Behavioral Profile: _____ Why? _____

© Copyright Icenhower Coaching & Consulting, LLC. All rights reserved.

# MODULE 13

# APPENDIX 13.6

# BUYER INVENTORY

## Buyer Agency Agreements (BAA) Signed

| # | Client | Agent | Pre-Qualified/Lender | City/Area | Source | Price Target | BAA Signed | BAA Expires | Status |
|---|---|---|---|---|---|---|---|---|---|
| 1 | Mark Fisher | Melissa | Yes- HomePlus Mortgage | NW/SW Visalia | Robyn SOI | $400,000 | 11/14/17 | 11/14/18 | Actively looking |
| 2 | Steve Ensslin | Melissa | No- HomePlus trying to contact | Visalia | Melissa SOI | $550,000 | 11/17/17 | 6/4/18 | Shown 15 homes. Actively looking |
| 3 | Dan & Karen Holloway | Kari | Yes- CC Mortgage | Springville | Open House | $495,000 | 2/26/18 | 6/26/18 | Actively looking |
| 4 | Maria Focha | Melissa | Yes- CC Mortgage | NE Tulare | Agent Referral | $225,000 | 3/13/2018 | 6/8/18 | Looking for 2 acre lot |
| 5 | Matt Kelly | Jessica | Yes- HomePlus Mortgage | Exeter | Robyn SOI | $514,900 | 3/16/2018 | 5/9/18 | Still can not make contact to reschedule |
| 6 | Ricardo Mora & Sylvia Lopez | Kari | No- Trying to connect w/ CC Mortgage | NW Visalia | Website | $210,000 | 3/22/18 | 9/18/18 | Still deciding between us & agent Uncle |
| 7 | Brian and Kara Martinez | Melissa | Cash | Visalia | Melissa SOI | $208,000 | 3/28/2018 | 9/21/18 | Still remodeling bathroom. List when done |
| 8 | Ron & Linda Watts | Melissa | Yes- CC Mortgage | Tulare | Website | $350,000 | 2/26/18 | 2/25/19 | Waiting for summer school break. |
| 9 | Don Evans | Kari | Yes- CC Mortgage | W Visalia | Kari SOI | $425,000 | 3/13/2018 | 3/12/19 | May/June |
| 10 | James & Maggie Wilson | Melissa | Yes- CC Mortgage | Visalia | Website | $310,000 | 3/16/2018 | 3/15/19 | Canceled/Reschedule |
| 11 | Debra Mattoon | Melissa | Yes- CC Mortgage | Tulare | Robyn SOI | $475,000 | 3/22/18 | 10/21/18 | Waiting on tenants to vacate |
| 12 | Dan & Abbie Johnson | Kari | Cash | Visalia | Robyn SOI | $850,000 | 3/28/2018 | 3/27/19 | Waiting on tenants to vacate |
| 13 | Jerry Washington | Melissa | Yes- Valley Credit Union | Visalia | Website | $500,000 | 2/26/18 | 2/25/19 | Sellers unsure if moving forward at this point |
| 14 | Jim & Cindy Stephens | Jessica | Yes- HomePlus Mortgage | Porterville | Open House | $285,000 | 3/13/2018 | 3/12/19 | early to mid May |
| 15 | Sarah Watson | Logan | No - Trying to connect w/ HomesPlus | Visalia | Website | $350,000 | 11/14/17 | 11/13/19 | Dead for now. Wating till next year or so |
| 16 | Maggie Henderson | Tasha | Yes- HomePlus Mortgage | SW Visalia | Website | $500,000 | 11/17/17 | 11/16/18 | Canceled & rescheduled for 4/15 |
| 17 | Jessica Tulane | Melissa | Yes- HomePlus Mortgage | W Visalia | Open House | $285,000 | 2/26/18 | 2/25/19 | May 3rd appointment |
| 18 | Mike & Angela Fountain | Melissa | Yes- CC Mortgage | Three Rivers | Melissa SOI | $350,000 | 3/13/2018 | 3/12/19 | Actively looking |
| 19 | Terry Wilkenson | Jessica | No - appointment w/ CC mortgage set | Visalia | Website | $425,000 | 3/16/2018 | 3/15/19 | Meeting Lender this week |
| 20 | Brandon Ames | Kari | Yes- CC Mortgage | NW Visalia | Robyn SOI | $400,000 | 3/22/18 | 3/21/19 | Actively looking |

| Totals - BAA Signed & Active | |
|---|---|
| Melissa | 10 |
| Kari | 5 |
| Jessica | 3 |
| Logan | 1 |
| Tasha | 1 |
| TOTAL | 20 |

## Active Buyer Leads - No BAA Signed, But Actively Looking

| # | Client | Agent | Pre-Qualified/Lender | City/Area | Source | Price Target | Status |
|---|---|---|---|---|---|---|---|
| 1 | Andrew Serna | Melissa | No | Exeter | Rob SOI Ref | $375,000 | Still can not make contact to reschedule |
| 2 | Thomas and Sherry Ferreira | Kari | No | Porterville | Website Lead | $425,000 | Still deciding between us and Uncle who is an agent |
| 3 | David & Lindsay Johnson | Melissa | Yes- HomePlus Mortgage | NW/SW Visalia | Open House | $400,000 | Still remodeling bathroom. Ready to list when done |
| 4 | Susan and Terry Malhman | Melissa | No- HomePlus trying to contact | Visalia | Robyn SOI | $550,000 | Waiting for summer school break. |
| 5 | Bill and Marina Meek | Kari | Yes- CC Mortgage | Springville | Farm | $495,000 | May/June |
| 6 | Terra Walker | Melissa | Yes- CC Mortgage | NE Tulare | Zillow Lead | $225,000 | Canceled/Reschedule |
| 7 | Jerry Davis | Jessica | No | Exeter | Open House | $514,900 | Waiting on tenants to vacate |
| 8 | Jerry Davis | Kari | Yes- Cousin is a lender | NW Visalia | Open House | $210,000 | Waiting on tenants to vacate |
| 9 | Miguel and Crystal Sanchez | Melissa | No | Visalia | Robyn SOI | $208,000 | Sellers unsure if moving forward at this point |
| 10 | Rafael and Sylvia Arzate | Jessica | Yes- CC Mortgage | Visalia | Robyn SOI | $425,000 | early to mid May |
| 11 | Albert Limon | Tasha | No | Tulare | Website Lead | $310,000 | Dead for now. Wating till next year or so |
| 12 | Brad Vickers | Logan | Yes- HomePlus Mortgage | Visalia | Robyn SOI | $475,000 | Canceled & rescheduled for 4/15 |
| 13 | Daniel Snead | Melissa | No | Visalia | Kari SOI | $850,000 | May 3rd appointment |
| 14 | Christine Akers | Kari | Cash | Porterville | Website | $500,000 | Sellers unsure if moving forward at this point |
| 15 | Neil & Paula Brockmeier | Jessica | No | Visalia | Website | $285,000 | early to mid May |
| 16 | Jake & Winsome Ullman | Logan | No | SW Visalia | Website | $350,000 | Dead for now. Wating till next year or so |
| 17 | Dan & Debie Cote | Jessica | Yes- CC Mortgage | W Visalia | Website | $425,000 | Canceled & rescheduled for 4/15 |
| 18 | Julian Werts | Kari | Yes- CC Mortgage | Three Rivers | Kari SOI | $400,000 | May 3rd appointment |
| 19 | Tom & Christy Blue | Melissa | No | Exeter | Open House | $650,000 | Actively looking |
| 20 | Ryan Atkinson | Jessica | Cash | Visalia | Jessica SOI | $550,000 | Meeting Lender this week |

© Copyright Icenhower Coaching & Consulting, LLC. All rights reserved.

# MODULE 13　　　　　　　　　　　　　　　　　　　　　　　　　　　　　APPENDIX 13.7

# LISTING INVENTORY

## Active Listings

| # | Client | Buyer too? | Address | City, Zip | Agent | Source | List Price | List Date | DOM | LA Expires | Today |
|---|---|---|---|---|---|---|---|---|---|---|---|
| 1 | Mark Fisher | Yes | 1701 S. Crumal St. | Visalia 93292 | Robyn | Robyn SOI | $159,900.00 | 11/14/17 | 235 | 11/14/18 | 7/7/2018 |
| 2 | Steve Ensslin | Yes | 143 Carmelita St. | Pville 93257 | Kari | Kari SOI | $329,000.00 | 11/17/17 | 232 | 6/4/18 | 7/7/2018 |
| 3 | Dan & Karen Holloway | Maybe | 2067 Linda Vista Ave. | Pville 93257 | Kari | Open House | $495,000.00 | 2/26/18 | 131 | 6/26/18 | 7/7/2018 |
| 4 | Maria Focha | No | 1104 S Whitney | Visalia 93277 | Robyn | Agent Referral | $225,000.00 | 3/13/2018 | 116 | 6/8/18 | 7/7/2018 |
| 5 | Matt Kelly | Yes | 763 Park Place Ct | Exeter 93221 | Robyn | Robyn SOI | $514,900.00 | 3/16/2018 | 113 | 5/9/18 | 7/7/2018 |
| 6 | Ricardo Mora & Sylvia Lopez | No | 996 E San Joaquin | Tulare 93274 | Kari | Website | $210,000.00 | 3/22/18 | 107 | 9/18/18 | 7/7/2018 |
| 7 | Brian and Kara Martinez | Yes | 1955 W Wall Ave | Pville 93257 | Kari | Kari SOI | $208,000.00 | 3/28/2018 | 101 | 9/21/2018 | 7/7/2018 |

## Listing Agreement Signed & Waiting to Go Active

| # | Client | Buyer too? | Address | City, Zip | Agent | Source | LA Signed | LA Expires | Notes |
|---|---|---|---|---|---|---|---|---|---|
| 1 | Hayley Tashjian | Yes | 216 N. Orange Ave. | Exeter 93221 | Robyn | Melissa SOI | 3/25/18 | 3/24/19 | Active on 4/15 |
| 2 | April Black | No | 2720 W. Caldwell Ave. | Visalia 93277 | Kari | Kari SOI | 1/31/18 | 12/31/18 | Active on 4/26 |
| 3 | Barbara (Heaher Saddler) | Yes | 3529 W. Howard | Visalia 93277 | Robyn | Robyn SOI | 3/5/2018 | 9/4/18 | Waiting for yard rennovation |
| 4 | Miguel Sanchez | Yes | 39 Brook Street | Visalia 93291 | Robyn | Rob PC Ref | 3/15/2018 | 12/31/18 | Active on 5/1 |

## Listing Leads - No Listing Agreement Signed Yet

| # | Client | Buyer too? | Address | City, Zip | Agent | Source | Status |
|---|---|---|---|---|---|---|---|
| 1 | Andrew Serna | Yes | 794 Sheffield Ave. | Exeter 93221 | Robyn | Rob SOI Ref | Still can not make contact to reschedule |
| 2 | Thomas and Sherry Ferreira | Yes | 1704 Cotton Ct. | Visalia 93291 | Robyn | Website Lead | Still deciding between us and Uncle who is an agent |
| 3 | David & Lindsay Johnson | Yes | 2822 W. Border Links | Ivanhoe 93292 | Kari | Open House | Still remodeling bathroom. Ready to list when done |
| 4 | Susan and Terry Malhman | Yes | 15016 Avenue 312 | Visalia 93291 | Robyn | Robyn SOI | Waiting for summer school break. |
| 5 | Bill and Marina Meek | No | 5837 W. Stewart Ave. | Visalia 93291 | Robyn | Farm | May/June |
| 6 | Terra Walker | Maybe | 1802 Marroneto Circle | Tulare 93274 | Robyn | Zillow Lead | Canceled/Reschedule |
| 7 | Jerry Davis | No | 24006 Road 224 | Lindsay 93247 | Kari | Open House | Waiting on tenants to vacate |
| 8 | Jerry Davis | No | 1825 E Fir St | Lindsay 93247 | Kari | Open House | Waiting on tenants to vacate |
| 9 | Miguel and Crystal Sanchez | Maybe | 2823 W Brooke Ave | Visalia 93291 | Robyn | Robyn SOI | Sellers unsure if moving forward at this point |
| 10 | Rafael and Sylvia Arzate | Yes | 3613 E. Harvard Ct. | Visalia 93292 | Robyn | Robyn SOI | early to mid May |
| 11 | Albert Limon | Yes | 1032 E. Academy Ave. | Tulare 93274 | Robyn | Website Lead | Dead for now. Waiting till next year or so |
| 12 | Brad Vickers | No | 4106 S. Bridge St. | Visalia 93277 | Robyn | Robyn SOI | Canceled & rescheduled for 4/15 |
| 13 | Daniel Snead | No | 3145 W. Ashland Ave. | Visalia 93277 | Kari | Kari SOI | May 3rd appointment |

© Copyright Icenhower Coaching & Consulting, LLC. All rights reserved.

# MODULE 13

## APPENDIX 13.8

# PENDING INVENTORY PIPELINE

| # | Client | B or S | Address | City, Zip | Agent | Source | Price | Open | Close Date | Total GCI | Notes |
|---|---|---|---|---|---|---|---|---|---|---|---|
| 1 | William and Erica Pine | Buyer | 1600 Palm Dr. | Exeter 93221 | Melissa | Melissa SOI | $500,000 | 12/21/18 | 4/19/18 | $13,500 | |
| 2 | Luis Guerrero | Buyer | 2148 W. Union Ave. | Porterville 93257 | Melissa | Website | $255,000 | 1/9/18 | 4/11/18 | $5,558 | |
| 3 | Chris and Crystal Smith | Buyer | 14663 Avenue 344 | Visalia 93292 | Melissa | Robyn SOI | $685,000 | 2/12/18 | 4/12/18 | $12,813 | Ray Jones (Uncle) 949-555-1243 |
| 4 | Carly Heinzen-Woods | Seller | 813 W. Reese Ct. | Visalia 93277 | Robyn | Robyn PC | $224,900 | 2/15/18 | 4/13/18 | $6,900 | |
| 5 | Jennifer De Mascio | Buyer | 813 W. Reese Ct. | Visalia 93277 | Melissa | Robyn PC | $350,000 | 2/15/18 | 4/13/18 | $6,900 | |
| 6 | Henry Hash | Seller | 644 W. Loyola Ave. | Visalia 93277 | Kari/Robyn | Kari Expired | $249,700 | 2/22/18 | 3/23/18 | $6,250 | |
| 7 | Henrique Guerreiro | Seller | 1000 Belmont | Porterville 93257 | Robyn | Robyn SOI | $205,000 | 2/23/18 | 4/9/18 | $6,150 | |
| 8 | Jessica De Mascio | Seller | 1025 Princeton Ave. | Visalia 93277 | Robyn | Robyn SOI | $219,900 | 3/1/18 | 4/13/18 | $6,810 | Also buying |
| 9 | Gary Garret | Seller | 1331 Laura Ct | Visalia 93292 | Kari | Kari FARM | $389,000 | 3/15/18 | 5/21/18 | $6,900 | Also listing/selling |
| 10 | Gary Garret | Buyer | 381 S Beverly | Porterville 93257 | Kari | Kari FARM | $310,000 | 3/21/18 | 5/1/18 | $5,125 | |
| 11 | Florence Ann Webster | Seller | 2400 W Midvalley | Visalia 93277 | Kari | Kari PC | $885,500 | 9/21/18 | 12/31/19 | $14,000 | |
| 12 | Daniel Snead | Seller | 3145 W Ashland | Visalia 93277 | Kari | Open House | $249,000 | 9/22/18 | 12/31/19 | $7,100 | |
| 13 | Donnie Brandon | Seller | 401 N. Powell | Visalia 93291 | Robyn | Robyn SOI | $814,900 | 3/13/18 | 12/31/19 | $16,200 | |
| 14 | Scott and Kirsten Hyder | Buyer | 131 W Putnam | Porterville 93257 | Kari | Kari PC | $750,000 | 3/27/18 | 5/21/18 | $18,400 | |
| 15 | Samuel Velasquez | Buyer | 893 San Ramon | Visalia 93292 | Melissa | Website | $350,000 | 3/28/18 | 4/26/18 | $8,900 | Melissa's cousin |
| 16 | David & Mel Johnson | Seller | 2822 Border Links | Visalia 93291 | Robyn | Robyn SOI | $750,000 | 2/25/18 | 4/16/18 | $14,750 | |
| 17 | Kimmy Berkley | Seller | 236 Feemster Ct | Visalia 93277 | Robyn | Open House | $550,000 | 2/29/18 | 4/13/18 | $9,550 | |
| 18 | John & Dani Kale | Buyer | 145 Beverly Glen | Visalia 93277 | Kari | Website | $350,000 | 3/1/18 | 4/1/18 | $7,525 | |
| 19 | Mark & Donna Griffel | Seller | 856 N. Fairway | Visalia 93291 | Robyn | Robyn SOI | $655,500 | 3/5/18 | 4/25/18 | $11,500 | |
| 20 | Omar & Katie Vaz | Seller | 435 Keogh Dr. | Visalia 93291 | Robyn | Website | $450,000 | 2/15/18 | 4/6/18 | $7,000 | |
| 21 | Katherine Florentine | Buyer | 231 Park Place | Porterville 93257 | Kari | Kari SOI | $350,000 | 3/13/18 | 5/12/18 | $6,250 | |
| 21 | Larry Burke | Buyer | 259 Hyde Way | Tulare 93234 | Melissa | Melissa SOI | $250,000 | 3/18/18 | 5/2/18 | $6,800 | Tenant's occupying property |
| 22 | Larry Burke | Buyer | 1342 Ames Ct. | Exeter 93221 | Melissa | Melissa SOI | $259,000 | 3/26/18 | 5/14/18 | $7,450 | |

© Copyright Icenhower Coaching & Consulting, LLC. All rights reserved.

# MODULE 13

# APPENDIX 13.9

## WIG – Wildly Important Goals

| Example WIG: $325,000 | Annual | Monthly | Weekly |
|---|---|---|---|
| Number of contracts (@ $7500 GCI each) | 43 | 3.6 | .9 |
| Number of prequalified leads | | | |
| Number of property previews | | | |
| Number of SOI Database contacts: | | | |

**Calculate the effort you need to put in to make YOUR number become a reality.**

WIG: _____

| | Annual | Monthly | Weekly |
|---|---|---|---|
| Number of contracts (@ $7500 GCI each) | | | |
| Number of prequalified leads | | | |
| Number of property previews | | | |
| Number of SOI Database contacts: | | | |

© Copyright Icenhower Coaching & Consulting, LLC. All rights reserved.

# Module 13

## Appendix 13.10

## Production Ratio Planner

### MY CONVERSION RATIOS

1. My gross commission income goal for this year is: _____

2. My average gross commission last year was: _____
   *(divide your last year's gross commission by the number of sides that you closed)*

3. To reach my goal of _____ (#1), I will need to do (#1/#2) transactions this year: _____ transactions

4. Last year, I went on (_) listing appointments: _____ listing appointments

5. Last year, I listed (_) properties: _____ properties

6. Last year I sold (_) listings: _____ listings

7. *(Divide #6 by #4)*
   My closing percentage on listings sold compared to listing appointments taken is:
   *(This helps you calculate how many appointments are needed to reach your goal.)* _____ closing %

8. This year, I want to close on (_) listings: _____ listings

9. *(Divide #8 by #7)*
   **Figuring that my closing % will continue to be _____ % (#7), I will need to go on (_) listing appointments to close on _____ (#8) listings:** _____ listing appointments

10. Last year, I met with (_) potential buyers: _____ potential buyers

11. Last year I worked with (_) buyers: _____ buyers

12. Last year, I sold homes to (_) buyers: _____ Buyers

13. *(Divide #12 by #10)*
    My closing percentage on buyers closed compared to buyers I initially met with is:
    *(This helps you calculate how many buyer appointments are needed to reach your goal.)* _____ closing %

14. This year, I want to sell homes to (_) buyers: _____ buyers

15. *(Divide #14 by #13)*
    **Figuring that my closing % will continue to be _____ % (#13), I will need to go on (_) buyer appointments to sell homes to _____ (#14) buyers:** _____ buyer appointments

*Note: "Last year" refers to the past 12 months*

© Copyright Icenhower Coaching & Consulting, LLC. All rights reserved.

# MODULE 13

# APPENDIX 13.10 CONTINUED

## MY PRODUCTION PLANNING

Now divide #9 (number of listing appointments needed) by the number of months you will work this year & number of weeks you will work this year for listing appointments needed below.

*(Note: there are 12 months & 52 weeks in a year)*

Now divide #15 (number of buyer appointments needed) by number of months you will work this year & number of weeks you will work this year for buyer appointments needed below.

| | | Per Month | | Per Week |
|---|---|---|---|---|
| Listing Appointments: | | Per Month | | Per Week |
| New Buyers: | | Per Month | | Per Week |
| **Total:** | 0 | **Per Month** | 0 | **Per Week** |

**My Gross Income Goal (GIG) for this year (from #1) is:**

_____

**I NEED TO CREATE ____0____ APPOINTMENTS PER WEEK**

**I NEED TO CREATE ____0____ APPOINTMENTS PER MONTH**

© Copyright Icenhower Coaching & Consulting, LLC. All rights reserved.

## HOLDING YOURSELF ACCOUNTABLE

Accountability. Along with mindset and perspective, accountability has probably been the most repeated word in this book next to prospecting and business-generation!

The truth is that you can't have one without the other. You must consistently and regularly hold yourself accountable to your business-generating activities if you want to succeed and exceed your stated goals.

To hold yourself accountable, you must find the motivation to do difficult things. Motivation must come from within, but no man is an island and an accountability advocate can act as a cheerleader as well as a reality-check when you need that extra motivational boost.

*Do or do not. There is no try." – Yoda*

As you know, real estate has a phenomenally high failure rate. 33% of all licensed agents don't make it to their second year in the business, and 87% of agents fail within the first five years.

These agents don't have a plan, don't commit to a regular systematic schedule, and don't prioritize lead-generation over customer-service. In short, though they might be the most wonderful and talented people in the world, they miss the mark by failing to hold themselves accountable to their priorities and responsibilities.

Avoid making the same mistakes by putting accountability on your agenda today.

## Learning Targets

In this chapter you will learn:

- The difference between Accountability and Responsibility.
- The key accountability characteristics of responsible people.
- The difference between Extrinsic and Intrinsic motivation.
- Why you absolutely have to have an Accountability Advocate.

## ACCOUNTABILITY & RESPONSIBILITY

The words 'responsibility' and 'accountability' are often used interchangeably, but while they're on the same spectrum of professionalism and answerability, they actually have slightly different—but important—meanings.

> *"It is not only what we do, but also what we do not do, for which we are accountable."* – Moliere

Imagine that a friend offers you a weekend at their lake house if you'll agree to feed their dogs and take them out for some exercise, make sure that there's gas in the boat before you leave, and let a repairman in on Sunday morning.

Excited for a weekend away, you happily agree to all of these terms, obligations, and conditions. When you arrive at the house on Friday evening, you let the dogs out but you forget to feed them until the next morning. And, on Sunday morning, you have to race back from the lake when you suddenly remember the repairman is coming.

On Sunday evening as you're packing up your car, your friend calls to confirm that the dogs were fed and let out, the boat was gassed up, and the repairman was given access.

You tell your friend that you fed and walked the dogs and the repairman was let in, but you forgot to put gas in the boat and will run down and take care of it now.

Though it's not the end of the world, you feel bad that you forgot to put gas in the boat, and that you were a little sloppy when it came to your other responsibilities, though you did *technically* complete them.

When your friend called and held you accountable, you realized that you hadn't taken true responsibility for the things they had held you responsible for, and you also didn't give them a completely honest account of the things that you did do.

You start to think about what you'd do differently next time: put an alarm on your phone for the dog's mealtimes, confirm an exact time, with the repairman, gas up the boat as soon as you got to the lake Friday evening, and take complete an honest ownership when your friend checks in with you.

This short story contains some of the key differences between responsibility and true accountability.

## WHAT'S THE DIFFERENCE?

The main difference between responsibility and accountability is that:

- Responsibility can be shared while accountability cannot.
- Responsibility can take place before or after a task, while accountability can only take place after a task was due to be completed.

In the example above, your friend is responsible for who *they* entrust and hold responsible to take care of their pets and home, and *you* are responsible for all of the things they have asked you to do.

From the moment your friend called you, and you agreed to take care of the dogs, gas up the boat, and let the repairman in, you were *responsible* for those things in the days leading up to the trip and for the entire weekend. It's not until your friend called you on Sunday night that you were actually *held accountable* for your responsibilities.

In other words:

- Being responsible involves *implementing a response* to designated tasks and activities.
- Being accountable involves *providing an account* or an answer of what did and did not actually happen at the time, or by the time, it was supposed to.

In the absence of accountability, it becomes easier and easier to avoid our responsibilities or create excuses about the lazy and sloppy execution of our tasks and duties.

Knowing that a moment will come when we will be answerable, one way or another, for our actions increases our moment-by-moment commitment to fulfill our responsibilities.

*"Accountability breeds response-ability." – Stephen Covey*

We all *have* responsibilities but we *take* responsibility when we implement actions and systems to ensure that the things we will be held accountable for actually take place.

When holding ourselves accountable, or being held accountable by a coach or partner, we take responsibility and ownership for our actions, we think about what happened and why, we don't tell half truths or twist what happened to make ourselves sound better, and we implement tangible strategies for how we will do things differently—and better—the next time.

## WHAT DOES THIS MEAN FOR ME?

While you are responsible for performing your daily SOI phone calls between 9AM and 11AM, you won't be *held accountable* for those calls until after the appointed time has passed. In the minutes between now and then, you must *take responsibility* and implement actions and systems to ensure that the things you will be held answerable for actually take place.

You are responsible for your business-generating activities each and every day, but if there is no formal and explicit moment of accountability where you provide an account or investigation of your actions, then it will become easier and easier to avoid these tasks and responsibilities on a daily basis.

You must consistently and regularly hold yourself accountable to your business-generating activities if you want to succeed and exceed your stated goals.

Responsibility is shared. You're not responsible if a prospect fails to show up to a scheduled appointment, but you are responsible for following up with them to reschedule, or making up the numbers by making some extra contacts.

> *"Accountability is not simply taking the blame when something goes wrong. It's not a confession. Accountability is about delivering on a commitment. It's responsibility to an outcome, not just a set of tasks. It's taking initiative with thoughtful, strategic follow-through." – Harvard Business Review*

Sometimes, a true emergency will arise during the time you had blocked off for income-producing activities, and sometimes you will have to choose between competing responsibilities.

However, you must still hold yourself accountable to your overall goals. When something prevents you from completing your business-generating activities on a given day, you cannot adopt the mindset that you had to something else *instead*. Rather, you have to do something else *as well*.

You must always take responsibility and hold yourself accountable for any lost hours of activity. When something comes up, you erase your time block for that day, but you extend your time blocks an hour each on the next two days. Being held accountable means that you cannot delete your responsibilities. Never erase your tasks or appointments without replacing them somewhere else in your schedule.

> *You must always take responsibility and hold yourself accountable for any lost hours of activity.*

Naturally, there will be moments where you technically fulfill your responsibilities or check off a task on your list, but you don't do it to the high standards you expect from yourself.

When you reply to a client's email, you are fulfilling one your customer-service responsibilities to respond to calls and messages in a timely manner, but if you respond with a rude and dismissive tone then you are probably not holding yourself accountable to your manners and attitude, and the way you want to communicate with others.

Accountability involves taking responsibility for our mindset, attitude and **the way that we do things** by implementing strategies for how we will do things differently—and better—tomorrow, and the day after that.

## 12 Characteristics of Accountability

Do you possess the qualities and characteristics of accountability? The chart is available in the Appendix.

**01 I BUY IT & OWN IT.**
I accept responsibility for the successful completion of the task at hand. I take ownership and accept the blame as well as the credit.

**02 IT'S A TEAM EFFORT.**
I have an external network or an in-house team for support, quality management, and timely delivery.

**03 I SET THE STAGE.**
I put myself in an environment where making progress & tracking progress are a way of life.

**04 I HAVE X-RAY VISION.**
I deliver a thorough needs-assessment to get clear on details, processes, gaps, and expectations.

**05 I MEET THE MARK.**
I have the ability to complete the tasks that reach the goal: skills, schedule, and stamina.

**06 I GPS.**
I set a schedule of frequent and effective feedback sessions. I don't just perform the activity: I track and monitor and elicit feedback for constant improvement.

**07 I BEAT THE CLOCK.**
I reach my goals on time and show up to activities on time. I use a calendar, stick to a schedule, and prioritize my time.

**08 I'M HACK FREE.**
I pursue processes in such a way that they're not leaving excessive carnage in their wake as I do it. No cheating and no cutting corners.

**09 I DO IT NO MATTER WHAT.**
I have the resourcefulness to overcome unforeseen obstacles. I'm empowered to not be risk-averse and get the job done no matter what.

**10 I BUY IT & OWN IT.**
My values are building & maintaining trust and reputation. I improve my conversion ratios by being accountable to building respect and rapport.

**11 I'VE BEEN THERE DONE THAT.**
I'm constantly referencing and recalling my track record of setting, reaching and exceeding goals to increase my motivation.

**12 I'VE BURNED MY SHIPS.**
I remember the reference to the Spanish conqueror, Cortés, who burned his ships when he reached Aztec shores to show that he was committed and there would be no turning back. When I hold myself accountable, I know that my ships are burned, and I am all in.

## Your Accountability Agenda

Throughout this book we have presented you with a wealth of time-management and scheduling strategies that will kick-start and elevate your prospecting career. At this point, you have all the sample calendars and lead-tracking sheets and forms you could ask for. All that's left for you to do is to put accountability as well as activity on your prospecting agenda.

Responsibility and accountability is a constant and continual process. In the days, weeks, and months ahead, you will need to both hold yourself accountable and participate in a system where you allow yourself to be held accountable by another person or persons.

**Responsibility** involves *implementing a response* to designated tasks and activities and following through on a daily and weekly basis. Responsibility can take place before, during or after a task.

Taking responsibility includes (among many other things):

- Managing your goals by managing your time.
- Committing to a regular and systematic schedule.
- Giving each task your undivided attention, from script practice to your daily SOI calls, and systematic lead follow-up.
- Maintaining a consistently positive perspective.
- Starting each day with a motivational recitation.
- Writing down your goals and breaking goals into manageable, actionable milestones.
- Scheduling and setting reminders for regular accountability sessions.

**Accountability** involves *providing an account* or an answer of what did and did not actually happen at the time, or by the time, it was supposed to. Accountability is the moment of truth. Accountability can only take place after a task was due to be completed.

Holding yourself accountable (or being held accountable by someone else) includes:

- Tracking and monitoring your actual business-generating activities.
- Calculating your results and numbers using accurate, precise and valid information.
- Reporting real data in an agreed-upon format.
- Analyzing, evaluating, and interrogating your data.
- Discussing data and outcomes, and answering tough questions to help you find solutions when something isn't working.
- Revaluating your existing schedule and implementing better systems when needed.
- Acknowledging that you allowed yourself to be interrupted and implementing tactics to prevent future occurrences.
- Reviewing your goals and regularly determining if milestones are actually being met.

# SCHEDULE ACCOUNTABILITY SESSIONS

You must consistently and regularly hold yourself accountable to your business-generating activities if you want to succeed and exceed your stated goals.

Depending on your particular accountability agenda, you might personally hold yourself accountable at the end of each day or working week, and have someone else hold you accountable at additional and regular points in between. We'll take a look at who that "someone else" might be in just a moment.

How often you plan to be held accountable by someone else can exponentially grow your productivity and your learning curve. Knowing that a moment is coming when you will be answerable for your actions will increase your moment-by-moment commitment to fulfill your responsibilities. The more often you are held accountable by another person the better!

Accountability advocate sessions can happen in person, over the telephone, via email, or a combination of both. What's important is that you actually report on and answer for your activities.

If you're brand new to being held accountable, it's a good idea to schedule a daily check-in to create a consistent habit and frequently reinforce your sense of responsibility.

Notice that a personal accountability session occurs at the end of each day, as well as a more formal accountability appointment and a reminder to submit an accountability agenda to your advocate and coach.

Your exact schedule will depend on you and your advocate's availability, but we find that it is very satisfying to email your reports at the end of each week, and then start each new week by reflecting on what happened the week before.

| Time | Monday | Tuesday | Wednesday | Thursday | Friday |
|---|---|---|---|---|---|
| 9AM-12PM | Business Generation Activities (SOI/Expired) | Business Generation Activities (SOI/Expired) | Business Generation Activities (SOI/Expired) | Business Generation Activities (SOI/Expired) | Business Generation Activities (SOI/Expired) |
| 12PM-1PM | Lead Follow-Up | Lead Follow-Up | Lead Follow-Up | Lead Follow-Up | Lead Follow-Up |
| 1PM-2PM | Accountability Advocate Appointment | Lunch | Lunch | Lunch | Lunch |
| 3PM-5PM | Business Generation Activities (Property Previews/FSBOs) | Business Generation Activities (Property Previews/FSBOs) | Business Generation Activities (Property Previews/FSBOs) | Business Generation Activities (Property Previews/FSBOs) | Business Generation Activities (Property Previews/FSBOs) |
| 6PM | All Paperwork/Tracking Forms Completed? | All Paperwork/Tracking Forms Completed? | All Paperwork/Tracking Forms Completed? | All Paperwork/Tracking Forms Completed? | All Paperwork/Tracking Forms Completed? |
| 7PM | | | | | Email Accountability Agenda to coach@aol.com |

## Prepare To Account For Yourself

The quality of your accountability meetings will depend on the system you implement to make sure you're getting the most out of your appointments. For example, you may decide to do the following:

- Deliver reports before the meeting so everyone can review and digest the information in advance.
- Anticipate questions and prepare answers—be purposeful not reactionary.
- Develop an agenda to ensure the best use of everyone's time—articulate what you want to achieve from your sessions and follow the agreed-upon system.
- Circle back to previous accountability meetings—report on progress and improvements that have happened since the last meeting/session.

## What's Not On Your Accountability Agenda

As a real estate agent, you have a lot of tasks to complete, and your daily and weekly schedule should be pretty jam-packed. There is no time or place in your busy agenda for complaints and excuses.

## No Excuses!

It's tempting to complain about the way things are, especially if you are not meeting your targets and converting prospects into transactions. Every day, we hear agents repeating the same excuses to explain why business isn't going well:

- "Sales aren't what they should be."
- "The real estate scripts are too complicated to memorize."
- "No one picks up their phone anymore."
- "No one wants to talk to you when you knock on doors during your property previews."
- "I didn't sign up for THIS!"

Like Zig Ziglar said, "Some people find fault like there's a reward for it." But complaints and excuses are not going to increase your business or reward you with a commission any time soon.

## Most Excuses are Missing One Thing....

Did you notice the problem with each of these excuses?

- *Sales* aren't what they should be.
- *The real estate scripts* are too complicated to memorize.
- *No one* wants to talk to you when you knock on doors during your property previews.

According to these statements, the problem lies with sales, the real estate scripts, and even the prospects themselves. Essentially, the problem is anyone or anything except the real estate agent.

Negative generalizations like these can derail a real estate agent's career, and diminish self-confidence. Real estate agents have more control over their outcomes than most people who are employed in sales, or even in other professions for that matter. An agent determines his or her schedule as well as which contacts are likely prospects. You have *complete* say in what you will and will not do every day you choose to work.

*"Some people find fault like there's a reward for it." -Zig Ziglar*

Bringing these types of statements to an accountability session means you're in the wrong place. These statements belong to someone who hasn't accepted responsibility and its terms, and is refusing ownership of results and outcomes.

Avoiding responsibility and accountability is a disease of the mindset and, left unchecked, can be terminal to your relationships and your career. Reformulate negative thought-processes into proactive and productive accountability statements:

| *Venting, Ranting, Complaining* | *Being Responsible & Accountable* |
|---|---|
| "Sales aren't what they should be." | Zero sales, 20 hours prospecting, zero appointments: The results, I'm realizing, are lower than my expectations. Is my activity level or skill level where it needs to be to deliver my goals? |
| "The real estate scripts are too complicated to memorize." | Based on the time amount (X) and process I've used to memorize scripts, I'm not where I want to be, yet. |
| "No one picks up their phone anymore." | From the X calls I made this week, I'm at a 15% connection rate; I'm curious to learn different strategies to increase the pick up rate. |
| "No one wants to talk to you when you knock on doors during property previews." | From the X doors knocked this week during previews, only Y were open to responding to the dialogue I've prepared. Can we address the script, time of day, and process I'm using to increase my success? |
| "I didn't sign up for this!" | I'm discovering that the process & results are different than what I understood & prepared for, specifically the time needed, and presentation skills; can we clarify & recommit on this? |

What's the difference here? Real numbers. Ownership. Reflection. Honesty. Looking for solutions and help. The phrases on the left are cul-de-sacs: they're going nowhere.

Generalizations don't include numbers, because numbers make things real. Real numbers offer proof of tracking—honestly, and with a level of intention. Looking for solutions shows that you're still committed to delivery, and open to feedback based on where you are now. You're being resourceful by asking for help, and using a network of people around you to increase the odds that what you're doing is the best way, not just the best way you know how.

## Your Accountability Advocate

Self-motivation may get you started in real estate, but when it comes to maintaining that motivation and continually increasing your momentum, we cannot stress the importance of an accountability advocate enough.

Having an accountability partner is crucial for keeping you on track with achieving the goals and results that you set for yourself. So who is your accountability advocate, and what characteristics should you look for in an accountability partner?

An accountability advocate could be another agent in your industry or a trusted friend or family member. Whoever they are, they should be:

- Reliable
- Available
- Honest
- Trustworthy
- Encouraging
- Challenging
- Constructive
- Objective
- Non-judgmental
- Candid
- Committed

An accountability partner is not a mentor, a taskmaster, a trainer, or your tutor. It's not your accountability advocate's job to tell you what to do.

Essentially, you invite your accountability advocate to sit co-pilot, check your trajectory compared to where you tell them you want to go.

An accountability partner can point out the gaps, make suggestions, point out potential pitfalls, collaborate on a plan, and set some deadlines—but only you can take responsibility for following through.

Your accountability advocate will help you own up to the truth about your work habits on some glaring red flags or disconnects. However, they may be limited by a couple of things:

- Their experience
- Their training & education
- Their relationship to you

### The Case For Paying For A Professional Coach Or Accountability Partner

While there is no one-size-fits-all approach when it comes to who your accountability advocate should be, the majority of top-producing agents in North America do employ the services of a coach or professional accountability partner.

Whether it's a personal trainer at the gym or a tailor-made suit, when you invest a significant amount of money in something, you're more likely to use it more often, take better care of it or treat it more seriously, and ensure that you get a good return on your investment.

While anyone you trust can be your accountability partner, you are statistically more likely to show up and commit to increasing your business activities and reporting your results if you have some sort of skin in the game.

A paid coach will provide you with a level of honesty and candid feedback that a friend or family member might not if they're worried about hurting your feelings. Likewise, you are more likely to provide an honest account of your activities and results to a neutral third-party than to someone you're afraid of disappointing.

While your accountability advocate should act as your cheerleader and offer you a great deal of encouragement and support, as a professional they will also challenge you and highlight your blind spots in ways that a friend or family member may not equipped to do. If your accountability coach has a background in the business, they have valuable insights and experiences that other people may not.

## EXERCISE: My Accountability Advocate

Select Your Accountability Advocate. On the left side of a piece of paper, write 10-15 adjectives describing what characteristics your ideal advocate would have.

On the right side, list the names of people who meet some or all of these characteristics. Determine how many characteristics each person has, and weigh up the pros and cons of your potential advocates. Those with the highest numbers of crucial characteristics (and more pros than cons) are the people you will approach about being your accountability advocate.

### THE 4 KEY ACCOUNTABILITY QUESTIONS

Once you identify your accountability advocate(s), it's up to you to train them how to help you if they don't have previous experience.

Fortunately, this person has only two tasks:

1. Ask the *Four Key Accountability Questions*
2. Listen

The Four Key Accountability Questions are:

1. How do you think you did?
2. What got in the way?
3. What do you need to do differently next week?
4. Is there any way we can help?

Notice that the questions are open-ended and reflective in nature. Your accountability partner is asking the questions, but you are doing the important work of looking within yourself for honest answers.

At every meeting, your accountability advocate will ask these four questions the same way each time. Before long, you will have memorized the questions, and can use these inquiries to 'self-coach' and guide you through your working week.

### How do you think you did?

As harsh as it may seem, either you met your stated targets or you didn't, and a good accountability partner will hold you to rigorous expectations no matter what. If your goal was to make 10 new SOI contacts, then anything short of that needs to be addressed.

However, your accountability advocate is not there to pass judgment on your effectiveness. Only you can do that. By asking how *you* think you did, your accountability advocate can get some perspective and context on your results.

**For example:**

> You might say: "You know what? I think I did pretty well. I got 8 contacts despite the fact that my uncle died and I was out of town at the funeral last week. I came into the office late on Friday and managed to get 8 contacts completed before 5PM."

Having said that, while a good accountability advocate will listen to your answers, they will still hold you accountable to make up for those lost hours and missing contacts when they check in with you the next week.

Being firm and holding a strong cadence of accountability right from the start will prevent a downward spiral.

### What got in the way?

This question makes you identify the obstacles that prevented you from meeting your goals. Again, notice there is no judgment and no negativity in the question.

Your accountability advocate is simply prompting you to reflect and self-identify whatever the challenge might be:

"I took two days off because I had the flu" and "I watched kitten videos" are both obstacles preventing you from meeting your prospecting goals.

So are these:

- I spent half a day making folders.
- The paper in the printer ran out before I could make presentation materials, so I had to go to the store.
- I doubled my phone contacts this week because there were no new properties listed in my areas.

Only you can decide whether the time you spent on an activity was worthwhile.

### WHAT DO YOU NEED TO DO DIFFERENTLY NEXT WEEK?

This question asks you to solve your own problems and decide your next course of action. Or in other words, you need to overcome your own objections!

Responsibility and accountability mean stepping up and taking control of your destiny, even if you're only taking small steps at first, like planning next week.

The word 'differently' implies that you can't use the same excuse and solution twice. If you fail a second time, you'll need to try something new.

### IS THERE ANY WAY WE CAN HELP?

There's a saying that when the universe knows what you're seeking, everything contrives to make it happen.

If no one knows your goals, you'll find it much harder to do them on your own.

When you need help, don't be ashamed or afraid to ask for it.

## ACCOUNTABILITY & MOTIVATION

In case you haven't realized, simply picking up this book was an act of taking responsibility and the first step towards achieving your goal of becoming a real estate prospector.

But what was the motivation behind that? Perhaps you wanted proven strategies that would increase your income and provide a path to a better quality of life.

If so, you are reading and studying ICC's material in order to gain external reinforcement (increased income), which means that your actions or behavior are *extrinsically motivated*. There's nothing at all wrong with that!

**Extrinsic Motivation** happens when we perform a behavior or engage in an activity in order to gain a reward or to avoid a punishment or something unpleasant.

Examples of extrinsic motivation are:

- Studying Biology to get an A in a test.
- Working out to reach a target weight.
- Cleaning your bedroom to avoid getting in trouble with your parents.

If, on the other hand, you picked up this book because you were simply interested in learning about prospecting and curious how real estate relates to mindset, time-management, and various aspects of human behavior, then that would be an example of *intrinsic motivation*.

**Intrinsic Motivation** happens when we engage in an activity because it is enjoyable or personally rewarding. Essentially, we do something for its own sake, rather than for an external factor.

Examples of intrinsic motivation are:

- Studying Biology because you are fascinated by plant and animal life and want to learn more about it.
- Working out because it's fun and you enjoy being physically active.
- Cleaning your bedroom because you personally like things to be tidy and organized.

### Which Motivation Is Best? Both!

To hold yourself accountable to your business-generating activities, you must find the motivation to do difficult things and push through discomfort on a daily basis. As we've said before, there is a lot of rejection in real estate, and you won't always enjoy or be completely comfortable with the activities you need to perform. Our advice is to take a two-pronged approach and tap into both extrinsic and intrinsic motivation.

Much of the time, your motivation will be boosted by external factors like the promise of a paycheck or a reward for reaching a specific goal. Another example of extrinsic motivation is accountability. Knowing that you will be held accountable and have to answer for your actions and inactions is a powerful motivator!

Extrinsic motivation can be extremely effective, but it can also take an emotional and physical toll if you absolutely hate the activity and are only doing it because you want the commission or to avoid an uncomfortable meeting with your coach or accountability advocate. Eventually, the business will wear on you to the point that it impacts your ability to lead-generate, which in turn will lead to reduced commissions and a failing business.

Extrinsic motivation is not sustainable in isolation or over long periods of time. It's very important that you actively seek out ways to find intrinsic motivation and frame your chosen career in a positive light. Yes, real estate offers real financial rewards, but prospecting is only sustainable over the long term if it's also personally rewarding and something you enjoy doing for its own sake.

Intrinsic motivation can be cultivated by taking pride in your profession and coming from a place of contribution and helping people. Those who feel that they are adding value and working for the greater good find it easier to persevere and stay motivated. Tap into intrinsic motivation by rethinking what the word 'reward' means to you.

When your work is its own reward and you genuinely enjoy the process of helping people achieve their real estate and financial dreams then it's far easier to stay motivated and hold yourself accountable to your own dreams and goals.

### Summary

You must consistently and regularly hold yourself accountable to your business-generating activities if you want to succeed and exceed your stated goals.

Being responsible involves *implementing a response* to designated tasks and activities. Being accountable involves *providing an account* or an answer of what did and did not actually happen at the time, or by the time, it was supposed to.

In the absence of accountability, it becomes easier and easier to avoid our responsibilities or create excuses about the lazy and sloppy execution of our tasks and duties. There is no room for excuses on your accountability agenda!

Knowing that a moment will come when we will be answerable, one way or another, for our actions increases our moment-by-moment commitment to fulfill our responsibilities.

Self-motivation may get you started in real estate, but when it comes to maintaining that motivation and continually increasing your momentum, we cannot stress the importance of an accountability advocate enough.

While there is no one-size-fits-all approach when it comes to who your accountability advocate should be, the majority of top-producing agents in North America do employ the services of a coach or professional accountability partner.

A good accountability partner will prompt self-reflection, self-discovery and self-made solutions by asking the 4 Key Accountability Questions:

1. How do you think you did?
2. What got in the way?
3. What do you need to do differently next week?
4. Is there any way we can help?

At ICC, our sincerest wish is to see you succeed and thrive in your chosen profession, and we encourage you to use every technique, tool and strategy at your disposal. Cultivate intrinsic motivation as well as extrinsic motivation, and don't think for a second that you have to do this alone. We've got your back and are always happy to help!

# MODULE 14

# APPENDIX 14.1

## 12 CHARACTERISTICS OF ACCOUNTABILITY

**01 · I BUY IT & OWN IT.**
I accept responsibility for the successful completion of the task at hand. I take ownership and accept the blame as well as the credit.

**02 · IT'S A TEAM EFFORT.**
I have an external network or an in-house team for support, quality management, and timely delivery.

**03 · I SET THE STAGE.**
I put myself in an environment where making progress & tracking progress are a way of life.

**04 · I HAVE X-RAY VISION.**
I deliver a thorough needs-assessment to get clear on details, processes, gaps, and expectations.

**05 · I MEET THE MARK.**
I have the ability to complete the tasks that reach the goal: skills, schedule, and stamina.

**06 · I GPS.**
I set a schedule of frequent and effective feedback sessions. I don't just perform the activity: I track and monitor and elicit feedback for constant improvement.

**07 · I BEAT THE CLOCK.**
I reach my goals on time and show up to activities on time. I use a calendar, stick to a schedule, and prioritize my time.

**08 · I'M HACK FREE.**
I pursue processes in such a way that they're not leaving excessive carnage in their wake as I do it. No cheating and no cutting corners.

**09 · I DO IT NO MATTER WHAT.**
I have the resourcefulness to overcome unforeseen obstacles. I'm empowered to not be risk-averse and get the job done no matter what.

**10 · I BUY IT & OWN IT.**
My values are building & maintaining trust and reputation. I improve my conversion ratios by being accountable to building respect and rapport.

**11 · I'VE BEEN THERE DONE THAT.**
I'm constantly referencing and recalling my track record of setting, reaching and exceeding goals to increase my motivation.

**12 · I'VE BURNED MY SHIPS.**
I remember the reference to the Spanish conqueror, Cortés, who burned his ships when he reached Aztec shores to show that he was committed and there would be no turning back. When I hold myself accountable, I know that my ships are burned, and I am all in.

© Copyright Icenhower Coaching & Consulting, LLC. All rights reserved.

## Next Level Commitment

Congratulations! You've made it to the end of *Prospect—The Lead Generation Manual*.

As we said way back in the beginning, we assumed you picked up this book because you were at a turning point in your life and your career. We pictured someone fresh out of school that was drawn to selling real estate, but didn't quite know where to begin. We also pictured someone who had been prospecting for some time with little success and was seeking a better, and proven, alternative.

We promised you the only prospecting plan you would ever need, and we trust you agree that we've delivered it—and that you are well on your way to a long and lucrative career in real estate.

In the past few hundred pages, you have learned:

- Discovered truths about prospecting—what it really is, and why it works.
- How to implement the techniques proven to boost sales.
- How to recreate the framework to do it again, and again, and again.

Specifically, we have taught you everything you need to know about the following prospecting methods:

- Prospecting for Expired and Cancelled Listings
- Prospecting through Open Houses
- Property Previews
- Prospecting For Sale By Owners (FSBOs)
- Circle Prospecting
- Generating business through your SOI Referral Database

Not to mention the techniques, tools and strategies necessary to secure your success:

- Memorizing and internalizing scripts.
- Time-management and honoring your schedule.
- Staging your prospecting arena for success, whether you generate business from your home office or a cubicle.
- Tracking numbers and lead-generation activity for motivation, accountability, and diagnosis.
- Holding yourself accountable and removing excuses from your vocabulary.
- Maintaining a proper mindset, attitude, and perspective to fuel and reenergize you through the inevitable setbacks and rejections that lay before you.

Chances are that some of you sat down and read this book from cover to cover in a single sitting. That's awesome—it's great to be prepared and know as much as possible in advance, but remember that you are just starting out and you still have a lot to practice, learn, and hone. Before you can go above and beyond in your prospecting career, you must first master everything we have taught you so far.

Much of this final chapter is designed for whenever you are ready to take your prospecting career to the next level—that is, to further improve and develop a career that is already successful.

For example, later in the chapter, we will discuss the next steps for agents who have reached a level of success and productivity that it's now time to consider hiring administrative help and support. We will also explore how to set longer-term goals and plan ahead for the next 18 months to 5 years while managing a growing budget.

However, much of this chapter applies to all prospectors at any stage in their career. It's never too early to make a next level commitment to prioritize your mindset and personal development. It's far better (not to mention easier) to recognize and remedy physical and mental burnout before it happens, so please read on and make sure that you don't skip over anything just because you're still in the early stages of your real estate journey.

## Learning Targets

In this chapter you will learn:

- The importance of practicing emotional hygiene, reframing negative thoughts, and taking care of your business by taking care of yourself.
- How to double your salary and diversify your business-generation activities.
- The importance of creating annual and long-term goals.
- What to consider when it's time to hire administrative help and support.
- How to evaluate and understand a Real Estate Team Production Growth Budget Schedule.

You've come so far, and are so close to finishing, but remember that reaching the end of this book is just the beginning of the challenging and exciting career ahead of you. Prospecting is a marathon, not a race, so make sure you set a healthy pace from the outset and maintain the mental and physical energy you will need to go the distance.

# Emotional Hygiene

When most people think of the word 'hygiene', they think of washing their hands or taking a shower, but hygiene is a much broader concept. The word hygiene comes from the old Greek *hugieinē tekhnē* meaning 'art of health' and, much like the art of closing, good hygiene is not a one-time activity or isolated skill; rather, it is a continual part of a seamless process or set of practices designed to prevent disease and preserve health.

In the same way that dental hygiene involves a set of daily and yearly practices—brushing and flossing every morning and night, and visiting the dentist every six months to prevent cavities and other serious problems—emotional hygiene refers to being mindful of, and attentive to, our psychological health, and is something we all need to practice each and every day to prevent bigger problems and pain points over time.

## Reframing Negative Thoughts

One of the best ways to practice good emotional hygiene is by attending to our thoughts. Human beings have thousands of involuntary and habitual thoughts a day—more than half of them negative and repetitive. Most of us experience a somewhat constant inner conversation or inner monologue—what is known as 'mental noise' or 'mental chatter' that never seems to stop.

While mental noise is universal and somewhat normal, the long-term effects of repetitive negative thoughts can be devastating. Numerous studies have shown a detrimental relationship between negative words and thoughts and our physical health. Ruminating and dwelling on negative thoughts increases our physical and chemical stress responses to the point where it can actually put us at an increased risk for chronic headaches, forgetfulness, difficulty breathing and cardiovascular disease.

**Cognitive Reframing** is a next level commitment to maintaining a positive mindset.

Reframing is a process of recognizing and identifying—and then disputing, disrupting, and re-describing—negative thoughts. Reframing is a way of looking at and talking about experiences, events and emotions to find more positive, productive, and effective alternatives.

---

*Reframing is a way of looking at and talking about experiences, events and emotions to find more positive, productive, and effective alternatives.*

---

For example, in the previous chapter we discussed the importance of finding intrinsic motivation in your work. Rather than focusing completely on external factors like your commission income, you can cultivate intrinsic motivation by *reframing the purpose* of your profession—to help people and find solutions to their wants and needs.

A negative mindset tends to think and speak in black-and-white, all-or-nothing, absolutist terms:

- "I'm never going to learn these scripts."
- "I always mess up at learning presentations."

- "All buyers are liars. All sellers are stubborn."
- "New licensees are idiots—they don't know anything!"

Reframing involves interrupting yourself in the middle of a negative thought and interrogating the accuracy and usefulness of the thought by asking the following questions:

**Is this thought true?** Is this thought based on an objective fact or hard data, or am I making an assumption or negative generalization? Am I leaping to conclusions? Are the words 'always' and 'never' factual and true, or am I overstating? Am I allowing one moment, person, or experience to cloud my judgment and taint my overall perspective?

**Is this thought constructive?** Will this type of thinking do anything concrete to change my current situation or make it actively better? Will this type of thinking achieve any tangible benefit, outcome, or positive result?

If the answer is "No" to any of the above questions, you have an opportunity to reframe your language and perspective towards truth, positivity, and productivity.

*"My life has been filled with terrible misfortunes, most of which have never happened." – Mark Twain*

Reframing involves replacing negative words and thoughts with neutral, factual, or positive expressions and statements.

"Frustrated" becomes "Fascinated". "Overwhelmed" becomes "Ready to Regroup". "Nervous" becomes "Excited". "I Guess So…" becomes "Sounds Good, Can't Wait!"

Another example of reframing is choosing to see something as a *challenge* or *opportunity* instead of a *problem*.

- Instead of "I'm never going to learn these scripts," try thinking: "I'm finding this script difficult to memorize. This is a great opportunity to reconnect with my prospecting role-play partner and brush up on our objection handling skills together."
- Instead of "All buyers are liars," try thinking: "It was hurtful and frustrating when that one buyer went directly to the builder to buy a home. From now on, I'm going to commit 100% to closing Buyer Agency Agreements with all my buyer leads."

Reinterpreting and re-describing our experiences and situation results in a changed and brighter reality, and is so much more constructive and empowering.

## EXERCISE: Set A Reframe Reminder

Set your phone to periodically remind you to stop what you are doing, look around, and note 5 positive things about the present moment. Chances are your phone will chime right in the middle of a negative thought and helpfully disrupt it! Soon, you will develop a habit of redirecting your negative thoughts back into the realm of positivity and productivity.

With your script expertise well underway, cognitive reframing is a skill you're more than ready to take on. Understanding how to use reframing with your own thoughts will help you in your business. A simple reframe can save the conversation, the sale, or the client relationship, and redirect the process in a more helpful and productive manner. When taking care of your own thoughts you're taking care of business. There is no separation between your personal health and the health of your prospecting career.

## Take Care, Then Take Care Of Business

It's well known, and often quoted, that you cannot pour from an empty cup. Oftentimes, new and enthusiastic agents will work up to 80 hours a week trying to generate leads and kick-start their new business, with the result that they dangerously deplete their physical and mental reserves.

While it's true that you will need to work longer and harder in the beginning stages of your prospecting career, and there will be moments of personal sacrifice and burning the midnight oil, if you're completely rundown and burnt out from a relentless schedule then your business will eventually stagnate and suffer.

Chronically low energy and high stress levels will ultimately prevent you from generating business, staying on target, and achieving your goals. You must maintain a balanced life because you are your own business—you are your own machine, and if your machine breaks down, so too will your livelihood and your career.

> *While it's true that you will need to work longer and harder in the beginning stages of your prospecting career, and there will be moments of personal sacrifice and burning the midnight oil, if you're completely rundown and burnt out from a relentless schedule then your business will eventually stagnate and suffer.*

Exhaustion repels rather than attracts. You might hear remarks like:

"You're so busy!"

"Seems like you're burning the candle at both ends!"

"Let's catch up when you have more time!"

You could be missing the underlying message of:

"You need help because you're taking on too much and it shows."

"Seems like you're overloaded, and work hours are pouring over."

"I'm going to wait to ask for help or send you business; I don't want to put one more thing on your plate."

Sometimes you'll hear these sentiments from other people, and other times you'll confess them to yourself. These are warning signs that you are struggling and your stress and visible exhaustion is negatively impacting your business. Pay attention to the signs and what your body and those around you are trying to tell you.

## Make Less More

It's especially important to create a better work-life balance if you're working a 70-hour week to sell 25 houses a year. Nobody needs 70 hours a week to sell 0.5 houses and service 0.5 clients. At some point, you will need to dial your working week way back and get used to achieving the *same results* and the *same service-levels* in a regular 40-hour week. Don't lose your life and personal relationships to unproductive and needless 'busy work'.

Cultivate the habit of checking how full your cup really is. Check your personal energy level battery as often as you check your smartphone's battery! Once that battery runs out, all those fantastic features don't mean a thing: it just takes longer to reboot, and you may lose some of your work.

Find the right balance between work and leisure for your life. While the job is paramount, so is your health, and health is a *multiplier* of talent.

Every year UCLA basketball coach, John Wooden, taught his nationally ranked basketball team the importance of proper foot hygiene and the art of putting on their shoes and socks—double-tying their laces and meticulously smoothing out every single wrinkle in their socks, from toe to heel to ankle. Blisters and athlete's foot have nothing to do with innate, raw talent, but they can take you out of commission just the same!

Likewise, you could be the most naturally talented prospector in the world, but you will still need to proactively and preventatively keep on top on your health to keep you in commissions.

- When you created your calendar for the year, did you schedule visits to your doctor, dentist, chiropractor, or massage therapist etc.?

- How often are you exercising and working out or practicing some sort of meditation or mindfulness techniques?

- Are you wolfing down junk food in your car between appointments, or are you eating healthy, nutritious, and energizing foods that will increase your stamina and vitality.

When your personal cup is full it will flow over into every other aspect of your life. By prioritizing your physical and mental health, you will increase your energy and endurance levels and find that you are able to prospect with more accuracy, efficiency, focus, and effectiveness and achieve better results in less time!

## Personal Development IS Professional Development

The time, energy, and effort you invest in yourself will return to you professionally as well as personally.

As we begin to wrap up and move towards the end of this book, we encourage you to take some time to look back and reflect on everything that you have learned so far, and the many ways that you have already grown and developed.

At the same time, as you go above and beyond in your prospecting career, we encourage you to maintain a future-oriented, growth-mindset, and continually focus on your personal and professional development.

No matter how busy you get in the day-to-day-operations of your business, you must always carve out time in your schedule for professional and personal growth.

To maintain your real estate license in the state(s) where you operate, you will need to participate in defined amounts of Continuing Education (CE) each year. Though somewhat time-consuming, practice maintaining a positive mindset about CE requirements and view it as an opportunity to network, stay abreast of new trends, and find ways to improve and enhance your business.

Some of the professional development opportunities you explore will be directly related to the real estate business. For example, joining a Toastmasters Club could help you with public speaking. You may also wish to strengthen your writing skills, learn more about digital marketing and social media, or study DISC behavioral profiles in-depth to improve your communication and sales performance.

However, remember the importance of cultivating *intrinsic* motivation as well as *extrinsic* motivation. Gravitate towards the hobbies, clubs, organizations, and pursuits that you are genuinely interested in. If you've always wanted to learn a new language or join a sailing club, then you should feel free to do so purely out of curiosity and personal passion.

The knowledge, insight, and connections you gain from the pursuit of things you love will return to you in unexpected ways. There's a real estate agent in Oregon who has grown a loyal, large, and steady client base over the past 20 years through her knitting and fiber arts community. Her main focus was on yarn and learning a craft. Growing her real estate business through a passionate community was an unintended but happy outcome. Real estate is about making connections and there are infinite ways that you can authentically connect your personal passions to your professional life.

## EXERCISE: Personal Development Brainstorm

Set a timer for 10 minutes and block out all distractions. In the first 3 minutes, write down as many answers to the following questions that you can think of:

> *Outside of prospecting, what am I most passionate about and interested in? What hobbies, interests and pursuits have I neglected over the years that I would love to tap back into?*

In the next 3 minutes, review the words and phrases that you wrote down, and rank your level of excitement, curiosity, and interest in each of them from 1-5 (1 being the most exciting to you and 5 being the least exciting to you).

With your remaining time, select the thing that is most exciting and interesting to you, and write down 3 concrete ways that you will make time for this personal pursuit this week, this month, or this year.

Ideally, your passions and interests would connect you to a broader community and network of possible prospects, but make sure to be guided by your curiosity and the things that genuinely captivate and interest you. When you come from a place of authenticity, your personal passions will find a way of connecting to your professional life.

## SHARPENING YOUR SKILLS: TO WHAT END?

Sharpening your skills requires more than learning the latest in real estate law or current interest rates on real property. By increasing your skill level, you will be more likely to persuade buyers to close a deal.

You need to improve your prospecting skills, so you can be at your best. That takes continuous practice based on the feedback you receive.

### EXERCISE TABLE: What Skills?

Take a moment to review the table below. The top bar categorizes five different areas that are crucial for prospecting success: Pipeline Development, Building Relationships, Sales Development, Winning the Business, and Sales Management. Within each of those categories are some related skillsets.

On a scale of 1-5, rank your confidence and expertise when it comes to the listed skills. For any skillset that you rate as a one or zero, pay close attention and hone in on that in your 18-month plan and start improving and moving those scores to five as fast as humanly possible.

| Pipeline Development | Building Relationships | Sales Development | Winning the Business | Sales Management |
|---|---|---|---|---|
| Market Intelligence RANK: _____ | Breaking the Ice RANK: _____ | Understanding the Decision-Making Process RANK: _____ | High Impact Presentations RANK: _____ | Interlocking prospect for long term commitment RANK: _____ |
| Target Qualification RANK: _____ | Creating Credibility RANK: _____ | Creating Reasons for Prospect to Switch Agents RANK: _____ | Negotiating RANK: _____ | Asking for Referrals & Recommendations RANK: _____ |
| Reverse Planning RANK: _____ | High Value Questioning, Probing, Listening RANK: _____ | Linking your Solutions to Prospect's Needs RANK: _____ | Overcoming Objections RANK: _____ | Sustainable Relationships RANK: _____ |
| Appointment Making RANK: _____ | Identifying Prospect's Unique Wants & Needs RANK: _____ | Leveraging Relationships RANK: _____ | Closing RANK: _____ | Next Step Clarification RANK: _____ |
| Sales Meeting & Plan Objectives RANK: _____ | Qualifying Opportunities & Consequences RANK: _____ | Excellent grasp of core values of your business and services RANK: _____ | Use of Trial Closes RANK: _____ | Efficient communication systems RANK: _____ |
| Your Value Proposition RANK: _____ | Excellent Listening Skills RANK: _____ | Product/Service Demonstration Skills RANK: _____ | Confidence to Assume the Sale RANK: _____ | Patience and Attentiveness RANK: _____ |

## Next Level Prospecting

In the early days of your prospecting career, don't be too frustrated if you're not as fast as you would like to be. It takes time to hone your skills and tap into an instantaneous flow or rhythm. It takes time to build your prospecting muscle memory and work as efficiently and effectively as you need to achieve those high conversion ratios we previously talked about.

Likewise, don't be frustrated if you haven't yet mastered every single type of prospecting method we've outlined in this book. In the very first days, your primary goal is to grow and develop your Sphere of Influence, and gradually incorporate other lead-generating methods into your schedule each day and week that passes.

In time, you will reach a point where you can double your salary in half the time and exponentially broaden your business-generating horizons.

## Double The Salary In Half The Time

Reaching specific prospecting targets is a Pass/Fail grade. There's no A, B, C, D, or F. Taking your business to the next level isn't about taking it from a B+ to an A-. It's about determining and reaching the exact goals you have set for yourself, and continually increasing your benchmarks for success when you have proven that you can consistently pass the test.

If your stated goal is to make 20 contacts a day then 18 or 19 doesn't qualify as achieving your target. While 18 or 19 contacts is certainly not 1 or 0, consistently falling short of your stated goals is a sign that you're not quite ready to make a next level commitment. Before you can go above and beyond in your prospecting career, you must first demonstrate the ability to consistently reach your stated goals and habitually stay on target.

Likewise, if your stated goal is to make 20 contacts "a day" then you should really be putting a more defined time-block around that goal, if you are not already doing so. In the first few weeks of prospecting, it might take you 3 or 4 hours to reach your 20-contact target, but once you are consistently reaching those goals, your aim should be to make the same amount of contacts, or more, in a lot less time.

> *Before you can go above and beyond in your prospecting career, you must first demonstrate the ability to consistently reach your stated goals and habitually stay on target.*

Taking your business to the next level means that you are constantly increasing your business and income while decreasing the amount of time you spend getting it. When you set your goals and targets, your aim should be to double your salary in half the time.

There is no magic trick to achieving more business in less time. There is no last-minute secret we forgot to tell you. The three pillars of prospecting success are Skill Level, Frequency and Number of Contacts. Skill levels increase in direct proportion to time on task and making the right connections.

It's very easy to double your salary without doubling the time you work if you can consistently and repeatedly condense your time-blocks and boost your conversion ratios by increasing your contacts per hour. We have seen clients who doubled and tripled their production levels simply by honing in on extreme time-blocking and meticulous tracking. You can always achieve more than you think you can.

## Broaden Your Business Generating Horizons

As your career progresses, you will be ready to make more and more next level commitments and begin to tap into other opportunities. Remember that taking your career to the next level means further improving and developing a career that is *already* successful.

Once you have demonstrated the ability to consistently reach your stated goals and habitually stay on target, you will be ready to broaden your business horizons in terms of price range, desired neighborhoods, and volume, as well as specializing in a particular area of real estate, or challenging yourself to get into new areas of the business or experiment with different types of marketing.

There are so many different ways that you can broaden your business generating horizons. Let's take a brief look at three strategies you might consider as your business goes from strength to strength:

- Boosting online leads with client testimonials
- Hosting a Client Appreciation event
- Deepening your neighborhood knowledge through Geographic Farming

### Client Testimonials Boost Online Leads

At ICC, as our client's business grows, we start adding in new layers of business. Typically, we start out by coaching people to grow their Sphere of Influence and then over time they might start focusing on growing online reviews so that they get more online leads from places like Zillow, Google, and Realtor.com, etc. Four out of five people in the market for a new home will turn to the Internet for their searches, so five-star online reviews have never been more important.

One way to take your business to the next level is my committing to consistently asking your clients and past clients for client testimonials that you can use as marketing pieces on your website, social media pages, buyer and seller presentation packages, and anywhere else you can think of to demonstrate your experience and expertise. Top agents ask for reviews and referrals early and often in a systematic fashion throughout transactions.

If you want a five-star review, you'll need to show and tell your clients what a five-star experience looks like. Getting great online reviews can often be as simple as asking for one. However, by setting an expectation of what a five-star experience looks like, you are also helping the client hold you accountable for superior service.

Envision what a five-star experience looks like for your client then create a checklist of everything you can do to make a true next level commitment to the people under your care.

## Show Your Appreciation

A great next level commitment is to host a client appreciation event. While you want to stay first of mind and in constant contact with people in your SOI, you don't want to feel as though you're hassling them. Holding an appreciation event for your clients, vendors, and affiliates can be a tremendous way to brand your real estate business, get referrals, stay out in front of your SOI, while providing something of value to them.

Remember that an SOI Database Contact Plan is a *systematic* process of staying in contact with the members of your SOI, and an effective plan with a solid conversion rate involves making 40 contacts, or touches, per year with each individual SOI member. When you host a client event, you can make 10-15 of those annual 40 touches just as invitations—a save the date mailer, a formal invitation email, 3-4 reminder emails, social media posts, a Facebook direct message and, of course, at least one personal phone call.

Hosting an appreciation event can be as inexpensive or as costly as you'd like, depending on the funds and ingenuity you have on hand. You could host coffee and donuts at the office or rent out a movie theater. Anything is possible. Get creative and stay organized!

For new agents starting out and are worried about enough people showing up, casual 'open house style' events, where people come and go throughout the evening, can make an event appear successful even if numbers are low overall.

While you want your event to be creative and successful, the contacts leading up to the event are more important than the event itself, so don't spend too much time agonizing over event ideas or spending lots of money. Your overall purpose is to maintain contact with your SOI and stay top of mind leading up to the event itself.

## Dominate Through Geographic Farming

In chapter 6, we discussed how Property Previews solve many of the problems and issues that face new agents when they first get into the business. Previewing property is a great way for new agents who do not yet have a large client database to quickly *gain* business while *learning* the business.

And in chapter 9, we taught you everything you need to know about Circle Prospecting, which, as you'll recall, involves contacting homeowners within a certain geographic area around a home that you have listed and asking them for business.

Geographic Farming takes previewing property and circle prospecting to a whole other level. Geographic Farming allows you to centralize your business in a specific geographic area, and assert yourself as the most knowledgeable real estate agent in town.

The goal of geographic farmers is to completely saturate and dominate a geographic area. Unlike property previewing which has no related expenses and is a wonderfully cost-effective lead-generation method for new agents, geographic farming implements aggressive marketing strategies and systems, and will require a fairly healthy marketing budget.

Geographic farming is a long-term lead-generation strategy that can reap amazing rewards. As your business grows and you deepen your knowledge and your skills, make sure to include farming as a further pillar of revenue to your business.

ICC has an entire course dedicated exclusively to Geographic Farming (*FARM: The Real Estate Agent's Ultimate Guide to Farming Neighborhoods*). This book explains how to create steady and predictable sources of commission income from targeted geographic communities, and all of the techniques, strategies, and methods you will need to quickly become a community's real estate expert of choice.

## SUCCESSFUL PROSPECTING WITH PROCESSES, PROCEDURES & SYSTEMS

A successful prospecting business is a complex machine with many moving parts and repetitive actions. Taking your business to the next level will involve implementing—and understanding the difference between—processes, procedures, and systems.

Essentially, the difference between a system, a process, and a procedure is scope, breadth, and depth.

A **System** is a set of things working together as part of an interconnecting network. Think of the body's circulatory system or our country's postal system. A system is the ultimate thing you want to implement or achieve within your business, and within that overall system, many different—but ultimately connected—processes need to take place. Often a system has an accompanying goal attached. In the example below, a goal might be to implement an Annual SOI Database Contact System.

A **Process** is a series of related tasks and methods. A process takes a broad, high-level view that further defines and describes the big picture and highlights the main elements on a wider, surface level. In the example below, a systematic SOI Contact plan involves different—but ultimately connected—processes.

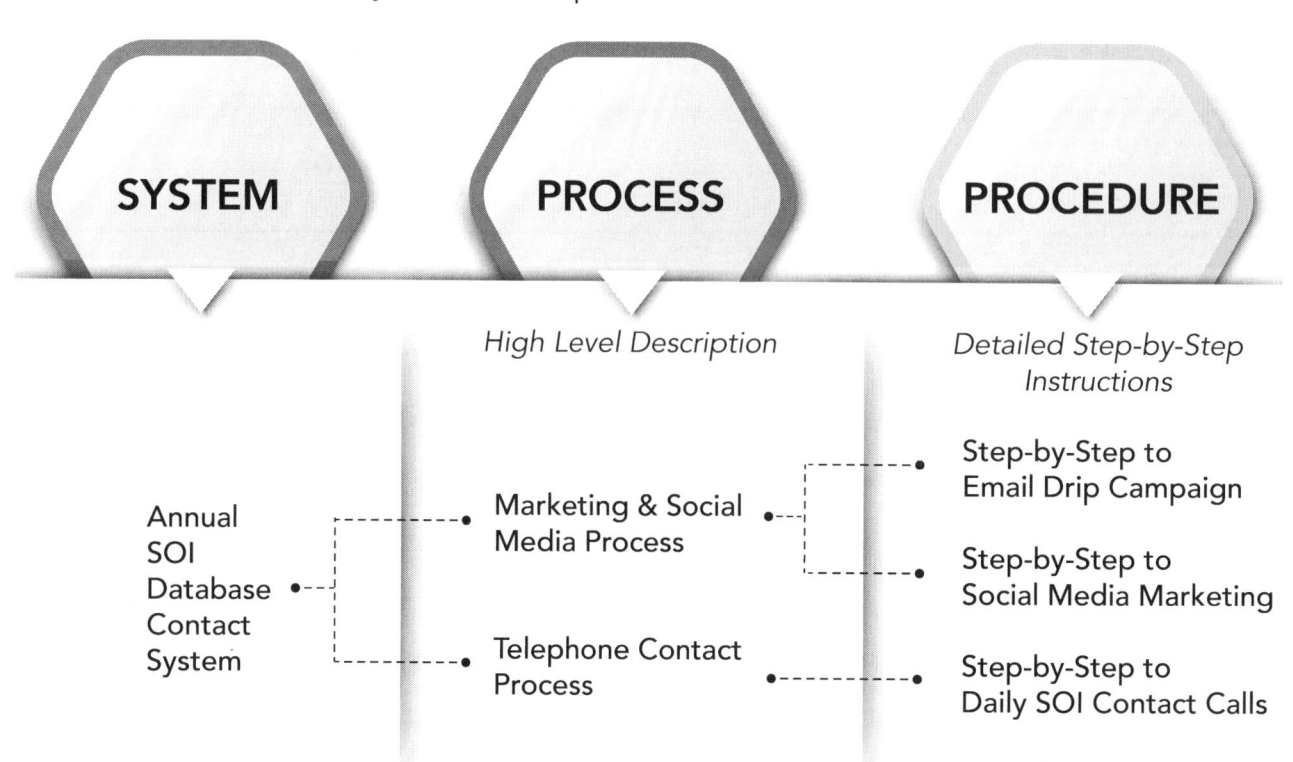

**SYSTEM** — **PROCESS** (*High Level Description*) — **PROCEDURE** (*Detailed Step-by-Step Instructions*)

- Annual SOI Database Contact System
  - Marketing & Social Media Process
    - Step-by-Step to Email Drip Campaign
    - Step-by-Step to Social Media Marketing
  - Telephone Contact Process
    - Step-by-Step to Daily SOI Contact Calls

A **Procedure** hones in on each of those elements and deepens the level of detail and information needed to complete the process. A procedure is the step-by-step instruction for exactly how to complete a particular task within the process. A procedure explains who is responsible for each part of a process and when a particular task or element needs to take place. In the example below, a successful SOI call could involve script practice, preparation, calling, asking a specific set of questions, prequalifying, closing for an appointment, scheduling the appointment, outlining the prospect's next steps, expressing gratitude and the hang-up.

A system is when everything combines to work together for the success of the business. A procedure tells you how to make a single phone call, but a system is designed to handle a volume of clients and overall business, and ensure that you can repeat the same processes over and over and over again.

Successful systems incorporate everything we have taught you, from daily time blocking and monthly scheduling to breaking large goals into smaller, manageable milestones, and tracking your conversions.

Each time you systematize something, you will get a much higher return of investment, an increased likelihood that a particular practice will actually work, and a therefore much higher likelihood that you're going to keep doing it.

For example, sending out a single 'Just Listed' mailer on a whim or as a stand-alone lead-generation method will not work. Your prospecting processes and procedures are most effective when they're consciously and strategically connected to a bigger and broader system.

If you have a listing you're excited about, you show your next level commitment by mailing the 'Just Listed' flyer *as well as* door knocking around the neighborhood for open houses and *as well as* emailing everyone in the neighborhood and *as well as* posting the listing on social media and *as well as* doing a sly-dial straight to voice message reminder to all the neighbors. Success never comes from a single, isolated action. Success is always the result of a well-oiled system of clearly defined processes and detailed procedures.

## EXERCISE: Are You Sufficiently Systematized?

Are your daily prospecting activities part of a seamless system of processes and procedures? Are you at a level where you know how to do something but it is not efficiently and effectively automated and you have to manually remind and motivate yourself to do it? Identify the areas and prospecting activities that need the most urgent attention and think about the systems, processes, and procedures you need to create and implement to take your business to the next level.

| Activity | Process | Procedure | System |
|---|---|---|---|
| Calling SOI | | | |
| Follow Up Calls | | | |

| Previewing Property | | | |
|---|---|---|---|
| Creating Plan for the Week | | | |
| Outlining Next Steps | | | |
| Showing Homes | | | |

## TAKING YOUR BUSINESS ABOVE AND BEYOND

In the early days and weeks of your prospecting journey, your focus will be firmly fixed on that first, sweet paycheck.

Right now, you might not be able to envisage a time when commission checks are coming through consistently and on a regular schedule you can count on and predict.

Right now, it might be completely unimaginable that a day will come when you can't keep up with the volume of business being generated, and that your success and productivity has reached a point that it is actually preventing you from further increasing your success and productivity!

Right now, you probably can't picture what the next five months will look like let alone the next five years!

But that day will come sooner than you think, and it's never too early to start creating the career you want, as well as visualizing a time when you will need to hire additional help, and preparing yourself to tackle and manage a steadily growing budget.

Let's flash forward to that future point in time by creating a series of short-term and long-term goals.

## CREATING THE CAREER YOU WANT

We've spent a lot of time talking about goals throughout this book. Setting goals has been a significant feature in almost every chapter, and goal setting will be a familiar feature throughout your entire prospecting future. Setting goals is not a one-time event. Creating the career you want is a conscious and constant proactive process.

Remember that if your goals are to be clear and realizable, they must be SMART:

- Specific
- Measurable
- Achievable
- Relevant
- Time-bound

When formulating your goals, the following five W questions can help kick-start your plan:

- **What** specifically do you want to accomplish?
- **Who** is involved?

- **Where** is the goal located?
- **Why** is this goal important to you?
- **Which** opportunities or obstacles are involved?

When thinking about the future and what you want to achieve, it can be hard to know quite where to begin, especially when you feel so far from where you want to be. Let's look at a slightly different approach to setting goals, starting with your 12-month goals.

## EXERCISE: 12-Month Goals

To create your 12-month goals, you need to look ahead but plan backward. Called *Pull Planning*, this new approach asks you to identify a future goal or project and work the goal or project in reverse order. Pull planning allows you to identify your action steps in detail. When you can visualize the details of what will make your plan successful, you are more likely to experience success in achieving it.

You can create as many goals as you want. You definitely want to create a specific and measurable Production Growth Goal, but you may also want to make a next level commitment by getting your broker's license which would include completing various education courses and sitting for the test. Whatever your goal is, make sure to break it out into manageable monthly, weekly, and daily steps.

- Write down the final goal.

_____

This is the exact thing that you want to see happen 12 months from now.

- Plan the monthly milestones, or mini-goals, that will make your final goal a reality.

_____   _____   _____   _____

_____   _____   _____   _____

_____   _____   _____   _____

- Create your plan for the week.

_____

_____

- Review weekly progress. If you are meeting your goals, keep doing what you are doing. If you are unable to meet the milestones, use the Four Key Accountability Questions to reflect on your progress. You may also want to discuss what's going on with your accountability advocate or your coach. The reflection part of this piece is critical to your success. Reflection will help you come up with solutions for getting back on track.

- Adjust as necessary*. Afterwards, you may find that you are exceeding your expectations and meeting goals more quickly. If you are not meeting your milestones, and you've spoken with your accountability advocate or your coach, you must develop a plan of action to get yourself back on track.

* Others on your team also need ownership in the process; their insight can be invaluable.

## EXERCISE: 18-Month Goals

**Develop your 18-month goals in a fashion similar to your 12 months goals.** Once you have generated six months of data, including your average monthly GCI and your sales conversion rate, you can extend your goals to 18 months by using a multiplier to forecast future success.

It's wise to forecast your revenues two ways: conservatively and aggressively. The conservative numbers are those with which you are comfortable. They cover your current living and business expenses, but not much more. The aggressive numbers are part of your Wildly Important Goals. These are the numbers you dream of achieving one day in the future. The bigger the better!

## EXERCISE: 5 Year Goals:

Using the same planning format as the above plans, create a 5-year or 60-month plan. Alongside these, add the following strategies for your success:

**Create a strategic planning team:** A board of directors, investors, even staff that will bring different perspectives from inside and outside your organization. You'll be covering all aspects of your business; from lead generation, to marketing, budgeting, investments, and allied business relationships.

**Compile Team Dream lists:** If you currently have people on your team, ask them to draft their goals for the next few years and add some of these into your plan. Do the same with some of your top referring clients: they're essentially investors in what you do, and their input can reveal some places where you'd be a great fit, you just haven't thought about it.

**Ask your mentor, your coach, and your family:** These are people who've seen your progress over the past few months. They may have ideas on where your trajectory could be taking you. Be a student of what they have to say, and you've created an incredible brain trust where you develop the best plan.

## WHEN TO CONSIDER HIRING AN ADMINISTRATIVE ASSISTANT

As a solo agent, it can be stressful and chaotic prospecting for new leads, conducting listing appointments and buyer consultations, writing offers and negotiating contracts, while also handling the entire transaction from listing until closing, coordinating home-cleanings and repairs, not to mention your marketing and social media, and making your own coffee (which always seems to go cold before you've had a chance to drink it!).

Understandably, many new agents wonder how soon they will be able to hire an administrative assistant, and that moment can't come quickly enough!

> *"No one is more cherished in this world than someone who lightens the burden of another." -Joseph Addison*

Meanwhile, for other agents, no matter how busy or successful they are, they fail to make that next level commitment to growing their business. They want to do everything themselves, or minimize their administrative staff, because they are focused on keeping expenses low, but this is not how successful real estate businesses thrive and survive. You must invest in your business in order to generate more business.

As a real estate agent, your primary responsibilities are:

1. Business-Generation: Prospecting for New Leads
2. Lead Follow-Up: Nurture and Convert Leads
3. Conduct Listing Appointments and Buyer Consultation Appointments
4. Write Offers and Negotiate Contracts

This is true whether you're a solo agent or have a large team around you. The more you can concentrate exclusively on business generation, lead follow-up, appointments and contracts, the more money you will make. An administrative assistant will take over the tasks that take you away from prospecting. In fact, an administrative assistant can also augment your sales, by tapping into their own Sphere of Influence and increasing your referral network.

## Running The Numbers & Getting What You Pay For

While you must be willing to invest in your business to build your business, your overall finances must reasonably support taking the leap to outsource additional help. At ICC, our opinion is that you can consider hiring a full-time assistant if you are comfortably closing 30-40 transactions a year.

It is also our strong opinion that you should pay your assistant a monthly salary every two weeks, as opposed to on a transactional basis. There are Transaction Coordinators that are paid a certain dollar amount per transaction, and some agents are drawn to this system because they only have to pay someone when they themselves get paid.

However, we have found that you generally will not tap into the best talent and get the best return on your investment if you approach your support staff in that way. Transaction Coordinators typically just handles the transaction to close process or perhaps listing to contract, but they will not handle your marketing or hold you accountable and they will not handle a lot of your client communication and general administrative tasks and duties.

> *Agents who want to make a next level commitment to their business understand that they need to invest in quality and committed administrative talent before anything else.*

In short, Transaction Coordinators will not free up as much of your time as a full-time administrative assistant will. Typically, agents who want to make a next level commitment to their business understand that they need to invest in quality and committed administrative talent before anything else.

While it's tempting to consider hiring additional real estate agents ahead of administrative support, this is a cardinal sin in real estate. Without administrative support everyone on the team will effectively be acting as their own administrative assistant, which means you can't specialize or diversify, and you are doing the same amount of work you would normally do as a solo agent but at a reduced commission split because you're paying something to the team. This is not a good business model or situation to be in. If you're considering expanding your business, make sure that your first and best hire is a talented administrative assistant.

> **NOTE:** Having said all of this, please talk to your ICC coach before taking the leap to hire administrative support. There are many considerations and variables to consider such as appropriate compensation relative to your GCI, the actual process of hiring that person, how to train and onboard that person, how to set proper expectations, as well as what their exact job description and workflow will look like.

ICC has written an entire book on this process (*ADMIN—Systematize Your Real Estate Administrative Process*), so please don't wing this one on your own or based on what other agents do. Every real estate business is unique, and you are responsible for people's lives and careers when you start bringing on assistants, so please get professional help to educate and support you through that process.

## Understanding a Real Estate Team Production Growth Budget Schedule

As you continually go above and beyond, and your business expands to the next level, you will need to master the art of evaluating and managing a budget.

Take a moment to review our sample *Real Estate Team Production Growth Budget Schedule*. This sample budget will give you a very good rough idea of where expenses go once you start involving other people on your team.

In our decades of coaching different real estate teams throughout North America, we have found that, while each of them may look and act and think and sell in

### REAL ESTATE TEAM PRODUCTION GROWTH BUDGET SCHEDULE

| Total Sales Volume | $8 Million | $13 Million | $18 Million | $25 Million | $40 Million | $60 Million | $80 Million | $100 Million |
|---|---|---|---|---|---|---|---|---|
| GCI | $240,000 | $390,000 | $540,000 | $750,000 | $1.2 Million | $1.8 Million | $2.4 Million | $3 Million |
| Units (Divide Sales Vol by Your Avg Home Price) | | | | | | | | |
| **OPERATING EXPENSES** | | | | | | | | |
| Administrative Salaries (12%) | $28,800 | $46,800 | $64,800 | $90,000 | $144,000 | $216,000 | $288,000 | $360,000 |
| Marketing & Lead Generation (10%) | $24,000 | $39,000 | $54,000 | $75,000 | $120,000 | $180,000 | $240,000 | $300,000 |
| Training & Education (5%) | $12,000 | $19,500 | $27,000 | $37,500 | $60,000 | $90,000 | $120,000 | $150,000 |
| Equipment & Supplies (2%) | $4,800 | $7,800 | $10,800 | $15,000 | $24,000 | $36,000 | $48,000 | $60,000 |
| Rent (0.5%) | $1,200 | $1,950 | $2,700 | $3,750 | $6,000 | $9,000 | $12,000 | $15,000 |
| Misc. (0.5%) Technology | $1,200 | $1,950 | $2,700 | $3,750 | $6,000 | $9,000 | $12,000 | $15,000 |
| Total Operating Expenses (30%) | $72,000 | $117,000 | $162,000 | $225,000 | $360,000 | $540,000 | $720,000 | $900,000 |
| Cost of Sales (Deductions from Commissions Checks to pay brokerage + sales agents) | $24,000 (10%) | $58,500 (15%) | $108,000 (20%) | $187,500 (25%) | $360,000 (30%) | $540,000 (30%) | $840,000 (35%) | $1.2 Million (40%) |
| NET INCOME | $144,000 (60%) | $214,500 (55%) | $270,000 (50%) | $337,500 (45%) | $480,000 (40%) | $720,000 (40%) | $840,000 (35%) | $900,000 (30%) |

*All percentages calculated as a percentage of Gross Commission Income (GCI)

very different ways, all of their budgets tend to look very similar. Their success leaves clues that we can now share with you and will help you when taking your business to the next level.

As you can see, your essential *Operating Expenses* will include:

- Salaries
- Marketing & Lead Generation expenses
- Training & Education (professional development)
- Office Rent
- Utilities
- Equipment & Supplies
- Travel (mileage for showing properties/attending events)
- Technology

Notice that your *Total Operating Expenses* should never exceed 30% of your *Gross Commission Income (GCI)*.

Furthermore, within that 30%, every operating expense item also has a corresponding % amount. For example, your professional development/training & education budget should not exceed 5% of your GCI. And, as much as you'd like to work in a super luxurious office, we recommend that your rent cannot exceed 0.5% of the GCI. Administrative salaries account for (a maximum of) 12% of your operating expenses. That's almost *half* of your total operating expenses. Yes, the administrative role is *that* important.

As you can see, *Total Sales Volume* and *Gross Commission Income* increases from left to right across the schedule as sales rise and the company grows and grows. However, your sales volume won't grow by itself. Expansion is a team effort. The more agents you hire for your team, the more revenue you will bring in. This increases your *Cost of Sales* (commission checks paid out to brokerage and/or sales agents), and your operating expenses will also increase as you continue to expand.

When you deduct cost of sales plus operating expenses from your GCI, you will arrive at your *Net Income* or profit—the very bottom row of the budget schedule. The % number in that row is your profit margin. The most successful real estate teams have the lowest margins and the highest net income.

The bigger the business the smaller the margin! Think of a big, successful business like Microsoft. They may have $100 billion in expenses and $101,000 billion in revenue, so their profit margin is only 1%, but they are making a billion dollars in actual profit. Obviously, Microsoft is not in the business of selling real estate. Each industry is very different and their optimal profit margins will vary accordingly. Our point, however, is that successful, growing businesses always decrease margins over time, *but they also increase total profit.*

As your team grows over time, your net income should go up, and your life balance should stay the same if not significantly improve. A good budget can also help you begin to create those big 18-month and 5-year plans going forward. However, once again, we highly recommend getting a coach if you are thinking of developing an actual real estate team. There are innumerable ways that that decision can go wrong, and we cannot emphasize enough how important it will be to put systems in place before making that kind of next level commitment.

## Budget with Goals

Set your growth goals in percentages, units, and dollar amounts. Over the course of the next few months, this becomes your *'stretch'* budget: month after month, you'll know whether your net would have room for the added expense you've projected you'll need.

Much like setting aside money for quarterly and annual taxes, creating a separate account for future investments can also work. For example, if you're planning on hiring an assistant for $3,500 a month, start setting aside portions of your profit to get a feel for the expense now. You'll have months of reserves for salary, thereby reducing the initial financial stress when the hire is made.

Though you're just starting out, it's never too early to make a next level commitment and start proactively planning for your future growth and success.

## Summary

We've said it once and we'll say it again: Congratulations! You've made it to the end of *Prospect—The Lead Generation Manual.*

Our sincerest hope is that we will continue to congratulate and applaud your prospecting successes and endeavors far into the future. We look forward to seeing what you do next and we look forward to deepening our friendship and professional relationship with you over time.

No doubt you will return to this book again and again as you incorporate more and more lead-generation methods and strategies into your prospecting toolbox. We've covered an enormous amount of material in the past few hundred pages, and there's a lot to digest and absorb as you take your first steps.

However, in essence, prospecting is quite simple really:

The three pillars of prospecting success are Skill Level, Frequency and Number of Contacts. When all three are in balance, they provide the structure and support that is essential to success. Skill levels increase in direct proportion to time on task and making the right connections.

We have seen people with the lowest skill levels become some of the most successful prospectors out there, because they worked on their skill development as they were actively prospecting for business.

Prospecting is an Organized Sales Process: a systematic, repeatable series of steps and actions that take an individual from Lead to Prospect to Client or, in other words, from Contact to Appointment to Contract.

Success never comes from a single, isolated action. Success is always the result of a well-oiled system of clearly defined processes and detailed procedures.

Your persistence in adhering to your schedule will reward you, and the motivational stories you collect will inspire you even when some days are tougher than others.

Mindset, attitude, and perspective are the bedrock of your business. Positive energy changes everything. Keep your chin up. Smile. Reframe negative thoughts. Avoid making excuses. Commit to constant personal and professional development. Take pride in your profession and your ability to advocate hard for your clients and meet their needs. Remember that when your personal cup is full it will flow over into every other aspect of your life.

Above all, more business cannot equal less personal time. Your ultimate prospecting goal is to increase your business and income to increase your personal freedom. As your career goes from strength to strength and prospecting takes you to new and challenging and unexpected places, never lose sight of what brought you here to begin with!

# MODULE 15

# APPENDIX 15.1

## SKILLSET RANKING

| Pipeline Development | Building Relationships | Sales Development | Winning the Business | Sales Management |
|---|---|---|---|---|
| Market Intelligence<br>RANK: 0 | Breaking the Ice<br>RANK: 0 | Understanding the Decision-Making Process<br>RANK: 0 | High Impact Presentations<br>RANK: 0 | Interlocking prospect for long term commitment<br>RANK: 0 |
| Target Qualification<br>RANK: 0 | Creating Credibility<br>RANK: 0 | Creating Reasons for Prospect to Switch Agents<br>RANK: 0 | Negotiating<br>RANK: 0 | Asking for Referrals & Recommendations<br>RANK: 0 |
| Reverse Planning<br>RANK: 0 | High Value Questioning, Probing, Listening<br>RANK: 0 | Linking your Solutions to Prospect's Needs<br>RANK: 0 | Overcoming Objections<br>RANK: 0 | Sustainable Relationships<br>RANK: 0 |
| Appointment Making<br>RANK: 0 | Identifying Prospect's Unique Wants & Needs<br>RANK: 0 | Leveraging Relationships<br>RANK: 0 | Closing<br>RANK: 0 | Next Step Clarification<br>RANK: 0 |
| Sales Meeting & Plan Objectives<br>RANK: 0 | Qualifying Opportunities & Consequences<br>RANK: 0 | Excellent grasp of core values of your business and services<br>RANK: 0 | Use of Trial Closes<br>RANK: 0 | Efficient communication systems<br>RANK: 0 |
| Your Value Proposition<br>RANK: 0 | Excellent Listening Skills<br>RANK: 0 | Product/Service Demonstration Skills<br>RANK: 0 | Confidence to Assume the Sale<br>RANK: 0 | Patience and Attentiveness<br>RANK: 0 |

© Copyright Icenhower Coaching & Consulting, LLC. All rights reserved.

MODULE 15                                                                                   APPENDIX 15.2

# SYSTEM PROCESS PROCEDURE

**SYSTEM**     **PROCESS**     **PROCEDURE**

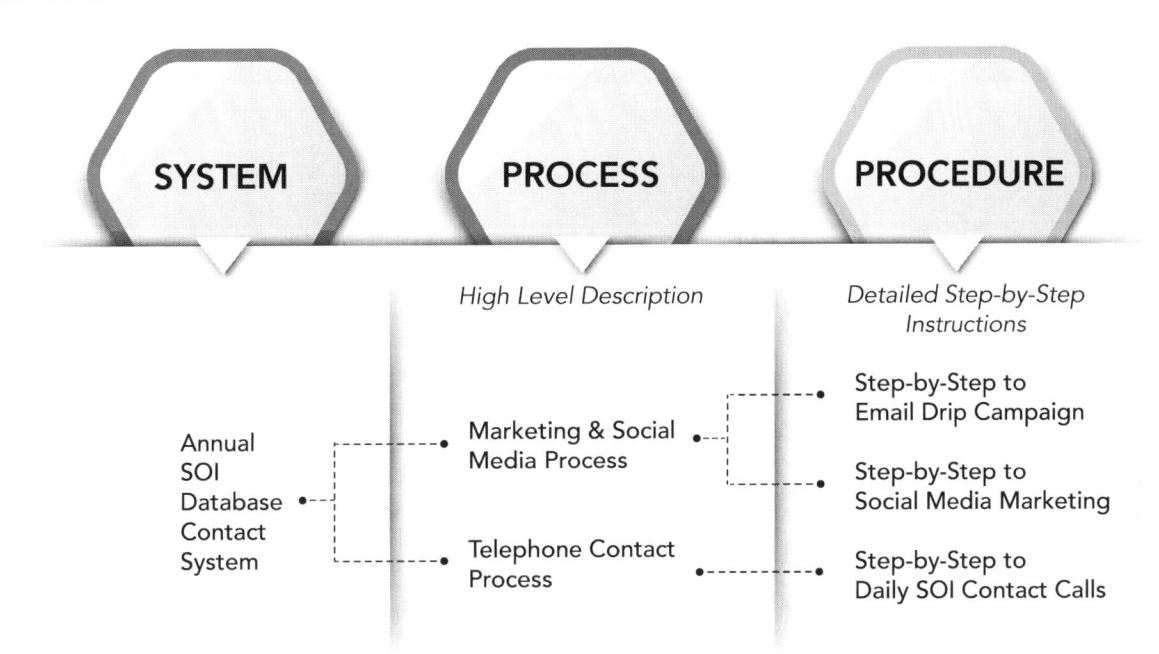

*High Level Description*     *Detailed Step-by-Step Instructions*

Annual SOI Database Contact System
- Marketing & Social Media Process
  - Step-by-Step to Email Drip Campaign
  - Step-by-Step to Social Media Marketing
- Telephone Contact Process
  - Step-by-Step to Daily SOI Contact Calls

| Activity | Process | Procedure | System |
|---|---|---|---|
| Calling SOI | | | |
| Follow Up Calls | | | |
| Previewing Property | | | |
| Creating Plan for the Week | | | |
| Outlining Next Steps | | | |
| Showing Homes | | | |

© Copyright Icenhower Coaching & Consulting, LLC. All rights reserved.

MODULE 15　　　　　　　　　　　　　　　　　　　　　　　APPENDIX 15.3

# PULLED PLANNING - GOAL SETTING

## GOAL

## 12 MONTH MINI-GOALS / MILESTONES

_____  _____  _____  _____

_____  _____  _____  _____

_____  _____  _____  _____

## PLAN FOR THE WEEK

☐ **REVIEW WEEKLY PROGRESS:**
The Four Key Accountability Questions are:

1. How do you think you did?
2. What got in the way?
3. What do you need to do differently next week?
4. Is there any way we can help?

© Copyright Icenhower Coaching & Consulting, LLC. All rights reserved.

# MODULE 15 — APPENDIX 15.4

## REAL ESTATE TEAM
## PRODUCTION GROWTH BUDGET SCHEDULE

| Total Sales Volume | $8 Million | $13 Million | $18 Million | $25 Million | $40 Million | $60 Million | $80 Million | $100 Million |
|---|---|---|---|---|---|---|---|---|
| GCI | $240,000 | $390,000 | $540,000 | $750,000 | $1.2 Million | $1.8 Million | $2.4 Million | $3 Million |
| Units (Divide Sales Vol by Your Avg Home Price) | | | | | | | | |
| **OPERATING EXPENSES** | | | | | | | | |
| Administrative Salaries (12%) | $28,800 | $46,800 | $64,800 | $90,000 | $144,000 | $216,000 | $288,000 | $360,000 |
| Marketing & Lead Generation (10%) | $24,000 | $39,000 | $54,000 | $75,000 | $120,000 | $180,000 | $240,000 | $300,000 |
| Training & Education (5%) | $12,000 | $19,500 | $27,000 | $37,500 | $60,000 | $90,000 | $120,000 | $150,000 |
| Equipment & Supplies (2%) | $4,800 | $7,800 | $10,800 | $15,000 | $24,000 | $36,000 | $48,000 | $60,000 |
| Rent (0.5%) | $1,200 | $1,950 | $2,700 | $3,750 | $6,000 | $9,000 | $12,000 | $15,000 |
| Misc. (0.5%) Technology | $1,200 | $1,950 | $2,700 | $3,750 | $6,000 | $9,000 | $12,000 | $15,000 |
| Total Operating Expenses (30%) | $72,000 | $117,000 | $162,000 | $225,000 | $360,000 | $540,000 | $720,000 | $900,000 |
| Cost of Sales (Deductions from Commissions Checks to pay brokerage + sales agents) | $24,000 (10%) | $58,500 (15%) | $108,000 (20%) | $187,500 (25%) | $360,000 (30%) | $540,000 (30%) | $840,000 (35%) | $1.2 Million (40%) |
| NET INCOME | $144,000 (60%) | $214,500 (55%) | $270,000 (50%) | $337,500 (45%) | $480,000 (40%) | $720,000 (40%) | $840,000 (35%) | $900,000 (30%) |

*All percentages calculated as a percentage of Gross Commission Income (GCI)

© Copyright Icenhower Coaching & Consulting, LLC. All rights reserved.

# Visit the ICC Online Learning Center

for a library of progressive online courses

- PROSPECT
- SOI
- FARM
- ISA Manager
- ISA Training
- DISC
- HIRE
- COACH
- ADMIN
- and many more courses

### icconlinelearningcenter.com

© Icenhower Coaching & Consulting, LLC.

Printed in Great Britain
by Amazon